W9-ACM-299

The Rise of Rome

Jacques Heurgon

The Rise of Rome
to 264 B.C.

translated by
James Willis

University of California Press
Berkeley and Los Angeles 1973

University of California Press
Berkeley and Los Angeles, California

First published by Presses Universitaires de France
as *Rome et la Méditerranée Occidentale*, 1969

First English language edition 1973
Copyright © Jacques Heurgon, 1969

Published in Great Britain by B. T. Batsford Ltd, London
Printed in Great Britain

ISBN 0-520-01795-1
Library of Congress Catalog Card No: 70-126762

Contents

Part Two – Research: Its Problems and Directions

Part Three – Instruments of Research: Bibliography

1 General Bibliography

2 Specialized Bibliography

List of Maps

Preface

I have aimed here at tracing the formation and earliest development of the peoples who appeared in the protohistoric and archaic periods around the western basin of the Mediterranean—in Italy and Sicily, in Gaul, Spain and North Africa. At the same time—indeed above all else—it will be the story, put into its proper setting, of the rise of Roman power, of the city long unnoticed among higher cultures and paying tribute to them, but which was one day to impose her rule upon them all. I end my narrative in 264, when Rome, having conquered all Italy apart from Cisalpine Gaul and the islands, proceeded thus to unify the peninsula for the first time: it was then that she revealed herself to the Greek world as the only state capable of buttressing Hellas in her age-old struggle against Carthage, and took her first decisive step as a Mediterranean power.

The present study, with its limited ambitions, cannot replace such excellent works as Piganiol's *Conquête romaine*, which has recently (1967) reappeared in its fifth edition, wholly recast, but reaffirming the same conclusions as before. My work was conceived and executed in the midst of a grave crisis in ancient history where these early periods are concerned. The nature of this crisis may as well be stated at once. The examination of traditional sources has led in very many cases to an impasse; archaeology is constantly bringing forward new facts which, once they have been digested, will lead, one may hope, to the solving of a great many problems.

First we have to recognize that a hundred years of criticism—and of hyper-criticism[1]—although great progress has been made in the setting-up of texts and in our knowledge of languages and monuments, have succeeded only in a few lucky instances[2] in definitively solving the big questions which the authority of Mommsen left unsettled or which have been reopened since his time. Thus in a recent dispute concerning the structure of Roman society in the early Republic and the significance of the struggle between plebeians and patricians, we find two scholars of equally high standing hopelessly and diametrically opposed one to the other.[3] On the other hand, we have seen many syntheses published, often artificial, in which an arbitrary element has always revealed itself to examination, thus producing in many scholars a feeling of confusion and discouragement. Consequently there has been a tendency to give up the battle and fall back on the tradition as its stands; and this has produced here and there an equally regrettable 'hypo-criticism'.

Amid these difficulties, which suggest most of the time that the historian should suspend judgement, there now appear the unlooked-for achievements and unbounded promises of the ancillary sciences, linguistics and, above all, archaeology. The perfecting of techniques in excavation has multiplied discoveries; increased precision of method—particularly in the stratigraphical study of deposits—has made research more fruitful; in addition new fields of study have opened up in the reconstruction of cities that have perished, in tracing the great works of city engineering and the improvement of cultivable ground: from this field comes an abundant harvest which is not always quickly classified or even published, which sometimes seems to undermine our hesitant knowledge of the basic facts, but at all events makes us remodel our views, sometimes confirms the tradition,[4] sometimes discloses unpalatable truths,[5] but undeniably is laying the foundations of a future authentic history of early Rome in the Mediterranean West.

In this area of history, the present time is one of analysis. We have to take up the strands of a tradition which was long distorted by too much love of system, to disentangle the threads that are sound, to keep the most sensible modern interpretations and to compare them with what the spade from time to time reveals. In the narrative, everything will still be problematical. But I hope that this restatement of the problems as they stand in 1968 will enable the reader to place himself as far as possible upon the line taken by current research.

Part One

Present Knowledge

Chapter One
The Original Population

A The peopling of early Italy and the origins of Rome

In tracing the conditions under which Mediterranean Europe, and Italy in particular, was peopled, we can go no further back than the Neolithic. At the end of that period some foreign infiltrations mingle with a very strong Mesolithic substratum to give some definable appearances to the populations and to raise the question how and how far they were Indo-Europeanized.[1]

The peoples of Italy

In the historical period Italy presents a mosaic of peoples. Some of them seem to be fixed in defined territories; others are still on the move.[2] The Latins are occupying the only plain in central Italy, between the Tiber and the Alban hills, overflowing the latter boundary towards the south in the Pontine marshes. Across the Tiber (the *Tuscus amnis*) the Etruscans occupy the littoral as far as the Arno and the upper valley of the Tiber as far as the Apennines. Downstream, a bend of the river, at the level of the lakes of Bracciano and Vico, enclosed on the right bank the territory of the Falisci; further upstream the Tiber divided the Etruscans from the Umbrians. The latter may perhaps have dwelt at some time on the coast of the Tyrrhenian Sea, for their name recalls that of the river Ombrone (Umbro) which flows near Grosseto, and it was in Umbrian country, according to Herodotus (1, 94), that the Etruscans first landed. To the north of Etruria, on the shores of the Gulf of Genoa and in the maritime Alps, was the stronghold of a backward hill-people, the Ligurians. The plain of the Po had been colonized by the Etruscans, except for the delta, which remained in the hands of the Veneti. The Celtic invasions, however, had

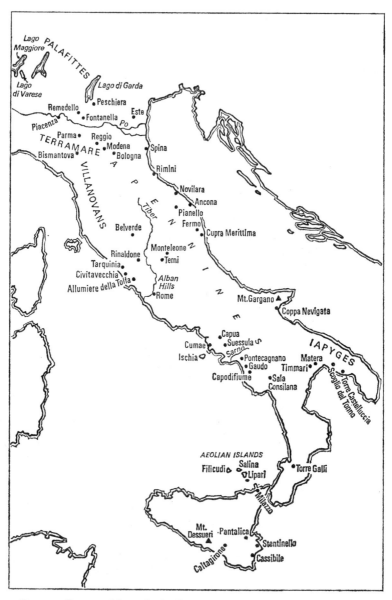

1 Pre- and protohistoric Italy

turned this area into 'Cisalpine Gaul', and on the upper Adige the Rhaetians were reckoned to be the barbarized posterity of those Etruscans who had been driven out by the Gauls.

To the east and south-east of Latium the whole chain of the Apennines was to be one day the domain of a nomadic, pastoral population, interrelated tribes with a common native name for themselves—Sabines near Latium, further south Samnites ('Safinim' was the name for Samnium in the tongue of the Samnites themselves).[3] Neighbouring on these 'Sabellian' peoples were those whom we find in the inland valleys, such as the Marsi on the shores of the Fucine lake, or those who had been put into motion by Marsian pressure—the Volscians, who in the early fifth century came down into the Pontine plain, and the Campanians, who a little later set up their state in the hinterland of Naples. They had been preceded here by the Ausones and Osci ('Opici' as the Greeks called them). More southerly yet, around the same time, the Lucani and Bruttii were spreading out in what is now Calabria and Basilicata, making contact with the Greek colonies founded in Magna Graecia from the eighth century onwards. Here they overlay more ancient indigenous peoples, called by the Greeks Oenotrii, Chones, Morgetes, Itali—for Italy in its proper original sense was the cape of Bruttium. Tradition represented the Sicilian Siculi as having come from Italy, pushing the indigenous Sicani before them into the western part of the island. We have still to mention the peoples of the Adriatic coast, starting with the Piceni, who had come into the region of Ancona, as the legend had it, in the course of a Sabine *ver sacrum* (below, p. 179). Next the Frentani and the Apuli, among whom the Daunii and Peucetii were singled out; finally the Iapygians and Messapians in the Sallentine peninsula about Tarento. We may notice that the name of the Iapyges turns up again in the Iapydes or Iapodes of Slovenia, and that the ritual of the Umbrians of Gubbio, in excluding from their festivals the Etruscans and Sabines, excluded also an *Iapudicum nomen*;[4] which makes it likely that Iapygians and Umbrians had come into contact sometime when they were both on the move.

The languages of Italy

Up to the time when the grant of citizenship to all peninsular Italy (89) made Latin the official language, all these peoples spoke different languages, some of them showing more or less close affinities. The latter belonged to the Indo-European group; the others appear to have had different origins.

Among the first group[5] we find Latin—the Latin of Praeneste differing from that of Rome[6]—Faliscan[7] and Venetian.[8] Umbrian is known to us from the inscriptions of Assisi, Ameria and Foligno, and especially from the bronze tablets found at Gubbio (the *Tabulae Iguvinae*).[9] Oscan was spoken throughout south-west Italy, by the Samnites, Lucanians and Bruttians.[10] Umbrian and Oscan by their obvious kinship form a special group of particular importance, which has been the theme of many special studies. To this group we may add the dialects (wretchedly enough documented) of the Sabines, Marsians, Volscians and the southern Piceni from the neighbourhood of Ascoli. The language of the Sicels[11] is also reckoned to be Indo-European, and in some respects close to Latin. All these languages show many correspondences in phonology, morphology and semantics, and they are capable of etymological interpretation based on their common roots and on those that they share with other Indo-European languages.

Among the pre-Italic languages[12] which were not Indo-European we may number Ligurian, infiltrated though it was by Indo-European, possibly Celtic, elements, Messapian or Iapygian,[13] which has certain features relating it to Illyrian, the language of the inscriptions at Novilara[14] to the north of Picenum. Etruscan also is non-Indo-European; so is the Etruscan-sounding language of the Rhaetians[15] and presumably the language known to us from the rock-inscriptions of the Val Camonica.[16]

That there were in Italy Indo-European languages cheek by jowl with others going back to the ancient Mediterranean stock, is beyond dispute; how we are to interpret this linguistic fact depends on the way in which we try to associate it with the coming of the peoples who spoke the languages.

In establishing the interrelations of the languages spoken in Europe and Asia from the Atlantic to India, that is to say (leaving aside the languages of Italy) the Germanic, Celtic, Hellenic, Slavic, Iranian and other groups, scholars had long persuaded themselves that the kinship arose from a common racial origin—that there was a primitive Indo-European people (*Urvolk*) with a single cradle (*Urheimat*) of its civilization. It was held that the original unity of this people had been subsequently broken, and that the groups making it up had successively parted from the main body, taking on their migration the particular dialect which they already spoke at home. This differentiation and diffusion of the Indo-European tongues was made easier to envisage by the picture of a family tree,[17] the trunk giving birth to an infinite diversity of branches. Thus certain neighbouring tribes, having set off together and travelled some way in company, had spoken a common Italo-Celtic, from which a common Italic in turn budded off. Our own age has had to give up what was shown to be an over-simplifying myth; no one now believes in either trunk or branches. We are more and more aware, at every stage of linguistic development, of the mutual influence and, as it were, osmosis, which draws the languages of neighbouring peoples together—so much so that some scholars are ready to make the resemblances stem from the arrival, not the departure, of the groups.[18] At all events the minute subdivision of groups, the complexity of their interaction, their divergences and convergences as we find them in Italy at the dawn of our period, seem to have existed ever since the time to which we can ascribe the formation of the Indo-European-speaking peoples, in other words in a gradual racial and cultural development during the Neolithic and Chalcolithic periods (4500–1800). The present state of research into the Indo-Europeans, says Bosch-Gimpera, shows how hard it is to make a coherent system out of this multiplicity of 'fluid cultures, with the same influences working at cross-purposes within them, and only at long last arriving at something like lasting coherence'. When the Indo-Europeans first appear in history in the near east and Aegean—that is, round about 2000, when the pressure of the people of the steppes had resulted in expansion at the periphery of the Indo-European peoples, witness the destruction of Troy II about 2150, the Hittite invasion of Cappadocia between 2000 and 1900, the invasions of northern Syria by the Mitanni, of Greece by the Achaeans—their movements can be traced back to two irreducible foci, the so-called 'Danubian-Central European' and the 'Pontic-Caucasian'. It was about this time, according to archaeologists and linguists, that Latin made its first appearance in Italy, being brought there by peoples from the Danubian area.

We speak of Latin, not of Italic. Not only is the notion of a former Italo-Celtic unity under attack, but the conception of a common Italic, a single branch comprising the different Indo-European languages of Italy, has been severely handled by Devoto and his school, who insist on the points of difference between them, established even before they spread through the peninsula. It is therefore necessary to consider two streams[19]—on the one hand, round about 2000 B.C. that stream which, with the Protolatini, brought Latin and Faliscan into central Italy, the Sicel language that was forced back by successive waves of pressure into Sicily, Venetian which held out in the angle of Venezia; on the other hand, about 1100 to 1000, the Umbrian and Oscan stream with its outliers Volscian, Marsian, etc. These Umbro-Sabellian languages in fact differed from Latin in phonology (e.g. Lat. *rubros*, Umbr. *rufru*; Lat. *quinque*, Osc. *pompe*) and in vocabulary (fire is *ignis* in Latin, as in Lithuanian and Indo-Iranian, but *pur* in Umbrian, as in Greek, Armenian and Germanic; water is *aqua* in Latin and Germanic, *utur* in Umbrian, cf. Greek ὕδωρ; the word *teuta*, found in Oscan-Umbrian and Germanic with the meaning 'people' is unknown in Latin). The conclusion reached is that Oscan-Umbrian had longer and closer contact with Greek, inter alia, than with Latin, and that the features which seem to relate it to Latin result from cohabitation in Italy and the ascendancy of Rome.[20] This is why the Italian school has chosen to limit the name Italic to the languages and speakers of the second group; but this nomenclature is unfortunately founded on a theory far from universally accepted. Considering how hard it is to know what sort of Latin the Protolatini spoke, we may perhaps more safely adhere to the definition recently proposed by Lejeune after a less sectarian survey of the facts: 'By Italic I mean those of the Indo-European languages spoken in Italy in the first millennium B.C. which show closer and more numerous affinities among themselves than any one of them shows with any other Indo-European language. These affinities are to be explained partly by the proximity of the speakers in continental Europe, partly by proximity in Italy itself; but to distinguish between the two explanations is not always easy. In this sense Oscan-Umbrian and Latin-Faliscan are Italic languages; so is Venetian, and more closely akin to the latter than to the former.'[21]

Sequence of cultures in Italy according to archaeology

The way in which Italy was Indo-Europeanized, according to the researches of the comparatists, the order and manner in which various Indo-European languages were introduced, developed and stabilized, are not enough in themselves to let us work out how Italy was peopled. Can archaeology decisively supplement the shortcomings of the linguistic approach?

Here again it must be said that, when we see how complex the facts really are, we have to abandon over-ambitious theorizing. Scholars have had to admit that, contrary to the supposed law of Kossinna, formulated in 1928, culture and race do not coincide, or at all events not necessarily.[22] The development of artefacts, shapes of swords, designs of brooches, decorations of pots, all attend the behests of fashion and progress, and may just as well reflect economic expansion as military conquest. Even funeral rites, which might seem at first sight more closely tied to the persons of those practising them, can no longer, one is forced to admit, be reckoned a sure token of racial individuality: burial and burning are found at once or successively in one and the same people. At the same time fewer and fewer scholars accept the notion that prehistoric and protohistoric Italy witnessed the pouring in of large ethnic groups, maintaining on their march their primitive unity. One thinks now more of infiltration, diffusion, cross-fertilization as having been the conditions under which foreign elements came in, in small, loose groups which were sooner or later assimilated.

In this situation, archaeological research in Italy has made vast progress in recent years where prehistory and protohistory are concerned. Important sites have been dug methodically, although to be sure only a small part of the subsoil has been explored; a mass of material has been assembled, classified and published; syntheses have been put forward, many of them brilliant. We are now in a position to see what civilizations took shape in a given area at a fairly closely limited time and what relations there were between these civilizations; but in most cases we are not able to identify the peoples representing these cultures with those whose names are given by tradition, nor to assign to each any one of the languages known to us.

The Neolithic

The Neolithic is beginning to be better known, thanks largely to the stratigraphical studies undertaken since 1950 by L. Bernabó Brea in Lipari and the neighbouring islands.[23] Brea's achievement has been to illustrate and fix the chronology of prehistory not merely in the Aeolian archipelago and Sicily, but in all western Europe. We now have reliable criteria for classifying the finds from Liguria (the grotto of Arene Candide) and Apulia (caves of Matera) and for dating them, with the culture of Stentinello (near Syracuse) and the cultures of Lipari as a starting-point. In the fourth millennium Italy was largely inhabited by peoples dwelling in caves or in villages of rude huts (sometimes fortified), living not only as hunters and food-gatherers, but also breeding animals and practising some elementary agriculture. They buried their dead without burning, laying the skeleton in the tomb lying on its right side, with the legs drawn up as if in repose. They had a full range of weapons and tools in polished flint, and even knew how to work more delicate materials, such as the obsidian that constituted the wealth of Lipari. They had hand-thrown pottery decorated by impression or incision, sometimes done with the help of a smooth-edged shell, making those series of chevrons which were simple at first, but in the end covered the whole surface of the pot, or sometimes concentric circles round the edge, with now and then the prophylactic representation of a human eye. This impressed pottery was followed by a phase of pottery painted in three colours—red bands or pennants bordered with black on a white ground. The neolithic people knew how to navigate along the coasts, and were already in touch with the East, whence they learned the use of metals, first among them being copper.

The Chalcolithic

The Chalcolithic is known to us in Italy (apart from the Aeolian islands and Sicily)[24] from a number of cemeteries, of which the most typical are those of Remedello in Lombardy, near Brescia (a hundred or so graves, stone implements with some bronze daggers and axes among them),[25] of Rinaldone in Tuscany, near Montefiascone,[26] and of Gaudo near Paestum in Lucania.[27] The last-named above all (known to us since the last war) provides an example of what the Chalcolithic culture of southern Italy was to become as far as funeral rites are concerned. The tombs, approached through a round vestibule, are hollowed out of the rock in the shape of ovens; they may contain two, or as many as twenty-five, skeletons. The necropolis, divided up by trenches intersecting at right-angles, had sacrificial wells at the end of each strip, which indicates that the cult of the dead was already well developed. With the dead man they buried his arms (mostly of stone: only two blades of copper have been found) and black-glazed pottery, not much ornamented, comprising pitchers of a flattened globular shape, with only one handle, and some vessels called salt-cellars, which may have been lamps. The necropolis can be dated about 2400–1900.

The pile-villages

To about the same period we may assign the appearance south of the Alps, around lake Maggiore (Lagozza), the lago di Varese and above all the lago di Garda (Lagazzi, Porada, Peschiera), of villages built on piles, or *palafitte*,[28] which find their parallels and presumably their older prototypes in the lake-villages of Switzerland, France and Germany. They continued in existence for many centuries: Peschiera, for example, renowned for its fiddle-bow brooches[29] was inhabited down to the full bronze age and even the iron age. But the first *palafitte* (Lagozza), which amid a great many weapons of flint show only a timid use of metals, appear by their almost undecorated pottery to be related to the neolithic traditions that were still alive in France (Chassey on the Saône) and in Switzerland (Cortaillod on the Aar).[30] There is hardly any specific pile-village culture, but their appearance in Lombardy and Venezia is none the less of the greatest interest; for it is with them that cremation first appears among the funeral practices of Italy. It is also undeniable that the principle of building on piles, attributable at once to the quest for security and to intensive fishing,[31] is next found on land in the terramaras, constituting an obscure but unmistakable link between them.

The terramaras

The culture of the terramaras is no longer that which the heated imagination of L. Pigorini held up for the admiration of the late nineteenth century[32]— an exact anticipation of Roman civilization, with its towns set out along the axes of a *cardo* and a *decumanus*, equipped with a *mundus* and a *templum*, surrounded by a rampart, flanked with cemeteries also set out with the surveyor's chain and reflecting in the poverty and uniformity of their urns the puritan discipline of an egalitarian society. Every textbook reproduced edifying sketches of the terramara of Castellazzo di Fontanellato,[33] up to the moment when criticism of Pigorini's methods, together with a scholarly study of the strata by G. Säflund, showed what a fraud it all was.[34] The fact remains that the terramaras are one of the most interesting forms taken by bronze age civilization in the marshy valley of the Po from the middle of the second millennium onward.

The terramaras (from *terra mara* or *marna*, 'rich earth', because these hillocks, which the peasants traditionally dug for manure, were so rich in organic matters) are strung out to a number of sixty or so on either side of the Via Aemilia west of Panaro, in the provinces of Modena, Reggio, Parma and Piacenza. They were villages of small (mostly circular) huts, built on a terrace which was often artificial and supported on piles, with an area of from two to seven acres; the cemeteries were laid out nearby on similar but smaller terraces. Some of these villages are surrounded by a bank

of earth, occasionally parallelled by a ditch, which served to give protection against enemies as well as against flooding. The fertility of the plain
brought these settlements into being; the battle against floods caused by the
sudden rising of streams dictated the type of construction—the more so
since it seems that the climate worsened and became wetter at the end of
the second millennium, and that this caused the final disappearance of the
terramara people. Building on piles was the local solution of a local problem, found only in the Po valley. The inhabitants were farmers: bronze
billhooks, hoes made of horn, and stone querns bear witness to their basic
pursuit;[35] their pottery, marked by raised, crescent-shaped handles and
decorated most commonly with incised grooves, shows no kinship with any
other neolithic or aeneolithic pottery. The terramara culture seems to have
no ties with the archaeological context of the neighbouring territory.[36]
Hence it is coming to be thought of as having come from outside, from
central Europe, with the practice of cremation, which, as we have seen,
first appears in the pile-villages, then in the terramaras. But despite the
efforts of Säflund, the chronology of the terramaras is very uncertain, and
should perhaps be brought down somewhat. A radiocarbon dating obtained
in 1959 for the terramara of Castione dei Marchesi gives us 986 plus or minus
105 years, i.e. 1091–881.[37] We must say that the level from which the
sample was taken is not precisely stated; Säflund gave the duration of this
terramara as Tm I A, I B and II B—and these periods extend from 2000
to 700 B.C.

'Apenninic' culture

A culture less limited in space and time is that which first appears in the
14th to 13th century B.C., to which U. Rellini[38] and S. M. Puglisi[39] have
given the name 'Apenninic' because it stretched all along the backbone of
Italy and derived its special qualities from its occupancy of the Apennine
highlands. It was a culture of semi-nomadic herdsmen, patriarchal and warlike in its structure; they built up herds which they maintained by raids on
the lowlands, and drove them through the mountain passes in regular
changes of pasture; perched on the heights, they formed their settlements
by preference at the heads of valleys or at watering places. Hence come those
villages of huts or cave-dwellings, those dolmen-like tombs where, faithfully clinging to inhumation, they buried their dead, of which we find the
remains in eastern Emilia, in the Marches (Spineto, Frasassi, Pianello), in

Tuscany (Belverde in the mountains of Cetona near Chiusi), in Latium (the Civitavecchia area, the megalithic centre of Pian Sultano), in the Abruzzi, in Campania (as far as the island of Ischia) and especially in Apulia (settlements on Monte Gargano, caves of Molfetta, grottoes of Matera, villages of Scoglio del Tonno[40] and Torre Castelluccia, both near Taranto). The pottery is hand-thrown, and shows great skill in making an incised or inlaid decoration, composed of zigzag bands decorated with dots, stand out on a black ground. It has certain typical forms, such as boilers and churns, belonging to the dairying industry. These 'Apenninic' peoples, whose pottery has lately been found on the side of what was to be Rome (in the Forum Boarium),[41] are perhaps the remote ancestors of the Sabellian tribes, Sabines and Samnites, who were ever threatening to descend from their thin mountain pastures and plunder the farmers of the Latin or Campanian lowlands.

In the bronze age it is still the Aeolian islands that furnish the most trustworthy data. The culture which has been christened 'Cape Graziano culture' (in the island of Filicudi),[42] though it crops up with the same features in the citadel of Lipari, shows a new wave of prosperity at an early date—to be set at *c.*1600—and this wealth may arise from closer commercial contact with the Aegean world. It has been supposed that the Aeolian islands were then the furthest point west reached by Minoan-Mycenaean shipping, and that they served as an entrepôt on the tin route.[43] We shall come back again later to the part played by Mycenaean imports in the first Hellenization of Italy. They are well attested in the middle bronze age in Sicily, in the culture of Thapsos and other villages near Syracuse[44] as well as in the hut-village and necropolis of Milazzo, on the north coast, where the Greek Mylae was to be built:[45] the cemetery shows inhumation, with skeletons in large jars, the legs drawn up. Here also, as in the Aeolian islands (Salina), we find pottery imported from the mainland, typical of the Apenninic culture,[46] and thus datable to about 1400–1250.[47]

The urnfields

Between the end of the bronze age (about 1200) and the beginning of the iron age comes a period of some centuries: how long it was depends on which of the rival chronologies one chooses to adopt.[48] It is sometimes cautiously called 'the age of transition'; by others, since the early iron age in Italy is most clearly represented by the Villanova culture, it is labelled 'pre-Villanovan'. Yet other archaeologists prefer to call it the urnfields period, from a culture practising cremation which originated perhaps in Lusatia or Transylvania, and subsequently covered a great part of Europe with its great uniform cemeteries, where the cinerary urns are packed in the earth side by side in their hundreds.[49] Intensive working of ore-deposits (as at Mitterberg in the Austrian Tyrol) and great advances in metallurgy made it possible to manufacture arms of much better quality, heavy swords in particular, which helped to assure the military expansion of those who wore them and the commercial expansion of those who made them.[50] The Germans, who have made a special study of the *Urnenfelder* culture, are fond of pointing to the synchronism between its first appearance and the great revolutions then affecting the East[51]—the onslaught of the Peoples of the Sea on Egypt, the Philistine invasion of Palestine, the collapse of the Hittite empire in central Anatolia, the sack of Troy and the collapse of Mycenaean power. In the west, the urnfields culture was first studied north of the Alps, especially in the Rhineland; it covered Gaul and a part of Spain. But it also penetrated into Italy, following a route which one thinks of more and more as passing through the Julian Alps by the pass of Mt Ocra (the Birnbaumer Wald); an alternative is to suppose that the expansion took a sea route across the Adriatic from the Illyrian coast.

Urnfields are known from the twelfth century onwards at Pianello di Genga in the Marches[52] and at Timmari in Apulia;[53] and it is tempting to see in this last-named necropolis that of the Iapyges, who, as we have seen, were probably kinsmen of the Iapydes of Slovenia and had made contact with the Umbrians of Gubbio;[54] they were to give trouble to the first settlers in Tarentum at the end of the Mycenaean age, as we shall see.[55] Pianello and Timmari developed in the course of a first phase, while in a later period, characterized by the evolution of brooches and pottery, other urnfields, destined to a more or less long duration, were appearing throughout the peninsula—in Venezia at Fontanella[56] and Este,[57] in Emilia at Bismantova,[58] in Umbria at Monteleone[59] and Terni,[60] in Etruria at Allumiere della Tolfa,[61] where the urnfields lasted on into the Villanovan period, and even in Sicily at Milazzo.

As the bronze age ends, the civilizations of Sicily and the Aeolian islands show some awareness of a threat that drives them to shun the coasts and take refuge in their citadels.[62] The threat becomes reality in the thirteenth century: the hut-village of the Lipari acropolis is destroyed by fire, and the pottery of the stratum above shows new links with southern Italy.[63] The settlements in the south-east of Sicily, mostly hidden away inland (Pantalica, Caltagirone, Monte Dessueri, Cassibile) are marked thenceforward by no Mycenaean imports, but by an abundance of bronze objects, while in the funeral furnishings of their large cemeteries they show typological features linking them to the Apenninic and sub-Apenninic cultures. They gradually adhere to burial in chamber tombs, but at Milazzo, after the dead had long been buried in jars unburned, we see around 1050 an urnfield appear which resembles in all respects those of Pianello and Timmari, with the ashes contained in urns covered with inverted bowls.[64] A little before, at Lipari itself, the hut-village rebuilt on the acropolis was accompanied by a cemetery in which burial in jars gradually gave place to burial in banded bronze situlae.

Bernabò Brea thinks that the events which then brought a dark age of four centuries (until the Greek colonization) upon Sicily and the Aeolian islands were those invasions of the Ausones and Sicels from the mainland of which Thucydides and the Sicilian historians tell us. We must remember that Sicily in general never adopted cremation; must we suppose that the newcomers were absorbed into the existing populations and adopted their habits?

The development of metallurgy in the *Urnenfelder* period was pursued in the early first millennium in two rich and rather similar cultures, both exemplifying at the same period the technical and artistic forms of the iron age—namely the Hallstatt and Villanova cultures,[65] both named after one of their most typical sites. Hallstatt, in the Austrian Salzkammergut, remained until 500 one of the principal centres of iron-age culture in central Europe and Gaul.[66] The culture of Villanova is a specifically Italian creation.

It derives its name from a village on the outskirts of Bologna, where its remains were first noticed in 1853. Bologna indeed was one of the most active centres, its continued prosperity being explained by its position in a very fertile plain, in contact with the civilizations north of the Alps and with the metal-shops of Hallstatt, within reach of the Adriatic and the Po delta, where Greek commerce was soon to flow through Spina, and at the lower end of the Reno valley which formed its link with central Italy and the Etruscan world.

The evolution of the Villanova culture at Bologna has been studied[67] through five successive phases from c.950 to 525, when the Etruscans conquered the country. These periods are named after the cemeteries where they are found: San Vitale, Benacci I and II, Arnoaldi, and finally Certosa, corresponding to the Etruscan phase. In the beginning, cremation is almost universal in the Villanova culture; out of 793 graves at San Vitale, 763 show cremation, i.e. only four per cent are inhumations. In the contemporary necropolis of La Savene there are 316 cremations, two inhumations. In the Benacci I period the proportion of inhumation to cremation is still less than five per cent (49 to 981). But later there is an increasing number of inhumations, reaching 50 per cent in the Arnoaldi period (27 of each).

The cremation-tombs in all the early phases took the form of a pit, at the bottom of which was placed a special cinerary urn, the shape of which is well established in the earliest sepultures and remains long unchanged, even after the clumsy pottery of the first phases has changed into artistic bronzework. This is the typical Villanovian ossuary, 'standing on a very narrow flat base, then swelling out like a bowl for about one third of its height; it then narrows gradually towards the neck, where it swells out again to form the mouth. It looks like two frusta of a cone set on top of each other.'[68] We must add that it had a single handle and incised decoration basically made up of Greek frets. The jar was covered with an inverted bowl; the dead man's effects were spread round the outside; inside, mingled with the ashes, were his personal ornaments—brooches either of simple bow form or shaped to represent a snake or leech, pins, bracelets, amber beads, half-moon-shaped 'razors'.[69] As we pass from S. Vitale-Savena to Benacci I, above all to Benacci II, the funeral furnishings become steadily richer; the cinerary urns of terracotta are replaced by bronze vessels which show that the technique of laminated bronze work was perfected from the eighth century onward.[70] A special favourite at Bologna in these later phases was the situla or bucket of truncated cone shape, with two handles.[71] These situlae, lavishly decorated in repoussé, were very popular in a zone stretching from Hallstatt in Austria to Este in Venezia, spreading out into all the present-day Slovenia. Their superimposed friezes show long strings of animals, scenes of farm work, of banquets and sacrifices, the personages being shown in their local costumes with their picturesque headgear. This 'situla-culture' imported into Bologna one of its masterpieces, the situla of Certosa.

It would be wrong to conclude from the accidents of archaeological discovery and from the richness of the Villanovan culture at Bologna that it was confined to that area or originated there. Setting its sights at all the northern half of Italy, it spread on a broad front south of the Po to Rimini and the Adriatic, and pushed with equal vigour into the south-west, through all Tuscany to the Tyrrhenian Sea and the marches of Latium; here the movement even seems to have propagated itself from south to north, starting from southern Etruria. The Villanovan culture in this area is thought to go back to the early tenth century; it ends after only two phases (Tarquinia I and II), to give place to the orientalizing Etruscan culture.[72] The Villanovan civilization in Tarquinia shows signs of great opulence: we find cross-hilted daggers and a rich elaboration of brooches and jewellery; the traditional double-cone ossuaries are often surmounted by crested helmets, either in terracotta or bronze—the latter find their analogues in central Europe, in fact at Hallstatt itself.[73] The ossuary is sometimes replaced by a hut-urn similar to those which we shall find characterizing ✓ the culture of Latium.

But the Villanovan expansion is not limited to Emilia or Tuscany. It was long thought to reach its limit west of a line from Rimini to Rome, whereas south and east of this line there began the domains of different cultures, practising inhumation only, where the Villanovans had no foothold.[74] Since the last war we have found that this boundary was not so hard and fast as we thought. A Villanovan nucleus has been found at Fermo, near Macerata, south of Ancona.[75] In particular the province of Salerno has recently brought to our notice a series of Villanovan cemeteries. At Sala Consilina in the Vallo de Diano a thousand or so graves have been excavated, revealing an iron-age culture which was for a long time turned inwards on itself, but gradually admitted outside influences and was finally Hellenized. In its oldest layers it shows heavy Villanovan infiltration (75 per cent of cremations), with the classic ossuary and even a house-urn.[76] Discoveries of the same kind at Capodifiume near Paestum,[77] and at Pontecagnano to the south-east of Salerno[78] have shown the surprising extent of this movement, although these Villanovan colonies were speedily absorbed by the native population. Even more surprising, and even wider in its implications, has been the discovery in the neighbourhood of the ancient Capua (S. Maria di Capua Vetere) of two Villanovan cemeteries dating from the eighth to seventh centuries, showing analogies with those of the Etruscan coast (Vulci), and providing some support for the traditional date of the founding of Capua (800).[79]

The 'foss-a-culture'

Despite this Villanovan penetration into their midst, the civilizations of eastern and southern Italy display a character of their own, marked perhaps by a more tenacious adherence to the ancient Neolithic and Apenninic forms, while the newer forms seem slower to establish themselves in equilibrium. Even in the historic period, this part of Italy was to remain for a long time in ferment, troubled by movements of peoples, among which the descents of the Samnites and Lucanians upon the coastal plains in the fifth and fourth centuries are the best known. In this complex of culture we may pick out, on the Adriatic coast, the civilization of Picenum,[80] practising inhumation in its two centres of Novilara on the one hand, Belmonte Piceno, Fermo, Cupramarittima on the other, a culture very sensitive to overseas influences from Illyria; in Apulia (or Iapygia), in sites which were already inhabited in the bronze age (Coppa Nevigata, Scoglio del Tonno, etc.), and which were early calling-points for Mycenaean navigators, encroached on by the Urnenfelder peoples (Timmari), a native civilization was developing its characteristic forms—a civilization whose originality was not to be quenched by the Greek settlement of Tarentum: witness the pitchers called *trozzelle* with their very tall handles decorated at the top with little wheels.[81] On the Tyrrhenian coast, notably in Campania at Cumae, Capua, Suessula and the valley of the Sarno,[82] and in Calabria at Torre Galli.[83] another culture was in the ascendant—the so-called *Fossakultur*,[84] named from the rectangular graves dug in the earth, with a pyramid of small stones on top, under which the skeleton was laid out straight; in Campania it was sometimes enclosed in a wooden coffin; the rich funeral furnishings included weapons (spears and axes), brooches either bow-shaped or in serpent form, pottery, among which we find occasionally biconic urns, but not made for funerary purposes, bowls with handles either horn-shaped or perforated, with ornamental bosses surrounded by concentric incisions or graffiti; the remains of animal bones show that *silicernia* or funeral banquets were held.

The cultura laziale

If we now look at the culture of Latium (*cultura laziale*), to which the first Roman settlements belong, we shall naturally suppose it to have been subject to two influences meeting and mingling in that plain and among those hills—the Villanovan influence from the north, that of the *Fossakultur* from the south.

Here we are in an area where we should like, more than in any other, to have solid facts at our disposal; but the recent essays in reopening an inquiry that is still not completed lead us rather to suspend judgement on many questions. Some very important discoveries made in Rome itself since the war have led to a re-examination of all the material previously brought to light in the Alban hills, in the hope of classifying the forms, determining their exact origin and fixing their chronology.[85] We have to admit that the distinguished archaeologists who have taken up this problem have not yet achieved a synthesis, and that at present they are not in agreement with each other on the results, or even on the methods to be followed. Let us try to pick out what emerges from the discussion that is now going on.

Tradition represents Rome as one Latin city among others, and indeed a colony of Alba Longa—the site of which is probably to be traced at Castelgandolfo.[86] And archaeology does inform us that these hills were covered—some say from the tenth century, some not much before 800, while a reasonable middle view says during the ninth century—with numerous villages whose graves show undeniable kinship with those of Rome. But in implying that the Alban villages were older than Rome, the tradition is disproved by the facts. The oldest finds in the Forum and Palatine are contemporary with the first manifestations of the *cultura laziale*.[87] They need to be examined together. Nevertheless for clarity's sake we will first describe the latter in its origins and development, and leave until later an examination of the strictly Roman material.

The cemeteries of the Latin villages have been found mostly on the western slopes of the *Colli Albani*, in the neighbourhood of Grottaferrata (Villa Giusti, Villa Cavaletti, Boschetto), of Marino (Campofattore, Monte Crescenzio, Riserva del Truglio), of Rocca di Papa (S. Lorenzo Vecchio) and near Castelgandolfo (Monte Cucco), but also on the southern slopes, at Lanuvio and Velletri, and in all the southern part of the Roman Campagna (Ardea, Anzio, Satricum, etc.). The whole complex is divisible into three groups, which have been named the Boschetto group, the Alban group and the Campagna group, but it must be remembered that the first name has archaeological rather than topographical significance,[88] being used conventionally to denote a typical form of culture represented not only at Boschetto (one kilometre south-east of Grottaferrata), but sometimes quite a distance away at other Latin sites, as Pascolaro (grave I) near Marino, at Velletri (Vigna d'Andrea), etc. The graves of the Boschetto group appear isolated in the middle of the other two groups, either because they go back to a period before the latter were fully developed,[89] or because they reflect only the settled way of life of a small number of individuals distinct from the mass of the people in the greater community around them.[90] Chronologically the evolution of the culture of Latium is divided into four periods,[91] sometimes with subdivisions;[92] it is universally agreed that it ends towards 600 or 575, when the Etruscan monarchy in Rome began;[93] but the dates and duration of each period are disputed. The adherents of the long chronology[94] make the first period start from the tenth century, as we have seen (period II 850, period III 750, period IV 675); the short chronology[95] starts with 800 (period II 775–750; period III 700–675; period IV 650–625).

A more serious difference of opinion concerns relative chronology: one and the same grave (e.g. the very important one of S. Lorenzo Vecchio near Rocca di Papa) is placed in Period I by H. Müller-Karpe and R. Peroni (the latter makes it I B), but in Period II by P. G. Gierow.[96] The reason is that, apart from stratigraphic indications, present at Rome but absent in the Alban hills, the first-named workers base their classification on the way in which the various types of pottery and bronze-work and other cultural elements are associated in funeral furnishings ('horizontal stratigraphy'),[97] while the others will not admit that objects such as brooches, which may remain in use a long time, have any value for dating, and they pin their faith to a purely stylistic criterion—namely the evolution of the form of pottery, which, whether it be in a carinate cup or a hut-urn, is supposed to pass uniformly from a convex profile of the belly (Expansive Impasto, period I), through an intermediate period (Normal Impasto, period II) to a slim and angular contour (Contracted Impasto, period III).[98] All this is concerned solely with hand-thrown pottery made in the home; the invention of the potter's wheel, which was to make the potter a specialized craftsman, did not come until Period IV (Advanced Impasto), at the very moment, moreover, when Etruscan imports caused a reduction in local manufacture.[99]

Let us turn from these doctrinal disputes to note only those points on which agreement is easily possible. The culture of Latium was not born in a vacuum; the form and decoration of its pottery in many cases necessarily imply the survival of Apenninic elements,[100] and we shall see that at Rome itself traces of bronze-age inhabitation have been found. The opening of the iron age is, however, marked by a sudden and considerable increase in population, which we must attribute to the arrival of newcomers from outside. The civilization which then arises practises at first cremation only (shaft-graves), but at a later date (which is commonly agreed to be the beginning of Period III) admits inhumation (*fossa*-graves). The latter practice is at first concurrent with the former, but finally becomes universal.

It seems then that the *cultura laziale*, basing itself on the Apenninic culture, absorbed, either successively or at the same time, some Villanovan elements from the culture of Allumiere della Tolfa (that is the appearance presented by the Boschetto group) and some elements of the *Fossakultur*, the latter dominating in the Alban group and that of the Campagna.

In the shaft-graves a large jar contains the ossuary and the different vessels and ornaments of the funerary furnishings. The ossuary may be an amphora or a pitcher; it is remarkable that the Villanovan ossuary with its characteristic design is entirely lacking: the Latian culture shows instead a partiality for urns in the shape of huts or cabins representing the house where the dead man had lived. These huts are of circular or elliptical plan; a doorway, with sometimes an opening beside it, is often shown in the walls; the roof is gabled and the ridge-piece and common rafters are indicated. They are very like the houses that we can restore from the foundations of huts found on the Palatine, with the post-holes of the central pillar and the supporting posts. We have previously noticed (p. 19) similar hut-urns among the Villanovans of Etruria (at Vetulonia, Bisenzio and Tarquinia), and it is not easy to know in what direction the type spread. Perhaps it came from southern Etruria: this is the view of R. Peroni,[101] who detects in it, as well as in the serpent-shaped brooch with circular needlecase, the influence of Villanovan culture. Yet if we bear in mind the high proportion of hut-urns at Rome and in the Alban hills (40 out of the 70 found in Italy), we may have to admit, with P. G. Gierow,[102] that we have here an original manifestation of Latian culture, and that its spread at Bisenzio shows a current of Latian influence.

Another feature that we may reckon characteristic of this culture is the little terracotta supports looking like the frustum of a pyramid pierced and surmounted with a tubular neck, which are usually described as chafing-dishes or braziers.[103] We should note above all the presence in certain graves (principally in the Castelgandolfo and Rocca di Papa areas, the sixth example being at Grottaferrata) of crude human figurines also of terracotta, some male, some female,[104] which have been taken to be representations of the Lares or Penates,[105] but which H. Müller-Karpe more properly recognizes as showing persons in the different attitudes of prayer and sacrifice.[106] We repeat, only six of these are known, and nothing like them has been found at Rome. Still the deep religious feeling that they show in close proximity to the future high places of the Latin League, Alba and the temple of Jupiter Latiaris on Monte Cavo, cannot but arouse the greatest interest. We have seen that Rome could not have been a colony of Alba, since the first villages in both places came into existence at the same time; but it is possible that from the first two periods onward the Alban hills assumed a religious authority to which all the Latins, including Rome, bent the knee.

In Period III—at the time *fossa*-graves were coming into use alongside shaft-graves—it seems that the Alban group suffered something of an eclipse, to the advantage of the Campanians. It is perhaps what is indicated by the tradition of the destruction of Alba or what can be glimpsed of her replacement at the head of the Latin League by Lavinium (Pratica di Mare).[107] There occurred a renewal of cultural horizons, of which there is also evidence at Rome in the development of the Esquiline necropolis and which, among other differences in the contents of graves, is signalled by a notable increase in the number of weapons.[108] Are these changes to be explained by the pressure of the *Fossakultur*, always present but now become irresistible, on the *cultura laziale*,[109] or by the intervention of new ethnic forces following the course of the Anio down into Latium?[110] We shall take up the problem again at Rome.

The origins of Rome

However, before discussing the Roman situation of the *cultura laziale*, it is necessary to point out the newly-discovered facts which prove that the site was inhabited long before the beginning of the iron age.[111]

The Forum Boarium, the cattle-market of classical Rome, stretched along Rome's first quays, the banks of the Tiber opposite the island which from the earliest times had made the crossing easier. Excavations begun just before the last war, close to the church of S. Omobono, revealed the foundations of temples to Fortuna and the Mater Matuta, dedicated by Servius Tullius, burnt in 213 and rebuilt. The entire history of these temples down to the Etruscan period became clear in the layers of one of the wells, known as *favissae*, in which it was customary to bury the sanctuary refuse. In 1959 the stratigraphical study was taken up again by E. Gjerstad; above the pavements of the buildings destroyed in 213 he found a made soil raising the level of the ground by 4.4 metres. This soil contained many

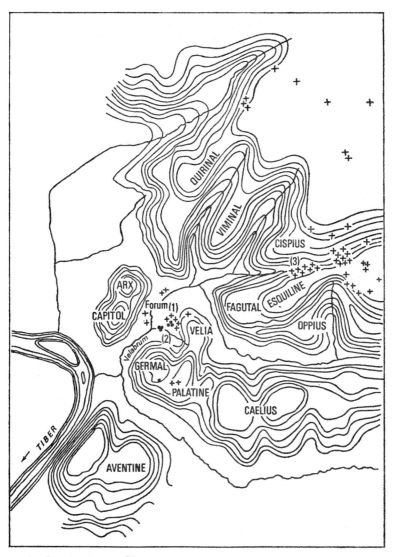

2 The beginnings of Rome

1 *Sepulcretum;* 2 *Graves found near the arch of Augustus;* 3 *Graves on the Esquiline.*

(*After H. Müller-Karpe*)

pieces of Apenninic and sub-Apenninic pottery, the oldest fragments going back to the fourteenth century. The earth had been carted from the slopes of a neighbouring hill—Palatine, Capital or Aventine. At all events, it was now established that there was at Rome, from the bronze age continuously down to the ninth and even the eighth century, a nucleus of population covering the ford of the Tiber. This discovery has its illustration in the tale of Hercules and Cacus: it was in the Forum Boarium that Hercules, driving back the cattle of Geryon from Spain, was attacked by the robber Cacus, lurking in one of the caves of the Palatine. But there is no proof that the harbour was used by long-distance navigators: Mycenaean potsherds are found in small numbers throughout Italy, but at S. Omobono there are none.

We have seen that the peoples of the *cultura laziale* established themselves simultaneously at Rome and in the Alban hills. We may imagine a community of tribes, not yet organized into a state, some of them being attracted to the neighbourhood of the Tiber, not immediately with the notion of founding a town, but because the locality (apart from the ford already mentioned) offered well-watered pasture for their flocks and hills with caves and natural defences as a refuge in case of raids by their neighbours or against incursions by wild animals.[112] The Latins immediately occupied the hills—all the hills rising above the Campagna, which in general is very flat.

The site of Rome (the point demands emphasis) was in the highest degree hilly and broken—indeed more steeply scarped then than it became later, when the raising of the ground-level over the centuries had ironed out some of the irregularities.[113] In several of the classic seven hills (Palatine, Aventine, Capitol, Quirinal, Viminal, Esquiline and Caelian), subsidiary heights were recognized. The Capitoline had two summits, the Arx or citadel and the Capitol proper. The Palatine was subdivided into the Germal and the Palatium, to which was added the Velia, projecting like a spur in the direction of the Esquiline. The term 'Esquiline' itself was a general one, including the Cispius, Oppius and, west of the latter, the Fagutal. The last name recalls the beech forest which covered its flanks, just as the Caelian was formally called Querquetulanus from the oaks that grew on its summit.

The valleys between these hills, starting with the Forum which had the Velabrum running through it, were little more than quagmires, subject to frequent flooding from the Tiber.[114] We may recall the story that the infants Romulus and Remus were set adrift during a winter flood, and that the waves washed them ashore at the Lupercal, at the western corner of the Palatine.[115] The Augustan poets liked to recall the time when one could go boating round the submerged Forum,[116] up to the days when the Cloaca Maxima and other drainage works of the Etruscan engineers dried out the swamp. All the low-lying parts of Rome were reclaimed in early times from the waters.

The legend which makes the hills the first part inhabited is then perfectly natural. The Arcadian Evander is supposed to have established his legendary Pallanteum in the Palatine, before Romulus and Remus had the notion of founding their town on the Palatine or Aventine. Titus Tatius is likewise credited with having occupied the Quirinal with his Sabines.

The archaeological facts strikingly confirm the story that the hills were dwelt in first. On the Germal, near the place where the Romans revered the hut of Romulus, S. Puglisi brought to light in 1949 some hut-foundations, some parts of which had been seen by D. Vaglieri in 1907;[117] the holes in which the roof-supports had been set indicate their plan—rectangular or oval, some five metres by three and a half, often with a central pillar, with a lean-to roof over the door and a lateral opening, having a channel dug in the rock all round the house to carry off water. These huts, with their walls of wattle and daub, were exactly the kind reproduced in miniature in the hut-urns used as ossuaries in Rome, in the Alban hills and in Etruria. But a hundred paces further east, on the Palatine, Boni had reported in 1912, under the peristyle of the Flavian palace, traces of other huts composing, on the other side of the ravine, part of a second village; for between the two groups, under the so-called house of Livia, G. Carettoni has found a cremation-grave,[118] and if the classical rule against burying adult dead within the inhabited area was already in force in these Palatine villages, this grave shows a significant break of continuity between the village on the Germal and that on the Palatine.

But vestiges of these hut-foundations have also been found above the cemetery of the Via Sacra, which we shall describe a little later. They belong to a phase in the peopling of Rome when the slopes of the hills were becoming habitable and when the living, as they grew in number, were beginning to compete for space with the dead.[119] Even in the middle of the Forum, near the Equus Domitiani, when Gjerstad took up again in 1949 a stratigraphical study begun by G. Boni in 1903, he found more hut-foundations in his strata 28 to 23 (there are 29 strata down to undisturbed soil).[120] Elsewhere, between the temple of Caesar and the arch of Augustus, hut-foundations are sandwiched between two sepulchral levels, as if the attempt to colonize the lower slopes had enjoyed some success at first, but that the position had been found too insecure and too unhealthy.[121]

The graves add a copious commentary to what the remains of the habitations tell us. There was a time when the Forum here and there must have looked like a great urnfield; it is not surprising that a place near the Cloaca Maxima had the name *doliola* from the 'little jars' that were turned up there and in which bone fragments had been found.[122]

The most important of these cemeteries is the one excavated by G. Boni in the early years of this century, having the Sacra Via as its northern boundary, east of the temple of Antoninus and Faustina.[123] It comprised 41 graves—circular shaft graves in which the ashes were often contained in a hut-urn,[124] and rectangular *fossa* graves at the bottom of which the unconsumed body was laid out amidst funerary offerings.[125] Here, as in the Alban hills, cremation was the only rite in use at first, and for a long time it was twice as frequent as inhumation, which first appeared in Period II. Furthermore, a large number of the graves had been dug over earlier shaft-graves.[126] One fossa-grave, of very early date, contained a hut-urn.[127] In another we find three sets of remains—two cremations and one inhumation.[128] At some time, as we have seen, the necropolis of the Via Sacra was covered by huts, and only children were then customarily buried within the huts themselves.

To the graves found by Boni we must now add ten or so others, discovered since the war about fifty metres further west, between the temple of Caesar and the arch of Augustus: these show that the cemetery extended that far, or more probably had started from there and had developed north of the Via Sacra; for the best preserved of these graves, to judge from their furnishings, (but here again the chronologies, relative and absolute, are in disagreement) are among the oldest in the cemetery and in Rome in general.[129] They are all cremation-graves, and most archaeologists make them contemporary with the grave of the 'house of Livia' on the Palatine; they are closely related to the Latin graves of the Boschetto group.[130]

It is customarily thought that this cemetery served the first dwellers on the Palatine, for, as the Esquiline, under whose first counterforts it lies, already had its own, one does not see to which of the hills it should be assigned. A difficulty arises from its being so far from the Germal and the Palatine, especially since we have seen that the villagers buried their dead near at hand. Recently traces have been found of a brook which in ancient times flowed down the western slopes of the Velian and went on to swell the Velabrum;[131] all our graves are located on the right bank, to the north. It has been supposed that the tufa of this bank lent itself to the task of the gravedigger better than the clayey strata on the left bank. It has further been maintained that this brook marked the frontier of the Palatine city and that its cemetery could only start on the far side of this limit:[132] but this would be admitting that the Palatine was unified by that time, and we have seen that it was not. This is why this writer is inclined to believe that it was the cemetery belonging to the Velian village, of which no traces have been discovered except a child's grave of rather late date, which proves indeed that the place was inhabited. In addition we shall see later that tradition kept alive the name of the *Velienses*.

On the other hills of Rome we are much less well informed. The temples, votive deposits and cistern of the Capitol have been carefully examined, and Gjerstad declares that it was not occupied before the sixth century.[133] But it appears that there was at a very early date a village on the Caelian (Querquetulani), although archaeology has told us almost nothing about it.[134] The Quirinal also remains a mystery at present;[135] some light, not enough, is cast on it by two small groups of graves, five in all—to the north of the hill, on the side where the Via Quintino Sella is, there are three inhumation-graves, the body being deposited in two of them in a terracotta sarcophagus (Period III);[136] to the south, on the site of the Forum of Augustus, two cremation-graves, comparable with those of the Forum, but going back only to Period II in the peopling of Rome.[137]

The Esquiline is a very different case. At its northern end, from the Via Giovanni Lanza to the Piazza Vittorio Emmanuele, astride the *agger* of Servius Tullius, we find 86 graves of Period III and IV in close-packed ranks.[138] They show two peculiarities which set them apart from all that we find in the other cemeteries—the almost exclusive practice of inhumation (only four cremations in all the 86), and the presence of weapons, lanceheads, daggers, breastplates, a helmet, a shield, and even a war-chariot, in 17 of the graves,[139] starting with the oldest of them. The oldest are in the west, for the cemetery expanded in a west-to-east direction.[140] Moreover, the character of the furnishings is distinct from that found in the graves of the Forum and the Palatine. The establishment on the Esquiline of this village of warriors burying their dead unburned, opposite the villages of the Palatine and Velian where no weapon has hitherto been found in any of the graves, is a fact of great historical significance—but at the same time it is hard to interpret. Briefly put, is this a new wave of the Fossakultur,[141] or is it the arrival of the Sabines[142] to whom tradition assigned such an important role in the constituting of primitive Rome, and whose arrival may be signalized archaeologically by certain finds at Rieti (*Reate*)[143] and Tivoli?[144] Here is a question which we have already posed in connection with the Latins (and we shall see later the provisional answer that can be made to it): Do the historical tradition and the excavations lend support to each other, and do they enable us to retrace with some accuracy the story of Rome's beginning?

We have seen that Rome cannot be reckoned as a colony of Alba Longa, detached—this is the view formerly cherished[145]—as an advanced post on the heights commanding the bend of the Tiber, at the point where the *insula Tiberina* made the river passable for commerce between northern and southern Italy.[146] This function was unforeseen and could only have been assumed later. But it is not impossible that the Alban hills, around the sanctuary of Monte Cavo, early claimed a religious authority which later engendered the legend that Alba was there first.

Thus we want to know whether, among the various villages that arose first on the hills of Rome, the Palatine possessed from the beginning that primacy which history attributes to it: founded by Romulus after consulting the auspices, its direction and boundaries set according to rites which must be those used by the Etruscans in founding their cities, surrounded by a quadrangular wall,[147] exercising sovereignty over all the countryside around. Some good historians still maintain that it was 'the first centre of organized life at Rome, at all events as a place of refuge'.[148] But what is surprising is that the first settlements were so scattered, clinging to all the bluffs rising above the marshes, and that the population was so thinly spread in groups of huts standing isolated amidst large areas where no one lived.[149] On the Palatine itself three villages occupied quite separately the three knolls—Germal, Palatium and Velia.

In recent years the list of 30 *populi Albenses* who took part, according to Pliny (N.H.3,69, probably following Varro), in the sacred meal of the *feriae Latinae* (*carnem soliti accipere*), has been invoked as a fairly trustworthy picture of the multiplicity of these villages;[150] among them we recognize who lived on the site of the future Rome or very near to it—the *Velienses*, those who dwelt on the Velian hill, the *Querquetulani*, living on the Caelian (*Querquetulanus mons*), the *Vimi*(*ni*)*tellarii*, presumably the inhabitants of the

Viminal; possibly also the *Latinienses*, in the *ager Latiniensis* or *Latinus* (beside the Tiber north of the city, opposite the *ager Vaticanus*), who gave their name to all the Latins.

When we look at all these scattered villages, it is hard to think that the founding of a town, the Palatine city, was the starting-point: the city could only have been the result of a gradual 'coagulation' of the *pagi* and their absorption by the one which was richest and best placed. In any case, if we accept the chronology of R. Peroni, which seems the safest, the cremation-grave between the Germal and Palatium is from the mid-eighth century, which corresponds exactly to the Varronian date for the foundation of Rome (754); but the village on the Velian is distinctly older.[151]

One of the first ways in which the *pagi* joined together is seen in the tradition concerning the Septimontium, although here also things are less simple than we were once taught.[152] According to several notices in Varro and Festus (*L.L.* 5,41 and 6,24; 458 and 476 Lind.) primitive Rome celebrated under this name every 11 December a festival in which the *montani*, the dwellers in the 'mountains', offered a sacrifice, some in honour of the Palatium, others in honour of the Velian, and so forth. It was held that, according to an etymology by Varro and seemingly self-evident, *Septimontium* meant the festival or group of *seven* hills. Now the texts all give a list of eight: *Palatium, Velia, Fagutal, Subura, Germal, Caelius, Oppius, Cispius*; hence expedients have been devised for suppressing one of them— as, for example, the pretence that the Subura, classically identified as a hollow between the Esquiline, Viminal and Quirinal, here meant a part of the Caelian, and that the name *Caelius* was a mere gloss on Subura and should therefore be excised.[153] More recent critics[154] have scouted this rather forced theory and suggested that the *Septimontium* was not the feast of the *septem montes*, but of the *saepti montes*, from the palisade or earthen bank that enclosed them and made them defensible; thus all the eight hills in the list, including the Subura on the slopes of the Esquiline (*clivus Suburanus*), have been at last admitted to the celebration on 11 December.

This being said, we can still recognize in the eight hills of the Septi-montium the three summits of the Palatine (Germal, Palatium, Velia), the three of the Esquiline (Fagutal, Oppius, Cispius), with the Subura as an appendage, and the Caelian. Now if we leave out the Caelian, whose subsoil has told us nothing, although its inhabitants (Querquetulani) figure in the list of *populi Albenses*, we find here the chief villages that are known to us by their cemeteries, gathered into a larger grouping which marks a stage in the unification of the town. They are not yet mingled together into one people, but they constitute a federation (at least in religion); the sacrifice is offered not *pro populo* but *pro montibus*, for each in its enclosure. Still the fact that all held it on the same day (11 December) shows a beginning of mutual dependence.

The community of the *Septimontium* seems to have had its frontier marked at the north-west by a stream which was canalized by the Etruscans (*cloaca maxima*), flowing from the Argiletum to the Velabrum through the Forum. A recent hypothesis[155] puts forward the very ancient god Janus as the *numen* properly attached to water-gates; to open the *ianus* was like opening a drawbridge—it cut the road that led across it, and vice versa. This is why the symbolic opening of the temple of Janus in later times signified war, its closing peace. Now the watercourse in the Forum was marked by three arches of this kind: Janus Quadrifrons in the Forum Transitorium, Janus Quirinus at the crossing of the Via Sacra and the Cloaca Maxima, and Janus Quadrifrons on the Velabrum.

This first grouping includes neither the Quirinal nor the Capitol, and this omission of two of the most important hills of Rome is in keeping with the tradition which consistently represents them as having been colonized by another people, the Sabines. Nevertheless archaeology has revealed no characteristic trace of their presence, and if one did not remember what great gaps there are in the material remains, one would be tempted to one of two conclusions. Either, as F. von Duhn has argued cogently and as many still believe,[156] one thinks that the 'Sabines of archaeology' are the warlike, inhumating people whom we find in the Esquiline cemetery; or one concludes with H. Müller-Karpe that the tradition is a lie:[157] the Sabine occupation of the Quirinal is a tissue of late legend, invented in the early third century to embellish the grant of citizenship then made to the Sabines. Neither of these solutions is satisfactory.

In the absense of archaeological evidence, religion and placenames shew that the Quirinal had a peculiar character in very early times, setting it apart from the Palatine and Esquiline, and pointing to different racial origins. Unlike the latter, which are the *montes* of Rome, it alone, with its eastern prolongation the Viminal, bears the name *collis*;[158] it is often spoken of simply as *collis* unqualified—'the hill' *par excellence*; the same name of *collis*, in the ceremonial attached to the festival of the Argaei, was given to the four heights that composed it—Collis Latiaris, Collis Mucialis or Sanqualis, Collis Salutaris and the Collis Quirinalis proper.[159]

Thus it seems impossible to assign to this *collis* the people who dwelt on the Mons Cispius or the Mons Oppius. Furthermore, whatever may be the worth of the etymology that connects it with the Sabine town of Cures,[160] the Quirinal had its own special gods, as Semo Sancus and Dius Fidius, certainly of Sabine origin, and special celebrants of its own cult, the *sodales Titii*, who were supposed to have been instituted by Titus Tatius.[161] The college of *Salii Palatini*, devoted to the cult of Mars, had its counterpart in the *Salii Collini*,[162] consecrated to the service of Quirinus and traditionally said to have been set up by Tullus Hostilius during his war against the Sabines. It is possible likewise that the distinction between *Luperci Quinctiales* and *Luperci Fabiani* had a topographical basis, the Fabii having a clan-sanctuary on the Quirinal;[163] it could thus have corresponded to a very ancient political duality reflected by the legendary alliance between Romulus and Titus Tatius (*civitatem unam ex duabus faciunt*, Liv.I.13,4). The story cannot be taken literally, but it enshrines a profound truth. If Rome was once a double city (*geminata urbe*),[164] this explains many of its primitive institutions too well for us to reject the unanimous voice of the ancient writers on this head. Besides, the annexation of the Quirinal to the *Septimontium* community represents a relatively recent development. Servius Tullius is credited with the creation of four urban tribes (*Suburana, Palatina, Esquilina, Collina*). It is significant that in the *ordo tribuum* the *Collina* regularly comes last.[165]

Servius Tullius was an Etruscan king; the creation of these four tribes will thus be the work of the Etruscans, writing finis to the pre-urban era (to adopt Gjerstad's terminology)[166] and ushering in the era of the archaic city. We will therefore end this chapter on the peopling of Italy, Latium and the site of Rome itself by passing a reasoned judgement in favour of tradition and finding the allegations of the archaeologists not proven. This seems to be the commonsense solution, and claims the support of Gjerstad, himself a great archaeologist, when he admits that Sabine infiltration could have taken place on the Quirinal 'without leaving any trace in the archaeological material'.[167] Let us provisionally admit the enigmatic character of the Quirinal, and hope that some unforeseen discoveries may throw further light on the problem.

B The peopling of France in protohistoric times

Ancient writers sometimes applied the name Ligurians to the primitive inhabitants of northern and western Europe, and some moderns, from Arbois de Jubainville to Camille Jullian,[168] have inferred from this the existence, notably in France, of a vast Ligurian bronze-age empire before the expansion of the Celts. Nowadays we tend to use *Liguria* in its classical sense: the domain of those barbarous peoples who repulsed Greek colonization from their shores, and whose name was applied as a contemptuous designation to the inland natives in general, stretching from the Rhône delta to the borders of Etruria.[169]

It is vain to try to give an historical appellation to the very dense and varied racial substratum which in the old bronze age (from *c.*1500 B.C. onwards) carried forward the strivings of the neolithic centuries (2600?–1600?), and which imparted its vitality to successive invading peoples.[170] We do not know whether the use of metals came in from the Iberian peninsula (civilization of Los Millares near Almeria)[171]—certainly the megalithic alignments of Brittany attest long and regular intercourse between France and Spain[172]—or from central Europe through the intermediacy of the Swiss lake-cities among others:[173] perhaps it was from both. At all events the spread of metal-working techniques is attributed to certain population movements which are traced by the use of bows and daggers of bronze and especially of a kind of pottery called 'bell beakers',[174] which is found in the dolmens of Brittany as well as in the tumuli of the Rhineland. These tumuli are the tombs of chieftains, attesting a feudal organization, which tend to become the typical form of sepulture of the bronze age; they have been studied especially at Haguenau in Alsace[175] and in the Côte d'Or.[176]

At the end of the second millennium the *Urnenfelder* movements, whose development in Italy we have already studied, affected all central Europe and the eastern parts of France.[177] Its two principal centres north of the Alps and in the Rhineland (the Rhine-Switzerland group and the Main-Swabia group) have their analogues in Franche-Comté, Burgundy, Lorraine and Champagne; thus there came to be 'a sort of prehistoric kingdom of Austrasia, bringing together south-west Germany and eastern France, and pushing out extensions along the principal valleys leading to the North Sea and the Atlantic'.[178] In all this domain, after a preliminary phase (CU I) which may be dated *c.*1100 there follow three more phases (CU II, III, IV) corresponding to the Hallstatt phases A, B and C,[179] in which the wide use of cremation is attested by numerous cemeteries; the ashes are laid mostly in levelled graves (this is the practice of the Urnenfelder proper), but sometimes under burial mounds reflecting indigenous tradition. Stelae, ritual hearths and cult-enclosures hint at strong religious feeling. Pottery is characterized by angular profile, incised decoration in festoons at first, but evolving with the arrival of new waves of settlers; among the metal objects one notices at first pins with poppy- or petal-heads, then from *c*.800 (when the iron age began in France) long swords and cross-hilted daggers appear, attesting the improvements in the manufacture of weapons.

Now it is certain that the establishment of the urnfields does not reflect a great, once-for-all invasion; rather it marks the start of a series of infiltrations that went on throughout the first half of the first millennium, each one bringing in beside the established occupants, sometimes without a blow struck, newcomers who helped to strengthen the network of Hallstatt settlements. Hence comes the disparity between cemeteries on the same site, e.g. at Aulnay-aux-Planches in Champagne,[180] where we find between 1000 and 550 the regular Urnenfelder practice mingled with returns to the tumulus of the bronze age—a token that tribes of different origins were living side by side. Alternatively, as J. Jannoray has suggested in connection with Ensérune,[181] we may have to distinguish between an Urnenfelder element, arriving earlier and by different routes, and a new set of invaders who brought mound-burial with them.

We have just mentioned Ensérune in Languedoc. The Urnenfelder expansion had in fact overflowed the limits of their primitive 'Austrasia' and had penetrated into the south-west of France, indeed even into Catalonia.[182]

Can we call the Urnenfelder civilization a Celtic civilization? It is a question not yet satisfactorily answered.[183] P. Bosch-Gimpera does not hesitate to identify all the Urnenfelder people with the Celts.[184] The appearance in Catalonia of place-names in -*dunum* in archaeological contexts going back to 900 or so (Hallstatt A)[185] 'attests a Celtic invasion amounting to a military occupation of the area covered by the urnfields civilization'; and again, 'There is no indication that any later invasion took place'. A. Grenier, while admitting that the arrival of the Celts en masse only took place at the end of the early iron age, also claimed as Celtic the whole western province of the Hallstatt civilization, and even the tumuli of the early bronze age. The reason that he found decisive was that in the British isles a sustained push by proto-Celts and Celts had brought in the Gaelic and Brythonic languages, and that the country which he calls Gaul even then must have witnessed similar scenes.[186] 'The establishing of the Gallic peoples in Gaul spread over more than a thousand years.'[187]

Far from destroying the earlier substratum, they became assimilated by it. Indeed its influence made itself so much felt that the Hallstatt culture in France came to be characterized more and more by mound-burial—in its last phase (sixth century) by inhumation in mounds.[188] The most striking and the most thoroughly studied examples come from Burgundy.[189] The fortified *oppidum* of Mont Lassois, with its three tumuli (la Garenne, la Butte à Sainte-Colombe, and especially Vix) is one of the most typical establishments of Hallstatt C, in a place whose prosperity is accounted for by its position on the tin route to Cornwall. 'Vix was at once the key to the navigable part of the Seine and the gateway to the south.'[190] These princely tombs, in which the corpse (according to a practice elsewhere attested in Burgundy and Franche-Comté) was laid out on his dismantled ceremonial chariot,[191] are remarkable for the richness of vessels and ornaments, both in bronze and gold, with which they were filled; they have many imported objects, Greek and Etruscan—among them the famous mixing-bowl of Vix.[192] These objects were conveyed into Burgundy perhaps over the Alps, perhaps by the Rhône valley if Marseilles, founded about 600, had yet made that route safe for passengers and goods.

Nevertheless, the fifth century marks a decisive turn in the peopling of France, with the influx of new settlers, this time undoubtedly Celtic;[193] insinuating themselves among the existing villages, filling up the empty spaces and annexing large areas previously unpopulated, they brought a great increase of strength to Gaul.[194] At the same time the transformation of funerary practice (abandonment of cremation and tumuli), changes in armament (long iron sabres meant for cutting with the edge), elaboration of pottery and jewellery under Mediterranean influence, these mark the change from the Hallstatt culture to the La Tène culture, so named from one of the settlements, near the outlet of lake Neuchâtel, where it was first studied.[195] The first period of La Tène culture is sometimes called the Marnian period because so many of its cemeteries (over 190) have been found in the Marne department.[196] Occasionally the term 'Jogassian invasion' or 'Jogassian wave' is used, because we find in the necropolis of Les Jogasses near Epernay two cemeteries significantly juxtaposed—both showing inhumation in levelled graves, but one of Hallstatt C, the other of La Tène I, being thus at the turning-point between the first and second iron ages.[197] The La Tène culture does not always appear with that brusque intrusiveness that Hubert ascribed to it; the transitions are often smoothed out: 'The La Tène sword is a cross-hilted dagger drawn out longer';[198] the last Hallstatt phase had already returned to inhumation, and in some La Tène cemeteries cremation is still practised.[199] At Haulzy near Sainte-Menehould the inhabitants did not venture to break completely with their ancient rite of cremation, but placed the urn in an oblong grave, as if to pretend an inhumation.[200] This type of essentially peaceful penetration, proceeding according to agreements made beforehand, is later exemplified in the projected migration of the Helvetii on the eve of the Gallic wars.[201] But often the changes were accompanied by violent conflict: at Malpas in the Ardèche and at Le Pègue in the Drôme, as at Heuneburg on the upper Danube, the Hallstatt settlement was burned and destroyed by the invaders.[202]

In this way a *Celticum* is supposed to have come into existence in the middle of Gaul and to have been unified under the leadership of the Bituriges of Bourges, having as its king 'in the time of the elder Tarquin' (Liv.1,34: i.e. towards 600) the old king Ambigatus. His empire embraced the Arverni, Senones, Ambarri, Carnutes and Aulerci; it was established, that is, in the same territorial limits in which Caesar was to find Gaul when he conquered it, 'overflowing with corn and men', and Ambigatus was obliged to send out the surplus population in search of new lands; he charged his nephews Bellovesus and Segovesus with the task of leading colonizing expeditions to Germany and Italy.

This legendary account can no longer claim our credence. C. Jullian, while not affirming the historicity of Ambigatus, held that 'the oldest Celtic realm was a political unit, and it obeyed a single ruler, dictator or priest, patriarch or king'.[203] H. Hubert considered the list of Ambigatus' peoples as 'a document of the highest importance, because it represents a fundamental grouping of the Gaulish peoples'.[204] What is certain is that the Bituriges, if they ever did exercise the paramountcy with which Livy credits them, were not yet fixed in Berry, where in La Tène I they have left no token of their presence. The *Celticum* was still taking shape, still in movement, with its vanguards in Switzerland, Champagne, Dauphiné and Provence: Livy fell into an anachronistic delusion in making the centre of Gaul the starting-point of their outward migrations.[205] We tend more and more to think—and Appian (*Celt.*2,1) is on our side here—that the Celts who came down into Italy came 'from the banks of the Rhine', or at all events from central Europe, that they came by the Brenner and St Gothard, not by the western passes of the Alps, and that the Insubres, Cenomani, Lingones, Boii and Senones whom one meets in Cisalpine Gaul had parted from their similarly named brothers on the journey, before the latter had definitively established themselves in Gaul.[206] Furthermore, of the two Gaulish invasions described by Livy, the first, that is the migration under Bellovesus, is only a projection into the past of more recent events; only the second, the massive expansion of the Gaulish peoples in the early fourth century, is an historical fact. Nevertheless, in the Romagna at Dovadola and Casola Valsenio Celtic cemeteries of the late sixth or early fifth century have been found,[207] which prove that the combined thrust of the Boii, Lingones and Senones to which Rome succumbed had been preceded by lesser infiltrations, lasting over some generations.

We hardly need mention here that at the same time and by the same impulse other Celtic hordes pushed towards the Danube,[208] plundered Greece (the oldest archaeological evidence of their passage is from the end of the fourth century;[209] the sack of Delphi came in 279), and even penetrated Asia Minor, where they founded the kingdom of Galatia. Apart from a few stelae from Bologna and some urns from Chiusi, the sculptures of Pergamum give us the most lively artistic representations of the Gauls.[210]

We leave unfinished this summary of the Celtic migrations into France; for the Belgae, the last wave to become settled, dwelling from the Argonne to the Channel, north of the *civitates* already established, were not to come on the scene until the middle of the third century.[211] We have to wait even longer for the Gaulish peoples to settle into stable political units: the kingdom of the Arverni was set up in the second century. We shall return to Gaul in discussing the founding of Marseilles and the Hellenization of Provence. But it is permissible to suppose that the Gauls of the archaic period had some of the features which were remarked in their descendants by the philosophic Greek traveller Posidonius of Apamea about 100 B.C. (his observations are recorded by Strabo and Diodorus), or even a little later by Caesar himself: an aristocratic social order, in which clientship (the *ambacti*) was very important, the *civitates* often squabbling among themselves, with a feeling of community kept alive by the federal assembly held periodically in the sanctuary of the Carnutes under the authority of the Druids.

C The peopling of Spain in the protohistoric period

The population of Spain also includes a foundation of pre-Indo-European stock, more sharply defined even than in France and presumably more resistant. Around the edges and even in the midst of this Ibero-Tartessian element various Celtic streams discharged themselves, in one part of the peninsula mingling with the Iberians to form the Celtiberi.[212]

In Andalusia, between the neolithic and the beginnings of the bronze age, the civilization of Los Millares (near Almeria) had developed, with a wealth of megalithic burials.[213] Its successor, the fabled kingdom of Tartessus, began exploiting the silver mines of the Sierra Morena and the copper of the Rio Tinto from the second millennium onward, and imported tin by sea from the Cassiterides: its attraction for Phoenician and Greek merchants will be discussed later.[214] Further north up the east coast, starting from Valencia, all the eastern part of Spain was the domain of the Iberes,[215] a domain which some writers in ancient and modern times have extended as far as the Rhône delta.[216] The connections between Tartessians and Iberians are still obscure: they were alike autochthonous (if we set aside some crossbreeding from Africa in the neolithic) and spoke distinct languages which were not Indo-European; and they both picked up from the Phoenicians and Greeks systems of writing partly alphabetic, partly syllabic.[217] But what we hear of Tartessus is mostly legend, and the kingdom seems to sink into obscurity about the middle of the first millennium—although the Tartessians are mentioned in the second treaty between Rome and Carthage[218]—at the very moment when the Iberes come on to the stage, so that one cannot help wondering whether the two peoples are in fact one, glimpsed at different periods and under different aspects.

Indo-Europeans came into Spain several times over.[219] We have seen that urnfields turn up in Catalonia towards 900, and they were already Celtic, according to Bosch-Gimpera. One may believe that the movements which took place in France during the Hallstatt period did not extend into Spain; but La Tène I witnessed the start of large-scale migration. Herodotus about 450 attests the presence of Celts south of what is now Portugal.[220] They did not merely occupy the still fairly empty spaces of Meseta and Galicia, but worked round to the southeast of the areas held by the Iberians. Where they came up against them and became mingled, in Aragon and in Old and New Castile (Numantia was to be one of their principal strongholds), they formed the Celtiberi: the name, first found in Timaeus, ought to mean not

the Celts dwelling in Iberia so much as a mixed race of Celts and Iberians—
of Iberianized Celts, in fact, since the Iberian component seems always to
have been the stronger.[221]

Although the resultant population was split into countless tribes, the
Iberians in the fifth and fourth centuries displayed great energy as a nation
and a living unity of culture; their original creative qualities, fertilized by
Greek and Carthaginian contributions, showed themselves above all in
sculpture and architecture: in the statues of the sanctuaries in the south-
east (Cerro de los Santos, Elche, Despeñaperros),[222] in the urban architecture of their *oppida* (San Antonio de Calaceite in lower Aragon).[223] Even
in southern Gaul at the same time the so-called 'Iberic' *oppidum* of Ensérune,
remaining almost immune to the *Urnenfelder* migrations and the movements
of the Celts, built its stone houses in a checkerboard pattern on its hilltop,
sheltered behind a surrounding wall. This reconstruction of Ensérune II is
not attributable to a supposed Iberian conquest; rather it attests the
'original oneness of the agricultural peoples settled on either side of the
Pyrenaean chain'[224] and the same Greek influences which were equally
felt by Languedoc and Catalonia.

Chapter Two
The Etruscans in Etruria

In an area of central Italy bounded by the Arne, the Apennines, the Tiber and the Tyrrhenian Sea, we find by about 700 a people firmly established, wonderfully gifted for active and artistic achievement, known to the Greeks as *Tyrrhenoi*, to the Romans as *Etrusci* or *Tusci*. Modern Tuscany, which derives its name from the people whose remote heir it is, occupies the northern part of ancient Etruria.

Let us reserve the question of Etruscan origins for later discussion.[1] Even if we admit that the amalgam of heterogenous peoples that made up the Etruscans incorporated some dynamic minority who had come from the east at some fairly early date in prehistory, the civilization thus produced, during the four centuries (700–300) while it was independent, is unquestionably much richer and more important than any cultural element or tradition brought in by those mysterious strangers. It was on Italian soil, in touch with Italian realities, assimilating all the ways of thought of Greece and the orient, but without losing its unquenchable originality, that Etruscan civilization arose; and we do not err in calling it the first great native civilization of Italy.[2]

The Etruscan towns

At a time when the rest of the peninsula, (except Magna Graecia) was vegetating in villages, the centres of this civilization were already towns, founded according to rites (*Etrusco ritu*) later adopted by the founders of Roman cities, which regulated the drawing of the boundaries, the disposition of the gates and the number of the temples.[3] The cities were often on Villanovan sites, sometimes near the coast—Veii, Caere (Cerveteri),

Tarquinii, Vulci, Vetulonia, Rusella, Populonia, Volterra—sometimes inland, along the valleys of the Tiber and its tributaries—Volsinii (Bolsena), Orvieto, Clusium (Chiusi), Perugia, Cortona, Arretium, Faesulae. The Roman historians tell us that the Etruscan nation in its centuries of glory consisted of a federation of twelve peoples;[4] to list their twelve capitals is not easy—we always find either too many names or not enough. But in addition to the towns just mentioned, which took a place in history through fighting against the Romans and thus finding a place in Roman texts, archaeology is constantly finding others, as Castro to the west of the Lago di Bolsena,[5] San Giovenale inland of Tarquinii,[6] and many more. The rise of Etruscan civilization, essentially urban in its nature, at first is like the spontaneous generation of countless towns, where wooden construction is superseded by architecture in stone.

Inhumation gradually gains ground at the expense of cremation, but we have seen that funerary rites are a function of time, not of nationality. In the cemetery of Sorbo at Caere, shaft-graves and *fossa*-graves are still found side by side.[7] Chiusi long remained faithful to the old usage, and here the development of belief is reflected in the transformation of the cinerary urn; set on a chair, it takes on more and more the lineaments of the dead man (*canopi*).[8] At Vetulonia we see even better the transition from the Villanovan shaft-grave, surrounded by a circle of dressed stones, with the first eastern imports already appearing in the furnishings, to the *fossa*-grave and then to the chambered tomb in its various forms.[9] At Quinto Fiorentino the chamber-tomb, often topped by a dome and approached through a sloping corridor, calls to mind the Mycenaean tombs of many centuries before.[10] In other places, as Norchia and Sovana, such tombs are hewn out of the cliff-face, and have a columned and pedimented façade, like the rock-cut tombs of Lycia.[11] At Caere the family-tombs have an atrium and chambers around it with beds of stone—different types for men and women—and a tumulus built over a drum.[12] The Etruscan cemeteries of the 6th and 5th centuries, with their little roads and squares, become the exact reflection of the rectangular cities of the living.[13]

The reasons for Etruscan prosperity

What marks the rise of Etruscan civilization is not a change of funerary customs in tombs which were soon packed with ivory and gold, but the amazing increase of wealth in a people which till then had scarcely stood out from its neighbours. And it is significant that in the south this wealth overflows the borders of Etruria. J. Bayet has observed[14] that the princely tombs of Populonia, Vetulonia, Vulci and Caere are closely approached in the make-up and the costliness of the furnishings by the Bernardini and Barberini tombs excavated at Praeneste in Latium, in a racially different milieu, at the start of the later Via Latina leading to Campania: 'Controlling long-distance trade, or gathering fat tolls at the junction of trade-routes by land and sea, both [i.e. Etruscan and Latin 'lords'] could afford to spend freely to keep up with fashion and to employ perhaps artists of orientalizing taste.'

Seen from this angle, Etruscan civilization does not seem any longer to be a purely geographical fact.

The causes of this wealth lie not only in agricultural prosperity, even though the soil of Etruria, indefatigably tilled, watered and drained with an admirable skill in hydraulic engineering that confined malaria to the coastal strip, must have offered the best pasture and arable land in Italy, especially in the interior between Arretium and Faesulae: the *Etrusci campi* were famous.[15] Nowadays we recognize increasingly that the sudden transformation of the Villanovan world was connected with the discovery of the mineral resources of Etruria. The island of Elba and all the west coast near Populonia and Volterra were full of tin, copper and iron deposits which had been exploited from the earliest times. The iron mines of Elba were reckoned inexhaustible, and its Greek name *Aithaleia* ('sooty black') came from the smoke of its manufactories. Opposite, on the mainland, Populonia depicted Vulcan with hammer and tongs on its coinage. In 205, when Scipio put all the Etruscan cities under contribution before crossing to Africa, iron was all he demanded from Populonia. Throughout the district archaeologists have found the shafts and galleries where the ore was dug out and the furnaces, dating back to the eighth century, where it was smelted. Even today Populonia lies under a great accumulation of iron scoriae, and the re-treatment of this slag was begun in the nineteenth century. It is not without reason that Populonia has been nicknamed the Pittsburgh of antiquity.[16]

It was the search for metals that had always impelled Phoenician and Greek navigators to sail the western seas. It is claimed that 'Aithaleia' has been made out on the Mycenaean tablets from Pylos.[17] Be that as it may, it is highly likely that the Chalcidians set themselves up at Pithecusae (Ischia) and Cumae in the eighth century in order to be well-placed on the trade route which the Etruscans had opened up towards Campania by way of Praeneste.[18] It has been supposed that a great deal of the ore from Elba was sent to Cumae to be smelted and wrought by methods in which the Chalcidians were unrivalled. The Chalcidians cannot have been the only people to concern themselves with the new Eldorado: the quantity and quality of Phoenician imports show how powerfully it attracted all the east. This primitive industrial revolution in Etruria best explains how the country suddenly appeared in history and achieved great-power status at the beginning of what is justly called the orientalizing period.

Etruscan territorial expansion

The Etruscans were in time to form a confederation of twelve peoples, whose delegates met every year to choose a common leader, the *zilaθ meχl rasnal* (*praetor XII Etruriae populorum*) in a sanctuary consecrated to the god Voltumna (Latin Vertumnus) and probably situated near Volsinii. This political assembly was accompanied by religious ceremonies, athletic and scenic games and a great commercial fair; participants in it were the kings (*lucumones*) of each city, or later—when the monarchy was abolished in the fifth century, as in Rome—the praetors and magistrates who succeeded them.[19]

The truth is that this federal organization of the Etruscan nation, which never entirely prevailed over the disunion of the cities, seems more the growth of time than an original feature: it was probably conceived on the lines of the confederation of Miletus,[20] and cannot be older than the late sixth century. In fact the *concilium Etruriae* is never mentioned in the texts before 434.[21] Likewise the establishment of the Etruscan empire, with the two provinces that it annexed in Campania and Cisalpine Gaul, where they formed two *dodecapoleis* like the motherland, was not so much a conquest carried on methodically by a unified state, but the work of one *condottiere* after another, bringing more or less firm coalitions: the systematic character which it afterwards assumed was the work of historians.

The fact of Etruscan expansion to south and north is now beyond dispute. It was long well-known from the texts that they had colonized Campania:[22] Capua, which they called *Volturnum*, confirmed the tale by Etruscan inscriptions, one of which, containing a funeral ritual, is among the longest that have come down to us.[23] More recently Etruscan inscriptions have been found also in the forum of Pompeii.[24] But more important than all, the discovery at S. Maria di Capua Vetere and at S. Angelo in Formis of two Villanovan cemeteries, in which the development from Villanovan to Etruscan is traceable unbroken from the eighth to the sixth century, has rehabilitated the early date (800) which the ancients assigned to the founding of Capua-Volternum, which few had been willing to accept.[25]

In addition to the profit derived from one of the most fertile of territories, by the possession of Campania and its extensions in the Salerno region the Etruscans were assured of immediate contact with Magna Graecia. Sybaris above all, during the two centuries of its existence (710–510) was to establish contacts with them at Paestum (Posidonia) and the mouth of the Sele (Silaros), by one of the isthmus portages which avoided the Chalcidian control of the Sicilian narrows. 'The Sybarites', says Timaeus, 'kept up close association with the Etruscans in Italy, and overseas with the Ionians'.[26] It was through Sybaris principally that not only Milesian mantles and rugs, but Ionian influences in general found their way as far as Etruria.

It used to be thought that the formation of Padane Etruria, with *Felsina* (Bologna), Mantua, Melpum (Milan) and nine others whose identity is disputed as its principal towns, took place later, about the end of the sixth century. It was presumably an ancient tradition that made the Pelasgi land there and go on to occupy Cortona.[27] But more recently the following question has been posed: Could not the same autonomous development that in Etruria proper led from Villanovan to Etruscan equally well explain the transition at Bologna from the Arnoaldi to the Certosa phase, accounting for the hiatus between them by a gap in the archaeological evidence? On this theory the Etruscanization of northern Italy would be reduced to 'the progressive acquirement of Etruscan consciousness—that is, a sense of political and spiritual belonging to the Etruscan world'.[28] Nevertheless, if we look further than Bologna and Emilia, Mantua with its Etruscan name derived from the god Mantus and its Etruscan magistrates, from whose title Virgil was to receive his cognomen Maro, the *pagus Arusnatium* north of Verona with its cult of *Cuslanus-Culsans*, the territory of Veleia where the placename 'Tullare' attests an old Etruscan boundary-mark,[29] all point to an artificial Etruscanization in non-Villanovan areas. This could only be the result of long-distance colonization in a territory which was afterwards partly overlaid by the Celtic invasions. As for Felsina-Bologna, it seems that when the early gradual evolution speeded its pace about 600, adopted urban organization, and began to use writing—specifically the Etruscan alphabet—

it did so only through the active intervention of elements from beyond the Apennines. There is an eloquent synchronism connecting the rise of the La Certosa culture with the economic rise of the Graeco-Etruscan port of Spina, which was brought to light by excavations in 1956 and later,[30] as also with the vicissitudes of Etruscan sea-power in the Mediterranean. The latter's decline, ending in 474 in a final defeat off Cumae, gave greater importance to the Adriatic route by which the Etruscans could re-establish and strengthen their contacts with Athens. The dates of Attic pots from Spina, Bologna and Marzabotto (on the Reno, guarding the descent into the plain of Emilia)[31] show that the number imported went up sharply starting from 470.[32]

Etruscan sea-power

The Etruscans had not indeed been content with deploying their forces on land. Before the battle of Cumae put an end to their former marine supremacy, they had been undisputed masters of the sea which bears their name.[33] Some of their more important cities, such as Vetulonia, Vulci, Tarquinii, and above all Caere (which Herodotus calls Agylla), although themselves withdrawn some miles from the sea, kept in their harbours (as Graviscae, the harbour of Tarquinii, Punicum and Pyrgi of Caere) fleets capable of throwing sixty ships into a single battle. Their reputation as pirates had spread terror as far as the Aegean; for a long time it intimidated foreign trade in the waters where they held sway, and it confined Greek colonization to the south of the peninsula down to the time when the Phocaeans towards 600 opened up a passage to the west beyond the islands of Sardinia and Corsica which the Etruscans (and the Carthaginians) had included in their sphere of influence. We shall see later[34] how Etruscans and Carthaginians joined forces to parry this threat, in an alliance which Aristotle quotes as being unusually closely drawn; it included commercial agreements as well as the military clauses. The discovery of bilingual inscriptions at Pyrgi, in which the magistrate of Caere, in a votive tablet, expresses his obligation to the Punic goddess Astarte, lets us judge how intimate their relations were at the beginning of the fifth century. But towards 540–535, off Alalia on the east coast of Corsica, the Phocaeans won a Cadmaean victory over the combined Etruscan and Carthaginian fleets, and thereby, despite their heavy losses, gained their objective. In the sequel, the Etruscan-Carthaginian axis suffered grave reverses; the Carthaginians were crushed at Himera in 480; the Etruscans, after harrying the islands of Lipari and the towns in the Sicilian narrows, suffered at the hands of Hiero of Syracuse the defeat previously mentioned. The Etruscan thalassocracy in the Tyrrhenian sea was smashed; but this does not mean that all activity ceased at the Etruscan ports on that coast. Thus we catch sight of Caere's fleet being used by the Romans at the outset of their maritime ambitions, before they built a harbour of their own at Ostia.[35]

Etruscan political and social institutions

The Etruscan peoples were at first ruled by kings (*lucumones*); in the fifth century these gave place to annually elected magistrates, called *zilaθ*, or in Latin *praetores*.[36] At the head of each republic (so far as we can infer from inscriptions, none of which are older than the fourth century) a *zilaθ purθ* or *purθne* (the name may be compared with Greek *prytanis*) had the assistance of a college of *zilaθ* or *zilc* whose powers are sometimes defined: thus at Tarquinii we find a *zilχ ceχaneri* (= *praetor sacris faciundis*) in charge of official worship; at Tarquinia, at Musarna in the *ager Tarquiniensis* and at Orvieto a *zilaθ eterav* entrusted with the interests of clients, while the *zilaθ parχis* of Musarna and Norchia perhaps protected those of the nobility. Some magistrates had the title of *maru*, which we find in various applications in the political institutions of other Italian peoples, notably the Umbrias of Assisi and Foligno: it was from this title that Virgil inherited his cognomen *Maro* via the Etruscan traditions of Mantua. The *maru* were at once priests and magistrates, and they have been compared with the primitive *aediles* of Rome; however, at Orvieto the Latin word *aedilis* was borrowed (*ailf.*). The Etruscans, who exercised such a profound influence on Roman political institutions, as we shall see, made some borrowings from them in return. Here as in other areas, the Etruscans and other civilized peoples of central Italy were working out, in a real community of culture, the answers to the questions posed by the abolition of monarchy.[37] However, the Etruscan republics with their supreme *zilaθ* presiding over a college of magistrates indeterminate in number do not seem to have had pairs of equal magistrates such as the consuls at Rome; except that just once, at Tarquinia, we find a deposition in a tomb dated by the mention of two eponymous magistrates. As for assemblies, the texts only mention a single senate, composed exclusively of the nobles (*principes*) of the cities; only much later, in the fourth century, after violent social conflicts, did it admit the lower orders who had hitherto been excluded from all political responsibility.

While neighbouring societies were gradually transforming their structures, Etruscan society remained archaic and almost feudal; the nobility—knights whose class-insignia were inherited by the Roman *equites*[38] —lorded it over an enormous servile class.[39] Everything that we learn from the documents and artistic remains, from the Regolini-Galassi tomb at Caere in the mid-seventh century down to the history of the Cilnii of Arretium at the end of the fourth, attests the opulence of the *principes*, with hosts of domestics in their city palaces and armies of peasants tilling their country estates. No middle class ever succeeded in establishing itself between the two.

Nevertheless, the Etruscan *familia*, i.e. the body of slaves owned by a single master, did know of degrees corresponding only roughly with the terms *servi* and *liberti* used by Latin writers.[40] There were the slaves of the ergastula, working in mines, quarries and in the draining of marshes, and the country serfs, whose conditions may have been a little more enviable, since, to the great astonishment of the Roman jurists, they enjoyed the right of property. Many of these slaves were freedmen (*lautni*); and although they remained subject to their patron, they contracted marriages, raised themselves socially, and could themselves have slaves and freedmen. Lastly, at the top of the ladder, freedmen could pass into the category of *lautneteri* or *etera*—clients who had the right to choose a place for themselves in the family tomb, sometimes equal with that of the sons, while in the city they had a special praetor (*zilaθ eterav*) to look after their interests.

Without sharing Bachofen's mistaken notion that Etruscan society was matriarchal, we can observe that women among them held a privileged position much superior to that which Athens or Rome accorded to the sex. Their status in society endowed them with a praenomen, as Tanaquil, Ramθa, etc.; in the epitaphs (even those of the Roman period) the mother's name is given as well as the father's; in the paintings from Tarquinia women take part in banquets and are present at games side by side with men; in the tombs at Caere the funeral couch of the materfamilias was enclosed within an elaborate sarcophagus. All indications go to show that the important social and political rôle assigned by the historians to such women as Tanaquil, the 'king-maker', the wife of Tarquin the Elder, or to the daughters of Servius Tullius, reflects a tradition going back to good Etruscan sources.[41]

Etruscan civilization, which we must now consider from the artistic, religious and linguistic aspects, has indeed basic characters of its own, but these are largely obliterated under the large borrowings from Greece and the orient. Works of art, ideas and techniques from the other end of the Mediterranean were always sure of a welcome from the Etruscans, who enthusiastically imitated them at home and spread them among their neighbours.

Etruscan art

This keen acceptance and emulation is already attested in the princely tombs of the seventh century.[42] Among their furnishings, side by side with typical Etruscan ceramic in the most brilliant and delicate *bucchero*, we find Phoenician imports—ivory bowls with repoussé decoration, caskets, combs and rods of carved ivory[43]—bronze bowls from Urartu decorated with heads of griffons and sirens,[44] brooches, bracelets and pendants in gold, wrought somewhere in Asia Minor with a consummate mastery in filigree and beadwork.[45] But the models were very speedily imitated on the spot by native artists; in some cases (e.g. in the ivory work) we can identify their productions.[46] It has also been possible to show how the Etruscan art of sculpture on a larger scale developed (at Vetulonia for example) from the enlargement of small imported caryatids and statuettes.[47]

The rôle of the Etruscans as the introducers of Hellenism into central Italy remained strongly marked throughout the sixth century. It appears at first in the influx of Attic pottery, which found a seller's market at Caere, Tarquinia and Vulci; their cemeteries 'alone have yielded thousands upon thousands of Attic vases, more than all the rest of the Greek world.[48] One tomb at Caere has provided some 150 vases, in black figure or early red figure of outstanding quality.[49] In the same city an Ionian artist set up shop between 540 and 510, making the hydriae of Caere, as they are called.[50] From 550 onward the series of so-called Pontic amphorae was issuing from an Etruscan workshop, possibly at Vulci.[51]

Apart from pottery, the Etruscan tombs, especially at Tarquinia, reflect in their frescoes the great archaic school of Greek painting, of which nothing survives in Greece itself:[52] there are scenes of heroic legend (tomb of the bulls), banqueting scenes (tomb of the leopards, tomb of the triclinium), scenes of athletic contests and horse-races (tomb of the chariots, tomb of the Olympiads); but the reproduction of Greek drawings is shot through with Etruscan elements, such as the sport of the demon Phersu in the tomb of the augurs and that of the Olympiads.

The Etruscans showed their capacity for plastic art not in marble (for the quarries of Luni were not worked until the Roman period), but in bronze—bas-reliefs and statuettes of bronze on tripods and candelabra[53]— and above all in terracotta.[54] The architectural adornment of temples, their superstructure being of wood, gave wide scope for artists in that material. In Campania (at Capua), in the Pontine marches (at Satricum), in Latium and throughout southern Etruria, the cornices were surmounted by painted antefixae showing female heads or Gorgon-heads or Sileni embracing maenads: these are often masterpieces, full of life and strong realism. The most expressive were moulded after 500 by an artist of Veii: we are lucky enough to know his name—Vulca.[55] The younger Tarquin commissioned him to make the quadriga which was to stand as an acroterion on the temple of Jupiter Capitolinus.[56] It is to his genius that we owe the group of Apollo and Hercules disputing the possession of the Cerynian stag, a work of which fragments were found at Veii in 1922 and later; we possess part of the stag, a head of Hermes, and the splendid Apollo itself.[57] It is for the art-historian to determine what is inescapably unhellenic in the vigour, rhythm and proportions of the walking figure.

Etruscan religion

In the sphere of religion the Etruscan foundation stood more firmly. Etruscan religion, unlike the religions of Greece and Rome, but like Judaism and Christianity, was a revealed religion: half-divine prophets (Tages, Cacus, the nymph Vegoia) were supposed to have imparted it to their people; what they taught had been codified in the *disciplina Etrusca*.[58] It prescribed in the most minute detail the ritual proceedings by which the will of the gods was to be found out and followed. The Etruscans lived out the ten centuries accorded to them under the burden of an obsessive belief in an immutable fate which was revealed to them by complex ways of divination. 'No people', says Livy, 'was ever more devoted to religious observances—the more so since they had unique gifts in that sphere.'

The *disciplina Etrusca* comprised several series of books. The *libri rituales*[59] contained 'the rules for the founding of cities, consecration of altars and temples, sanctifying of walls and gates, and everything pertaining to war and peace'. The *libri fulgurales*[60] dealt with the interpretation of thunder and lightning: each god had distinct kinds of lightning at his disposal; Jupiter, either by himself or on the advice of his counsellors, threw three kinds of thunderbolt, benevolent or more or less destructive, while eight other gods had one kind apiece. The Byzantine writer Johannes Lydus has preserved a 'brontoscopic calendar' translated from the Etruscan at the end of the Roman republic, which taught what thunderclaps meant on every day of the year.[61] The *libri haruspicinales* enshrined the experience gained by the Etruscans in examining the entrails of sacrificial victims. The learning of their haruspices was so generally recognized that the Roman senate used to appeal to them when any difficult portent had been reported. Examination of the liver (hepatoscopy) is represented on Etruscan mirrors. A model of a liver in bronze,[62] probably coming originally from Cortona,[63] has its convex side divided into 44 compartments, each one marked with the name of one of two gods; it is an image, set out according to the points of the compass, of the Etruscan heaven, showing the place occupied by each divinity.

We know a fair number of Etruscan deities,[64] but their functions and relations are largely unknown, particularly since their original significance has been lost or modified through their being lumped in with the Italic gods and contaminated by Greek or oriental influence. At their head was *Tin* or *Tinia*, identified with Jupiter; with *Uni* (Juno) and *Menrva* (Minerva) he formed a trinity worshipped in tripartite temples: the best known of them is the temple of Jupiter Capitolinus at Rome, which sheltered the 'Capitoline trinity'. But *Voltumna* (= Voltumnus or Vertumnus) was reckoned at Vulsinii as 'foremost among the gods of Etruria';[65] *Turan* was equated with Aphrodite, *Fufluns* with Dionysus, *Turms* with Hermes, *Sethlans* with Hephaestus. The inscriptions of Pyrgi attest the introduction of a Punic goddess, Astarte, into a sanctuary of *Uni*.[66] Apollo, Artemis and Heracles retained their Greek names, but as *Aplu*, *Aritimi* and *Hercle* they sometimes display unexpected traits in Etruscan mythology. The Greek Charon, with a supporting cast of funerary deities—*Tuchulcha*, *Mantus* (cf. the name of Mantua), *Calu*, *Letham* etc.— plays an important part in the paintings and reliefs of the tombs, since punishment after death had assumed great prominence in a religious imagination that tended naturally towards darkness and cruelty.[67] Others such as *Nethuns* (Neptune), *Maris* (Mars), *Veive* (Veiovis) come up again in the religion of the Romans. Many others are now no more than names.

Etruscan religious ceremonies, with the sacrifices that were offered and the priests who performed them, are described in some inscriptions which we can only partly understand, on the Capuan tile and the mummy-wrappings from Zagreb.[68] We can also detect certain aspects of them in Roman adaptations, for example in the *ludi scenici* introduced in 364.[69]

The Etruscan language

The Etruscan language does not belong to the Indo-European family, despite the efforts of some linguists to associate it with Indo-European by way of Hittite,[70] and (of course) despite its borrowings from Greek and the Italic dialects. It is known to us (apart from a small number of glosses) by some 10,000 inscriptions. Most of these are epitaphs, short and usually late (third to first century), and the proper names,[71] ages, names of degrees of kinship and of magistracies contained in them no longer pose any great problems. Only a few are richer in content and go back sometimes to the fifth and fourth centuries: these are the mummy windings of Zagreb (1190 words), the Capuan tile (300 words),[72] the leaden tablet of Magliano,[73] the cippus from Perugia,[74] and the inscription of the magistrate of Tarquinia.[75] To these we must now add the inscriptions from Pyrgi, which are partly bilingual in Etruscan and Punic.[76] These important texts have been approached by three methods. The etymological method, attempting to interpret Etruscan through Greek, Finnish, Albanian etc., is now given up, or ought to be. Only the combinatory method, by its vigilant empiricism, has given good results. Some useful hypotheses have been suggested by the so-called bilingual method, which is based on the parallelism existing between the religious and juridical formulae of the Etruscans on the one hand, and of the Latins and Umbrians on the other.[77] Thus we are enabled nowadays, not indeed to translate the texts literally, but at least to know fairly accurately what they are about: we can recognize the Capuan inscription as being a funerary ritual,[78] that of Zagreb as being a liturgical calendar[79] in which one can analyse the composition, its repetitions and responses, and can pick out the names of deities, of sacred objects and of particular actions in the ritual. In addition, the advance in our understanding of the grammar has made it possible to reach some valuable conclusions.[80]

It is particularly instructive to see how the Etruscans got their alphabet and how its use spread.[81] We find this alphabet in two forms. Some examples of writing for teaching purposes, engraved on ivory tablets and vases and appearing in the seventh century, set out 26 letters drawn from a west Greek alphabet furnished perhaps by the Chalcidians of Cumae, some part perhaps being played also by Phoenician merchants.[82] Out of these 26 letters the Etruscans kept for their own use an archaic alphabet of 23 letters (seventh to fifth century); later the number went down to twenty. In most of the inscriptions, even the oldest, the words are separated by dots, usually two or three. Exceptionally, in the mid-fifth century in certain regions (southern Etruria and Campania), we find a syllabic punctuation, which has been interpreted as an obscure survival of ancient contacts with the Aegean world.[83] The Etruscans spread the use of their alphabet among the Latins, Oscans, Umbrians and Venetians. Thanks to them, all Italy became literate. This is one of the most indisputable achievements of Etruscan civilization.

Chapter Three

External Influences on Civilization in Italy

A Mycenaeans and bronze-age Italy

As an historical fact, Sicily and southern Italy only began to be colonized by Greeks in the middle of the eighth century; but the poets and mythographers and local traditions were full of legendary colonizations making the movement start very much earlier. The *Aeneid*, recounting how Trojan refugees sailed to Sicily, to Campania and at last to Latium in search of a new home, is only the most famous of a whole series of fables which represented victors or vanquished at Troy as having found refuge at last in Italy after long wanderings by sea.[1] The adventures of Ulysses in Etruria, those of Diomede in the Adriatic, had given rise to countless inventions. There was scarcely a fishing village in Calabria or Apulia that did not claim to possess the grave of Orestes, scarcely a sanctuary that did not count Nestor's cup among its relics, scarcely a colony that did not boast of having been founded by Heracles, Jason or Minos. One might have supposed these to be pure inventions, whose only basis was the desire of late Greek grammarians to explain a placename or an institution, or to invest a recent alliance with the glamour of antiquity. The fact is, however, that the *Odyssey* of Homer, in its oldest parts (ninth century onward), shows a detailed knowledge of the coasts of the western Mediterranean that owes nothing to the experience of colonists. 'It is possible', wrote Jean Bérard in 1941,[2] 'that the author of the *Phaeacian Tales* had acted as a guide to the first Greek explorers who were then reopening the Italian sea-routes . . . He could not have been their disciple.' All these legends may then have, to a certain degree, a basis in history; they may preserve the memory of immemorial relations between Greece in the days of the Trojan war and bronze-age Italy.

This view has been confirmed more and more in recent years by the discovery in Italy of very many shards of Mycenaean pottery. The Achaean kings who were to be Homer's theme, whose fortresses, palaces and tombs have been uncovered at Mycenae, Tiryns and Pylos, whose writing has been deciphered in our own generation, were the inheritors of Cretan civilization, and in the second half of the second millennium, especially from the fourteenth to the twelfth century,[3] exercised a maritime supremacy with Rhodes and Cyprus as their principal bases outside the Peloponnese. Their power did not only rule the Aegean, but extended westwards into the Ionian, Tyrrhenian and Adriatic seas.[4] Mycenaean pottery has in fact been found in Sicily, in various sites around Syracuse, and especially in the Aeolian islands, Filicudi, Salina and Lipari, where the Mycenaean imports, which are very abundant and go back sometimes to the late Minoan period (sixteenth century) are the oldest hitherto known in the west.[5] Ischia and Vivara opposite Cumae have yielded many shards.[6] Quite unexpectedly, five have been found in the heart of Etruria, at Luni sul Mignone, between Tarquinia and the Lago di Bracciano.[7] Along the Adriatic, some have been found at Coppa Nevigata at the foot of Monte Gargano. But it is especially at Scoglio del Tonno in the gulf of Taranto, just at the entry to the roadstead of the future colony, and at Porto Saturo, Porto Perone and Torre Castelluccia, dotted along the coast within a dozen miles of Taranto, that the richest deposits have been found—750 shards at Scoglio del Tonno alone. This Mycenaean penetration reached the hinterland also, where traces of it are found at S. Cosimo d'Oria, which was anciently Hyria, between Taranto and Brindisi.[8]

All that coast of Italy and Sicily which faced the Ionian sea was easily accessible to the sailors of Cephallenia, Olympia and Pylos as soon as they would venture into the open sea.[9] Pylos was Nestor's kingdom in Homer, and now the American archaeologists have unearthed its palace and inscribed tablets in Linear B. The decipherment of the latter has recently seemed to throw some new light on the history of Mycenaean expansion in Italy.[10] Among the demes subject to the kingdom of Pylos we find a Metapa, probably to be equated with the name of Metapontum, originally Metabon; now this town was supposed to have been founded by the Pylians accompanying Nestor on his return from Troy.[11] The same tablets also record the importation into Pylos of minerals coming from Cyprus and at the same time from Aithale—i.e. from Elba which Virgil describes as *inexhaustis generosa metallis*.[12] Are we to infer that exploration for metals in Tuscany, which had been one of the objectives of Chalcidian colonization in the eighth century, was already among the motives behind Mycenaean expansion in the west? We must suppose also that the quest for Baltic amber took a high place; the amber route by the Adriatic normally ended at Pylos,[13] while the tin route from Britain, after hugging the west coast of Italy, found it necessary to use Lipari as a stage point.[14]

The Aeolian islands seem to have played a central rôle in this commercial activity.[15] Lipari was perhaps the furthest point reached by Achaean navigators, and it has been plausibly supposed that they established a profitable check-point on east-west trade, as the Chalcidians did later in the Sicilian narrows. There are too few Mycenaean objects found in the Tyrrhenian, in Ischia and Etruria, for us to believe that there were real Achaean settlements there. Contrariwise, they are so thick in the Taranto area that we must believe that there was a fully-fledged colony—the more so since the pottery of Scoglio del Tonno, during the three centuries of its accumulation, remains uniformly original, with no local imitations.[16] Its close resemblance in form and decoration to the pottery of Ialysos has led some scholars to posit a Rhodian colony.[17] The most recent researches, however, conclude that Cypriot and Rhodian imports were preponderant only in the later stages of the Mycenaean thalassocracy (Myc. III B 2, III C 1: 1265–1125), while during the first two centuries (Myc. III A, Myc. III B 1: 1425–1265) there was a very close tie with the cultures of the Argolid and of Athens.[18]

The permanent settlement of the Achaeans at Tarentum may be reckoned as a civilizing leaven which helped to transform southern Italy, leading it from its pastoral and half-nomadic traditions into a settled agricultural economy.[19] This was what Italos had done, according to legend, for the most ancient people in Italy, the Oenotrians.[20] In support of this view it is remarked that the introduction of the sickle into Apulia and southern Italy coincides with this first distant flight of Greek colonialism.

However that may be, the consequences were to be lasting, even after Mycenaean power had collapsed. Scoglio del Tonno was abandoned in the twelfth or eleventh century,[21] but at Porto Saturo, Porto Perone and Castelluccia the native civilizations kept going virtually uninterrupted until the Greeks came. The stratigraphy of Porto Saturo shows that occupation was continuous throughout the first iron age, in two successive phases (tenth to ninth and ninth to eighth centuries) illustrated by Iapygian protogeometric and geometric.[22] The Aegeans, moreover, came less often to those coasts, but never ceased coming altogether.

When the Lacedaemonian Phalanthos came in the latter half of the eighth century to colonize Tarentum, he landed first at Satyrion, which is clearly to be identified with Porto Saturo, and was received favourably by the barbarians and Cretans dwelling there.[23] We may believe that the mention of these Cretans was not a stroke of later invention. That the Aegeans should still have been remembered in southern Italy, and that some Iapygian families claimed descent from them will not seem improbable if we recollect that in north Africa a tribe of the Numidian Sahara was still boasting in 1860 of its descent from the Romans.[24]

B Phoenician expansion and colonization in the west

After the Mycenaean empire had collapsed in the twelfth century, the Phoenicians came forward to make sure that eastern influence on the west should not flag or fail. Their performance as explorers, traders, colonizers and spreaders of civilization was very considerable, and few achievements have left a deeper mark on history.[25] It goes without saying that the existence of Carthage opposite Rome, on the other side of *mare nostrum*, was a determining factor in Rome's history. But long before this historic rivalry arose, Phoenician influence had made itself felt on the coasts of Italy and to the western extremity of the world: by passing the columns of Hercules and venturing over the river of Ocean (as Homer spoke of the straits of Gibraltar)[26] the Phoenicians won the power to exploit two sources of fabulous wealth—to the north their colony of Gades (Cadiz), next-door to the kingdom of Tartessos, received the silver of the Andalusian highlands and the tin which the sailors of Tartessos brought back from the Cassiterides,[27] while to the south, Lixus, on the Moroccan coast opposite Gades and founded (so it was said) at the same time, stored the gold of the Sudan which their fleets fetched from the mysterious Cerne, at the end of a long coastwise navigation which Hanno was to retrace in the fifth century.[28]

These great achievements of Phoenician colonization in the west were assigned by tradition to a very early date.[29] The Phoenicians were supposed to have gone straight to their most distant target and occupied the two keys to their Atlantic enterprises, Lixus in Morocco and Gades in Spain: the latter was founded, according to Velleius Paterculus, in 1110 B.C., while Lixus, according to Pliny, was even older. Utica was said to have been founded shortly afterwards. Punic sources also listed Hippo (Bône or

c

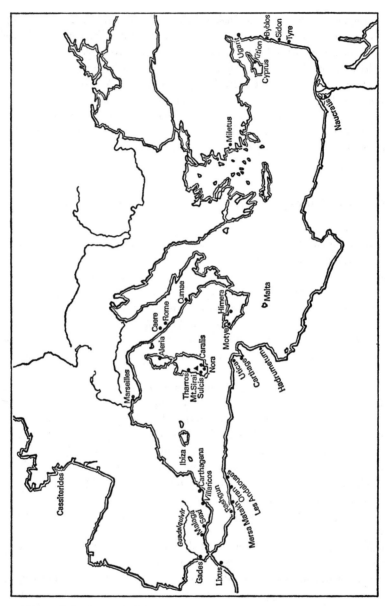

3 **Phoenician expansion**

Bizerta), Hadrumetum (Sousse) and Lepcis Magna, and Tyrian annals spoke of another African colony, the mysterious Auza (Aumale, Oran, Algiers?), as having been founded in the first half of the ninth century. To Carthage some authors assigned a date before the siege of Troy—namely 1213,[29a] but the date which Timaeus derived from Tyrian documents—814–813— gained general acceptance. In Sicily, according to Thucydides, the Phoeni- cians were established on the promontories and off-shore islands before the Greeks began to arrive in large numbers (from *c.*750 onwards).[29b] Finally the Carthaginians, carrying on the colonial policy of the Phoenicians, set up one of their trading depots at Ebusus (Ibiza) in the Balearic islands.[29c]

Phoenicomania and Phoenicophobia

Down to the end of the last century, these dates were accepted without dispute. When F. C. Movers was writing his *Phoenizier* (1841–49) men knew, or thought they knew, what a fundamental rôle the Phoenicians had played in the Aegean in the second millennium and how they had been virtually the sole formative influence on nascent Greek civilization; and all this fitted in well with the early date assigned to their colonizing activity in the west. These fearless navigators had taught the Greeks to be a mari- time nation; inventors of the alphabet, they were credited with the discovery of astronomy, geometry, arithmetic and all the learning of the east. The enchantment of 'an oriental mirage', in Salomon Reinach's phrase of 1893, had fallen on even the best of scholars; in our own day the charm was still working on Victor Bérard, when he tried to show, with much ingenuity, but not without some forced equating of placenames, that Homer had taken the material for the descriptions and legends in the *Odyssey* from a Phoenician source—'some record of voyages, some periplus drawn up by a professional'.[30] But excessive credulity provoked a reaction of scepticism (itself excessive) from the pen of J. Beloch in his article of 1894 *Die Phoeniker im aegeischen Meer*,[31] reissued later in his *Griechische Geschichte*. The resurrection of the Aegean world from the excavations of Mycenae and Cnossos strongly affirmed the originality of early Greek civilization, at the expense of the supposed bringers of culture, and Reinach drew the singular conclusion that it was necessary to continue 'vindicating the rights of Europe against the pretensions of Asia'. The dispute also took on the semblance of a battle between the classical scholars who still sat at the feet of Herodotus, Thucydides and Strabo, and the archaeologists, who demanded, as Bérard put it with his usual vigour, 'an archipelago free from all foreign penetration for centuries, nay, for millennia, to accommodate the successive cultures, all native, all independent, whose deposits were banked up in the walls of the Minoan trenches'.[32] Archaeology, preoccupied with 'trifling external details', and guilty, as its detractors thought, of not having sufficiently confirmed by its findings the tradition which made the Aegeans the pupils of the Phoenicians, was pronounced 'incapable of resolving the problem of Hellenic origins'.[33]

Archaeology has equally failed, despite the most extensive investigations, to confirm the early dates assigned to Phoenician colonization in the west, and the critical impulse first given by Beloch has been followed sometimes even to extremes. Thus in 1958 Rhys Carpenter in his *Phoenicians in the West*[34] brings their first colonizing movement down as late as the seventh century, and claims that the Greeks of Samos towards the end of that century were the first to exploit the riches of Tartessos. But there is a limit imposed by chronology in the other direction: historians of Etruscan civilization,[35] of Chalcidian colonization[36] and of Carthage[37] consider that the Phoenicians, whose home bases in Sidon, Tyre and Cyprus felt the weight of Assyrian arms in the beginning of the seventh century, were thenceforward cut off from the western Mediterranean. This would reduce to a minimum the time available to the Phoenicians for so great an achievement.

In recent years there has been a trend away both from Phoenicomania and Phoenicophobia; the problem is now treated with more balanced judgement and with an attempt to evaluate the various kinds of evidence in the confused welter of data—literary, epigraphic and archaeological. Some recent reassessments and a number of new facts help us to grasp the complexity, reality and duration of Phoenician expansion in the west.[38] It now appears indeed to have begun later than tradition said it did, but not so late as some critics would maintain, and to have continued well after 700, side by side with Greek colonization, often in rivalry, sometimes in commercial cooperation.

Phoenician 'pre-colonization'

We have used the word 'expansion', because colonization proper, i.e. the permanent establishment in trading posts of men to defend and maintain them, in numbers sufficient to constitute a New Town (Qarthadasht—Carthago),[39] presupposes continued naval activity beforehand, voyages of exploration, raids from time to time, regular commercial runs in which the crews only landed to load the gold of Ophir or the silver of Tarshish. The Homeric poems[40] refer to the arrival of these 'greedy sailors with a thousand tawdry gewgaws in their ships'; they stayed only long enough to debauch the women and stock up with food, then they would pack their bags, dismantle their 'one-night pirate camp' as A. Moret has fitly called it, weigh anchor and be seen and known no more. Sometimes all contact between the parties was eliminated by the 'silent barter' whose immemorial rules are described by Herodotus and sixteen centuries later by the Arab historian El-Yacout in dealing with the Sudanese gold trade.[41] Modern historians have tried to form a picture of the physical mechanism of these untraceable voyages:[42] they have certainly shown that the stage-points along the African coast were determined by the presence every evening of an islet sheltering a shore where they could beach their ships, together with a watering-point. Some writers have also speculated on what the Phoenicians could sell to savages who were not interested in silver bowls or ivory caskets:[43] glass beads, consumer goods, slaves?

The only trace left by such trading might be the modification of a culture in its archaeological aspect, as for example in Sicily in the Cassibile culture (1000–850): in that period Bernabò Brea has found articles of bronze—brooches, razors, axes—which on typological grounds are akin to similar articles commonly found in Spain and along the Atlantic coasts of England and France.[44] Or, as a clue to such traffic, we may appeal to some unusual objects—ivory combs at Carmona in Andalusia,[45] the bronze candelabrum of S. Vittoria di Serri in Sardinia.[46] When in 1956, off Sciacca on the south coast of Sicily, a figurine was discovered of a goddess brandishing a weapon in her right hand, identifiable with Melqart or Reshouf, the adherents of the high chronology took new heart: the statuette, which is very like many bronzes from Ras-Shamra (Ugarit) dating from the fourteenth to thirteenth centuries, and which was presumably re-used later to adorn the prow of a ship, is proof that Phoenician ships visited the Selinus area at a time something like the twelfth century[47]—unless indeed it goes even further back in history, to a time when sailors from Byblos perhaps took part in Mycenaean expeditions.[48]

The fact is that, although from the earliest times the Phoenicians practised their calling as carriers of cargo and as merchants banding together into companies to exploit markets, the invasion of the Peoples of the Sea towards 1175, with the difficulties that it put in the way of coasting trade between the Lebanon and Egypt,[49] must have meant the beginning of an age that was unpropitious to the great colonial expeditions which tradition in fact assigns to that very period—about 1200–1000. The expeditions seem much more likely to have resulted from a real renascence that came about only when the Assyrians had re-established order on the coast. Moreover, the forests of Libanus may have provided the Phoenicians with ship-building timber from the dawn of time; but it was the beginning of the first millennium that witnessed decisive improvements in technique, such as the use of pitch to make the planking watertight,[50] and the invention of the framed hull—from which the longship, intended to face the high seas, derived its classic silhouette and its prospects of success.[51]

The problem of Tarshish

Tyre was the principal seat of this renascence. The progress of its power in the tenth century is illustrated by Biblical texts. At this time Hiram I, king of Tyre (970–936) helps his son-in-law Solomon to build himself a fleet by providing him with buildings and equipment; the two monarchs organize joint expeditions towards Ophir (on the coasts of Arabia and India),[52] where their combined fleets went to look for gold, and towards Tarshish, whence once every three years they brought back 'gold and silver, ivory, and apes, and peacocks'.[53] The proposal to identify this Tarshish with Tartessos—which would be the Greek transcription of the Hebrew name—is an old one.[54] Now in fact the 'ships of Tarshish' do not necessarily go to Tartessos; we find them on one occasion based at Ezion Geber on the Red Sea and sailing towards Ophir.[55] It seems likely that *Tarshish* in that expression is a common noun, meaning etymologically 'mine' or 'mining region'; thus it could have been applied to various countries in east or west—Tarsus,[56] Tunis,[57] Tartessos. In favour of its having a singular denotation, meaning only Tartessos (although the evidence for it is rather late) we may note that the second treaty between Rome and Carthage mentions a Punic town in the south of Spain, *Mastia Tarseion*, a name in which the Tarseians are undoubtedly confused with the Tartessians.[58] Ezekiel, in a prophecy dated to 586,[59] is able to say that up to his time Tarshish kept the markets of Tyre supplied with silver, iron, tin and lead— and these are precisely the metals that made Tartessos rich.[60] But one could not venture to declare that the Tarshish of king Solomon, with its ivories and its peacocks, was already that of the Pillars of Hercules, and that the ambitions of Hiram I were already directed towards the western trade-routes.[61]

The traditions always talk in terms of colonies being founded, and that is a very different thing from the exploratory voyages which we have just described, voyages which did no more than visit the coasts where settlements were later to be made. The foundation of a Phoenician colony can be recognized by certain uniform features: having chosen a suitable site, in an islet where throughout the west, from Cadiz to Motye, they reproduced the image of their native Tyre,[62] the colonists, on the very place where they had just landed, consecrated a sanctuary to their gods.[63] To these, according to the ancient custom of the *mol'k* sacrifice, they offered up children over a period of centuries.[64] The sacred area, called the *tophet*, where the cinerary urns and stelae gradually accumulated, often lets us get back to an earlier date than the cremation-cemeteries—shafts sunk in the rock, shallow *fossae*, tombs built variously according to country and date—that spread out in the island and soon invaded the mainland.

Now throughout the Phoenician empire there is no archaeological trace of their settlement earlier than the eighth century. Even in Cyprus, where one might suppose that they would have gained a secure footing before advancing further, the founding of their colony of Kition, according to Gjerstad's chronology, is no earlier than 800.[65]

Malta

The Italian excavations in Malta in 1963–65 at Tas Silg[66] have brought to light a great Phoenician-Carthaginian sanctuary, established on a site of prehistoric worship, and consecrated to Astarte and Tanit before at last, under Roman rule, it became the *fanum Junonis* mentioned by Cicero.[67] Ivories, various fragments of statuary and buildings, etc., show a persistent oriental tradition; from the point of view of chronology we can say no more than that it goes back at least to the fourth or fifth century.

Motye

Motye, near the western tip of Sicily, is one of the places where the features of Phoenician colonization are most deeply marked and maintained without external influence.[68] The site, exactly like that of Cadiz, is typical: a small islet in a natural roadstead further protected by a larger island.[69] The small island comprised some 120 acres, with a tiny inner harbour (*cothon*) and a sanctuary; it was later walled about with a rampart and connected by a causeway with the mainland. This islet saw the first Phoenician settlement in the eighth century, to the latter half of which we can assign the oldest pottery, cinerary urns, pear-shaped and socketed jugs that are found in the primitive necropolis.[70] Attention has often been drawn[71] to the resemblances between this pottery and the contemporary pottery of Carthage, founded, according to tradition, in 814, and it was very tempting to conclude that Motye was a Carthaginian colony. The recent excavations, which have aimed at clearing the sacred enclosure of Cappidazzu and the *tophet*, have brought to light various features that cannot be explained by exclusively Carthaginian influence. They tend to confirm the guess of T. J. Dunbabin, who believed in an independent immigration coming from a point on the Phoenician coast.[72] Possibly Motye was only later brought under Punic hegemony; certainly it maintained throughout its history close connections with the Greek world.

Hadrumetum, Utica

Let us leave Carthage aside for a moment. On the Tunisian coast, Hadrumetum,[73] a thriving trading-post serving as outlet to a fertile hinterland, may have been founded before Carthage; but its *tophet*, which has been partly excavated, has shown nothing older than the sixth or possibly the seventh century. Further west, in the bay of Porto Farina, Utica, halfway between Tyre and Tartessos, was said to have been founded in 1101; it is now ten miles inland, and the silting of the Medjerda has rendered the site unrecognizable. In the excavations conducted there in 1946 and 1950, P. Cintas has laid bare, under masonry tombs going back perhaps to the seventh century, deep *fossae* with pottery dating possibly from the eighth.[74]

Sardinia

In Sardinia[75] the eighth century again is the date assignable to the oldest pottery discovered at Sulci (S. Antonio).[76] But the island has been keeping some surprises in store for recent years. Archaeological research, which has been endeavouring to distinguish under the Roman and Carthaginian strata the features of an early Phoenician period associated with the native culture of the *nuraghe*,[77] is now busy in its sixteenth year at Nora (already famous for a Punic inscription which the Semitists assign to the ninth century,[78] and for a temple of Tanit and a sixth-century cemetery),[79] at Caralis (Cagliari) and at Tharros (S. Giovanni di Sinni).[80] At Monte Sirai,[81] near Carbonia in the south-east of Sardinia, a previously unknown fortified town has been discovered, which is the only example so far found of Carthaginian penetration into the interior. The monuments and objects are very varied, strongly marked by Greek influence, and show close connections with Carthage, with Cyprus and with the Syro-Palestinian world; and there is talk of graves whose typology would take us back very nearly to the Phoenician graves of the beginning of the first millennium.

Oran and Morocco

If we now continue westwards along the African coast, we shall find nothing of such antiquity. In the Oran region, the stage-points of the Phoenician coasting voyages, which were later organized by Carthage— Les Andalouses, Mersa Madakh near Cape Sigale, the island of Rachgoun at the mouth of the Tafna[82]—have been carefully excavated in the last few years, and they take us back only to the sixth or seventh century. In Morocco, Lixus (Larache) may have been frequented from the eleventh century onward by vessels on their way to Cerne, but the fragments of pottery with a lustrous red glaze, which are found immediately over virgin soil and which mark the founding of a permanent settlement, date from the sixth century at the earliest.[83] Further south, 400 miles from the Pillars of Hercules, the tiny island of Mogador,[84] a site like those typical of Phoenician settlement, has aroused lively interest through the discovery of Attic and Ionian amphorae (the latter from Smyrna or Miletus) dating from approximately 650 B.C.;[85] in the same stratum, which they thus date, numerous fragments have been found of the red pottery from Lixus just mentioned, and of archaic Phoenician pottery. The presence of Phoenician and Greek imports in deposits of the same date is an important fact which is verified elsewhere, particularly at Carthage. The small number of the Greek shards (a score or so) suggests that they came to Mogador (and to other sites in Morocco) only by indirect commerce, the intermediaries being Phoenicians, and more probably the Phoenicians from around Tartessos than those of Tyre or Carthage; for there seems to be a community of culture, marked by distinctive and original elements (e.g. the red-glazed pottery), associating the far west of north Africa with the Punic civilization of southern

Spain and with the radiating influence of Gades, the doyenne of the Phoenician colonies.

Spain

Unfortunately changes of the coastline at Gades have so profoundly altered the characteristic roadstead that all we know now is a cemetery with about 150 hypogea, the oldest dating from the late sixth century.[86] In the hinterland the valley of the Guadalquivir was colonized for agriculture: traces of this colonization at Carmona and Osuna are of the sixth or perhaps the seventh century.[87] On the south-east coast the cemetery of Baria (Villaricos) is of the fifth century and has strongly marked Carthaginian features.[88]

But in the region of Malaga two Phoenician settlements have been successively revealed which are certainly much older.

At Torre del Mar, twenty miles east of Malaga, where A. Schulten had proposed to locate the settlement of Mainake, on a site very rich in Phoenician pottery, there have been found two Proto-Corinthian shards of the first half of the seventh century and a fragment of an Attic amphora from the beginning of that century. The excavators confidently claim the site of the discovery as that of the oldest Phoenician trading establishment in the Iberian peninsula, founded probably in the late eighth century.[89]

A comparable date may be assigned to the very interesting cemetery which has been recently excavated 35 miles further east, near Almuñécar, which is known to have been the site of Sexi.[90] Here there are a score of cremation-graves sunk into the rock, forming only part of a much greater necropolis rising up the sides of the hill. Two Proto-Corinthian subgeometric *kotylai*, found in one of the niches of grave 19 (one of the most recent), enable us to date this tomb to the first half of the seventh century. But we may well believe that the cemetery as a whole is of rather earlier date. We find in some of the graves indications of two successive interments, and the furnishings of the graves seem to become richer as one goes up the slope of the hill: all this suggests a chronological series with grave 19 as one of its last terms.

A particularly remarkable feature is the strongly Egyptian atmosphere of the necropolis: as cinerary urns, large jars of alabaster are consistently and exclusively employed, four of them bearing cartouches of ninth-century pharaohs—Osorkon II (870–847), Sheshank II (847), Takelot II (847–823) —but, strange to say, none of any later pharaoh. Three of them also have inscriptions in imitation hieroglyphics, while another has a Phoenician inscription.

That these cartouches and hieroglyphics were used for magic purposes is beyond dispute. Nevertheless they show that the Phoenicians of Almunecar felt a singular and special devotion to three successive pharaohs who, like Osorkon II for example, seem to have been especially popular in Byblos and Samaria.[91] Possibly the expedition which ended in the founding of the colony was the work of client Phoenicians, like those who at Byblos piously kept alive the memory of their Egyptian patrons until the advances of Tiglath-Pilesar, Shalmanezer and Sargon in the latter half of the eighth century brought all the coast under Assyrian rule. Occasionally flight or exile, as in the tale of Dido, may have added a particular motive to the general commercial motivation of Phoenician colonialism.

One might also on this hypothesis give some meaning to the tradition preserved in Megasthenes and Strabo, that some pharaohs, like Taharka, carried their victorious arms as far as the pillars of Hercules:[92] they would have taken the glory for navigations that should properly have redounded to the credit of Phoenicians sailing under their flag.

Finally it is worth while to recall a passage of Strabo[93] that applies fairly well to what we have learned from the necropolis of Almuñécar: 'An ancient oracle having commanded the Tyrians to go and found a settlement at the Pillars of Hercules, a first expedition went off to discover the places referred to; having arrived at the strait of Calpe [i.e. Gibraltar] the sailors who composed the expedition dropped anchor this side of the strait, where the town of Sexi now stands, and offered sacrifice to the god on that point of the coast.' It matters little that Strabo should go on to say that the sacrificial victims proved unsatisfactory and the expedition had to return to Tyre, and that a second and finally a third expedition were needed to reach Gades at last. Local tradition, preserved by Posidonius, allowed to Gades its accepted primacy in the order of colonies, but did not forget the great antiquity of Sexi. It has also been noted that the point where the colonists established themselves was at the issue of a valley route now followed by the road from Malaga to Seville, by which one could easily gain the valley of the Guadalquivir between the Sierra Nevada and the Sierra de las Nieves.[94]

The date that seems to emerge for the foundation of Mainake and Sexi, before 700, allows us to settle the old problem raised by the claims of the Ionian Greeks, who pretended to have anticipated the Phoenicians in the discovery of Tartessos. Herodotus had chosen to echo these pretensions, and he told of the odyssey of the Samian Colaios, who around 630 was driven by a storm beyond the Pillars of Hercules and thus opened up 'that centre of commerce which had not yet been exploited'.[95] He also dwelt on the friendly welcome accorded to Phocaean colonists by the king Arganthonios —a name suggesting at once the silver-mines of his kingdom.[96] The archaeological evidence now shows that the Phoenicians were there a little before the Greeks, and at the same time confirms the commercial relations existing between them, which at Mogador around 650 brought in Attic and Ionian amphorae, and at Sexi the two Proto-Corinthian sub-geometric *kotylai* which, in a colony firmly tenacious of its national usages, were allowed to help furnish one of its latest tombs.

Carthage

Let us now return to Carthage. On the date and circumstances of its foundation, if we set aside the rather late legend that takes it back to the thirteenth century, the sources are much more numerous, coherent and authoritative.[97] Tyre, like all the states of the east, drew up public chronicles analogous to the Babylonian and Assyrian chronicles, or to those whose value we can now estimate from the archives of Ras-Shamra in northern Phoenicia. The Tyrian annals, giving lists of kings together with the duration of each reign and the principal events occurring in each, have an a priori claim to be taken seriously—as when they declare, for example, that king Ithobal (873–842) founded in Africa a town, unfortunately unknown, called Auza.[98] These annals were consulted by Timaeus[99] about 300, translated about 200 by Menander of Ephesus, and fragments of them are cited (in his Greek version) by Josephus about A.D. 100 in his *Contra Apionem* and the *Jewish Antiquities*.[100] They placed the foundation of Carthage in the seventh year of the reign of Pygmalion. In the chronology of the kings of Tyre this corresponds to 819, but other calculations have set it at 814 (with Timaeus) or 824 (with Justin).[101] This insignificant variation of a few years is to be explained by mistakes in conversion to different eras; the basic agreement is obvious. Furthermore, Timaeus and Menander and Justin (the latter with much more detail) relate in generally similar terms the palace drama which led Elissa, the sister of Pygmalion who had slain her husband, to flee from Tyre with some of her compatriots; she arrived in Libya after various wanderings which earned her the name of Dido among the natives. Timaeus and Justin add that the king of Libya wanted to marry her, but she ascended the funeral pyre rather than be unfaithful to her first husband. Everyone knows what the Latin poets and Virgil above all have made out of this story.

Some years ago, the Assyriologist E. O. Forrer put forward a bold theory bringing the foundation of Carthage down a century and a half later.[102] Despite the cuneiform documents to which it appealed, while mixing in an element of pure fantasy, the theory will not stand examination. The author thought he could show that Qarthadasht or Carthage did not mean 'New Town', but 'New Capital', the element *qart-* having the pregnant meaning of 'town *par excellence*', a town such that there could not be two like it. He therefore looked for a time when Tyre, torn between the rival ambitions of its powerful neighbours Egypt and Assyria, and reduced at last to extremity, had no alternative but to 'transfer the capital from the kingdom of Tyre to that of Ethiopia to rescue it from Assyrian attack'. This historic moment he claimed to find between 673 and 663: in 670–671 king Ba'al was besieged in Tyre by Assar-Haddon and had to capitulate; another siege, after 666, put him at the mercy of Assur-Banipal; he had to yield up his daughters and his brother's daughters to the latter's seraglio. Forrer imagined that two other daughters of Ba'al, Dido and Anna, seized the opportunity to execute their father's project of transferring the capital to Africa. He pointed out that Dido in Virgil is the daughter of Belus (Ba'al),[103] and accounts for the 'mistake' which placed the foundation of Carthage under the reign of Pygmalion by a confusion with the Cypriot Qarthadasht, Kition, which he supposed to have been conquered by Tyre in 814. Against this entrancing construction one may object that neither at Kition nor at Cartagena did Qarthadasht mean 'New Capital', implying that its foundation meant the replacement of the metropolis; that Tyre, which had been under an Assyrian protectorate since the end of the second millennium, was taken and retaken in many campaigns, from Shalmaneser in 841 to Nebuchadnezzar in 587, and that the purpose of these campaigns was not to destroy Tyre—which continued to be siege-proof on its island and to send its fleets into the western seas—but simply to enforce payment of arrears of tribute. As for the father's name, the authority of Virgil cannot prevail against the tradition which calls him Mutto (Matan). Finally, the date 673–663 is controverted by the discovery under the soil of Carthage of archaeological material that is beyond dispute much older.

It is possible that the first graves of Carthage, contemporary with its foundation, have not been discovered yet.[104] Several parts of its vast necropolis,[105] on the slopes of the hills of St Louis and of Juno, on the beach of Dermech and especially at Douimes, abundantly cover the seventh and sixth centuries, the oldest graves being of the eighth; they show that at the end of the eighth century the colony had active relations with the outside world (pot-bellied aryballoi from 730–710, Cycladic cups).[106] The tophet of Salammbo, excavated by D. Harden[107] and later by P. Cintas,[108] perhaps went back to a yet more ancient past. Under the lowest of the strata in which, from the beginnings up to the fall of Carthage, the bones of child victims and the accompanying stelae to Tanit had been deposited, Cintas brought to light a vault contrived in a natural irregularity of the ground; this, roofed over with stone, may have been the sanctuary constructed on the beach when the colonists first arrived. Some Greek vases found in a hiding-place there may have been the foundation offering: two skyphoi, three small oinochoai, and a sprinkler, all proto-Corinthian 'from the period of the pot-bellied aryballoi' (725–700), together with a Cycladic amphora which on the most generous dating cannot be older than 750. It has also been supposed[109] that the 'chapel' discovered under the tophet had been constructed in memory of Dido on the site of the pyre which was later to be the centre of her cult. However that may be, the gap between the traditional date of the founding of Carthage and the archaeological discoveries, although it is tending to close, remains visibly open.

Punic colonization

After the foundation of Carthage it is sometimes hard to tell what instances of Phoenician expansion, commerce and influence in the west stem from the metropolis and what from the colony. Carthage soon began to send out settlers in its turn, for Iviza in 654 is given by tradition as a Carthaginian colony. The historians of Carthaginian civilization often tend to suppose that Tyre, succumbing to the Assyrian onslaughts in the late eighth century, was thenceforth striken with paralysis, and that Carthage at once took up the reins of empire.[110] But in fact the inexhaustible vitality of the Phoenicians survived the successive sieges of Sennacherib (701), Esar-Haddon (671), Assurbanipal (666) and even Nebuchadnezzar (587):[111] under the flag of Egypt or of Assyria, the Tyrian fleet was active near the Pillars of Hercules in the time of Taharqa (689–683) and Nebuchadnezzar (605–562), thus giving rise to the obscure tradition that the region had been conquered by those rulers.[112] It was again the pharaoh Necho who towards 600 entrusted Phoenician sailors with a circumnavigation of Africa which is celebrated in the history of exploration.[113] Even after Phoenicia had submitted to the Persian empire (539), her fleets continued to play a leading part in the naval battles of the fifth century, and it was only in Alexander's day, when the causeway linking the island to the mainland was built, that Tyrian naval activity came wholly to a stop.

In all this time, and up to her final destruction in 146, Carthage had never ceased to keep up bonds of friendship and even dependence with Tyre. At Carthage no trace has been found of a metropolitan 'governor' like the one who administered Cyprus in the mid-eighth century in the name of the king of Sidon.[114] But for a long time Carthage paid to Tyre a tribute originally fixed at one tenth of her revenues;[115] she sent an annual embassy to the festivals of the Tyrian Hercules, and filled the hero's temple with offerings after her victories.

There is reason to think that these bonds, never entirely to be broken, became relaxed when Carthage had proved her military might in the middle of the sixth century, with Malchus' expeditions in Africa, Sicily and Sardinia, and his victory over the Phocaeans at Alalia. The conquest of Tunisia and the development of agriculture is placed by S. Gsell in the fifth century. At that time, says Dio Chrysostom, a certain Hanno 'turned the Carthaginians into Libyans, from having been Tyrians before.'[15] Carthage was then indeed in a position to replace Tyre completely as the leader of the Phoenicians in the west. It is significant that the first treaty between Rome and Carthage, at the end of the sixth century, confines Carthaginian suzerainty to Sicily, Sardinia and the African coast east of Cape Farina, while the second, at the end of the fourth century, includes Utica and Spain, but at the same time expressly mentions Tyre, Carthage assuming thenceforth the responsibilities of the fallen metropolis.[117]

This replacement of the metropolis by the most powerful of its colonies had important consequences: 'Carthaginian support, Carthaginian power and political direction were needed to render fruitful the activities of the Phoenicians in the west.'[118] Not only did she breathe new life into the still feeble trading depots (the Punic cemeteries in Sardinia, Morocco and Spain are often the only ones hitherto discovered and always the most numerous), she also vindicated their independence against threats from the native peoples, as Gades taken by storm from the Tartessians; she strengthened and organized on a systematic basis the chain of stage-points along the African coast, firmly establishing them at 22-mile intervals (the normal distance sailed in daylight hours; they are strung out along the western trade-route like beads—Carthage to Utica, Rusicade (Philippeville) to Cullu (Collo), Icosium (Algiers) to Tipasa, Iol (Cherchel) and Gunuga (Gouraya), Les Andalouses to Mersa Matakh and the island of Rashgun.[119] The periplus of Hanno in itself is enough to show that Carthage took upon herself the work of exploration by sea which the Phoenicians had earlier initiated beyond the Pillars of Hercules.[120] But from the sixth century onwards, it was Carthage that strove to defend (in concert with the Etruscans) the monopolies enjoyed by the old trading depots and now menaced by the progress of Greek colonization.

Phoenician influence in Italy

Before that time, Phoenician commercial activity, either directly or through Carthage, but without allowing its own routes to become confounded with those used by Chalcidian and Phocaean ships, had been actively carried on in the west, particularly on the coasts of Etruria and Latium, where fairly clear traces of it were left.

The history of Etruscan culture begins with an orientalizing phase, and it was formerly fashionable to attribute the formation of this phase to Phoenician influence. Then an attempt was made to show that Phoenician influence was insignificant. A reasonable synthesis now seems to be emerging. We are not concerned solely with the Egyptian or pseudo-Egyptian knick-knacks like scarabs, amulets and ostrich eggs that fill the Etruscan tombs[121] from the oldest onwards—one of these, at Tarquinia, is dated by a piece of faience with the cartouche of the pharaoh Bocchoris (720–715). In the second half of the seventh century, the great princely tombs of Caere and Praeneste contain some very fine objects either imported from Phoenicia or made under the influence of Phoenician models. Were they imports? One remembers some verses of Homer on a silver mixing-bowl: 'Skilful carvers from Sidon had wondrously adorned it; Phoenicians had then borne it over the misty sea and offered it in harbours . . .'[122] Two silver bowls of composite artistry, resembling some found in Cyprus in their mingling of Egyptian and Assyrian motifs, figure among the treasures of the Bernardini tomb; one of them bears some imitation hieroglyphics and a Phoenician inscription with the name of the owner—Eshmunazar, the son of Asto.[123] But the very numerous ivories—the arms and hands of the Barberini tomb, the pyxis with bands of figures from the Regolini-

Galassi tomb—also go back to the same source.[124] One of these pyxides has been very carefully analysed:[125] it originated at Nimroud in Assyria shortly after 1000, and each of its decorative themes—chorus of women, sphinx-tamer, lion-tamer, Phoenician palmettes—can be shown to have been current around 700 in Palestine, Syria and Cyprus. If the object was made in Etruria, the artist, like the contemporary goldsmiths, had a range of images at his disposal, coming from the near east under Phoenician dominance. At about the same time another archaeologist[126] announced 'some cases of direct contact between Etruria, Cappadocia and northern Syria towards 600 B.C.', and suggested that archaic Etruscan sculpture in stone had come into existence at Vetulonia by the scaling up of small caryatids in ivory or bucchero—the prototypes of these also coming from the same source.[127]

If the Phoenicians frequented the coasts of central Italy, did they leave nothing there but precious objects and models for artistic imitation? Did these images not have some influence in the religious sphere also? F. Altheim[128] in 1930 drew attention to some verses of the Odyssey in praise of another Phoenician silver *krater*:[129] 'It is a work of Hephaistos,' says Menelaus, 'I have it from the lord Phaidimos, king of the Sidonians.' Now according to some scholiasts, *phaidimos* is simply an adjective meaning 'brilliant, shining', and the real name of this king of Sidon was Sethlos; it is an odd fact that one of the names of the Etruscan Vulcan, worshipped at Populonia, the centre of the metal-working trade, was *Sethlans*. The question has been taken up again from various different angles in connection with the origins of the cult of Hercules: J. Bayet[130] has traced its course starting from the Greek colonies of southern Italy as far as Rome, in his temple of the Ara Maxima in the Forum Boarium. Bayet does not rule out 'a purely oriental influence', and he observes the close ties between the Roman Hercules and the Tyrian Baal-Melqart, whose sanctuary was also out of bounds to women, dogs, pigs, and flies.[131] A. Piganiol[132] has recently shown that the parallelism which the calendar reveals between the festivals of Hercules at Athens and those at Rome implies a common pre-Hellenic origin, and that the oldest statue of Hercules in Italy, showing the god brandishing his club in the right hand, endows him with the features of Melqart—the attitude, we may add, is that of the Melqart of Sciacca: the Roman Hercules had been brought to the Forum Boarium, the site of Rome's most ancient harbour, by Phoenician merchants. At the same time, D. van Berchem[133] has also underlined the oriental features of the ritual, comparing the tithe offered to Hercules with the tax imposed on eastern markets for the coffers of the god, and above all furnishing a perfect solution to the problem of the *Potitii*, who appear in the tradition as one of the two families charged with the service of the sanctuary. J. Carcopino[134] had already suggested that their name, unknown in the Fasti or as a Latin proper name at all, concealed a sacerdotal function: the college of the Potitii corresponds literally to that of the *Katochoi*, 'those possessed of the god', who are known at Baetocaece and elsewhere in Syria. Finally, R. Rebuffat[135] in an article entitled 'Lés Phéniciens à Rome', has assembled all the evidence that leads him to believe that a Tyrian colony was very early established in the Forum Boarium, where it founded and administered the Ara Maxima until the censor Appius Claudius in 3 1 2 transferred its management to the Roman state.

All this still remains very obscure. There is one much more clear-cut and indeed vital contribution which the Phoenicians made to the rise of civilization in the west—the alphabet. It is well known that the Phoenician alphabet, in use at Byblos from the end of the second millennium, was the basis of the Greek alphabet and the Etruscan alphabet from which the Roman was derived.[136] It was long supposed that the Etruscan alphabet was a Chalcidian alphabet which came to Etruria by way of Cumae. The recent discovery at Ischia of a skyphos from the latter half of the eighth century, bearing the name Nestor followed by two hexameters,[137] has tended to support this thesis: it shows that the Chalcidian alphabet was in use near Cumae at an earlier date than that of any Etruscan inscription. But it does not wholly invalidate the arguments by which A. Grenier,[138] taking as his basis the tablet from Marsiliana d'Albegna (first half of seventh century), had sought to show that the Etruscans had borrowed their alphabet from a pre-Hellenic alphabet, without the intermediacy of Cumae. A recent study by J. A. Bundgård[136] shows that in any case the Phoenicians played a large part in teaching the Etruscans to write, as they had taught the Greeks.

This ivory tablet, bearing on its upper margin 26 characters of the alphabet, was found in an orientalized tomb belonging to an Etruscan prince, surrounded with objects certainly of Syro-Phoenician provenance—a pyxis, a comb, two fan-sticks of carved ivory, and a silver bowl. Similar ivory writing-tablets of the same date and the same type of manufacture have been found at Nimroud. The pyx, comb and tablet had been sent to their Etruscan recipient by a Tyrian merchant in payment for some goods (perhaps wheat) which the former had delivered to him. But the tablet, with its alphabet so carefully engraved in the east, also constituted an invitation to write and to practise a form of correspondence which the eastern business houses had found useful and which they now wanted to spread more widely. It is a specimen alphabet of 26 letters, intended generally to meet the phonetic needs of various languages: the speakers could leave out any characters that they did not need. And in fact several pots in impasto or bucchero of slightly later date show us these model alphabets, conscientiously, often clumsily, recopied by docile disciples; soon we find mingled with them syllabaries from which the unwanted consonants have been removed, and inscriptions written in the practical Etruscan alphabet of 22 and 20 letters. This is the way in which writing and all that went with it seems to have been disseminated in Etruria and later in a great part of the western world during the first half of the seventh century—on the initiative of Phoenician merchants who wanted to facilitate their transactions and accounts with their unsophisticated customers. This striking example shows how important and how productive was a civilizing contact which should never be pushed out of mind by the more obvious impact of Greek civilization.

C Greek colonization

In southern Italy and Sicily

The Greek colonization of southern Italy, Sicily, the coasts of Gaul and Spain constitutes the third and most important of the civilizing influences in the western Mediterranean. It began, in the Tyrrhenian as in the Aegean and Black Seas, during the eighth century, under the pressure of the same economic and social causes which then compelled the dispossessed elements of the population to seek their fortunes abroad.[140] The Aegean navigators had never, as we have seen, completely forgotten the western sea-routes; the practice of piracy or the kind of scouting voyages made by the Phoenicians were enough to maintain some sort of maritime activity on those coasts; but, there is no credit given now to the notion of 'pre-colonization' —sporadic and unrecorded ventures which on such or such a site might have been the prelude to the definitive appearance of a Chalcidian Naxos or a Corinthian Syracuse. The founding of a Greek colony was an official religious and political action—the nature of which we shall later analyse— which in every instance ushered in a new era.

Chalcidian colonization

The pioneers of this colonization were the Chalcidians and the Eretrians of Euboea.[141] Their first foundations were Cumae in Campania, reputed the oldest of all Greek colonies in the west,[142] and Naxos in Sicily, which was officially recognized as the oldest in the island. It was at Naxos, on the altar of Apollo Archegetes, that the representatives from the different cities of Sicily made their sacrifice before leaving for the Hellenic games.[143]

The foundation of Cumae took place in two stages. Livy[144] has preserved a tradition according to which the Chalcidian colonists landed first on the island of Pithecusae (Ischia) before venturing to set foot on the mainland opposite. This has been demonstrated, and is still being confirmed, by the excavations of G. Buchner on Ischia. The site of Cumae has yielded many proto-Corinthian pots, but Ischia has specimens of geometric pottery older than the oldest of the proto-Corinthian, together with some of the latter belonging to series as yet unknown at Cumae.[145] The period separating the two foundations may be estimated at 30 years—from 770 to 740 if one likes. On Ischia the site where the Greeks installed themselves, near the native village of Castiglione on the promontory of Monte di Vico at the north-west corner of the island, offers a terrace that could not be attacked by sea and could easily be defended by land[146]—a holding position which enabled the colonists to make contact with the barbarians of the coast until they should be able to transfer their installation to the mainland: the acropolis of Cumae was on the edge of the fertile plain whose potential as farmland they were anxious to exploit.[147]

The initial object, however, of Chalcidian colonialism seems not to have been so much the search for good farmland as the conquest of a market and the creation of a trade-route. Cumae and Pithecusae are not only the oldest but the farthest from home of the early Greek settlements in the west,[148] and it would be hard to believe that their oecists had sailed all that distance, past the rich plains of Magna Graecia and Sicily, just to find room to dispose of their surplus population. They went in one bound, as the Phoenicians had done at Tartessos, to the ends of the earth, attracted not only by the cereals of Campania, but by the mineral riches of Elba and Etruria—tin, copper, bronze,[149] and wanting to seize the market in them by making contact as near as possible to the centres of production.

Once they had secured this advanced position, the Chalcidians went to work with a will during the years immediately following. They set up the

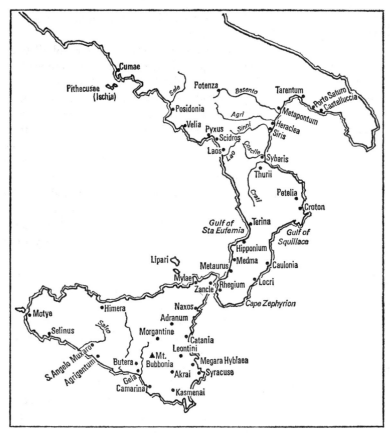

4 Greek colonies in southern Italy and Sicily

intermediate stages on the route, and as first priority laid their hands on the Sicilian narrows. Zancle (Messina) was founded on the Sicilian coast: here again there were two foundings—first by 'pirates' from Cumae, then by a contingent sent from Euboea:[150] Cumae and Chalcis each furnished one of the two oecists. On the Italian shore Rhegium was founded, the oecists this time coming from Zancle and Chalcis.[151] We can see that the great plan as it took shape was powered not only by commands from the metropolis, but by the active collaboration of the colonies themselves.

The colonies of Zancle and Rhegium are said to have been founded shortly after Cumae, hence a little after 740.[152]

From then on, the Chalcidians were in a position to control all trade through the straits, and the greater part of the Greek imports into western countries had to pay their tolls. G. Vallet has shown that the dominant position thus obtained by the Chalcidians in the Tyrrhenian sea resulted in the almost complete elimination of Corinthian pottery. The very wide spread of Corinthian ware in Sicily and at Tarentum as the standard pottery shows that Corinth had created in those areas 'a sort of monopoly in the exchange of its manufactured products for raw materials'; but at the same time the only Corinthian imports in Etruria are a few luxury articles: Corinthian trade stopped short at the straits.[153] On the other hand the good understanding between the Chalcidians and Phocaeans made it possible for many splendid examples of Attic pottery to find a wide distribution through the cities of Etruria, starting from the straits through which they were forwarded.[154]

This lucrative rôle as intermediaries on the trade-route between Greece and Etruria was the basis of Chalcidian prosperity; the colonies that strung themselves out along the Sicilian east coast during the eighth century— Naxos, Leontini, Catania—formed the starting points for the penetration of Hellenism to the interior by way of the fertile valleys. It is pleasing to note that, unlike the brutal expansion of the Dorians of Syracase and Gela, this Hellenization worked by peaceful means.[155] On the north coast, before the end of that century, Zancle had established at Mylae a fortified post which gave her command of a rich wheat-land and of a flourishing native population, among whom the Milazzo culture had arisen at the inception of the iron age;[156] then towards 650, some 120 miles from the straits, in the still virgin west of Sicily, they founded their colony of Himera.[157] It was the Himerans a little later (570–560) who used Spanish silver, imported through the intermediacy of Carthage, to strike the first coinage of western Europe. Zancle and Rhegium soon followed suit, taking the same Euboean-Chalcidian monetary system as their basis.[158] Thus from Campania to the borders of the Carthaginian world, the Chalcidians, firmly based on the Sicilian narrows, where they dominated the Hellenization of the Etruscan coasts, had erected a veritable empire for themselves, commercial, naval and military; their cities were united by the consciousness of forming a community—the γένος χαλκιδικόν of which Thucydides speaks;[159] they found aesthetic expression through such sculptors as Pythagoras of

Rhegium,[160] such poets as Stesichorus of Himera,[161] and kept up high-quality manufactories which produced the Chalcidian style of pottery[162] and bronzes of which the vase from Vix may be a specimen.[163]

Progress of Greek colonization

The example set by the Euboeans was soon followed by other peoples, particularly the Dorians, on both sides of the straits: by Megarians, Corinthians, Achaeans from the north of the Peloponnese, Lacedaemonians, then, from farther afield, by Rhodians and Cretans, and by Ionians from Colophon in Asia Minor. From Cape Pachynos (capo Passero) to the Iapygian promontory (capo S. Maria di Leuca), Sicily and Italy held out to Greek emigrants a continuous coastline uniformly rich in arable land; and this they colonized completely before going further. Gela on the south-west coast of Sicily was not founded until c.689, and the bold seizure of Pithecusae and Cumae (inspired, as we have seen, by more specifically commercial motives) was not followed by any further colonization on the Tyrrhenian coast until the middle of the sixth century. The Adriatic was not opened up to Greek colonization until the time of Dionysius of Syracuse in the fourth century.[164]

The order in which the colonies were founded along the coast that bounded their horizon seems to have been determined by individual circumstances. The legends of their foundation make the colonists come coasting along the shores of the Ionian, hugging the coast of Magna Graecia before reaching Sicily: Myscelus, the oecist of Croton, met there another oecist, Archias, bound for Syracuse.[165] If that is true, how is it that the convenient harbour of Tarentum and the rich plains of Metapontum failed to attract the Corinthians and Chalcidians, and were colonized so very late? We must perhaps suppose that Thucydides' distinction between 'the Ionian gulf' where one followed the coasts, and 'the Sicilian gulf' where one sailed straight across, goes back to a very early date.[166] At all events, the success of the Chalcidians at the narrows seems to have encouraged the first colonial settlements to follow in their tracks: they are all concentrated on the east coast of Sicily. Thucydides' chronology, if one could accept it, suggests that in a brief period of six years there was a veritable contest to see who could seize the most favourable positions:[167] Naxos 734, Syracuse 733, Leontini, Catana and Megara 728. It is true that the archaeologists would now modify these dates and have Naxos founded towards 757, Megara towards 750.

Sicily

If the Megarians were ahead of the Chalcidians of Leontini and Catana and the Corinthians of Syracuse, we have to admit that the spot they laboriously chose for their colony, after two abortive attempts in the neighbourhood, was not the best.[168] Restricted to doing what they could with the coastal plain, without any good routes into the interior, squeezed north and south by the expansion of their better situated neighbours, the Megarians, after an initial hundred years of tolerable prosperity but without a future,[169] saw nothing for it but to go and form a sub-colony—one of the oecists being provided by the metropolis—at Selinus on the south-east coast, near the borders of the world of Carthage. The date may have been 650 or 627.

We have remarked that the Chalcidians had acquired the richest lands, and the Corinthians the best harbour—Syracuse. The island of Ortygia, where they established themselves at the entrance to a bay which ought to have tempted the Phoenicians, was one day to be the base of one of the greatest naval powers in the Mediterranean; but despite the future that awaited Corinthian commerce, partly thanks to Syracuse, it is commonly agreed that this expansion was a consequence, not a cause, of the colonization;[170] it was initially an agricultural venture. The hill-folk of Tenea near Corinth who almost wholly made up the contingent under the oecist Archias, went as bearers of a *kleros*, that is, a title to a country property. The colony was at first governed by the *gamoroi*; the name ('those who have received an allotment of land') points to a land-owning aristocracy.[171] From the island of Ortygia and the plateau of Achradina they extended their territory unceasingly until they held all the south-east corner of Sicily, founding the two military colonies of Acrae (Palazzolo Acreide) and Casmenae (Monte Casale near Giarratana: Thucydides gives 663 and 643 as the dates), and in 598, on the coast facing Africa, the prosperous Camarina, which was not long content with subservience.[172]

Gela[173] brings us to the last colony to be founded in Sicily from overseas; this time the colonists were Rhodians and Cretans, comrades of old in sea-going enterprises[174] which had led them to these waters in Mycenaean days and later since the trade routes to the west had been reopened. They were later to send a contingent of emigrants to Cyrene,[175] and the Rhodians were to take part, about the same time, in the founding of Lipari; but their activity strictly as colonists in Sicily was confined to Gela. They set themselves up on the south coast, the only one still vacant, perhaps lured by ancestral memories of Daedalus and Minos,[176] about 688 according to the traditional chronology. The necropolis in fact provides no specimen of the pot-bellied aryballoi, but begins with the period of ovoid aryballoi and the sub-geometric style.[177]

It is remarkable that the colonists forgot their old calling as sailors, and, once they were in Sicily, gave no thought to developing their little river harbour, but turned determinedly to the exploitation of the great alluvial plain that stretches behind the coastal hills—Virgil's *campi Geloi*[178]—and, after the first generation, to the conquest of the hinterland.[179]

This expansion was crowned at last (in 580, says Thucydides) by the founding of Agrigentum, 120 miles further east, with the collaboration of the two mother-cities. But the sub-colony soon broke free from the colony; the celebrated tyrant Phalaris manned his frontiers on the east against Gela just as much as on the west against Selinus and the Carthaginians, and took up the war against the natives of the interior on his own account. In the fifth century, under Theron, Agrigentum was to become one of the richest and most populous cities of Sicily, with its 200,000 inhabitants; Pindar would sing of it as 'fairest of mortal cities'; the grave of Simonides and the cradle of Empedocles, it boasted among its temples—still partly standing— an Olympeion that was one of the wonders of the Greek world, which the Carthaginians respected when they razed Agrigentum in 406.[180]

It was in the Dorian cities of Sicily, Gela and Agrigentum especially, that a spirit of aggression and conquest first raised its head; and it was their coalition, in the early fifth century, that ended the anarchic separatism of the Sicilian cities and brought about the hegemony of Syracuse. Gela at first conquered the Chalcidian colonies, then Syracuse in 482; but the victor, the Dinomenid Gelon, transferred his nascent empire to the conquered city. Some years later (480), Gelon and his father-in-law Theron defeated the Carthaginians before Himera, which by that time was under Theron's rule. This joint triumph ushered in a new era in the history of the Greeks in Sicily—an era in which, despite revolutions and wars, the history of Sicily was to be that of Syracuse.

Magna Graecia

Not only Sicily, but the whole of southern Italy was covered with Greek colonies, particularly the part called Magna Graecia. This name properly speaking applied only to the *frons Italiae*,[181] the coast facing the Ionian sea, from Locri to Tarentum. By an extension of usage, the sub-colonies of the Tyrrhenian side, such as Terina, founded by Croton in the bay of S. Euphemia, claimed the honour of belonging to it.[182] Once only, in Strabo,[183] is the term used to include Sicily. The name 'Great Greece', first found in Polybius,[184] presumably goes back to the sixth century, and reflects the enthusiasm with which the Greek settlers viewed the wide horizons open to their exertions and the great projects that where being realized there. It may be, as is often said, a coinage of the Pythagoreans of Croton, or rather a piece of bombast on the part of Sybaris, dreaming of setting up in the west an empire quite distinct from 'little Greece' in the east.[185] At all events, it did not replace the more natural designations derived from the names of native peoples, Oenotria and, above all, Italia. (The latter name was at first restricted to the tip of Bruttium, then extended to all southern Italy, finally to the whole peninsula.)

The dates of the colonies of Magna Graecia are very uncertain. In general they seem rather more recent than those of Sicily, although an artificial synchronism represents Croton, Syracuse and Corcyra as founded at the same time.[186] The traditional dates are Sybaris 721–720; Croton 709–708; Tarentum 706–705; Locri 679–678 and 673–672. But it has been shown that the two dates for Sybaris (Dunbabin preferred 721–720[187] and Jean Bérard 709–708)[188] are obtained from a genealogical calculation working back from the siege of Sybaris by Croton in 476–475, allowing either 35 or 33 years to a generation: the two dates are then equally arbitrary.[189]

Archaeology is not yet able to make good the deficiencies of the texts, except where Tarentum is concerned. Among the thousands of tombs of the necropolis there, abundantly furnished with proto-Corinthian pottery of the seventh century, there is only one which, by the presence of an almost spherical pot-bellied aryballos of *c.* 720–710, together with a sub-geometric skyphos, can be firmly dated to the end of the eighth century, or certainly no later than the beginning of the seventh.[190] But a short distance away, at Satyrion (Porto Saturo), where the colonists first established themselves, proto-Corinthian geometric is more widely exemplified, with some pieces even of early geometric.[191] All this is in perfect agreement with the foundation-date of 706–705.

Around this fixed point we may arrange the chronology of the other colonies as tradition and historical probability suggest. It is possible that the Spartan enterprise against Tarentum may have been held up by the presence of a well-organized native population, the Iapyges, who were disconcertingly hostile and hard to subdue. Earlier, in the last quarter of the eighth century, Achaean settlers had installed themselves at Sybaris and Croton (the foundation-legend implies that Sybaris was the earlier),[192] at no great distance apart. The Sybarites chose wealth, according to the oracle, the Crotoniates health;[193] or, if we prefer, the former chose a rich and fertile plain with a mediocre harbour, the latter an excellent harbour with fewer agricultural possibilities. At all events their rivalry recalls the haste which the Chalcidians had made, a few years before, to lay hands on the plains of Leontini and Catana. Perhaps we may assign to the same epoch the founding of Caulonia, further to the south, near Punta Stilo; this was another Achaean colony conventionally dated 690–680, but the excavations made by P. Orsi have revealed geometric pottery which suggests a some-what earlier date.[194] It was around 700 also that other Achaeans settled at Metapontum, to contain the possible northward expansion of Tarentum.[195]

Magna Graecia then seemed to be reserved for Peloponnesians. But in the seventh century colonists of different origin came to push in among the Achaeans: in the north some Ionians from Colophon, driven from their homes by the conquests of the Lydian Gyges between 680 and 670, chose the plain where the Sinni and Agri rivers join the sea as the site of their colony Siris; as prosperous as Sybaris, the city was defeated and brutally razed a century later by an Achaean coalition.[196] In the south some Locrians from Ozolian Locris on the north shores of the gulf of Corinth, or Opuntian Locris on the mainland opposite Euboea, perhaps even from both, founded at the same period (673–672 according to Eusebius), near cape Zephyrion (now Capo Bruzzano) the town of Epizephyrian Locri; also attacked by Croton at the time when Siris fell, Locri hurled back their onslaught at the memorable battle of the Sagra, and survived until the Roman conquest.[197]

Confined to the Ionian coast, Locri reached over the mountain chain to the Tyrrhenian coast by colonizing Metaurus (Gioia Tauro), Medma (Rosarno) and Hipponium (Vibo). The other colonies, encouraged by the narrowness of the Calabrian isthmus, followed suit; we shall return later to the necklace of sub-colonies that were successively established on that coast: Terina (S. Eufemia), a dependency of Croton; Laos, Skidros, Sirinos, Pyxous and, most important of all, Posidonia in the Sybarite sphere of influence: the last-named (Paestum, as it was later called) probably goes back to the middle of the seventh century.[198]

Mother-cities and colonies

The colonies of Sicily and Magna Graecia proclaimed themselves as coming from a metropolis which had supplied an oecist and (after consultation with the Delphic oracle)[199] the bulk of the contingent of settlers. It is true that nationals of another city were sometimes associated, for example Messenians with the Chalcidians who founded Rhegium, Troezenians with the Achaean colonizers of Sybaris.[200] But the occasional participation of a minority from outside did not prevent the contingent as a whole from stemming from a single mother-city which had officially organized the expedition. In the traditions concerning the foundation of a colony, the most trustworthy datum is the name of the oecist, whose memory was preserved with regular and permanent observances. As a typical indication of dependence, the 'ancient usage' attested by Thucydides[201] demanded that a sub-colony should only be founded with the collaboration of the metropolis, which provided one of the two oecists. Thus Hyblaean Megara, after being in existence for a century, did not fail, when founding Selinus, to associate Megara in the common task.[202]

Nevertheless there were many divergences and anomalies in the early colonial laws: there were some mixed colonies, like Gela, which was founded by Rhodians and Cretans, each group conducted by its oecist, and one wonders to which of its two mother-cities the colony felt more closely tied. There were perhaps, according to a recent theory,[203] 'quasi-federal colonies': Sybaris, Croton, Caulonia, Metapontum are always described as πόλεις Ἀχαιῶν, Αχαιῶν κτίσματα; Is of Helice was the oecist of Sybaris, Myscellos of Rhypes that of Croton, Typhon of Aegion that of Caulonia; who was oecist of Metapontum we do not know. Now Helice, Rhypes and Aigon were little towns in that region of the northern Peloponnese which retained in classical times the name of Achaea, where the Homeric Achaeans had finally settled after long wanderings.[204] But Sybaris and her sisters were reckoned as founded not by Helice and her neighbours, but by the Achaean people as a whole, conscious no doubt of their glorious past and thinking to recapture its memory in a land perhaps already visited by their ancestors. In the end there was a pan-Hellenic colony, Thurii; set up in 444 on the site of Sybaris, it united representatives of all Greece under the aegis of Athens.[205]

The story of relations between colonies and their mother-cities is a complex one. It is at first the history of the inheritance which the colonists brought to flower on alien soil. In this connection the linguists pay attention to the fate of the various dialects that were imported.[206] A late eighth-century inscription from Pithecusae is written in the Ionian dialect of the Chalcidian colonies—an Ionian strongly tinged with Homeric influences. Mingling with foreigners might diminish loyalty to a mother-tongue; Himera, as Thucydides notes,[207] where Syracusan exiles had joined the Zanclean colonists, spoke 'a mixed language halfway between the Dorian and that of the Chalcidians'. In Sicily the mingling of peoples gave rise to a Doric koinè in which Rhodian elements predominated (through the importance of Gela). In Magna Graecia the original dialects maintained themselves more distinctly—Ionic in the Chalcidian colonies, Achaean at Sybaris and Croton, Laconian at Tarentum, sometimes concealing older Aegean borrowings, as the names for the olive tree and olive oil.

The religious bond, first established by the transfer to the new site of sacred objects chosen for that purpose in the mother-city, remained alive for centuries, and the survival of cults from the metropolis in the religious life of the colonies[208] (e.g. the laconian divinities at Tarentum)[209] is a rich theme for research.

From the political point of view, the sentiment of filial piety which should subsist, according to Plato,[210] between colonies and mother-cities only displayed itself fairly late, and did not prevent, as Plato himself admits, the differences that set them so often at loggerheads; above all, it did not prevent the parents from watching with indifference while their children slew each other, as the Achaean colonies did, or suffer extinction, as befell Siris among others. It was only towards 345 that the Spartan Archidamus heard the appeal of the Tarentines, menaced by the Samnites, and came διὰ τὴν συγγένειαν, to die in their defence at the head of his hoplites.[211] In the classical period the ambassadors of the metropolis were received with peculiar honours in the colony, and colonists who returned to the metropolis recovered their citizen status.

From the beginning, Sicily and Magna Graecia naturally based their institutions on those of Greece proper, not without some adaptation to local conditions. This obscurely attested transmission of institutions is another rich field for research; the documentation is late and scanty, and intermediate links are often lacking. Thus the ephors of Sparta are found again not in Tarentum, but in Heraclea, founded by Tarentum in 423 near the site of Siris.[212] We must add that the colonies, once founded, did not fail to go through the political vicissitudes of Greece proper, and that tyrants began to appear from the late seventh century with a remarkable degree of success: 'No country has ever been so fruitful of tyrants as Sicily.'[213]

One might suppose that the colonies kept up special economic ties with their mother-cities[214] and offered a preferential market for the latter's exports. This seems to some degree true of Tarentum, where Laconian cups were highly favoured. Corinthian ceramic, on the other hand, far from being limited to Syracuse, was widely used at Tarentum, Hyblaean Megara and Naxos. We may think in fact that in general they organized their trade without any consideration of their own origin: Sybaris was the principal trade outlet for Milesian manufactures. The study of the circulation of currency from the end of the sixth century onwards suggests the same conclusions.[215]

Taking these facts together, we may conclude that, if the ties between mother-cities and colonies remained alive in language, religion and sentiment, they were very soon severed in the political and economic field. The western Greeks led a very independent existence, grappling with new problems for which they had to find novel solutions. The history of their relations with the native populations among whom they set themselves up and with the other colonies is more important than the history of their origins and traditions.

The colonists and the natives

Pious fiction has in some cases lent an idyllic colouring to what was doubtless a brutal reality,[216] but in general the establishment of a colony began with the eviction of the 'barbarians'.[217] We see this particularly clearly at Tarentum. Antiochus of Syracuse declared that the Spartans had been welcomed both by the barbarians and by the Cretans who had been there before them.[218] The oracle which, according to legend, had led Phalanthus to Magna Graecia had been nearer the truth: it told him to 'go and colonize Satyrion and the rich lands of Tarentum and to be the scourge of the Iapygians'. Following the coastline, the colonists touched land first at Castelluccia, where their arrival brought native inhabitation to an end;[219] they next landed at Porto Saturo (the Satyrion of the oracle): there the stratification shows huts abandoned in all haste, their food untouched, the furniture still in place, while the next stratum, levelled in order to build a temple, is full of Laconian, Argive and proto-Corinthian potsherds, corresponding to the first Greek occupation.[220] Reaching Tarentum at last, they occupied Scoglio del Tonno, deserted for centuries, as we have seen,[221] then Citta Vecchia, which was their citadel—here archaeology tells nothing of the protohistoric and archaic periods—and Borgo Nuovo, where they came up against an Iapygian village whose existence in what is called the 'geometric Iapygian' period is attested by some 350 pots.[222] It was a hard task to found the colony, and it was only done stage by stage; folklore preserved the memory of Phalanthus' discouragement before the obstinate resistance of the Iapyges.[223]

But even when Tarentum was founded, the conquest of the interior came up against insurmountable obstacles. If one traces an arc of some seven miles radius around the town, one finds a series of cemeteries containing material (Corinthian and Attic black-figure pottery) identical with that in the necropolis of Tarentum for the seventh and sixth centuries, but no native pottery at all. Outside another arc, following the rim of the limestone plateau of Murge, the cemeteries of Iapygian type show some penetration of Greek pottery, but maintain their own traditions for two centuries. The relations between Tarentum and Apulia are summed up in this veritable iron curtain: it was a case of co-existence, not colonization.[224]

Elsewhere Greek colonization met with more success; and this is a subject which the archaeologists have taken up energetically since the war, especially in Sicily—not just the fact of conquest, but the penetration of Hellenism into the native cultures, the successes and failures of cultural assimilation.[225]

We saw that when the Greeks arrived, the whole of Sicily—the Sicel peoples of the east and the Sicanians of the west—had reached the level of culture shown in the sites of Pantalica, Finocchito, Cassibile and Sant' Angelo di Muxaro. Of these native centres, built on hill-tops or positions of natural strength, in every place where good soil and a supply of water promised a living, only a few had been found and dug at the beginning of this century, by P. Orsi. In the hinterland of Gela, for example, only four were known; in 1968 the number has reached fifteen.

After the first collision with the earlier inhabitants, the newcomers pursued unflaggingly a policy of expansion. It is possible that the Chalcidians, whose objectives were primarily commercial, proceeded by peaceful means, establishing themselves for example at Mendolito (Adranum), Serra di Orlando (Morgantine), next door to, sometimes in the middle of, native villages whose autonomous development they did not hinder, so that Hellenization came about gradually by contact and by import trade.[226] A quite different picture is presented by the Syracusan conquest of the south-east corner. Once the natives had been driven from the island of Ortygia, those who were conquered on the mainland were reduced to slavery; under the name of Kyllyrioi[227] they formed the basis of the servile proletariat which one finds taking a hand in the Syracusan revolutions of the fifth century. The first colonies founded by Syracuse, after a prudent westward infiltration between the forts of Pantalica and Finocchito, were military colonies, Acrae and Casmenae, dominating the two forts and gradually, by their strategic position, encompassing their submission.[228] Then, turning towards the south-west, she finally reached the south coast, where Camerina, placed at the outlet of a vast and fertile country and provided with a good river port, followed a different policy towards the natives: historians have spoken[229] of a kind of 'Sicel reserve' established around Hybla (Ragusa), Modica and Ispica, where Camarina could have markets and find allies in her revolt against Syracuse.

But the most exciting discoveries have been made in connection with the expansion of Gela and Agrigentum towards the centre and west of Sicily, into what was almost *terra incognita*. All the hills sourrounding Gela had been protohistoric strongholds, φρούρια τῶν Σικελῶν, which were one by one converted into φρούρια τῶν Ἑλλήνων.[230] Here, at Butera and Monte Bubbonia (where it has been thought we may recognize the *Mactorion* and *Omphace* of Diodorus), and in the many centres of the interior, and further west beyond the Salso valley where Agrigentum carried on the task of her metropolis, cemeteries of several superimposed strata permit us to trace the advance of Greek cremations beside the inhumation practised by the natives, the introduction and imitation of imported pottery amid the local wares, while at the same time sanctuaries were being built, natural defences were strengthened by masonry-work, farms were laid out in the plains and Hellenization gradually gained the upper hand. Under the tyrant Phalaris, Agrigentine expansion towards the north was especially vigorous; he gained possession of Camicos (Sant' Angelo di Muxaro), the capital of the legendary king Cocalus: legend had it that his impregnable fortress was built by Daedalus, and that he received king Minos in his palace, where he had him strangled in the bath.[231]

So by slow degrees the Hellenization of the island went forward, and became complete not only in the cities, but in a zone some thirty miles in from the coast. It only stopped before a nucleus of tribes in the centre of Sicily—tribes exposed to the influence not merely of the colonies, but also of the Hellenized native tribes, yet in the mass defying conquest or assimilation. It was among them that in the mid-fifth century a native chief, Ducetius, recruited a large part of the armies with which he essayed for ten years a hopeless war of liberation.[232]

The expansion of the colonies and the Hellenization of the interior perhaps presented special difficulties in Magna Graecia[233] owing to the relief: the coast was dominated by a mountain barrier not far inland, broken only where small rivers found their way to the sea, forming alluvial plains widely separated one from another. In addition we do not have much knowledge (except at Tarentum, as we have seen) of the native inhabitants with whom the Greeks came into contact when they landed. Tradition calls them in general the Oenotrians, associating with them the Chones, Morgetes and Itali. The protohistoric sites where one has tried to study the development of their cultures reveal—e.g. at Torre Galli—discontinuities which give the impression of some instability.[234] We must suppose that the racial movements which in the fifth century were to stock the mountains of Calabria and Basilicata with new tribes of Lucanians, Bruttians and Samnites, threatening the Greek colonies and putting them on the defensive, had sent out their preliminary skirmishers as early as the first iron age. In the eighth century the native villages seem to have been too scattered to offer stern resistance to the newcomers.

Traces of these villages and especially of their citadels have been found near all the colonies—a fact which is easy to explain, since both barbarians and Greeks were swayed in their choice of a site by agricultural potential and ease of communication. This we find at Torre Galli near Hipponium, at Canale and Janchina near Locri, at Torre del Mordillo and Francavilla near Sybaris,[235] to mention only the most important. The archaeologists are now working to establish their cultural affinities—decidedly continental, with a few elements reminiscent of Sicily—and to establish their relative chronology.

This juxtaposition has furnished an argument for those who believe that the colonization was pacific: instead of taking over the place inhabited by the natives, the Greeks let them live as neighbours, leading a life which was altered only by commerce with the colonists.[236] Such a conclusion must be checked by examining the chronological relations between the various centres. The traditional tale of the founding of Locri (673) relates how the Sicels living there were terror-stricken at the sight of the newcomers, then

D

came to an agreement by which the two parties would occupy the land in common and live as good neighbours; finally after a little while they were expelled.[237] We now have a valuable archaeological confirmation: the cemeteries of Canale and Janchina near Locri seem to come to an end in the second quarter of the seventh century, at the very moment when at S. Stefano di Grotteria (inland, a dozen miles north) a new cemetery starts up in which the local culture runs its course, with some imported pots or imitations of them, down to the middle of the sixth century. In the neighbourhood of Sybaris, Torre del Mordillo, at the point where the Coscile flows into the plain, yielded in the closing years of last century nearly 300 native graves closely contemporary with those of Canale and Janchina, with some fragments of proto-Corinthian geometric at the end of the eighth century;[238] a little distance away on the same hill, a large number of Greek potsherds from the fifth century attests a Greek settlement. But it is ten miles further north still, on the southern rim of the plain of Sybaris, at Francavilla Marittima, that the most interesting results seem likely from excavations begun in 1963 in a cemetery and an acropolis. The cemetery shows a native people of the eighth to seventh century; at first they show the features common to the cultures of Calabria and Lucania, during the seventh century they gradually admit Greek material, in the sixth they become completely Hellenized. The acropolis and the sanctuary that crowns it are purely Greek from the eighth century onward; it has been suggested that here we have the legendary Lagaria which is placed by Strabo, in his description of the coast of the Ionian sea, immediately north of Sybaris.[239]

The expansion of Sybaris is attested by ancient sources: in the middle of the sixth century, that is, at the height of her power, she had 25 subject towns; the names of some are preserved, and just a few can be identified. Their location is significant: *Cossa* is presumably Cassano Ionico, *Ninaea* is S. Donato di Ninea, *Arinde* and *Menecine* are Rende and Mendicino respectively; all four dominate the wide gap carved in the mountains by the Coscile and Crati and their tributaries. The last two, near Cosenza, show that Sybaris had fortified that natural route by retracing the Crati almost to its source.[240]

The portage routes

Here we meet the problem of the portage routes. Magna Graecia presents a series of constrictions or isthmuses which bring the Ionian sea very near to the Tyrrhenian. Two of these are especially apparent on the map: from the bay of Squillace to that of S. Eufemia is little more than twenty miles as the crow flies, or about half a day's march;[241] between the mouth of the Coscile and that of the Lao there is less than 40 miles.[242] Now we know that the colonies of the Ionian coast founded their sub-colonies on the part of the Tyrrhenian coast nearest to them—e.g. Locri and Hipponium, Croton and Terina, Sybaris and Laos; what they did was not to go sailing off again along the coast, but to push through the interior, going up one and down another of the valleys that connected the one slope with the other, just as today the Taranto-Naples railway first follows the Bassento valley as far as Potenza, then the Sele valley down towards the gulf of Salerno.

Since Lenormant's time[243] many daydreams have been indulged on the lure of the 'sure and practically direct routes'[244] held out by the great openings in the mountains made by the wide valleys of the rivers and *fiumare* as seen from the sea; unique importance has been ascribed to these routes in the economic life of Magna Graecia. The import trade from Greece and the orient completely avoided (it was believed) the Sicilian narrows, the proverbial perils of Scylla and Charybdis, and the burdensome exactions of the Chalcidian cities; traders preferred to break bulk at the ports on the Ionian sea, principally at Sybaris, and to use the portage routes across the Calabrian isthmus leading down to the Tyrrhenian coast. There the southern outposts of the Etruscan empire beyond Salerno served their only purpose by receiving the products of Ionian civilization directly, avoiding Cumae. There is unambiguous testimony to the friendship of Miletus and Sybaris, and to a sympathetic understanding between Sybaris and the Etruscans.[245]

Some heavy blows have recently been dealt against this sweeping theory, and it has been claimed that Rhegium and Zancle played a part of exceptional importance in trade, especially in the distribution of Attic pottery in the west.[245] Between the two extreme positions, it becomes necessary to accept a more qualified solution as the truth: the two routes, by sea and by land, coexisted but specialized in different trades. The narrows and the portage routes were both in regular use, with more or less traffic density at different periods and for different classes of merchandise.

The exponents of the portage theory enumerate at least five crossings: this is probably too many.[247] The one which connected Sybaris with

Skidros and Laos is beyond dispute: it followed the course of the Coscile until it was joined by the Esaro, at Torre del Mordillo, then followed the Esaro as far as S. Agata (Artemisium?); an easy pass (2400 ft) allowed passage to the Tyrrhenian slope, followed by descent into the bay of Belvedere (Skidros?).[248] It was on this route that the Thurians in 389, while traversing a wooded defile into which they had imprudently ventured, fell into a barbarian ambuscade.[249] An inscription of the sixth century at S. Agata, referring to a sanctuary of Hera,[250] proves that two centuries later, before the Lucanian people had come into existence, the route was safe and open to religious and commercial traffic.

Another and much longer route followed the Basento to Serra di Vaglio (near Potenza) and then went down the Sele valley to Posidonia. An inscription recently found at Olympia[251] has acquainted us with a treaty of perpetual alliance concluded in the sixth century between Sybaris and her allies and the people called *Serdaioi*: this treaty was put under the guarantee not only of the gods, but also of the city of Posidonia. We may suppose that the Serdaioi were a small native tribe in the mountains where the route went through from Sybaris to Posidonia, who were disposed to accord passage to none but their allies, and to them only on payment of a toll. Sybaris and Posidonia at the two ends of the line were working together to make their communications by the inland route as safe and well-regulated as possible.

It has been thought unlikely that such fragile wares as Attic pottery would have been taken by such routes on mule-back. On the other hand it is agreed that textiles were taken along them: deep-pile carpets and richly ornamented cloaks. Milesian woollens were famous throughout the ancient world, but Sybaris was where they sold best—Sybaris and the Etruscan cities that imported them from there. The Latin word *laena*, from which the French *laine*, is a Greek loanword χλαίνη brought in through Sybaris. Moreover, these stuffs were not merely articles of luxury; they were factors in civilization. Like the Sassanid and Coptic textiles in the European middle ages, they spread the images and fashions of the Ionian east into Italy. 'This trade in perishable objects', says G. Vallet, 'may well have had a subtle but profound influence on Etruscan civilization in the second half of the seventh century.'[252]

Magna Graecia followed the example of Miletus in setting up a textile industry, which was made easier by the abundance of sheep. Tarentum and Sybaris were rivals in this field.[253] In the institutions of Sybaris we find several features that anticipate Hellenistic economic policy.[254] Fishers and importers of the purple-fish were exempt from taxes—not as a concession to luxury, but to support local manufacture of dyed woollens. Similar tax-concessions applied to those who caught or marketed eels; we know that potted fish and meat from Sybaris was highly prized abroad. Athenaeus waxes indignant that the inventor of a new delicacy was granted the monopoly of it for one year; what emerges is that the first instance known of patenting an invention goes back to the economic policies of Sybaris. Only the moralizing of ancient writers has preserved such details as these, but they let us glimpse the vigour of life in Sybaris, both in agriculture and in trade. It is likely that Sybaris (and all Magna Graecia with her) practised a policy of preferential tariffs that conflicted with the interests of rival cities. This policy no doubt had its share in the animosities which led to the destruction of Siris by Sybaris and of Sybaris by Croton.

Numismatic evidence

On the economic life of the Greek colonies in Sicily and southern Italy the numismatist can give invaluable information, quite apart from finding an incomparable series of artistic masterpieces. The striking of coin began at Himera and Selinus[255] about 570–560, at Sybaris and Croton[256] about 550; but the use of coin must have been preceded by a long period in which money was used by weight; this in turn implied the acceptance of certain systems of weights which determined the basis of the future coinages, and these were to maintain themselves in economic areas with clear geographical boundaries—so much so that we can infer from metrology the entire history of Greek colonization.[257] It is noteworthy, for example, that the Achaean colonies, Sybaris, Croton, Caulonia and Metapontum, all struck incuse staters to a standard of 8.25 grammes; this stater, with its subdivisions (thirds, sixths and twelfths) is in conformity with the details of the Corinthian system and with the commercial pre-eminence of Corinth. The colonies of Campania and Sicily, on the other hand, even the Corinthian Syracuse, adopted under Chalcidian influence the Euboean system of fractions, while to meet the needs of their trade in the Tyrrhenian sea they had two systems of weights—one Etruscan (5.70 gr.), the other 'Phocaean' (in reality of Phoenician origin) of 7.60 gr. One token of how important the local factor was is that Posidonia, a colony of Sybaris, followed the technique of incuse coinage practised in their metropolis, but preferred the standard of 7.60 gr. for their didrachm. It is true that the fall of Sybaris at the end of the sixth century, with its grave political and economic repercussions throughout southern Italy, drove Posidonia, which had received many refugees from Sybaris, to change her system also to the Corinthian. The hoards that have been found have often been on the portage routes:[258] they are made up exclusively of coins of the Achaean colonies and their sub-colonies, with an admixture of Tarentine money, and thus confirm the regional limits within which those coinages were current.[259] Much the same may be said of the Sicilian coinages; but the currencies of Greece proper were accepted there (for example, to facilitate trading with Corinth), as we may infer from the overstriking of incuse staters on Corinthian 'foals'.[260] A particular interest attaches to the alliance-currencies struck in the name of two cities. Thus in the early fifth century, under the hegemony of Croton, staters were struck with the names of Croton and Sybaris, others of Croton and Locri, combining the types of the cities concerned. Some of the sub-colonies on the Tyrrhenian coast formed alliances with the native peoples of the interior: hence the *Pal-Mol* staters and the *Pyxous-Sirinos* staters.[261]

Tyrannies in Sicily: Syracuse

Now that we have outlined the social and economic bases of the Greek empire in Sicily and Italy, we shall not go into the details of the revolutions and wars of the various cities. We shall only point out the importance of two of them which we shall often discover in the background of archaic Italy or of the nascent Roman empire—Syracuse and Tarentum.

The despotism of the Dinomenids[262] established by Gelon (482–478), the victor over the Carthaginians at Himera in 480, continued by his brother Hieron (478–467), who defeated the Etruscans at Cumae in 474, had made Syracuse a very great power. Their fall did not cripple the city's progress: about 440 she was the most brilliant, the most free, the most prosperous city in the west;[263] her fleet cruised in the Tyrrhenian sea and dominated trade with Etruria. We know of course that before the end of the century her increasing dominance, with its threat to Leontini and Segesta, brought down the thunders of Athens upon her at the height of the Peloponnesian war; the Sicilian expedition almost overthrew her, and her victory at the eleventh hour filled her with national pride.

Some time after this, Carthage, which had not intervened in Greek

Sicily since her defeat in 480, took advantage of the rivalry of the Siciliot cities to take her revenge and reopen hostilities: Selinus was sacked, Himera razed, Agrigentum pillaged, Gela beseiged (408–405). Then it was, when catastrophe seemed imminent, that Dionysius the Elder seized power[264] and held it for 38 years (405–367), during which three 'Punic wars' (398–392, 383–374, 368) saved the cause of Hellenism in Sicily, not merely thanks to the defensive works that he carried out at Syracuse (fortifying Euryale and Epipolae) and to his strengthening and modernizing the artillery and the fleet, where he introduced quinqueremes, but also to his creation of a mercenary army which for the first time included Campanians together with Iberians and Celts. In an alternation of victories and setbacks, he succeeded, not indeed in driving the Carthaginians out of Sicily, but in throwing them back nearly to their former possessions in the west. At the same time he had himself recognized not just as tyrant of one city, but as 'archon of Sicily'. His military ambitions and the progress of his conflict with Carthage led him to challenge the Carthaginians' allies, the Italiot confederation in Magna Graecia, where he himself joined forces with the barbarous Lucanians; in the event he remained master of the whole coast as far as Thurii. In the Tyrrhenian sea he made naval demonstrations against the Etruscans; he even established some control over the Adriatic by founding colonies at Ancona and on the island of Issa off the Dalmatian coast, and by establishing contact with the Celts. The personality of Dionysius, which was harshly judged by the ancients and by the moderns until recent times, is now being better evaluated. The ambition which drove him at once to liberate the Sicilian Greeks and to create a vast empire in the west is not so much in the tradition of Greek despotism as an anticipation of the Hellenistic monarchies. At the same time the precursor of Alexander appears, in his effort to build on the indigenous forces of southern Italy and Sicily—the Campanians, Lucanians and Sicels—like 'the heir of the ancient kings of Oenotria, the descendant of Italos or Morges'.[265]

The succession to Dionysius was disputed by his brother-in-law Dion, Plato's pupil, who was assassinated in 354, and his son Dionysius the Younger, who was deposed in 344. This period of anarchy was ended by the arrival of the Corinthian Timoleon, who had come from the metropolis in answer to the colony's appeal, to found it, as it were, over again.[266] He restored democracy at Syracuse and carried on the fight against Carthage with his victory on the Cremisos, and against the tyrants who were cropping up almost everywhere and were betraying Greek ideals, and against the

Campanian mercenaries who had formed independent states. He repeopled the ruined and deserted towns[267] and re-established Sicilian unity and prosperity.[268] After seven years (344–337) he abdicated, his task completed. Timaeus anticipated Plutarch in writing his life as that of a model hero.[269]

Twenty years later there arose at Syracuse a second Dionysius the Elder, Agathocles (317–289) who claimed the title of king.[270] Some confused campaigns were to lead him into Magna Graecia, to Corcyra and to the Adriatic. What we shall principally remember is that in the vain hope of freeing Sicily from the grip of Carthage he conceived the design, pregnant with future possibilities, of carrying the war to Africa: he landed south-west of Cape Bon, burned his ships to make retreat impossible, ravaged all the territory of Carthage, and finally abandoned the struggle (310–307).[271] On his death his Campanian mercenaries took possession of Messina and founded there the Mamertine state.

Tyrannies in Magna Graecia: Tarentum

The cities of Magna Graecia, Rhegium, Tarentum, Croton, with Thurii established in the midst of them since 445 as a pan-Hellenic colony on the site of Sybaris, had worn themselves out during the fifth century in un-ceasing rivalry, while in the mountains an aggressive spirit was rising among the Lucanians, who cut the lines of communications between the two coasts and threatened the coastal plains.[272] To meet this threat a defen-sive alliance was formed (about 430) between Croton and several Achaean cities—Caulonia and Sybaris on the river Trais, subsequently joined by Thurii, Velia, possibly Posidonia, and finally Rhegium.[273] We have seen how the elder Dionysius, supporting the Lucanians, went to war with this Italiot confederacy (390); he defeated them on the Elleporos (Galliporo), captured Rhegium (386), and turned all the point of Italy as far as the bay of Squillace into a redoubt which, after the destruction of Caulonia and Hipponium, assured him complete possession of the narrows with Locri as his centre.[274] Hostilities were resumed with the second of his Punic wars, the Italiots being the allies of Carthage: he gained possession in 379 of Croton and the confederation's sanctuary of Hera Lacinia, and annexed all Magna Graecia as far as the bay of Thurii.[275]

Tarentum remained the only great free city in southern Italy.[276] She had always been contained in her expansion towards the interior by the resistance of the barbarians of Apulia—Iapygians, Messapians, Peucetians—

who had even inflicted a memorable defeat on her in 473, and she had had to hold her own in a ten-year war (443–433) against Thurian designs on the Siris valley, where she had set up her sub-colony Heraclea, with ephors like those of Sparta herself. Presumably she stayed aloof from the Italiot confederacy, although her frontiers also were menaced by the Lucanians; she certainly kept clear of the hostilities between the confederacy and Dionysius. In the first half of the fourth century she was governed by a very wise statesman, Archytas the Pythagorean, friend of Plato, musician, engineer, universal genius, and shrewd politician. His seven successive terms as strategos (367–361), if Wuilleumier's calculations are correct,[277] began in the very year that Dionysius died. However that may be, the eclipse of the other colonies in Magna Graecia enabled Tarentum to make tremendous advances: having become president of the Italiot confederacy, she extended her power throughout southern Italy from Metapontum to Croton (which had thrown off the Syracusan yoke), from Velia to Naples, where in 326 she met for the first time the ambitions of Rome. For Tarentum the fourth century brought a new advance in her commercial prosperity, her naval strength, and her skill in bronze and goldsmith's work.[278]

Influence of Sicily and Magna Graecia in central Italy

The influence of the Greek colonies did not wait for the latest triumph of Greek arms or diplomacy to spread itself far afield among the barbarians. From their earliest days there was unofficial but regular intercourse between the shores of the Ionian sea and of the Sicilian narrows and the most remote cantons of the peninsula—principally by sea, but also by the inland valley routes, especially through Campania and by way of the Etruscans. Livy[279] wonders how Numa Pompilius (whom men called a Pythagorean in the teeth of chronology) could have been inspired in his Sabine homeland to undertake so long and perilous a voyage. There are in fact some Etruscans in the list of the first Pythagoreans which is preserved by Iamblichus.[280] The discovery in 1959 at Lavinium of a dedication in Greek to the Dioscuri[281] has confirmed that in the years around 500 Tarentum and Locri were not so very far from Rome, and that their voices were heard there more easily than one has imagined.

All the forms of western Hellenism—religious, philosophical, artistic and literary—under the particular aspects which they had assumed when their roots were watered from new streams[282] quickly found their way to central Italy. We can trace the gradual advance of the Greek divinities:[283] Demeter and Kore become Sicilian bringers of fertility;[284] the Argive Hera travels from Metapontum and Croton to the Heraion of the Silaros and to Posidonia, then on to Capua, Lanuvium, Tibur, Caere, Falerii;[285] Heracles travels also, for the theory that Hercules-Melqart was directly introduced at Rome by Phoenicians does not hinder us from tracking the progress of a Greek Heracles from Magna Graecia.[286] Orphic beliefs touching the after-life took deep root in this soil—witness, inter alia, the gold plates of Thurii and Petelia (fourth to third centuries), inscribed with formulae to help the dead man find his way in the underworld; we find similar objects at Pharsalus and Eleutherna;[287] comparable prayers and sacrifices are prescribed in the Acherontic books of the Etruscans and in the inscription on the Capuan tile.[288] A similar representation of the journey to the under-world and the torments there inspires some of the frescoes of Tarquinia.[289] Pythagorean philosophy, conceived in Magna Graecia in the late sixth century by the Samian exile who set up his school of wisdom at Croton,[290] found its adepts in that city, and later at Metapontum and Tarentum; we have seen how successfully Archytas applied its doctrines to the government of the Spartan colony; it had an influence on the origins of Plato's thought, and made itself felt throughout Italy and at Rome: 'When first Italians acquired a national consciousness, it was a Pythagorean consciousness'.[291] Likewise the artistic debt of Italy to Magna Graecia and Sicily from the archaic period onward is incalculable,[292] whether in architecture,[293] in the decoration of temples[294] or in terracotta sculpture.[295] The debt of Latin literature is no less great: the first epic and tragic poets were to come from Tarentum and Apulia (Livius Andronicus, Ennius, Pacuvius) or from Capua (Naevius); in the field of comedy, invented by the Sicilian Epicharmus, the humorous vein of the phlyax-farces and the *hilarotragoediae* of the Tarentine Rhinton were to provide one day, by way of the popular 'Atellane' farce, food for the genius of a Plautus.[296]

D Greek colonization in Gaul and Spain

In the far west, on the Mediterranean coasts of Gaul and Spain, a new people took a hand a little later in the carrying on of Greek colonization, under rather more complex conditions. The movement as a whole is dated by the foundation of Massalia (Marseilles) about 600, which was also its fairest creation. Its authors were the seamen of Phocaea in Asia Minor; they fitted out a fleet of penteconters (long, swift vessels of fifty oars) and sent it 'on a voyage of conquest beyond the Sicilian narrows and the African sea to carve out for themselves a commercial empire in the farthest west'.[297] In the western basin of the Mediterranean they encountered the common interests and the combined forces of Carthage and the Etruscans.

We have seen[298] that the Phoenicians had gained a firm monopoly of the riches of Tartessos in Andalusia, with a prior claim going back to the twelfth century, as the literary sources would have it, and at least to the end of the eighth, as archaeological evidence confirms: the Samians and Phocaeans did not venture into these waters until 630 or later. It is likely that they had been preceded on the coasts of Gaul and Spain by Rhodian sailors, who seem to have found their way around the west very quickly in the wake of their neighbours the Phoenicians: the Rhodians are credited with the founding of Rhode (Rosas) in Catalonia, also perhaps of Agathe (Agde) and Rhodanousia on the banks of the Rhodanos (Rhône). It is very likely that etymological guesswork may have added to this tradition of Rhodian 'pre-colonization', but now that Rhodian pottery going back to the latter half of the seventh century has been found inter alia at the *oppidum* of Saint-Blaise, which dominates the étang de Berre, we know that Rhodians were in southern Gaul near the mouths of the Rhône about that time.[299] Much more important, however, and still before the arrival of the Phocaeans, is Etruscan imported pottery—canthari in *bucchero*, wine-amphorae, and imitations of the proto-Corinthian aryballoi.[300] These are being found more and more throughout Provence, Languedoc and Catalonia, and they point to a great wave of Etruscan commercial expansion using sea routes—witness the sunken vessel off Antibes[301]—which began in the last quarter of the seventh century and was suddenly broken off about 580:[302] a direct consequence of the foundation of Marseilles, and a clear token of the bitter commercial rivalry between Phocaeans and Etruscans.

Phocaean colonization

The dating and interpreting of Phocaean colonization rest upon two distinct sets of texts.[303] One places the foundation of Marseilles about 600: among these authors is Justin,[304] who attributes the Phocaean venture to the smallness of their lands and the poverty of the soil. We must say at once that, disregarding the anecdotal details of his story, the date is confirmed by archaeology: from the beginning of the sixth century, especially from 580 onward, the markets of Marseilles were opened up to large-scale imports of Ionian pottery, particularly to common earthenware with painted bands, greyish bucchero, large undecorated amphorae, which were the wares of every-day use or were employed for the transport of wine.[305] These were imports of a colonial character, consisting essentially of mass-produced articles; but there are some luxury products among them—Attic, Corinthian and Laconian wares.[306]

Another group of sources—their most eloquent exponent being Herodotus,[307] connects the great rise in Phocaean enterprise with the threat of the Persians under Cyrus, which would have borne heavily on them about 545–540. Rather than submit to the tyranny of the Great King, some of the Phocaeans chose to leave their country, and turned their bows towards Corsica, where twenty years later (i.e. 565–560), on the advice of an oracle, they took possession of the town of Alalia on the east coast. They dwelt there for five years with the former inhabitants, practising piracy 'on all the neighbouring peoples'—the Etruscans of Tuscany and the Carthaginians of Sardinia. Hence came the combined riposte of Etruscan and Carthaginian forces about 540–535, when a famous naval battle took place off Alalia, with sixty Phocaean ships against 120 of Agylla (Caere) and Carthage. The Phocaeans won a 'Cadmean victory',[308] dearly bought indeed, but assuring them success in their objective, which was the founding of Velia on the Lucanian coast (by refugees who had first collected at Rhegium) and the dominion of the western waters.

It will be seen that the Herodotean account, probably inspired by traditions current in Magna Graecia about the founding of Velia,[309] has not a word to say of Marseilles; and the somewhat obscure allusions of Thucydides,[310] Strabo[311] and Pausanias,[312] which have set going the idea that Marseilles was founded very late or was re-colonized in the middle of the sixth century,[313] do not find any acceptance nowadays. It was Alalia, not Marseilles, that the Phocaean exiles had chosen, after their own city went down, as the site of a new capital, a colony of permanent settlers, and one also excellently situated on an important sea route.[314] For the rest, the tale told by Herodotus has the air of a moralizing fable, grouping around the battle of Alalia events that were in fact more widely separated in time. He himself admits a 'pre-colonization' of Alalia in 565–560. Excavations on the acropolis of Velia have recently revealed a Phocaean settlement which the pottery enables us to date back to 580–570.[315] Lastly, the facts

disprove the story of the Phocaean's abandoning Corsica after their Cadmean victory: Etruscan expansion into Corsica does not seem to be attested
until the fourth century, and certainly the importation of Attic pottery went
on unhindered from the middle of the sixth to the middle of the fourth
century.[316]

It is doubtful whether Marseilles took part in the battle of Alalia, unless
a Massiliot contingent took its place anonymously among the Phocaeans.
The only naval battles with which her name is linked are those that she
fought against the Carthaginians:[317] she is supposed to have gained her first
victory in the latter half of the sixth century—this is the one commemorated
by the tablet of a votive offering at Delphi[318]—and another about 490 off
Cape Nao on the Iberian coast.[319] Archaeologically speaking, her hostility
to the Etruscans goes back to the eviction of their import trade into
Provence almost as soon as the colony was founded: the same applies to
Punic imports.[320] The economic conditions which in 540–535 lined up the
Etruscans and the Carthaginians together against Phocaean 'piracy' and led
to their permanent alliance, founded on trade agreements and pacts for
mutual support,[321] were already present in the nature of things. The
political forces in being in the western Mediterranean in the sixth century
sufficiently explain the inevitable antagonism between the Chalcidians and
Phocaeans on the one hand and the Etruscans and Carthaginians on the
other, even if we avoid over-simplification and admit that political actions
do not necessarily coincide with cultural developments. We can say that
Marseilles very quickly understood the part she was to play in the complex
interaction of these rival thalassocracies. Her relations with the Rome of
the Tarquins may have to be taken with a grain of salt,[322] but her bonds
with Velia, to whose foundation she probably contributed,[323] are clear
from the texts and from local nomenclature—for example Ἰταλία
μασσαλιωτική for southern Italy, and Μασσαλία τῆς Ἰταλίας for
Posidonia.[324]

Expansion of Marseilles

Let us now return to the founding of Marseilles to try to see what is meant
and exactly what followed from it, both in the history of power-conflicts
in the western Mediterranean and in that of the Hellenizing of Gaul.

This foundation was only one point in a vast programme of colonization,
which some writers have thought may have begun in the south of Spain

and only moved to the coasts of Provence for the sake of peace, in face of the barrier erected against it by the old Phoenician hegemony, which was now under the vigorous management of Carthage.[325] We recall the offers of help made by Arganthonius, king of Tartessos, to the Phocaeans—offers which they are not likely to have disdained. But while we hear of numerous Phocaean colonies in Andalusia—Mainake (Malaga?), Hemeroscopion (Denia) etc., it must be allowed that we know little of where they were or how they began.[326] In Catalonia, Ampurias is much better known: its *palaeopolis* on the island of San-Martin seems no earlier than 575.[327] Thus the Phocaean attempts at colonization in the far west seem to have been roughly contemporary, and the one which completely succeeded, at Marseilles, was not a miserable second-best, stumbled upon by chance on the homeward road,[328] but rather a judicious and well-informed choice, taking into account natural resources of all kinds—tin, wine, salt, fisheries, coral, etc.[329]—that could be held out by a site near the delta of a great river—a site where the hardy sailors of Phocaea felt also their 'continental vocation'.[330]

The charming story occurring as early as Aristotle of the foundation of Marseilles—the marriage of Protis and Gyptis under the fatherly eye of king Nannus—depicts an atmosphere of happy understanding between the first colonists and the natives.[331] Their relations speedily became embittered, and it was only by continual struggles with the Ligurians (joined in the fifth century by the Gauls)[332] that the Phocaean trading-post, first set up on the spur of the fort of S. Jean and then extending up the north bank of the Lacydon, was able to maintain itself within the narrow girdle of hills that limited its horizon to the north and east.[333] The city itself, even in the third century, felt the need of the defensive rampart flanked with towers of which the imposing foundations were discovered in 1967. Its territory, which at the latter period reached as far up as Glanum (Saint-Rémy-de-Provence), was at first restricted to a narrow ribbon of land which, south of the Étang de Berre, ended at Saint-Blaise, perhaps at the Rhône delta, and in the east scarcely reached ten miles along the valley of the Huveaune.[334] In contrast to the smallness of her possessions on land, Marseilles numbered in her overseas empire a good many colonies—Strabo[335] lists Rhodanousia and Agathe (Agde) in the delta, Tauroentum (Le Brusc), Olbia (Hyères), Antipolis (Antibes) and Nicaea (Nice), without reckoning the Phocaean foundations with which she had links. The list could be extended by adding numerous posts along the shore to mark the Heraclean way that was fortified against the Ligurian brigands.[336] It must be admitted that there is little agreement on the chronology of these sub-colonies. The document-ation is late, and they may not go back before the fifth to fourth centuries.[337] The *oppida* like Ensérune still kept their native character,[338] but this did not prevent the inland areas of Provence and Languedoc from being very soon flooded with Greek and Massiliot pottery.[339]

The distinction between the territorial extent of Marseilles and her cultural influence and commercial penetration is nowadays more and more sharply realized. The last stage of the Hallstatt culture is marked, as we have seen,[340] especially in Burgundy, by the appearance in its tumuli of Greek and Etruscan objects (pottery and bronze), but the route by which they came there is disputed. In the Hellenizing of Gaul a great part seems to have been played by Massiliot commerce.

It is of course possible that these objects reached their destination by the Alpine passes—the Simplon, the Great and Little St Bernard—which witnessed heavy traffic and levying of tolls[341] from the bronze age onward. Even under the Roman empire these passes kept the corporation of *negotiatores Cisalpini and Transalpini* in business.[342] Charles Picard has also found in Herodotus the traces of a strange tribe of professional travelling merchants (κάπηλοι) who plied their trade on wagons from the Danube to the confines of Venetia, and who were known to the Ligurians 'above Marseilles'.[343] No one can doubt that the transalpine routes contributed largely to the dissemination of Greek and Etruscan imports in southern Germany, Switzerland and Franche-Comté. Thus Rhodian oenochoae have been found at Vilsingen and Kappel;[344] a Greek hydria in bronze at Grächwyl near Berne;[345] a bronze Etruscan amphora at Conliège (Jura).[346] These finds sometimes seem to be dotted along a route leading into Burgundy.[347]

Now, however, the discovery of the *crater* of Vix[348] has set off a lively reaction. The honour of having forwarded this masterpiece and the pieces from the same source is now claimed for Marseilles and the Rhône valley.[349] Certainly, while the area dominated by Massiliot commerce—the so-called Gallia Graeca[350]—was long thought to stop at the Durance, Le Pègue's re-searches, which seem to have turned up Ionian pottery of the sixth to fifth centuries, have now extended its frontiers to the Isère.[351] Between the Isère and Burgundy or the Jura, there is still a blank patch on the map show-ing the distribution of painted pottery.[352] All the same, it is at Vix itself that Massiliot pottery is claimed to have been discovered ('notably some plates with painted bands').[353] The *oppidum* on Mont Lassois may have been in the sixth century the principal focal point and favourite market for Massiliot trade, but amidst a more 'capillary' distribution of Greek wares than had been previously thought.[354]

The importance of this site as an entrepôt on the overland tin route is nowadays almost undisputed. Tin from the mines of Cornwall and Devon, universally in demand for metalwork in the Mediterranean, was at first one of the sources whence the Tartessian merchants drew their wealth. They sailed to the islands of the Cassiterides, opposite the mouth of the Loire,[355] to pick up their supplies, and the Carthaginians, taking over from the Phoenicians, had done all they could to keep the secret of this sea-borne commerce to themselves. But an overland route through Gaul had been opened up to break the Punic monopoly:[356] starting from Ictis (the Isle of Wight), where a new despatching centre had been set up (mentioned in this connection by Timaeus and Posidonius), the route went up the Seine valley and down the Saône, after taking the shortest passage between the two basins, by the Ource and the Tille.[357] Mont Lassois, in the Châtillonais on the upper Seine, was in a position to control the traffic, to hinder or help it as desired: hence came the splendid gifts with which the 'Lady of Vix' had embellished her tomb; hence came the prosperity of Vix, and indeed that of Marseilles, if we may suppose, very reasonably, that the picture drawn by Timaeus, Posidonius and Diodorus is equally true of protohistory: 'They convey their wares by an overland route across Gaul, in thirty days approximately, as far as Marseilles.' And the links thus courageously forged between Marseilles and Vix from the sixth century on fit too well into the background of Massiliot-Punic rivalry and enmity for us to find anything implausible in the hypothesis which has been brilliantly and powerfully sustained, by which tin would have been the prime objective of Massiliot inland trade,[358] the cause of Marseilles' early prosperity, and indeed the real purpose of its foundation.

But our conclusions must not be too categorical: 'The Alpine-pass route and the Rhône valley route are not mutually exclusive.'[359] There is also an oenochoe with trefoiled spout in the treasure from Vix;[360] we have already mentioned the Etruscan amphora from Conliège, etc. Had these also passed through Marseilles on their journey? Could not the two export routes for tin have been in competition with each other? Current research, however, is aimed rather at analysing the distribution in time of Greek and Etruscan imports. Did they coexist in the sixth century?[361] Did one trade succeed to the other—Greek imports in the sixth century, Etruscan in the fifth?[362] It appears at all events that Marseilles in the fifth century went through a severe economic crisis which suspended for a time her imports of Greek pottery. It is hard not to connect this recession with the arrival of the La Tène Gauls, which must have broken the connection with her inland markets and dried up the principal spring of her revenues.[363] Efforts are being made to elucidate the obscure vicissitudes of her power and prosperity in the latter half of the sixth century, her decline in the fifth, her vigorous renascence and colonial expansion in the fourth—a period when Aristotle held up her laws as the model of an aristocratic constitution,[364] and when Rome began to hail the city as her traditional ally.[365]

Chapter Four

Rome Under the Kings

A Political and social institutions

At the outset of Rome's political history we must give the first place to those basic social units whose strength, traditions and ambitions seem to have been displayed long before the city was established and to have constantly dominated its development thereafter—the *gentes*.[1]

In its etymology *gens* manifestly implies a relation of kinship; it is the class of all those who go back to a common ancestor. This community of blood is expressed by the use of a common name, the *nomen gentilicium*, derived from the individual name of the founder: thus the Caecilia gens claimed descent from the Praenestine Caeculus. Each gens maintained its own cemeteries and practised religious rites of its own. P. Valerius Publicola had been buried at the foot of the Velian, which takes us back to a time when the hill was not yet incorporated into the city, and all the Valerii long afterwards went through a token cremation at that place.[2] The Aurelii had a special devotion to the god Sol, whose name in fact they bore, since *ausel* was the Sabine for 'sun'. The Potitii and Pinarii jointly took care of the cult of Hercules in the Forum Boarium until the state took responsibility for this *sacrum gentilicium*.[3] The gentes called their members together to reach common decisions, as for example forbidding or requiring the use of a particular praenomen by its members.[4] Other decisions, like that which sent the Fabii in 475 to war with Veii with only the forces of their own gens,[5] were of greater consequence. The main task of the *comitia curiata* under the republic was to maintain the integrity of the gentes and to see that their *sacra* did not fall into desuetude.[6]

The gens did not comprise those only who were bound by natural kinship. Apart from the *gentiles* properly so-called, it included a great many clients (*clientes*): the name is unexplained, but denoted a special form of dependence also found elsewhere among Italic peoples, among the Etruscans (*etera*),[7] and among the Celts (*ambacti*).[8] *Clientela* was a species of moral obligation, founded on good faith (*fides*), which assured the client of the protection of his *patronus* in return for obedience to him. The *patronus*, as the name implies,[9] had a relation with his client analogous to the father-son relation: the same designation, *liberi*, properly applied to legitimate children, was extended to clients *qua* free men.[10] The civil law was later to define rigorously the mutual duties of patron and client. The law of the Twelve Tables curses (*sacer esto*) the patron who wrongs his client.[11] He is bound to help him in court, decline to bear witness against him, defend him if need be against his *cognati*, who are kinsmen only on the distaff side. He must accord him a preferential place by his side— recalling the place of the client beside the eldest son in Etruscan tombs. In return he demands from his client certain no less stringent *obsequia*, services of a military, political, judicial, even financial character. The client bore the gentile name of his patron, and his condition was transmitted from father to son: the gens could always make good its *jus gentilitatis* over the descendants of those who had once been *in fidem accepti*.[12]

In historical times one of the chief ways of recruiting a *clientela* was manumission, since the freed slave continued to be dependent on his old master as client to patron (*cliens libertinus*);[13] but before the burst of expansion in the fourth century it seems unlikely that the Roman gentes had many slaves or, in consequence, many freedmen in their *clientelae*. Another way was *applicatio*, a legal act by which an individual sought to be attached to a gens. A mutilated notice in Festus[14] indicates that patrons assigned to their clients (the text says *tenuioribus*, 'the poorer people') parcels of land to be held *precario*, on condition presumably of their cultivating them. We come thus to the conclusion that the primitive kernel of *clientela* was made up of tenant farmers subject to the gentes who possessed the land. It was among these peasants, then, that they levied their private armies.[15]

To help us work out what strength the gentes could field, we have only the figures (consistent in themselves) furnished by the annalists in connection with more than half legendary events in the early days of the republic: the Sabine Atta Clausus came to settle at Rome with 5000 clients;[16] the Fabii in their private war against the Veii fielded 306 gentiles and 4000 to 5000 clients;[17] for his *coup de main* the Sabine Appius Herdonius got together his clients 'and the boldest of his slaves' to form a troop of 4000 men.[18] But this period marked the beginning of the expansion of the *ager*

Romanus and the creation of the Claudian and Fabian *tribus*; on these lands the two powerful gentes of those names could keep up a fairly dense population.[19] The primitive gentes must have been much smaller.

The families

This organization into gentes, which might seem to have provided a strong framework for Roman society, shows on closer examination a certain instability and some centrifugal tendencies that seem at variance with what its long survival would make us believe. Its origins and development during some very ill-documented centuries present difficult problems. It is a fact, however, that in the oldest legal texts the family, not the gens, shows up as being the living cell of Roman society. This sub-division of the gens, bearing the gentile name further qualified by a *cognomen*—Cornelii Scipiones, Cornelii Lentuli, etc.—comprised everything under the power of the *paterfamilias*—children, slaves, cattle, real estate. It forms a restricted group within the gens; in the cult of *parentes* it goes no further back than the third generation (the *proavus*, great-grandfather); in the collateral line it extends no farther than the sixth degree (*sobrini*, the issue of cousins-german).[20] The *familia*, not the gens, is treated by the Twelve Tables as the basic unit of society, when it is necessary to define the *patria potestas* or to safeguard property in a succession *ab intestato*. When a *paterfamilias* died intestate, the goods only went back to the *gens* in default of *agnati*. And in the political sphere the predominance of the *familia* is no less clearly apparent if in fact the *patres* forming the Senate are the *patres familiarum*, or at all events chosen from among them.

Under these circumstances it is not surprising that the relation between *gens* and *familia*, commonly taken as arising from genealogical subdivision, has lately been the subject of contrary hypotheses. Those who prefer to explain the evolution of social and political structures by 'the concrete factor of formation' rather than by 'the abstract factor of derivation'[21] have supposed that the families were there first, the gentes being of secondary and local origin because the families lived together in a single *vicus* or in adjoining *vici*. A word like *adfines*, meaning kinsmen by marriage, but properly signifying 'neighbours', strikingly underlines the local factor in this extension of the family and its domain. The feeling of solidarity arising from being neighbours would beget the illusion of original kinship, an illusion kept alive by having the same name and common cults. The difficulties in such hypotheses are not denied by their proponents, and they can only sustain them by pushing the rise of gentes out of familiae back to a time before Rome was settled. Such theories at least leave one with an idea of the complex pressures on the coherence of the gentes that arose from the accidents of their wanderings and their encounters with other ethnic elements. P. de Francisci has shown, in dealing with the Julii and Mamilii, how subject they were to splintering by the dispersion of their familiae.[22] But against such centrifugal tendencies they had the opposite reaction of religious loyalty and aristocratic pride. The Potitii (whose existence as a gens has been disputed) were on the way to extinction in 312, when they numbered no more than thirty adults; but they had maintained intact the structure of their twelve families.[23]

The plebs

Alongside the *gentes* was the *plebs*, long distinct from the *populus*, as in the ancient votive formula *ut ea mihi populo plebeique Romanae bene verruncent.*[24] In fact its essential quality was that it was excluded from the organization into *gentes*: *gentem non habet.*[25] It was an amorphous mass, its name implying etymologically nothing more than multitude; for *plebs* is to be compared with Latin *plus*, *plenus* etc. and Greek πλῆθος, 'multitude'. Dionysius of Halicarnassus calls them τοὺς πολλούς.

The origins of the Roman plebs are even more disputed than those of the gentes. Among the solutions which are gradually forcing themselves on historians today the most interesting suggests that the plebs had arisen from the age-long infiltration of isolated elements coming up against the impregnable barrier of the gentes—starting with the landless and lordless men to whom Romulus had thrown open his *asylum*.[26] Stress is laid on the economic factors which must have brought about the influx of foreign workmen and merchants, attracted by the prosperity of Rome and forming gradually a mainly urban plebs; and the theory of course ties up this immigration with the new wealth of the city under the Etruscan kings, who were presumably in favour of it and used it as an instrument of social policy.[27] But we should note that the influx of people whom the Athenians would justly have called metics, on however large a scale, could hardly have earned the designation of plebs, which implies that the true *populus Romanus* felt in a minority. These new arrivals were certainly important, but we should perhaps look elsewhere for the substratum to which they became attached. A theory formerly proposed by Mommsen[28] but now abandoned, identified the plebs with the client body—not only because, as is universally allowed, the clients of an extinct gens relapsed into the plebs, but because, even within the gentes, the clients remained plebeians. This was the opinion of the ancients: Romulus, says Cicero,[29] *habuit plebem in clientelas principum discriptam*. The argument brought forward against this, that in the fifth century the clients mostly detached themselves from the bulk of the plebs to vote with their patrons from the gentes,[30] only shows how strict a discipline the latter imposed. But the major objection remains: one cannot say of the client body, *gentem non habet*. The clients were part of the gentes, bore their name, took part in their cults. On the other hand, many historians have maintained that the plebs was composed of conquered and transplanted peoples,[31] or by the original native stock (Latins, for example) in thraldom to its Sabine or Etruscan conquerors.[32] And although the most recent studies on the way in which Latium was peopled tend to discourage the idea of large-scale invasions, the theory has to accommodate an unassimilated stratum of tillers of the soil, made up of the 'survivors of the ancient populations prior to the expansion of the Protolatini, Sabines and Etruscans'.[33] We may conclude that the sources from which the plebs was recruited remain uncertain, and that there were certainly many of them. We should also take care not to falsify the problem by assuming from the earliest times a dualism which is now thought to have been the work of time—the division between plebeians and—a word that we have hitherto avoided—patricians.

Constitution of the patriciate

One of the most considerable advances of modern research, and one of the most solidly established, is the dispelling of the illusion, fostered and spread by the annalists, that the conflict between patricians and plebeians was as old as Rome herself. Does not Livy assign to Romulus the artificial creation of two classes which immediately became rivals?[34] Hugh Last[35] has now taken up again the rather scattered observations of some of his predecessors, and has been able, he thinks, to show that their mutual animosity showed itself only at the beginning of the republic, when an oligarchy of *patres*— their sons being now for the first time called *patricii*,[36]—tried to corner for themselves all the benefits of the revolution, to close the Senate to plebeians, keep them out of magistracies, and even (in 450) to forbid marriage between patricians and plebeians. But in the perspective of a one-way progress towards democracy (which was the annalists' viewpoint, readily adopted by modern writers in relating the victories of the plebs) the plebeians must have started from nothing, and the patricians must have been (as Mommsen suggested) at first the only citizens. If plebeian consuls turned up in the Fasti before 486, it must be late interpolation, and the law of the decemvirs suppressing *conubium* must have been a reactionary attempt to reopen a gulf which the early advances of the plebeians had already succeeded in filling. Thus, by inverting the meaning of events and re-arranging them artificially, one could make them say what one wanted to hear, thus concealing the troublesome truth that the conflict of the classes burst out only in a secondary phase of social evolution at Rome.

Yet there are many indications still surviving that run counter to the common opinion. For example, four of the Roman kings had plebeian gentile names—Pompilius, Hostilius, Marcius and Tullius—and Livy cannot deny the plebeian extraction of Numa, Lucius Tarquinius and Servius Tullius.[37] The names of three hills of the Septimontium (Oppius, Caelius, Esquilinus) are also personal names never borne in history except by plebeians, while the 21 rustic tribes created in 495, according to Livy, all had patrician names. For these reasons and some others, Last, without of course denying that the kingly period knew those inequalities of rank and fortune that exist in all societies, concluded that the Romans of that time formed one political body in which all members had the same private rights and, at the same time, an equal share in the few public rights conceded to them. This conclusion has attained such authority now that in his recent *Primordia Civitatis*, P. de Francisci has been able to unroll a vast panorama of the pre-republican centuries at Rome without alluding to a problem which was not yet posed or to a dualism which, in his opinion, was not older than the beginning of the fifth century.[38]

More recently, however, Last's theory, while admitted in essence, has undergone some revisions in detail which only make it more fruitful in understanding the development of monarchy in Rome. It has become apparent that the dramatic confrontation produced after the fall of the kings had its immediate causes in the royal period, at least the latter part of it. A. Alföldi, describing the insignia of the equestrian nobility, has shown how soon the *equites* displayed their political aspirations.[39] A. Momigliano has pointed out that the nomination of the *interrex*, membership of the Salian brotherhood, the functions of *rex sacrorum* and *curio maximus* and the right to take the auspices, were either permanently or for a very long time during the republic restricted to patricians, and has stressed that these privileges could only have been granted by the kings.[40] The patriciate as a class had taken form gradually as certain gentes emerged from the mass of the people, 'gradually monopolizing religious and political rights, until the crisis of the monarchy gave them the opportunity to take the reins of government wholly into their own hands'. The ambitions of an aggressive aristocracy will then have shown themselves even before the fall of the monarchy, at the time when the prosperity of the city was swelling the ranks of the plebs; the story of the Tarquins, the target of hostility from the *primores patrum*, the 'liberal' policy of Servius Tullius, inspired by the wish to abolish the hierarchy of blood in a constitution based on wealth, find here their true significance.

The king

At the head of the state that was built essentially on the gens system that we have just described, tradition from the earliest times places a king—*rex*. The root of this word is found also in Celtic and Indo-Iranian, which proves well enough that kingship at Rome predates the Etruscan domination, even though the Etruscans had kings (*lucumones*) and the Italic peoples (Umbrians, Sabines, Samnites) seem to have had none:[41] when they first appear in history they have lost all trace of monarchy, which has been replaced in most instances by a federal magistrature. A valuable fragment of Epicharmus (early fifth century) lets us know that there was a king with augural functions, named ῥῆσος, among the Sicels,[42] who were akin to the Protolatini; the name of the city Rhegion in Bruttium confirms this testimony. We shall also see that the political divisions of primitive Rome —the *tribus* and *curiae*—establish a unitary and systematic order over the gentile basis of society, and that this order was presumably created on the initiative of a royal legislator—he whom tradition calls Romulus.

It is natural that the traits of Roman monarchy should have altered during the 250 years or more of its life. The annalists distinguish a first series of four Latin-Sabine kings, to whom they happily ascribe high patriotism, patriarchal manners and respect for the gentes, from a later sequence of three Etruscan kings, wealthy and lawless, whose despotic power (symbolized by the lictors' axe) profoundly changed the aspect of the régime in accordance with Etruscan national character—in accordance also with the general tendencies of the seventh and sixth centuries, which witnessed the spread of despotism from one end of the Mediterranean to the other. But this summary classification does not properly take account of the details of a transformation which the historian tries to see more clearly in its successive stages, going back even into prehistory.

The origin and extent of the king's powers are disputed. The traditional theory maintains that the kingship had a contractual basis, defining the king as a magistrate chosen by the federation of the gentes to take charge of religious and military affairs, while a Senate with wide responsibilities, especially in foreign relations, remained the depositary of sovereignty.[43] But many historians and jurists, analysing the nature of Roman kingship, insist on the absoluteness of the king's powers. Some, in defining his *imperium*, are more and more sensible of the magical elements which went into the making of kingship.[44]

This imperium was in its essence divine, and could only be conferred through two acts of religion—the augural act (*inauguratio*) and the taking of auspices (*auspicatio*).[45] Under the republic the terms *augurium* and *auspicium* became almost interchangeable, because of their superficial resemblance and because of a false etymology which derived them both from *avis*, and the jurists have great difficulty in distinguishing them. *Augurium* is connected, like *augustus* and *auctoritas*, with the root *aug-* as in *augeo*,[46] the augur was the priest who embodied in himself supernatural power in all its plenitude, and communicated it to persons and things—in particular to the king by touching the latter's head with his right hand. *Auspicium* (*avi-spicium*) was the observation of the flight of birds and of other signs whereby the will of the gods was declared. It seems likely that the originally factitive force of *augurium* was only subsequently added to the consultative force of *auspicium*: one made inquiries of Jupiter whether the proposed king possessed the fullness of power that rendered him capable of reigning. In the investiture ceremony of Numa which Livy[47] describes on the basis of later inaugurations, *augurium*, by the laying-on of hands, is associated with *auspicium*, by which the augur asks Jupiter to express his consent to the enthronement.

Roman kingship was not hereditary, although parentage might constitute an extra claim. Nor was it based on adoption of a successor by the reigning monarch, although formal recommendation seems to have played some part. Was it then an elective monarchy, as the annalists represent it, claiming that the nomination came from a vote of the people ratified by the Senate?

The clearest indication is really derived from an institution which persisted down to the end of the republic under the anachronistic name of *inter-regnum*,[47a] to which recourse was had when the two consuls died or abdicated in the course of a year, or when civil strife prevented elections from being held. Under the kings, the patres chose ten of their number, alternating every five days, whose task it was to find out what possible candidate (even a foreigner: most of the Roman kings came from abroad) would pass the test of the auspices; having found him, they put him forward for the solemn inauguration. The traditional formula to describe this machinery being put into motion—*res ad interregnum redit*[48] or still more significantly, *auspicia ad patres redeunt*—constitutes a very strong argument for those who think that the Senate was the source of the royal power, as being the depositary of the *auspicia populi Romani*, the continuity of which it was their prime duty to ensure.

Lastly, it is possible that a *lex curiata de imperio* confirmed in the name of the comitia the imperium with which the king had been ritually invested.[49]

The king's religious powers

The king exercised religious, judicial, political and of course military powers. His religious powers are those best known to us.

There were in fact some precious survivals of them right down to historic times. On the coming of the republic, the consuls inherited the other regal functions, but not the priestly ones. They allowed the king-priest to survive in the person of the *rex sacrorum* or *rex sacrificulus*, sometimes simply called *rex*. In the priestly hierarchy he held the first rank, as being 'the most powerful' (*quia potentissimus*),[50] well above the *pontifex maximus* who later took over the precedence and the direction of things religious.[51] He dwelt, with the *regina sacrorum*, in the midst of the Forum, near the temple of Vesta and the *domus Vestalium*, in the 'royal residence' (*regia*), a modest building which was reputed to have been Numa's house, and which later became the residence of the pontiff.[52] The *rex sacrorum* on his nomination was consecrated by inauguration, like the kings, and his priesthood ended only with his life.

The early Roman calendar

This ever more insubstantial shade of the ancient kings had certain functions known to us which certainly go back to his remote predecessors. He came forward in particular to dictate the calendar to his people:[53] at the Calends,[54] when a minor pontiff whose duty it was to watch the heavens had reported to him the appearance of the new moon, the rex offered a sacrifice; a minor pontiff then called the Roman people together and, by repeating either five or seven times the word *calo* (from the old verb *calare* 'call'), told them whether the Nones would fall that month on the fifth or the seventh day—for the country folk had to be given notice in time to hear the rex himself on that day pronounce which days of the month would be *fasti*, which *nefasti*, i.e. on which days it would be permissible or forbidden to summon an assembly and to dispense justice. It is a striking picture: the only republican innovation in it is perhaps the increased rôle of the *pontifex minor* in place of the *calator* or herald who accompanied the king in order to announce his decisions in a loud voice; it illustrates and authenticates in its atmosphere of reverent attention, where every word echoes like an incantation, all that tradition associates with the name of Numa, the inventor of the lunar month and of every detail of religious ceremony.

Some other significant survivals occur in the fragments of inscriptional calendars. They retain the part played by the king in the second Consualia on 15 December. Above all, they mark 24 March and 24 May not with the usual abbreviations[55] F. (*fastus*), N. (*nefastus*), and C. (*comitialis*, i.e. when the comitia could be held), but by the four letters Q.R.C.F. (*quando rex comitiavit, fas*). The meaning of *comitiare* in this formula (to appoint or hold comitia, to come to comitia) is disputed; we can only see that the king's initiative could turn a day (or part of a day) from being *nefastus* to being *fastus*.[56] There is a third day in the calendar (24 February) that can be compared with the two preceding;[57] it was called the *Regifugium*, 'the king's flight', which was classically interpreted as the anniversary of the flight of Tarquinius Superbus, but which in truth perpetuated a far more ancient rite, still not adequately explained: the rex sacrorum, in the presence of the Salii, offered a sacrifice at the comitium, and then decamped as fast as he could. It seems likely that this flight was the magical representation, made manifest in the bodily actions of the king, of the flight of the year, which ended on that day.[58] The king did not merely dictate the calendar; 'he lived it'.

Lastly, the basically religious character of kingship at Rome is further confirmed by an inscription of the utmost importance, discovered in 1899 under the Lapis Niger in the Forum: its essential significance has been worked out by G. Dumézil.[59] The rex who is explicitly mentioned in it (together with the *calator* who proclaims his edicts) is perhaps the rex sacrorum of the infant republic; more probably (for there is more and more agreement now that the inscription is of 550–500) he is a king in the full meaning of the word. Now the law engraved on this stone concerned certain precautions to be taken when the king was going along the Sacred Way to an *inauguratio*, to see that no unfavourable auspices should vitiate the ceremony. It is interesting to note that at the time of that inscription the Etruscan kings, Servius Tullius and Tarquinius Superbus, had given up none of the augural functions which had been assigned to royalty by Numa, as tradition had it, at the very beginnings of monarchy in Rome.

The truth is that we cannot distinguish that part of Roman religious institutions belonging to the primitive stock from that which was added by the Etruscans; the latter seems to have consisted essentially, as in all the domains where they made their influence felt, in organizing material which was no doubt abundant but still amorphous. While it is evident that the basic means of communicating with godhead—by consulting auspices and by *inauguratio*—go back to the earliest times; while it is equally clear that the majority of the gods and their priests—vestals, flamens and pontiffs—often reveal, either by their names or by details of cult in some cases, details of personal taboos in others, that they have a very long history behind them, nevertheless no one now believes that the oldest Roman calendar that Mommsen has constructed from the *Fasti* can justly be called the 'calendar of Numa', despite its agreement with what tradition relates as Numa's work.[59a]

Mommsen had observed that our calendars in stone, dating from the end of the republic onward,[60] exhibit in their columns, in regard to each day, two distinct series of notices; the one, in big letters or in red, represents a primitive condition, the other, in small letters or in black, has more recent additions or comments. The old part comprises the nundinal letters (i.e. the letters A-H marking the eight days between *nundinae* or market-days), indications of Calends, Nones and Ides, names of 45 public holidays, and signs denoting the nature of each day, whether *fastus*, *nefastus* or *comitialis*. For example, under 25 July one finds: *F. FVR. N.*, i.e. day F (6) of the nundinal 'week'; *Furrinalia* (feast of Furinna); *Nefastus*. We leave aside the mention that follows in small letters of the *ludi* celebrated in honour of Caesar's victory.

The pre-Julian calendar which thus stands out almost immutably pre-served in its structure and contents, bears every token of great antiquity. Of the 45 feasts enumerated[61] scarcely a single one occurs before the Nones, recalling the custom by which the king announced only on that day what feasts there were to be that month. A *terminus ante quem* was fixed by Wissowa, who pointed out that, among the deities whose cult appears as established (with no Greek gods among them, such as Castor and Pollux or Apollo), the absence of any allusion to Jupiter Optimus Maximus and the Capitoline trinity suggests that the calendar as a whole antedates the build-ing of the temple of Jupiter Capitolinus in 509. In conclusion he inclined towards an even earlier dating: 'If a name has to be attached,' he wrote, 'the organization of the feast-days and the system of the gods point to Numa as the author.'

The most recent researches tend to throw doubt on this calendar of Numa. They stress the Etruscan elements which, by their combination with a Latin substratum, permit us to date this calendar and the religious codi-fication from which it arises to the age of the Tarquins. The lunisolar calendar assigned to Numa by tradition, and even perhaps the lunar calendar whose deficiencies he corrected, are not of the old Latin stock; the lunisolar calendar was brought in by the Etruscans. Amidst the Latin names of months, the name *Aprilis* is Etruscan.[62] While the names of Calends and Nones are Latin, the word *Idus* is an Etruscan importation. The list of feast-days includes the Volturnalia, in honour of Volturnus, to whose service a *flamen Volturnalis* was assigned and who was the principal deity of Etruria, and the Saturnalia in honour of Saturn, whose name betrays the same provenance. In short, there is almost complete agreement in dating the appearance of the pre-Julian calendar to about 550[63]—unless indeed we reject Wissowa's *terminus ante quem* (for the omission of Jupiter *O.M.* is not so decisive an argument as had been thought), and bring it down to the age of the decem-virs, without of course denying the strong Etruscan imprint that remained upon it.[64]

Under that same influence the religious meaning of kingship had taken on a more sinister form. The quality of divinity that was conferred on Numa by *auspicium* and *augurium* had become in Tarquin's case total assimilation to Jupiter Optimus Maximus. The tokens which showed off his imperium to the world were all of Etruscan origin: the twelve lictors, armed with axes, who cleared the way for him, the ivory chair on which he sat in majesty; the purple toga brocaded with golden stars that enveloped him, the sceptre

with an eagle on top that he held in his hand, the crown of gold.[65] Some of
these insignia of royalty identified him with the king of the gods.[66] This
significance is confirmed by their having been those used under the republic
by the *triumphator* in the ceremony which also was imported from the
Etruscans, when he ascended to the Capitol in a chariot drawn by four white
horses, with the *toga picta*, the sceptre, and the kingly crown. Livy well
says,[67] it was the costume of Jupiter himself, *Jovis Optimi Maximi ornatus*,
and by wearing it the king by virtue of his investituture and the triumphator
on exceptional occasions embodied the power and the cosmic rôle of the
king of gods.

Judicial powers of the king

The judicial functions of the Roman kings are less clearly attested than the
religious, but tradition and the analogy from known facts in other primitive
societies make plausible reconstruction possible. We are also helped by the
close ties between justice and religion—ties which tend now to be more
and more stressed. The two virtues which marked out Numa for the throne
were inseparable—*justitia religioque*. The Indo-European root from which
Latin *ius* is derived, with some of its surviving usages, have enabled us to
see its basic sense—'more than human, more than logical, mystical'.[68] The
classical distinction between *fas* and *ius*, opposing the divine to the human
order, was only brought about by a long-sustained effort to secularize a kind
of 'pre-law' which was originally sacred in its nature.[69] P. Noailles has
made a masterly analysis of the way in which these meta-juridical factors
act upon the already secularized religious law of the *Lex Duodecim Tabularum*.
It presupposes a body of law, of which it is content to define the details, and
which cannot have been worked out except in the kingly period. Furthermore, are not the *dies fasti* the days on which civil law could be administered? The *dies fasti* were properly, so to speak, law-days.

The king pronounced the law *qua* priest. Tradition ascribed to the kings
in general (or to this or that one of the seven in particular) a certain number
of *leges regiae*, which, like those ascribed to the legendary Papirius, a
supposed contemporary of the Tarquins, are of recent redaction.[70] That
there could at least have been some *leges regiae*, the spirit of which is more
or less reflected in the pretended *leges*, and which were not mere customary
laws, but written edicts, is proved by the Lapis Niger inscription.

The relation between the king's justice and that of the gentes is a vexed question. Under the republic, the state long kept aloof from private litigation; the magistrate, when a complaint was laid before him, did no more than arrange the hearing and appoint judges (*dare judices*). Those who still hold the theory that kingship was contractual at Rome are driven to believe that the king left to the paterfamilias the full exercise of rights over all his dependents. Others think that his powers, religious in their origin, made him the sovereign arbiter who became necessary when the rivalry of the clans became a threat to order in the city, [71] and that the transition from public to private law was easily made. Now in fact, while the lex regia in which Numa limited the patria potestas by forbidding the father to sell his son into slavery is no doubt apocryphal, [72] the story of Tullus Hostilius' intervention in a domestic matter which should not have gone outside the Horatia gens may very well correspond to a real step forward in the evolution of the law. It is remarkable that Horatius, after the murder of his sister, was charged with *perduellio*, i.e. high treason. By this rather disingenuous interpretation the king claimed the right to bring into his court a case that previously would not have been in his competence. [73] He created for this occasion, as judges of the case, two duumvirs (*duumviros qui Horatio perduellionem iudicent secundum legem facio*), from whose decision an appeal lay to the people (*provocatio*). [74] We can probably also refer to the kingly period the institution of *quaestores parricidii*, whose job it was to draw up charges of *parricidium*; [75] unfortunately we know nothing of the nature of this crime, one of the oldest recognized by the Roman law. We know only that it involved a murder (*caedere*), and that it only later came to mean the murder of a father. The most interesting etymologies that have been proposed—murder of a patrician (*pater*), [76] and murder of a blood-kinsman (cf. the Greek πηός), [77] dash themselves on the rock of phonetics. A lex regia attributed to Numa convicted of 'parricide', or punished as for it, anyone who murdered a freeman. [78]

The punishments prescribed for *parricidium* (the condemned criminal being sewn in a sack and thrown into the Tiber) and for *perduellio* (hanging from a tree sacred to the infernal gods) have a quality of magical expulsion or expiation about them that bespeaks very great antiquity. The most common punishment seems to have been to declare the culprit *sacer* 'accursed', so that any who wished could kill him with impunity. But the appearance of rods and axes in the retinue of the Etruscan kings implies ordinary, secularized executions by the lictors. [79]

The place assigned to the spear (*hasta*), the Latin emblem of royal sovereignty, in auction sales and in the procedure of *actio legis per sacramentum* also seems to be a vestige of the part played by the king in the origins of Roman civil law.[80]

Political powers of the king

The political powers of the king were exerted upon a unified people, and it was this very unification of the *populus Romanus* that was the first task of the kings. On top of the gens-structure a new political mode of organization was superimposed—Romulus, according to tradition, divided the Roman people into three tribes and thirty *curiae*.[81] This new organization now demands our attention.

The tribes

The three tribes played a definite and fundamental role in the history of primitive Rome. They formed the basis of recruitment for the early army, with its three legions of infantry commanded by the *tribuni militum* and its three centuries of cavalry commanded by *tribuni celerum*. In historical times (after Servius Tullius, when there were four urban and 31 rustic tribes) the word *tribus* had a purely geographical acceptation, or had it no longer. Thus also in Umbrian *trifu-* denoted the territory of a city.[82] It is not impossible that this acceptance corresponds to the original meaning.

But the Romans, in addition to the classic territorial divisions, retained the memory of an ethnic division of their people. They had no doubt—as modern linguists have—that *tribus* was derived from *tres*[83] as the direct expression of a ternary division; in their original three tribes they were pleased to identify the three ethnic elements, Latin, Sabine and Etruscan, which had been united in the synoecism of Romulus.[84] Modern historians for a long time looked with favour on this notion of a tripartition on ethnic lines, and even thought to see in it an Italic national characteristic, visible also in the Umbrians and Sabellians.[85] More recently G. Dumézil has seen in the three Roman tribes the three social functions (priests, peasants, soldiers) that are imprinted in Indo-European ideology.[86]

The obscure names of these tribes do not help to solve the problem. Tities or Titienses, Ramnes or Ramnenses, and Luceres—that is the official order of their enumeration, giving precedence, as it seems, to the Tities. The annalists thought that the Tities had their name from Titus Tatius, the

Ramnes from Romulus, and the Luceres (rather more doubtfully) from an Etruscan king Lucumo. What is certain is that under the republic these names only survived to designate the six most ancient equestrian centuries (*sex suffragia*). These were originally formed, to the number of three, by Romulus, and later divided each into two by Servius Tullius. On the other hand, *Tities*, *Ramnes* and *Luceres* are Etruscan names,[87] or rather the Etruscanized transcription of Latin names already existing; it seems that this transcription must have been made at the time of the reforms of Servius Tullius, for the texts stress the requirements of augury: the centuries were doubled 'under the same names that had been given to them from their inauguration'.[88]

Beyond this *interpretatio Etrusca*, it is hard to identify the names of the three centuries and consequently of the three tribes in which they were recruited. *Ramnes* might be a distortion of *Romani*; the *Luceres* were perhaps the inhabitants of the *luci* on the Esquiline and Celian;[89] the Tities, if it be true that the college of the *sodales Titii* or *Titienses* who inherited their cults were devoted to 'the keeping up of the Sabine rites',[90] may have been connected with the Quirinal.[91] Thus the three primitive tribes would reflect a temporary regrouping of the villages of the Septimontium, the Sabine collis being included and indeed put at the head.[92] Other interpretations are possible. The essence of the matter is that the creation of the three tribes clearly predates the Etruscan dominance at Rome; and so does the creation of the curiae, inseparable from that of the tribes.

The curiae

The curiae,[93] which were subdivisions of the tribes, are much better documented than they, and had a much longer history, continuing under forms that were still living down to the first days of the Empire. *Curia* is an Indo-European word, apparently from **ko-wiriyā*, meaning 'a collection of men'[94] (cf. a Volscian inscription from Velletri where *toticu covehriu* is translated *publico conventu*)[95] this meaning agrees with the classical acceptation 'a group of persons' (the Thirty Romulean curiae) and 'the place where such a group assembles' (*curia* = senate-house). It is a natural supposition that at all times the inhabitants of the villages came together to discuss common interests and to hold their religious rites, and this spontaneous activity of the curiae still went on after a general reorganization had incorporated them, to the number of thirty, in the three tribes.

E

The names of the curiae (we know eight of them)[96] mostly fit the theory of a local origin. The curia Rapta, with its unexplained name (= *rapax*, 'greedy'?), may have suggested the legend that the tribes got their names from the ravished Sabine women;[97] the others bear either gentile names (Acculeia, Faucia, Titia, Velitia) or adjectives from place-names (Veliensis, cf. Velia: Foriensis, cf. *forum*); if the curia Tifata really was a curia, it may have been located near a grove of holm-oaks.[98]

The curiae of Rome find their analogues in other towns of Latium and the Italic world. At Gubbio the *acta* of the brotherhood of the Atiedii[99] have preserved a record of the sacrifices held in common by a group of ten *decuviae*, some of them split into two under the same name, with sometimes a gentile name (e.g. *Clavernii*), sometimes one derived from a locality (e.g. *Casilas*).[100] It is possible that these ten decuviae together made up the one tribe of Gubbio. It has been shown in other connections that the principle of decimal division held sway throughout the Indo-European world.[101]

Each curia had a president, the *curio*, a man of mature years, served by a flamen and a lictor. Each curia celebrated sacrifices and banquets in common: Dionysius of Halicarnassus was able to be present at one.[102] Each had its special gods, as the Dea Angerona[103] of the curia Acculeia. All in common honoured Juno *Curitis* or *Quiritis*, who may have been 'the goddess of the curiae'.[104] But their principal festivals were the Fornacalia, at the end of February, when the members of each curia gathered around the communal oven for the roasting of grain,[105] and the Fordicidia of 15 April, when a pregnant heifer was offered up to Tellus in each curia.[106] The agricultural character of these festivals is obvious. One important step (which must have corresponded to the systematic establishment of a body of 30 curiae distributed into three tribes) was taken when the seats of the thirty, previously dispersed, were all gathered at the eastern corner of the slopes of the Palatine.[107] This concentration marks a decisive stage in the unifying of the community, and the choice of site clearly betokens the precedence which the Palatine had gained over the rest of the city. That is where we find them in the historic period, so firmly rooted that when it was proposed, at some date unknown, to rearrange them more spaciously on the Caelian (*novae curiae*), four of them could not be shifted, but kept their place at the *curiae veteres*, because the inauguratio which had placed them there was quite indefeasible.

The religious life of the 30 curiae was co-ordinated by a *curio maximus*. Down to 209 he had to be a patrician,[108] but this does not imply that such an obligation was original. In Ovid's time it was still the *curio maximus* who took charge of the Fornacalia,[109] although in the Fordicidia the pontiffs had supplanted him.[110] The Fornacalia was always a moveable feast; in the course of it he fixed, in set phrases, the date appointed for the assemblies of the different curiae, at the same time posting up notices allocating them a place in the forum. The last day, properly called *Quirinalia*, was also popularly called the 'Feast of Fools', because those who did not know their curia or had not been able to leave their work in time[111] had the right to sacrifice on that day. It seems to follow from this that the system of curiae allowed for some isolated individuals, more or less artificially attached to one or other of them. We shall bear this in mind when studying the *comitia curiata*.

The curiae had a part to play in the allotment of military duties, for each was the basis from which a unit of 100 foot-soldiers (the century) was recruited; thus the infantry amounted to 1000 men per tribe, and their commanders bore the title *tribuni militum*. The three centuries of cavalry, on the other hand were levied on the basis of the tribe,[112] one from each, and under their commanders (*tribuni celerum*) they bore the name of the tribe whence they came—Titienses, Ramnes, Luceres. Thus the effectives of the primitive Roman army numbered 300 horse and 3000 foot.

The comitia curiata

Lastly, in politics the curiae formed the popular assembly of the *comitia curiata*. This was perhaps not the oldest assembly known at Rome; it had presumably been preceded by the *comitia calata*, which assembled, as we saw, on the Calends and Nones at the call of the *calator*. That they met at the Capitol is an idea entertained, from Varro's time onward, only from a false etymology:[113] the Capitol was not a part of primitive Rome. The *curia calabra* which antiquaries had identified there near a supposed 'hut of Romulus' derived its name from a root quite different from *calare* (cf. Calabria, the river Calabros in Bruttium, the *kalaprenas* at Volsinii :[114] it may have been the seat of one of the curiae. There is nothing to suggest that the comitia calata were summoned by curiae when all that the country people had to do was to come to town to hear the king's announcements on the calendar. But the comitia calata survived within the comitia curiata, which were summoned for the occasion with peculiarly archaic formulae and ceremonies.[115] In consequence the activities of the two types of comitia (which we only know from the jurists of the Empire) are very hard to distinguish. Both concerned themselves with questions of law touching the life of the gentes and the state of cults belonging to them: the comitia calata lent its presence twice a year to testamentary declarations whereby a *pater*, in the absence of natural heirs, appointed a *heres* charged with assuring the continuance of the family rites (this is the oldest form of *testamentum*), and to acts of *detestatio sacrorum*, by which a gens solemnly abjured its *sacra* ;[116] but *adrogatio*, the adoption of a person not under the *patria potestas*, was the concern of the comitia curiata—yet it implied a *detestatio sacrorum* and attachment to another cult.[117] The inauguration of the king (later of the rex sacrorum) and of the flamines was the business of the comitia calata, but the *lex* conferring *imperium* on the king (subsequently on certain magistrates) was a *lex curiata*.

It was certainly the king who convoked and presided over the comitia. Under the republic, indeed, the sessions of the comitia calata and curiata were held in the presence of the pontiffs *(pro collegio pontificum, arbitris pontificibus)*,[118] and the role played by Julius Caesar in 59, in his capacity as *pontifex maximus*, in the *adrogatio* of Clodius is well known. We should not infer from it (as is too often done) that the pontifex maximus anciently presided over the comitia calata.[119] We have already seen how a pontifex minor had usurped the functions of the *calator* in the comitia calata on the Calends and Nones: on all fronts the pontiffs succeeded in eliminating the rex sacrorum. Under the monarchy the king could consult with them on matters of religious law without yielding up his sovereignty.

It is generally agreed that the assembly had no legislative, judicial, or electoral competence,[120] and that its function was simply to be present and to approve. There are two words which strikingly express this passivity. The *testamentum* made in the comitia requires only the presence of a witness *(testes)* ;[121] the oldest way of voting was shouting *(suffragium* cf. *fragor)*.[122] When the king was presented to the assembly by the interrex, the *lex curiate de imperio* was voted by acclamation. Thus the *consensus populi* was far older than the *jussus populi*.[123] But it has been remarked on the other hand that the resolutions put before it were of particular gravity, concerning as they did the entire gentile organization and the economic and political structure of the family.[124] We know that the curiae voted successively, the order being dictated by lot.[125] At the end of the republic, they were represented only by their thirty lictors.

But of all the qestions raised by the curiae and their comitia, the most important is that of their composition. A jurist of the second century, making perhaps too systematic a division between the centuriate assembly, based on the *census*, the tribal assembly, based on place of birth, and the curiata comitia, says that in the latter voting took place *ex generibus*,[126] which can only mean according to birth.[127] The basic position held in the curiae by the gentes is manifest from the religious character of their activities and of the questions on which they had to decide. Nevertheless it was recognized as early as Mommsen's day (when the prevailing notion was of an original distinction between patricians and plebeians) that the comitia curiata were open to plebeians.[128] In our own day, when a less black-and-white view is taken and we see the antagonism of the two classes as a relatively late development, it is being admitted that 'any citizen could take his place in the comitia curiata.'[129] A very interesting view has been put forward by F. de Martino, who sees this assembly, for all its gentile basis, as one of the instruments by which individuals were emancipated from the gentes: in it the *filius familias*, oppressed at home by the full rigour of the *patria potestas*, could take heart and acknowledge his ambitions as an individual.[130] We may reckon Eduard Meyer's formulation as very near the truth: 'While composed primarily of noble families, the curiae were open to non-noble families also.'[131] We must admit, of course, that families did not become definable as noble (i.e. patrician) until fairly late, and that non-noble families, from then on constituting the plebs, were increased by the adherence of the detached individuals who were brought to Rome by her increasing prosperity. F. de Martino, who thinks that the organization of the curiae reached its zenith under the Etruscan kings, refers to that period the admission of plebeians to the comitia curiata.[132] We must remember what we said in connection with the 'Feast of Fools': 'those who did not know their curia' were not thereby excluded from the Fornacalia.

The senate

The rôle of the senate has been more keenly debated as it is more complex. Tradition makes it a creation of Romulus' out of nothing; modern writers are agreed in looking for its origins in the natural development of village life: the villages, as they joined one with another, were led to establish, over the head of the local curiae, an assembly where the whole body of patres familiarum was represented by those among them who had the most influence.[133] They were patres familiarum, abbreviated to *patres*; there is no mention at all of any supposed *patres gentium*.[134] The connection between the curiae and the senate was still perceptible at the end of the fourth century, when an obscure legal text prescribes that the censors shall proceed to the *lectio senatus curiatim*—i.e. by curiae.[135]

Romulus' senate, however, had only 100 members, a figure which does not go well with the division of the people into three tribes and 30 curiae, which is also attributed to Romulus: Dionysius of Halicarnassus[136] has a detailed explanation of how one chose 100 senators from 30 curiae. The number of senators increased gradually as the city grew greater, reaching 300 (a multiple of three) at the end of the monarchy. The stages in this increase are variously described by the historians.[137] The most important, however, dates from Tarquinius Priscus, who made 100 new senators.[138]

It is certain that in the Etruscan period the selection of patres, which may at first have belonged to the gentes, had passed into the king's hands.[139]

The senators created by Tarquin were called *patres minorum gentium*, to distinguish them from those of the old gentes, who were called *majores*. This is the first time that any principle of inequality appears in the organization of the gentes, and it seems likely that the patriciate as a class was established at the same period. The term *patricii*, 'descendants of patres',[140] must have been coined when certain gentes claimed or obtained the right of automatic son-to-father succession in the senate.[141]

On the powers of the patres there is a direct conflict of opinions, these being founded mainly on probabilities and on the notion which one forms a priori of Roman kingship. The assembly of the patres was the sovereign assembly of the city, says one school; to the senate belonged in principle a power which it subsequently shared with the king, and to a slight degree with the comitia:[142] this is the view of those who stress the federative character of the primitive community and think that it delegated to the king part of its own responsibilities, retaining the power to check the use that he made of it and keeping the upper hand in foreign relations. Others interpret the *regia potestas* in terms of *patria potestas*, considering the king as an absolute *dominus* who left to the senate, as *regium consilium*, only that authority which was granted to the family *consilium* in domestic life.[143] This conception, which goes so far as to deny that there was any *patrum auctoritas* during all the kingly period, draws some of its main arguments from the religious aspect of royalty: the *rex inauguratus* is the projection in human society of Jupiter Rex.

While scholars are thus profoundly divided, it is still possible to note certain points: the fundamental role of the *interregnum*, which is an emanation of the patres, in the nomination of the king, and the formula by which the auspices return to the senate on the king's death, allow us to believe that in decisive moments of public life the senate had a basic importance that is incompatible with its complete effacement during the reign. The notion of patrum auctoritas, in the original meaning of auctoritas, 'that which, as it were, augments (*augere*, cf. *augurium*) an action and makes it fully efficacious', is too much part of archaic ideology to be dated from the Republic only:[144] moreover, we cannot separate it from the interregnum among the privileges later claimed by the patrician senators as having been theirs from the first:[145] but the religious meaning of the term was quite different from the political meaning that it took on in the later relations between the senate and the popular assemblies.

We should not go too far in this direction and assign to the senate a deliberative power, since the annalistic tradition never shows it as playing a part in the king's decisions, only in his nomination; its pretended competence in foreign affairs is an anticipation of its known functions under the republic: the institution of fecials, declaration of war, conclusion of treaties—all this in our texts is the job of the king.[146] We shall therefore content ourselves with assigning to the senate consultative functions, in agreement with the definition of it as *consilium regium, consilium publicum,* given by Cicero and Festus.[147] What marks off a tyrant like Tarquin from the kings before him is that he *domesticis consiliis rem publicam administravit,*[148] without ever availing himself of its advice.

Rome and the Latin League

Before leaving the institutions of monarchical Rome, it is important to note that the city's sovereignty was naturally limited by the ties which from the earliest times united her to the Latin peoples as a whole.

At the beginning was the Latin League, which some modern historians tend to think took form on the spot out of ethnic elements of different kinds, while others follow the traditional conception (now vigorously re-asserted by A. Alföldi) and see it as the legacy of an old tribal formation which had existed before the Latins came to the site of their final settlement.[149] These Prisci Latini, whose number was religiously kept at thirty, no more, no less, met once a year, or more often if circumstances required it, in a federal sanctuary where they held a common sacrifice and a common meal. Here also the delegates of each people, presided over by a *dictator latinus* chosen in rotation from each, took diplomatic or military decisions by which they were all bound.

The sanctuary of the League was at first *in monte Albano* (now Monte Cavo) where thirty *populi Albenses* listed by Pliny[150] celebrated in honour of Jupiter Latiaris the *feriae Latinae* which were later accepted and perpetuated at Rome. But it shifted as one or other of the Latin towns carried it off as a status-symbol. After the destruction of Alba Longa the political and religious centre of the Latin peoples became Lavinium, where later legend was to place the landing of Aeneas—where also the Trojan Penates were preserved.[151] But the sacred grove of Diana at Nemi, near Aricia, had also claimed this position at the end of the same century; we know from Cato the dedicatory inscription attesting that the functions of dictator Latinus in that year were exercised by a magistrate of Tusculum.[152] As early as Servius Tullius' time, according to Livy,[153] Rome had tried to secure the first place in the Latin League by removing the federal cult to the temple of Diana on the Aventine. From the beginning of the fifth century onward the Latins met at the *aqua Ferentina*, a spring on the Appian way below the Alban hills.[154]

B History of the kings: the growth of the tradition

The history of Rome does not truly begin until the end of the sixth century, with the date commonly accepted for the foundation of the republic; it is only from then on that she had a firm chronological framework to which she could attach the events that made up her destiny. The beginnings of the city went back much farther, for she had not only been at one time ruled by kings, but she claimed to associate her origins with the arrival of Trojans in Latium shortly after the fall of Troy.[155] The story had had to combine two distinct cycles of legends, one borrowed from the Greek mythographers, with Aeneas as its hero, the other more directly inspired by national traditions and connecting the foundation of Rome with the fable of the twins Romulus and Remus suckled by the she-wolf. At first the storytellers, untrammelled by chronology, had made Romulus the grandson of Aeneas; Ennius still held to this story in the early second century. But from the third on, after Hellenistic learning had pinpointed the date of the fall of Troy (Timaeus put it in 1193, Eratosthenes in 1184), they had tried by hook or by crook to fill up the gap of nearly seven centuries between then and the founding of the republic by adding to the 240 years or so during which the seven kings of Rome had been on the throne a whole dynasty of Alban kings. These were already known to Fabius Pictor, and when inserted between Aeneas and Romulus they finally covered a period of some four hundred years.

Trojan origins of the Romans

The legend that Rome was founded by Trojans is no more than a legend; the only real element reflected in it is the dim memory of relations between the Aegean world and Italy in the second half of the second millennium. It has sometimes been thought to have been invented holus bolus by the mythographers of the third century in obedience to the political interests and ideological tendencies of the age of Pyrrhus.[156] Such interests and tendencies may have given further impetus to the legend, but they did not beget it. The discovery at Veii of terracottas depicting Aeneas carrying his father Anchises has shown that at the very gates of Rome in the first half of the fifth century there existed a cult which can be shown, by the closer study of other representations—some even older—to which these terracottas furnish the key, to have been widely spread in Etruria, whence it was introduced into Rome under the Etruscan domination.[157] In this sense Alcimus, the fourth-century disciple of Plato who is the first to mention Romulus, could say that the latter was the son of Aeneas and the Etruscan Tyrrhenia;[158] likewise a dedication of the fourth to third century, recently found near Lavinium, gives Aeneas an Etruscan praenomen—Lare Aineia (dat.).[159] Thus from the fourth century on the Romans had accepted this image of the son sustaining the failing strength of his father as representing their own natural conception of *pietas*.[160]

Three years after Aeneas had arrived in Latium, he founded Lavinium, where his son Ascanius reigned for 30 years and later founded Alba Longa, where his descendants ruled in succession until Romulus, the last of them, founded Rome in his turn. The part played in this story of Roman beginnings before Rome itself by two Latin cities which Rome always venerated as her mother-cities has some historical foundation. We have seen that the first Roman settlements were attached to the *cultura laziale* which is particularly well attested in the ninth century in the cemeteries of the Alban hills.[161] We have also seen that there is no reason in archaeology to suppose these older than the oldest cemeteries of Rome;[162] there is nothing to support the traditional theory that the first inhabitants of the Palatine were colonists from Alba Longa occupying an advance post by the Tiber. The Alban dynasty seems to have been artificially elaborated and completed in the last centuries of the republic. It has recently been suggested that we should identify its founder Silvius with the Agrios whom pseudo-Hesiod represents as reigning with Latinus over the Tyrrhenians: the presence of these two names in the interpolated verses of the *Theogony* would point to the double importance of Lavinium and Alba in sixth-century Latium.[163] The fact is that they then constituted the two main federal sanctuaries of the Latin League: the discovery of fourteen archaic altars and votive inscriptions in the neighbourhood of Lavinium has further proved its character as a religious centre: it was there that the penates of Rome were preserved. There Aeneas was venerated under the title of *Pater Indiges*; every year the Roman magistrates, before leaving for their provinces, went in procession to Lavinium to offer a sacrifice. Alba, however, disputed this rôle of metropolis with Lavinium, as we may see from the rite of the *feriae Latinae*, which was celebrated down to the end of the empire; on that occasion the delegations of the peoples of the old federation took part in a sacrifice and communal banquet in the presence of all the magistrates of Rome.

When was Rome founded?

To determine the date when Rome was founded, antiquarians from the third century on undertook calculations which tended finally to set it in the middle of the eighth century. First Timaeus in his *History of Pyrrhus* thought he could show that Rome was founded in the same year as Carthage—814; by this synchronism he took pleasure in pointing out that the young power whose appearance in the west he was the first to hail was of the same age as the old enemy of the Siciliot Greeks.[164] The fixed point here was the foundation of Carthage, which he obtained from the annals of Tyre. It would be hard to think that he took it on himself so boldly to declare the contemporaneity of the foundations if he had not possessed some data to support him, even if the interpretation was twisted. A lover of precision and of synchronisms, he is usually content to push together two dates not very far apart. It is probable that the archives of Lavinium, from which the people of Lavinium had given him certain information, contained a tradition making the foundation of Rome go back to the late ninth century.

At Rome itself the arithmetic was to be rather different. When Fabius Pictor created the nation's history during the Hannibalic war, he proposed a rather later date—748–747. The annalist Cincius Alimentus, who trod in his footsteps, brought it down to 729–728. Polybius went back to 751–750, Piso to 752–751; Varro arrived at 754–753, which became canonical.

These oscillations about 750 are to be explained by subsequent re-adjustments; in choosing the middle of the eighth century as the foundation date, Fabius Pictor was assuming that the kingly period lasted 245 years (the traditional figure is 244),[165] which corresponds to seven generations of 35 years each. That being given, the exact date depends on what year one assigned to the inception of the republic. This varied by some years: if Fabius Pictor made it 504, that gave 748 for the foundation; if Varro placed it in 509, that gave 753.[166]

It is hard to know whether (as is commonly believed) there was a list of seven kings before this calculation was made. If so, the date of the founding of Rome would result from adding 244 to 504 (or 509), and it would represent no more than the result of an artificial speculation. But one might equally think that the number of kings was kept down to seven because the foundation dated from the middle of the eighth century.

Thus just as the priests of Lavinium preserved a tradition concerning the date of Rome's foundation the pontiffs in Rome had also accepted one, distinct but not incompatible, and which agrees to a large extent with the archaeological data. Rather than write this off as pure coincidence, we may see in it the proof that from the earliest times Rome was able to keep alive the memory of certain great events.[167]

The fact is that it is the list of seven kings which bears the marks of deliberate manipulation. Why seven, unless it was necessary that their successive reigns should cover two and a half centuries? It is probable that Roman legend knew of others who have not found their way into history. On the Capitol stood eight archaic statues which were taken to be the kings of Rome, but no one knew any longer who the eighth was: Titus Tatius, the Sabine king who reigned with Romulus? Brutus, who drove out the Tarquins?[168] Manipulation is particularly apparent in the story of the Etruscan dynasty. Servius Tullius had been clumsily stuck in (*insertus*)[169] between the elder and the younger Tarquins, not without injury to the chronology; hence the annalist Piso was led to make Superbus the grandson, not the son, of Priscus.[170] Moreover, the numerous repetitions in the reigns of the two suggest that they are no more than the reduplication of an original single Tarquin. Everything suggests that Fabius or his immediate predecessors cut and sewed the stuff available to them until it came out to the right size.

The annalistic tradition then retained seven kings: four of them—Romulus, Numa, Tullus Hostilius, Ancus Marcius—form a Latin-Sabine group; Tarquinius Priscus, Servius Tullius and Tarquinius Superbus make up an Etruscan dynasty.

Are the kings the expression of a functional mythology?

One cannot easily believe that the task of differentiating and coordinating these reigns was done quite arbitrarily, and modern research is trying to trace the origin of the legends peculiar to each reign. But first we must give the credit that is due to the brilliant hypotheses of G. Dumézil, who regards the history of the kings of Rome as fundamentally mythological. In a series of studies in the religions of the Indo-Iranians, Germans, Celts and Italiots, he has pointed out many striking coincidences between parts of their folklore; in the battle of the Irish hero Cuchulainn against three brothers one after the other before coming up against a battalion of shameless women, he sees a sequence of episodes comparable with the battle of Horatius with the Curiatii and his encounter with his sister;[171] in the treachery of Tarpeia, bribed by Sabine gold, he sees a theme that has its counterpart in Scandinavian sagas, where in the course of the war between the Asen and the Vanen, Gullveig (=gold-drunkenness) is similarly seduced and punished.[172] Behind these lingering survivals he has reconstructed a common fund of mythology, and shown that the Indo-Europeans looked upon the world as formed of a hierarchy of three organs assuring the three primordial functions of religious sovereignty, military strength and fertility; a similar ideological structure had imposed itself on the emerging separate peoples and formed their peculiar myths—even their history, in the case of Rome. 'The materials coming from a historical basis (if any such existed) have been in any case so thoroughly rethought and remoulded along the lines of traditional ideology . . . that for us its only interest is as the dramatic expression of that ideological structure; hence to interpret that structure, as a structure, is our first task.'[173]

Hence the double aspect of sovereignty—magical on one side, juridical on the other—which was expressed in India by the pair Varuna–Mitra,[174] has put at the very head of Roman kingship the antithetical figures of the terrible and capricious Romulus and the pious and pacific Numa, the worshipper of *fides*, 'good faith'.[175] The second (the military) function, which there gave rise to the myths of Indra, here begat the cult of Mars and the exploits of Tullus Hostilius;[176] the third (fertility and abundance) owned Quirinus as its divinity and gave rise to the reign of Ancus Marcius after the fleeting appearance of Titus Tatius, 'a peasant who blundered into power'.[177] Ancus may in some of his features recall Romulus and Numa; but does he not reveal himself by his defensive wars and his taste for commerce on the grand scale as being the champion of peace and economic values?[178] 'The four national kings [unlike the three Etruscan kings in that respect] are figures harmoniously composed and arranged; there is not one who can be spared or who is a doublet of any other.' But the 'functional characterization of the kings' did not stop with the fourth; it extended to Tarquin and Servius Tullius, figures modelled by the ideology of the third function.[179]

In presenting these principles of interpretation, Dumézil hoped for a constant symbiosis, as he called it, between comparatists and specialists: 'Let the comparatist prospect for the subjects; the specialist scholars, if they take his thumb-nail sketch seriously, will do better with it than he himself will.'[180] The method has found real success in the interpretation of Roman and Italic religion. As regards political history, the history of kingship at Rome, which specially concerns us here, it has not given rise to the hoped-for collaboration. It has certainly appeared that transitions from the area of function to that of chronology and the mutual interference of one domain with another (as for example in the Etruscan kings, where Indo-European mythology and definite traditions are intermingled) could be very usefully studied.[181] But however subtle these characterizations, however eloquently urged, they have not carried conviction. Their author is indifferent to the complex stratification of Latin annalistic tradition, and is so firmly convinced that the ideological structure which he posits held the upper hand over the originality of writers through many centuries, that even in Propertius and Virgil, Livy and Dionysius of Halicarnassus he sees an unconscious purpose[182] which, for all their talent and despite the sources that they were following at any given point, made them still the interpreters of a primitive mythology and called them to witness on its behalf. It is impossible to believe that traditional ideology, if it existed, could have exercised this constraint and control, through long ages constantly modified by historical events, over intellects so diverse, in which ideology was so exposed to the erosion of history. In particular it is impossible to admit that the tradition concerning the seven kings was put together in the fourth century[183] (why not earlier? why not later?) as an organic closed system, a 'vulgate' codified once for all. On the contrary, all that we know points instead to the artificial combining of heterogeneous elements, directed by the desire to fill up a given extent of time.

How the legends took shape

Romulus, the oldest of the seven kings, is the one whose historicity is the most doubtful, even to the minds of those who accept all the others as historical.[184] Varro did not shrink from declaring that *Roma* came from *Romulus*,[185] which is absurd. The derivation is more complex and more meaningful. There was a *gens Romilia* (or *Romulia*), which gave its name to one of the oldest of the rustic tribes, the *Romilia tribus* which extended along the right bank (the Etruscan) of the Tiber, comprehending the *ager Vaticanus*; this was the original domain of the gens, or more likely annexed to its possessions subsequently (mid-fifth century).[186] The Romilia gens boasted as its ancestor one Romulus; but *Romulus* (*rumlna*) is a name well attested in Etruscan, and W. Schulze has been able to detect in it a form derived from a gentile name *ruma*. It was the *Ruma* whose name—under what circumstances we do not know—became attached to the city, *Roma*, where they had settled.[187]

Where Romulus is concerned we can grasp a stage of tradition before it became fixed by writing. The story of the twins who founded Rome became officially recognized in 296 when Cn. and Q. Ogulnius, two curule aediles of Etruscan stock, set up in the Comitium the statues of the two infants suckled by the she-wolf;[188] in 269 we find the scene figured on the reverse of one of the first series of Roman didrachms.[189] The constituent elements of the legend here seem very complex: an old totemic wolf-cult, natural enough in a culture of shepherds and reflected in the age-old rite of the Lupercalia; influence of certain Graeco-Etruscan themes of mythology (Telephus suckled by a doe, a child suckled by a she-wolf on a stela from Bologna);[190] two etymological approximations to the name of the eponymous hero of the city, one Greek (Rhomos), one Latin (Romulus), both being maintained to reflect a racial or political duality (Romans and Sabines? Romans and Campanians? patricians and plebeians?), the whole being enriched with various motifs developing about well-known sites, such as a grotto on the Palatine (the Lupercal) and a sacred fig-tree (the *ficus Ruminalis*).

The name of Titus Tatius who shared his reign, and the names of his successors Numa Pompilius, Tullus Hostilius, Ancus Marcius, differ from the single name of Romulus in that they agree with the laws of Latin nomenclature, having a praenomen (often not a very common one) and a gentile name of normal formation like an adjective.[191] It will be noticed that the gentile name never attaches them, as one might have expected, to any great patrician family. It could not have been in Roman *atria*, amid images of the glorious ancestors of the *gens*, that their legend was begotten and took its form. Neither Sextus Pompilius, tribunus plebis in 449, nor M. Pomponius Rufus, military tribune with consular powers in 349, was responsible for the legend of Numa. The Hostilia gens does not appear in the Fasti before the Hostilii Catones who were praetors in 207. Even the Marcii, despite the splendour achieved by the Marcii Rutilii in the latter half of the fourth century, never thought of claiming Ancus Marcius until a century later, when M. Marcius, although a plebeian, was named rex sacrorum :[192] this priesthood (an honour which he passed on, as it were, to his descendants by the hereditary cognomen Marcius Rex)[193] provided him with a pretext for claiming kinship with the fourth king of Rome. Thereafter the biography of Ancus Marcius was embellished with anticipations of the great deeds treasured up in the traditions of the Marcia gens.[194]

The history of Numa likewise was refurbished in the second century by the cult accorded to him by various 'Numaic'[195] families—the Marcii again, the Pomponii, Aemilii Mamercini, Calpurnii—who claimed descent from him and who, having at that time been won over to Pythagorean doctrines, sought to associate the two objects of their devotion by making Numa a pupil of the Samian sage and bidding chronology go hang.

Before that time[196] we possess up till now no image, coin or inscription enabling us to say what milieu had seen the genesis and development of the tradition concerning this Sabine king who was the organizer of religion. His provenance and his austere and pious character might well lead us to think that he first took shape in the national consciousness of the Sabines. But the content of the 'national stories'[197] in which the Sabines told of their legendary beginnings is pretty well known to us through Cato, who divulged them at Rome, and later through Varro and Dionysius; and it is striking that they ignore Numa. We ought rather to suppose that, as a great sage and religious legislator and one to whom all the religious constitutions of the city were attributed—the calendar which was the basis of all regular worship, the minute specification of most of the rites, the priestly colleges themselves, Vestals, Salii, flamens and pontiffs—must have lived on for a long time in the memory of those colleges as a supreme referee and guarantor of their orthodoxy; there he found the ideal milieu in which his memory could be preserved and his biography elaborated.

In other cases the personality of the king seems to have been formed in an atmosphere of heroic poetry. Cato referred to the custom, given up in his day, of singing at banquets hymns in honour of one's ancestors.[198] No doubt these *carmina convivalia* are responsible for some of the features of the legend of Tullus Hostilius. The annalists represent him as a warrior king, more in love with fighting than Romulus himself,[199] one to whose lot had fallen the dreadful duty of destroying Alba; but also as a lawgiver king concerned with international law,[200] and a judge-king who had personally presided in his court over the case of Horatius—a case of *perduellio* into which he was credited with having brought for the first time the right of appeal to the people (*provocatio*).[201] The basic outline of this personality[202] was not, as we have seen, drawn by the historical Hostilii. It is easier to believe that it was sketched in the margin of the tale of Horatius. The gens Horatia was one of the most powerful at the beginning of the republic,[203] and the combat of the Horatii and Curiatii, like the exploits of Horatius Cocles, must have been the theme of epic songs.[204] The war against Alba, which could not have taken place in the middle of the seventh century (the cemeteries of Castel Gandolfo show no sign of being abandoned at the date assigned to the reign of Tullus, i.e. 672–641), formed the background of the picture: the king who waged this cruel war of Rome against her mother-city has the same savage boldness (*ferocia*) as Horatius himself. The punishment that he inflicts on Mettius Fufetius is one of the cruellest possible, and Ennius, in the verses in which he describes it, has no doubt simply caught the barbarous tone of the primitive *chanson de geste*.[205] But from the fact that Horatius slew his sister and stood trial for it, Tullus inevitably became transformed into a judge; the arguments over which he presided stirred the juridical imagination of the Romans, and the merciful verdict ascribed to him tended to make men refer later softenings of legal rigour back to his reign.

The differentiation of character among the kings seems then not to result from historical happenings (largely unknown to us) which may have distinguished their reigns, nor yet from an a priori differentiation of function, but rather from the diversity of milieu in which their legends were fostered—that of Numa among priests, that of Tullus among epic singers.

The Etruscan dynasty

With the Etruscan dynasty the elements of reality become suddenly more substantial. That is the time when we first have attestation, sometimes contemporary, at all events very old; Rome enters then the sphere of action of a higher civilization that can read and write—and the name of Aulus Vibenna, tied up, as we shall see, with the legend of Servius Tullius, is read on a dedication at Veii about 550,[206] and the same name is inscribed on an Etruscan cup of about 450.[207] The Etruscans also represented the events of their history in plastic art: witness the frescoes of the François tomb at Vulci (latter half of fourth century), which traces the exploits of Mastarna (Servius Tullius) in a war that brought him to grips with Cn. Tarquinius of Rome;[208] witness also the series of intaglios dating from the start of the third century, in which a representation has been recently identified of Tarquin at the founding of the temple of Jupiter Capitolinus, contemplating a head that has come out of the ground at his feet, an omen presaging the future greatness of Rome.[209] In addition, the Etruscan people had their oral traditions and their historiography before ever there were annalists in Latin. Their historical works (whether in Etrucsan or in Greek versions) are known to us only by an author's name, Promathion[210] (with a fragment in Latin) and by a brief reference of the Emperor Claudius to *scriptores Tusci*.[211] It was from Etruscan sources that the annalists took their detailed and circumstantial accounts of Roman monarchy in its Etruscan phase.[212]

C Etruscan rule in Rome

The annalists anachronistically centre everything on Rome; the Etruscan ascendancy, which must have affected equally all the peoples of the Latin League, is seen by them only through Roman spectacles, in the succession of the last three kings, Tarquin the Elder, Servius Tullius and Tarquinius Superbus. Certainly, however artificially the story of these three reigns may have been put together, the fact of Etruscan ascendency in Latium cannot be doubted: it was simply one of the results (the most pregnant result, no doubt) of the expansion of a people who were known to have conquered most of Italy before conquering Rome.[213] The beginnings of their province of Campania have lately been illustrated by the discovery of further cemeteries at Capua and S. Angelo in Formis; dating from the end of the ninth century onwards, they show Villanovan features very like those that we find in central Etruria,[214] and for those who identify the Villanovans with the proto-Etruscans they confirm the early dating of 800 that Velleius gives for the foundation of Capua.[215] This Villanovan phase is succeeded by another in which, during the seventh century, ties with southern Etruria become ever closer; it is now, about 680, that those who reject the identification would date the arrival of genuine Etruscans on the heels of the Villanovans.[216] At all events, this move towards Campania took place along the two routes which have always connected it to central Italy: one route went from Caere to Veii, crossed the Tiber at Fidenae, reached Praeneste without going through Rome, and thereafter, going between two folds of the Apennines, followed the course of the Trerus (Sacco) and Liris (Garigliano); this was the future Via Latina, and its importance in the seventh century is clearly shown by the orientalizing tombs at Praeneste, as ostentatious as the Regolini-Galassi tombs at Caere.[217] The other route— the future Appian way—had to go along the coast. The Etruscans were well aware of the facilities for crossing the Tiber offered by the ford at the foot of the Palatine, and the advantages of the harbour of the Forum Boarium, where Greek and Phoenician ships used to come up the river.[218] Military and commercial considerations bade them establish themselves firmly on the site of Rome.

Epigraphical and archaeological traces of Etruscan rule in Rome

Some epigraphical discoveries have confirmed the presence of Etruscan elements at Rome: a graffito of the seventh century recently found in the Forum Boarium shows that this district of the city, where commerce was coming to life, was early frequented by Etruscan traders.[219] Two inscriptions on bucchero pots from the sixth century, found at the foot of the Capitol and on the top of the Palatine, have confirmed that some of them were settled in the heart of the city.[220] But the archaeological study of the subsoil has shown that this was not a matter of scattered infiltration; several considerable public works cutting across the stratification point to the coming of powerful rulers. E. Gjerstad's stratigraphy demonstrates that, at a date which he reckons to be 575 B.C., but which other equally competent archaeologists put at the end of the seventh century,[221] the Forum was paved for the first time, when a well-compacted bed of small stones was put down to let water run off. This paving (followed by two more during the sixth century) implies preliminary drainage works, the story of which is perpetuated in innumerable underground channels and especially in the Cloaca Maxima:[222] the last-named was a typical achievement of the Etruscan civil engineers. Thenceforward, instead of the huts scattered along the valley floor there was a vast public area which was to be the political centre of the city. This remodelling of the Forum may have been completed by the building or the realigning of streets—perceptible possibly in a section of the Sacra Via[223]—so that the Rome of the Tarquins corresponded to the shape of cities founded *Etrusco ritu*. At all events, stone buildings with tiled roofs everywhere replaced the old thatched cabins. New temples arose, like that in the Forum Boarium over which the church of S. Omobono was later built, and which was presumably the temple dedicated to Fortune by Servius Tullius. Two series of excavations, in 1938 and 1959,[224] have enabled us to study the accumulation of votive offerings: it includes much Greek pottery (Corinthian, Laconian, Attic) together with Etruscan pottery and some architectural terracottas very similar (often indistinguishably so) to those of the temples at Veii and Caere, or south of Rome at Velletri and Satricum. Thanks to these remains, we can picture more clearly the temple that the Tarquins built then on the Capitol to lodge in a triple *cella* the trinity Jupiter, Juno and Minerva; to adorn it they brought in the school of Vulca, the contemporary artist who modelled at Veii the famous group of Apollo and Hercules quarrelling over the Cerynian stag, and who perfected the Gorgon-head antefixae.[225]

Thus the new amplitude given to the overall plan, the replanning of streets and open places, the beauty of her new stone buildings won for Rome during the next 100 or 150 years the title that some historians bestowed on her—πόλις Τυρρηνίς, 'Etruscan city'.[226] But one can readily see that this programme of utilitarian and aesthetic construction, which involved forced labour for the 'plebs', as the annalists tell us,[227] made heavy demands on manpower which could only be met by a large influx of Etruscan technicians and workmen[228] and by economic changes which profoundly altered social equilibrium at Rome.

In every area of life the influence of Etruscan civilization on Rome in the kingly period shows the relatively subject status of the city. We have already seen that the calendar attributed to Numa contains several Etruscan gods, and that all the insignia of royalty and of the triumph were borrowed by Rome from the Etruscans. We should add that it was the Etruscans who taught the Romans to read and write by introducing among them an alphabet derived from the Greeks, which the Romans then adapted to the needs of Latin.[229] These represent the limits of a domination the depth of whose penetration cannot be overemphasized; but it would be a mistake to suppose that it dried up the original springs and shattered the native traditions of the subject people. Rome under the Etruscans remained a Latin city, where Latin was the language; two Etruscan potsherds with graffiti do not stop the rex in the Lapis Niger inscription from publishing his decrees in Latin;[230] the Etruscan corruption of the names of the three ethnic tribes (*Tities, Ramnes, Luceres*) does not affect the names of the principal Roman gentes.[231] In Rome there was a crowded street of ill repute alongside the Velabrum, which was called the *Vicus Tuscus*; here, it was said, Caelius Vibenna's or Porsenna's veterans had been settled.[232] However that may be, it seems that the mass of merchants, tradesmen and labourers who came from Etruria to Rome, while great enough to upset the social balance in the city, was easily assimilated, and that the relatively few who directed the occupation had to come to terms with nationalist forces. Praeneste also, despite the Etruscan lords who controlled from there the road to Campania, remained Latin and kept its own dialect: the Bernardini tomb (about 600) has furnished, on a brooch of gold, the oldest known Latin inscription.[233] We can estimate the proportions of the mixture of the two cultures at Rome by thinking of what we see at Falerii, 20 miles further north at the mouth of the Tiber: it also is a double town linguistically and ethnically; the Roman conquest in the middle of the third century broke off the process of Etruscanization before it had wholly absorbed the indigenous elements.[234]

Intervention by different Etruscan cities in turn

The annalistic tradition made the Etruscan kings of Rome into a coherent dynasty, the sceptre being transmitted peacefully according to ties of blood and of marriage. It seems, however, to be well established that the reigns of the Tarquins, and of Servius Tullius among them, represent several successive waves of invasion[235] coming from different points in Etruria and directed by condottieri whose plans were not (or not at first) coordinated nor their rivalries restrained by the federal assembly at the *fanum Voltumnae*. Legends of these events were nurtured by the popular imagination in Rome and in Etruria: there they had taken literary form and obtruded themselves on Fabius Pictor when in the third century he tried to put them in order and fit them into a chronology.[236] In this artificial construction three kings were retained; others might have been: it has recently been suggested that the cruel Mezentius, king of Caere, was one of these temporary masters of Rome.[237] From a passage of Cato[238] it appears that the Rutulians of Ardea paid him as tribute the first-fruits of their crops, not that the other Latins were subject to him; but Caere was certainly attracted by the coastal route to the south. At all events, the picture which the annalists present of the sequence of the Etruscan conquests contains one undeniable element of truth: the Etruscan kings follow one another at Rome in the same order in which the cities of Etruria gain the ascendancy. First come the Tarquins from southern Etruria, the cradle of Etruscan power, and in fact from Tarquinii, one of the most quickly maturing of its cities; then from Vulci, which begins to expand at the start of the sixth century, Servius Tullius sets out to dispute the kingdom with them; but when the hour strikes for Chiusi, in inland Etruria and slower to awake, it is the end of the sixth century, too late for Chiusi and her master Porsenna.

The Tarquins

But it would be dangerous to attempt too systematic an exposition of a sequence that remains obscure. That the Tarquins came before Servius Tullius may be in agreement with the local developments of Etruscan power; but it is a fact (and a fact of genuine history) that a Tarquin was still reigning at Rome at the end of the sixth century, for the revolution of 509 drove him out. It has been imagined that the conquest of Rome by Vulci was followed by a restoration of the Tarquins;[239] this would explain and justify the two reigns of Tarquin the Elder (616–579) and Tarquin the Proud (534–509), which we have mentioned as being probably doublets of each other,[240] Servius Tullius having been interpolated in the middle. In reality, Tarquin (or the Tarquins) and Servius Tullius are the contemporary leading figures in a very confused period. In Etruscan tradition (the frescoes of the François tomb) a Cn. Tarquin of Rome was killed by Mastarna (Servius Tullius). The praenomen perhaps does not exclude his being identified with one of the L. Tarquinii of Rome.

From this legend of the Tarquins, which was very greatly elaborated, especially in Etruria, there emerge elements to be kept in mind:

Their coming from Tarquinii, as expressed by the name that they took on arriving at Rome.[241] The element *tarch-* enters into the formation of a large group of proper names, including Tarchon, eponym of Tarquinii. The attempt to infer from a recent tomb of the Tarchna-Tarquitii[242] in one of the cemeteries of Caere that the Tarquins came from there is mistaken. The equation is unsatisfactory in itself, and could not stand up against a unanimous tradition which agrees with the facts of civilization in Etruria.

The arrival at Tarquinii of the father of Tarquinius Priscus, the rich Corinthian émigré Demaratus, driven from home by the usurpation of Cypselus (*c.*657):[243] this seems to illustrate the wide economic influence of Corinth and her western colonies, which is attested by the diffusion of Corinthian pottery and terracotta.[244]

The important part assigned to women (Tanaquil, Tullia) in the elevation and proclamation of the king, conformably to the place held by women in Etruscan society;[245] in Tanaquil's case we may add a typical instance of divination.[246]

A policy whereby the Tarquins, facing the economic and social transformation of the Roman people, sought the support of the *plebs* and opposed the new pretensions of the patrician gentes.[247]

The great projects of sanitation and urban improvement, in which tradition, drawing upon distinct sources, strangely assigns no part to Servius Tullius: his work had to be that of a reformer of institutions: it was he who enlarged the city,[248] bringing into it some new districts, built a wall round it and marked out the *pomerium*: all this was concerned with defining the administrative framework of the city. The Tarquins' contribution is of a quite different style: they were great builders, constructed drains, the Circus Maximus, the shops round the Forum, above all, the temple of Jupiter Capitolinus. The annalists, to tell the truth, never knew which of the Tarquins should have the credit, and in their uncertainty they assigned the draining of the valley-bottom to them both,[249] with a 45-year suspension of work, believe it or not, during the reign of Servius Tullius. Yet the work must have been completed early in the Etruscan period—witness the first pavement of the Forum (575 even in Gjerstad's low chronology), which implies previous completion of the drains. Likewise they supposed that the Capitoline temple was vowed by the elder Tarquin, but he never got further than levelling the site;[250] then there was not a whisper of the project while Servius Tullius ruled; finally the younger Tarquin started again from scratch a half-century later. It is he in Livy[251] who takes in hand the 'exauguration' of the cults formerly practised on the site of the future temple, together with the ceremonies preliminary to the founding. Attention has often been drawn to the doublets by which later annalists tried to magnify the role of Tarquinius Priscus, against Fabius Pictor, who presumably credited him with none of them.[252] Thus Pictor represents Superbus as meeting Roman expenses with the booty taken at Suessa Pometia in Volscian territory;[253] Valerius Antias claimed that Priscus financed his works with the booty taken at Apiola in Voscian territory:[254] Pometia and Apiola are probably two names of the same town. As for the temple, Superbus pushed on with building it, so far indeed that he had ordered up from Veii the acroterion which was to crown the work. The revolution took him by surprise (the annalists go on) and he left the honour of dedication to the republic in its first year.

Incessant warfare between the king and the Etruscans, ending (so the annalists pretend) in the victory of the elder Tarquin and the submission of all Etruria to his sceptre.[255] It has recently been suggested[256] that the verses of pseudo-Hesiod (late sixth century) which speak of Latinos and Agrios, the eponymous heroes of the Latins, as having a kingdom embracing all the Tyrrhenians, confirm the establishment of such an empire. It is sure that the Greeks, according to Dionysius of Halicarnassus, gave that name without distinction to the Latins and to all the peoples of Italy.[257] Nevertheless, the 'Greater Rome' of the Tarquins must have pushed its areas of dominance and its sphere of military action (which included Vulci) much further than the narrow limits of its territory. Etruscan rule opened up new horizons for Rome; those who ruled her in the sixth century made her a sharer in their vast enterprises, and aroused a spirit of imperialism which survived their going. Even if they pretended to respect the federal organization, they encouraged the Romans to claim independence and sovereignty among the Latin peoples.

Servius Tullius

Of the three Etruscan kings of Rome, it is Servius Tullius whose personality takes on an ever clearer shape and emerges more and more from legend into history. Roman tradition was anxious to paint his accession in the comforting colours of legitimacy, and pretended that from servile origins (even the lowness of these was elaborately dissembled) he found favour with Tarquin by his singular qualities, so much so as to be chosen as his son-in-law and, on the king's death, to be imposed on the Roman people by a ruse of the imperious Tanaquil. But there was an Etruscan legend, brought to light by the emperor Claudius from Etruscan sources, which made Servius Tullius, under the name Mastarna, play an important part in the history of Vulci.[258] As the faithful friend of the brothers Caelius and Aulus Vibenna, princess of Vulci, he had followed their standard through long and ill-fated campaigns; then, taking command of what remained of their army, he came to lend his support to Tarquin, who recompensed him by letting him settle with his old soldiers on the hill which he called *mons Caelius* in honour of his former chief. But the frescoes of the François tomb at Vulci itself[259] display the battles around Vulci in quite a different light: there one sees Mastarna cutting the bonds of the captive Caelius Vibenna, and many of his allies slaughtering their adversaries; among the latter (inscriptions tell us who they are and where they come from), cheek by jowl with a warrior from Vulsinii and one from Sovana, we find Cnaeus Tarquinius of Rome. In this old and unsweetened version of the Etruscan legend we capture the memory of the real conflict which had formerly set Mastarna-Servius Tullius and the Tarquins at each other's throat.

A. Alföldi[260] has recently re-examined, in the light of further documents and allusions, the tradition partly preserved in the François frescoes and the speech of Claudius; he concludes that an Etruscan army coming from Vulci had gained possession of Rome in the middle of the sixth century and driven out (a provisional hypothesis) the Tarquins. Now the testimony of the texts when thus interpreted can only be confirmed by our increasing knowledge of the power of Vulci at that time and the rapid growth of her trade relations with Rome. Vulci was a late-comer among the Etruscan towns; throughout the seventh century she had been far behind Tarquinii, Caere and Praeneste economically, politically and artistically. But after 600 she rapidly became the first city in Etruria in wealth and influence. A single fact will let us estimate the volume of her trade with Greece at that time: of the Attic black-figure pots imported into Etruria 40% come from Vulci as against 25% from Caere.[261] It is only natural that the rising power should have tended to assert itself on the battlefield also. It has been claimed that the Etruscan conquest of Campania was partly the work of Vulci.[262] In this perspective, the expedition of Mastarna and the Vibennas against the Tarquins becomes perfectly credible and it is confirmed by some archaeological observations. It is noteworthy, for instance, that the white Etruscan pottery found among the votive offerings at S. Omobono in the Forum Boarium, dated *c.*550–525, comes from Vulcian workshops. Commercial penetration and political expansion went hand in hand.[263] If it is true that this temple was indeed the one dedicated by Servius Tullius to Fortuna, to whom he was especially devoted, the presence of imports from Vulci among its votive offerings acquires a yet sharper significance.

Servius Tullius is a mysterious figure, born one knows not where nor of what parents. Dionysius of Halicarnassus, stepping for a moment out of the rut of the vulgate tradition, sums him up exactly in three words— ξένος καὶ ἄπολις, a foreigner, a stateless person.[264] Now here we may have the meaning of the praenomen Servius under which he was known at Rome. The word is no doubt from *servus*, and well calculated to suggest to the poets and annalists the story of his servile origin in the common meaning of the word. But an excellent discussion by H. Lévy-Bruhl has shown that in early Roman law slavery was a concept of an international nature:[265] 'In other words, at this period a slave is nothing more than a foreigner without rights,'—ξένος καὶ ἄπολις. An attempt has even been made to show that *servus*, inexplicable as Indo-European, is a loan-word from Etruscan.[266] If Servius was a foreigner in Rome, he was not less so in Vulci. Having put his sword at the disposal of the Vibennas, he was known in Etruscan legend under an Etruscanized form of a Latin name, Mastarna, or, as the François tomb has it, *macstrna*, which (allowing for the suppression of vowels in written Etruscan) is *magister-na*, or roughly, 'The General'.[267] Thus this condottiere, bearing an Etruscan name at Rome and a Latin name at Vulci, after fighting on every battlefield of Etruria and Latium, became in the end king of Rome—'to the very great advantage of the state', *regnum summa cum rei publicae utilitate obtinuit.*[268]

In Roman tradition the reign of Servius Tullius was reckoned one of the most fruitful. To him a unanimous tradition assigned a corpus of institutions —the creation of a modern army, the political reorganization of the people, a new division of the territory—which were destined long to determine the forms of public life in Rome.

The Servian constitution

Livy and Dionysius have left us a detailed account of the 'Servian constitution'.[269] Together with a remodelling of the army it included a distribution of political rights on the basis of wealth. The Roman people comprised essentially five classes of citizen. The first class consisted of those who had a capital (*census*) of 100,000 asses (120,000 according to Verrius Flaccus),[270] the second those who had 75,000, the third 50,000, the fourth 25,000 and the fifth 11,000 (12,500 according to Dionysius).

From the military viewpoint, each of these classes furnished a certain number of centuries, or groups of 100 men, half of them (the *juniores*, up to the age of 46) serving on the active list, the rest (*seniores*) in the reserve. From the first class were recruited (apart from 18 centuries of cavalry) 80 centuries of infantry, 40 of juniores, 40 of seniores; in the second, third and fourth, 20 centuries (10 + 10); in the fifth, 30 (15 + 15). The reason for this disproportion, which bore most heavily on the first class, was that each soldier had to provide his own equipment. Those of the first class had complete armour of bronze: helmet, round shield, greaves and cuirass as defensive armament; for offence a spear and a sword. The second class had no cuirass, and instead of the round shield (*clipeus*) they bore the old rectangular shield (*scutum*); the third class had neither breastplate nor greaves. In the last two classes there was a radical change: they had no defensive armour, but the fourth class had a spear and a javelin, while the fifth were armed with slings. There was also a pioneer corps of two centuries of carpenters and smiths, and two centuries of musicians. Those whose *census* was less than 11,000 asses, and who were only counted by heads (*capite censi*) were exempt from military service.

Just as each class contributed unequally to the army, so the Servian constitution gave them unequal political rights. In the new 'centuriate assembly', which met like an army outside the *pomerium* on the Campus Martius, each century, as it was a fighting unit, was also a voting unit. The *capite censi* on these occasions were all lumped into one century. The two *centuriae fabrum*, as a mark of respect for craftsmanship, voted with the first class; the two centuries of musicians with the fourth. In total there were 193 centuries, in which the 18 centuries of cavalry and the eighty centuries of the first class possessed an absolute majority. Late republican writers who commented on this system never wearied of lauding its balance, which abolished the privileges of blood while at the same time preserving the state from the tyranny of numbers.

This new organization of the army and introduction of a timocratic assembly, which our texts ascribe to Servius Tullius, poses a problem which has split modern historians into warring schools.[271] For a long time it was regarded as an elaboration of later date, say the fifth or fourth century. Some have even called it a forgery of the early second century.[272] The date proposed by de Sanctis,[273] viz. the early fourth century, still has many adherents, but the general tendency is to accept, with a varying degree of reserve, the traditional account.

We should say first of all that the Servian constitution, in its whole spirit, in its double aspect, political and military, seems to fit well with the profession of the man and the needs of the times. It is perfectly reasonable that Servius Tullius, 'The General' who had led the armies of the Vibennas at Vulci and of Tarquin at Rome, should have the credit for Etruscanizing the Roman army by a reform which took into account not only the growth of the population, but also the improvements in strategy and technique which had already been realized in Etruria Our sources tell us that it was the Etruscans who taught the Romans to fight in close formation (φαλαγγηδόν) and with the round shield of bronze. This was in fact the introduction of heavy hoplite armour into the army. Throughout the Mediterranean world it was goodbye to the old Homeric ways of fighting, with deeds of derring-do by nobles in chariots surrounded by their retainers on foot: from Greece to Etruria, during the seventh and sixth centuries we see cavalry and especially heavy infantry with regulation armament being organized for general engagements. It is obvious that Rome under the Etruscans, like all other states at that time, had to try to bring its army up to date. On this hypothesis an ingenious explanation has been offered of the disparities between the arms of the five classes—the Romans were then not all rich enough to provide complete equipment for a whole army. 'They were content to put in the field a first line of hoplites, behind which the old army remained unchanged.'[274] But we have other references to such distinctions: as late as the second century, Polybius says that only the citizens of the first class had the right to a mail-coat, the others having a simple breastplate.[275] It is of course obvious that the gradual undressing of the infantryman, in steps of 25,000 asses each, first taking his cuirass, then his greaves etc., results from a late and artificial reconstruction. In politics the introduction of a timocratic assembly has a special justi-fication in the middle of the sixth century, not only in the precedents of Draco and Solon in Athens, but in the economic and demographic develop-ment of Rome under the Etruscans. This was the time, as we have seen,[276] when a number of gentes were to label themselves patrician and lay bold claim to hereditary privileges in face of an ever-increasing plebs: 'The kings must have had their work cut out to keep their subjects quiet within the framework of the curiae.'[277] The patricians, with bodies of clients at their disposal and armed bands in their pay, could be a threat to public order; to meet this threat the centuriate organization looks like 'an attempt to arrest the drift apart of the two classes'. Attention has been drawn to the arrangements that were made, even in the organization of command, to break the ties with the gentile basis of the old tribes; from henceforth the military tribunes, who in the old army of 3000 foot had each commanded one regiment of 1000 men, formed a group of staff-officers who took it in turn to command all the infantry of the legion.[278]

But it is not only in the spirit that informed it, but also in the details of its structure and its numbers of effectives that it demands—as an indivisible unity, say some—the belief of the historian.

No one will of course deny that the picture presented by Livy and Dionysius reflects social and economic conditions which cannot be those of the sixth century.[279] The assessment of capital in asses is meaningless for a period in which they were reckoned in acres of land and heads of cattle (*pecunia*). The figures given by the annalists can only be the end-product of a long and complex evolution; when Rome began to admit the use of money (she struck none herself until the early third century), they had to convert, on some basis or other, real-estate values into monetary values, and then to revalue from time to time according to the successive reductions of the as. The figures fit fairly well with the money values current in the second century: 10,000 drachmae, i.e. 100,000 asses (perhaps 120,000), according to Polybius for the first class,[280] while an edict of the censor in 169 makes it 30,000 sesterces, i.e. 75,000 asses.[281] The only difficulty is in the census of the fifth class, which Polybius puts at 400 drachmae (4,000 or perhaps 4,800 asses); this reduced figure is perhaps explained by the need during the second century to enrol a large number of proletarians in the army.[282] It seems likely then that the *Commentarii* known in the late republic under the name of Servius Tullius, containing a *discriptio centuriarum*, were compiled in the early second century.[283] The work was no doubt apocryphal, expounding the ancient material in modern terms, but there is no reason to think it was a 'historical fraud' in its content; apart from the question of form, the basic problem of the origin of the Servian constitution remains untouched.

On the political aspect of the question, it appears that we are near agreement that Servius Tullius can be left with the credit of having brought in a classification of the Roman people according to wealth and of having set up the *Comitia centuriata*—allowing of course that it was a continuous creation which went on after his time. That there was such an assembly before 450 is firmly established by the law of the Twelve Tables, which calls it *comitiatus maximus*.[284] But it seems that at that time, apart from the knights, only one *classis* was known—the *classis* in its original sense, from *calare* = *appellare*, of all those who could be called up, the people in arms, the army—and below that were those *infra classem*.[285] The fact is that *classis* and *classici* even in Cato's time still meant the citizens of the first class, as if in earlier days they had been the only ones to merit that name. This simple antithesis agrees with the references in the Twelve Tables, where Roman society is divided into *adsidui* and *proletarii*;[286] the proletarii are confounded with the *capite censi*, the *infra classem*, while *adsidui* or *locupletes* is an all-embracing term for the rich. But when in 443 a special office, that of censor, was set up to carry out the census work formerly done by the king and later by the consuls, this must have marked an important stage in the elaboration of the century-system: that is perhaps the date when the *classis* was subdivided into four classes, or when four lower classes were added to the *classis* proper.[287]

The question is more open where the army is concerned. Up to 1931 the general opinion was that the establishment of such a large army of hoplites was unthinkable before the end of the fifth century. G. de Sanctis[288] claimed to have found proof of this in the multiplication of the tribuni militares: invested with consular power from 444 onwards they numbered at first three, then four, then in 405, when the war against Veii began, they went up to six: surely this doubling of their number must be a function of the number of men available for service, going up step by step from 3000 to 6000 men?

But in that year P. Fraccaro published an acute and epoch-making study,[289] formulating the argument which, in his judgement, would destroy 'the theory of those who refer the timocratic organization of the Roman state to the fifth or the fourth century—one of the most pernicious inventions of modern critics, which has clouded our knowledge (miserable enough as it is) of early Roman history'.[290] In the seemingly arbitrary numbers allotted to the centuries provided by the Servian classes, he was able to recognize the exact definition of the classic Roman legion. If we set aside the fourth and fifth classes, which provided only skirmishers, the centuries of the first three—the only ones with heavy armour, constituted the line infantry. Now if we total up the centuries of *juniores*—40 + 10 + 10—we arrive at a total of 60 centuries, which reflects the standard composition of the Roman legion at all times. This composition was religiously maintained throughout the republic, even when the number of men in each century was reduced (despite the name century which it still bore) to 60 (hastati, principes) or 30 (triarii), and even when Marius introduced the cohort as the tactical unit. The essential fact is that 60 continued to be the number of centuries and centurions.

Now if we recall that the primitive army numbered 3000 foot, the new one, with its 6000 hoplites (100 x 60) represents a doubling of the effectives, corresponding to the increase of the population up to Servius' time. In the sequel, at a date still to be fixed, a second legion was created, but only by halving the old one, keeping in each new one the same framework of the Servian legion, which served as a model for all subsequent legions. Fraccaro accepted 'an intuition of Delbrück's,[291] namely that this splitting of the legion must have taken place when the consulate was set up, so as to assign a whole legion to each of the consuls out of the same numbers as before. He concluded that the single legion of 60 centuries and the centuriate organization inseparable from it are older than the republic and can only be attributed to Servius Tullius.

This brilliant study has exercised a veritable fascination over the minds of subsequent workers in the field, claiming the adherence—either complete or with reservations—of historians so varied and so distinguished as Last,[292] Mazzarino,[293] de Martino,[294] Bernardi,[295] Schönbauer,[296] von Lübtow,[297] Staveley,[298] Friezer,[299] de Francisci,[300] Scullard[301] and Momigliano.[302] The reservations, be it said, are sometimes considerable. All are agreed that Fraccaro's explanation of the change from one legion of 6000 men to two of 3000 each is beyond cavil; but it has been pointed out that the date proposed—the beginning of the republic—rests only on an 'intuition'. Here we are still far from unanimity. Some writers[303] incline towards a much later date, viz. 366, when the consulate as a double magistrature was restored after seventy years or so of *tribuni militum consulari potestate*. On this hypothesis, despite the efforts made to distinguish these tribunes from the tribunes *ad legiones* and to show that they were only chosen from among the latter for an essentially political function,[304] the increase in numbers of the tribunes with consular power reassumes all the significance that de Sanctis[305] attached to it. We should also admit, with Stavely, that Fraccaro's theory 'ought to be accepted more or less *in toto*'.[306] If we admit at all (and one can scarcely help doing so) that in the field of politics the institution of a *classis* embracing all between the knights and those *infra classem* preceded the division into five classes, then the real centuriate army, which depended on the latter for its recruitment, could only have been formed, as they were, in the latter half of the fifth century.

Servius Tullius, then, keeps the credit of initiating the change: it was in the sixth century, not in the fifth,[307] at the zenith of Etruscan power, not in the dark days of Rome's 'middle ages', that the transformation, or partial transformation, of the Roman army into a hoplite phalanx took place: representations in art, at Rome and in the immediate neighbourhood, attest the wide spread of hoplite armour around 500.[308] On the other side, it was when increases in numbers and in wealth were bursting the seams of an archaic society that Servius Tullius set up a timocratic constitution and a *comitiatus maximus* which seemed to posterity more liberal that the gentile organization and the comitia curiata; this was his title to be lauded as the one *qui libertatem civibus stabiliverat*,[309] and to be reckoned as having accomplished a work which certainly did not spring fully armed from his head, although he established the basis of it before it evolved according to the trial-and-error of history.

At the same time that he created a legion of hoplites, Servius Tullius was traditionally supposed to have greatly strengthened the cavalry arm; from his time on it comprised 18 centuries, which voted first in the comitia. They were made up of two different elements: 12 new centuries recruited among the aristocracy (*ex primoribus civitatis*),[310] and six centuries of a singularly venerable character: these were the three Romulean centuries, already several times expanded as regards their effectives[311] but unswervingly faithful to their ternary grouping and their time-honoured names of *Tities*, *Ramnes* and *Luceres*. Servius Tullius first found the way of doubling them while preserving their Etruscanized names; thenceforth men would speak, for example, of the *Tities priores* and *Tities posteriores*. Under the republic they were reserved for patricians; they voted together and hence derived their name of *sex suffragia* ('the six votes'). It is possible that the expression *centuriae procum patricium*,[312] the two archaic genitives being in asyndeton, described the 18 Servian centuries taken together—the 12 centuries of *proci* or *proceres* and the six centuries of *patricii*.[313]

Here again it is hard not to think that the annalists have anticipated by providing Servius Tullius with so large a body of horse. There can be no doubt but that the twelve centuries were created later. But the *Tities, Ramnes, Luceres priores* and *posteriores*, although referred by some to the same period when the legion of 60 centuries was formed, i.e. the fifth century,[314] seem rather to go back to the kingly period. As for the texts, they are very confused: Livy seems to contradict himself within the space of a few chapters;[315] various legendary traditions, which the first historians put into order as best they could, ascribed to Tullus Hostilius, Tarquin the Elder, or to Servius Tullius the intention of breaking the framework of the Romulean centuries.[316] Now to fight on horseback (as formerly from a chariot) was in that age, when the heavy infantry battalions were coming to the fore, the ever more valued privilege of the nobles. It seems likely that one of the first campaigns waged by the patricians to set themselves apart from the other gentes was for the exclusiveness of the *sex suffragia*; but they only gained a partial success if it is true that the antithesis *priores—posteriores* among the knights reflects that of *patres majorum* and *minorum gentium*. Among the privileges peculiar to the first, one often cited is that of going to war with two horses at the state's expense. What does appear quite clearly, on the other hand, is that Servius Tullius' cavalry was quite independent of the centuriate organization. Eighteen centuries or *sex suffragia*, they are superimposed on the timocratic system, not built into it; and one cannot find out exactly what boundary divided them from the first class. Cicero[317] simply says that they comprised the citizens with the most wealth (*censu maximo*). They represent a compromise where tradition has won the day; this was the part of the reformer-king's task, it would seem, in which he met most resistance and in which the patrician opposition measured swords with him.

Creation of the tribes

Finally, Servius Tullius is the reputed author of a division of the city and the *ager Romanus* into tribes,[318] the word being taken now in the sense of defined territories. This division, replacing the ethnically based tribes of

Romulus, fitted into the general plan of the Servian constitution. The new tribes substituted a classification of citizens according to domicile for classification according to *gens*, and was thus the basis of the survey required to assess landed property for the purposes of compiling the census rolls and assessing tribute.

In the middle of the third century the number of tribes increased, the final figure being 35—four urban and 31 rustic tribes. The question is: Which of these go back to the time of the kings?

No one disputes that Servius Tullius set up the four urban tribes, *Suburana* (i.e. the mons Caelius), *Palatina, Esquilina, Collina*. Only then— although Varro in the late republic tried hard to prove that the Palatine village was rectangular and thus earned the name[319]—did Rome become *Roma Quadrata*, i.e. Rome in four parts.[320]

The Servian wall

The new Rome had a surrounding wall, which the texts attribute to Servius Tullius, and which modern critics, after some attempts to lower its date, now unanimously refer to the Etruscan period.[321] The most certain part of the wall of Servius is an *agger* or earthen levée, more than 25 feet high and paralleled by a ditch, which can be traced on the plateau to the east of the Quirinal, the Viminal and the Equiline, which Servius included within the city. A fragment of an Attic red-figure *kylix* found in the foundations may perhaps date the construction to the late sixth century. The stone wall, built in large blocks of tufa of *grotta oscura* which doubles this primitive earthen wall in places (e.g. near the Termini railway-station) dates from shortly after the Gaulish invasion of 390. But here and there—at two places on the Capitoline, on the Palatine, even the Aventine—fragments have been discovered of walls composed of flagstones of *cappellaccio*, and it is hard to see how they fitted in with the Servian rampart, but they also seem to be of the archaic period. They may have been defensive walls for one or other of the *montes*. The line of the Servian wall coincided with the *pomerium* or religious boundary of the city, which marked the limits of the urban territory within which auspices could validly be taken. The pomerium remained the same, leaving out the Aventine, until the beginning of the Empire.[322]

The history of the 31 rustic tribes is even more obscure. The annalists, as is their way, anticipate events: Fabius Pictor credited Servius Tullius

F

with the creation of 26 rustic tribes; added to the four urban, they give the total of 30—a suspiciously round number.[323]

Fourteen of the rustic tribes, however, were created in the historical period, at known dates from 387–241, punctuating the progress of Roman conquest. Of the 17 that remain, the *Crustumina*, around the town of Crustumeria in the north of Latium on the Tiber, was set up in 495, according to Livy;[324] in consequence the *ager Romanus* in the Servian constitution would have been divided into 4 + 16 tribes, the round figure 20 being perhaps connected with the centuriate organization.[325]

However, the date of the tribe Crustumina is disputed; it seems to imply the previous submission of Fidenae, between Rome and Crustumeria, yet Fidenae was not conquered until 426.[326] It is possible to reply that territorial acquisition is not necessarily continuous, and that certain 'pockets' may be bypassed before being reduced.[327] What chiefly renders the tradition suspect is that it halts the expansion of Rome for the whole of the fifth century, from 495–387; this halting of the frontiers in annalistic tradition seems to result from the absence of documentation for the period before the Gaulish conquest in 390.[328]

The ager Romanus antiquus

The question has been recently reopened by Alföldi in an important discussion.[329] Since Mommsen[330] the general opinion had been that the 16 original rustic tribes had a peculiarity of nomenclature which strikingly set them apart from the urban tribes on the one hand and the later rustic tribes on the other. The urban tribes were named from places (*Palatina*, *Esquilina*); so were the more recent rustic tribes (e.g. *Arnensis*, *Falerna*). But the 16 original rustic tribes bore the name of a patrician gens whose private property they had at first been. For ten of them (e.g. *Aemilia*, *Fabia*) there can be no doubt; but the other six (*Camilia*, *Galeria*, *Lemonia*, *Pollia*, *Pupinia*, *Voltinia*) can only be brought into this interpretation if we suppose that they were named after gentes which do not appear in the Fasti and later became extinct as patrician gentes.[331] But Festus tells us that 'the *tribus Lemonia* was named from the *pagus Lemonius*, which begins at the Porta Capena on the Latin Way'.[332] Alföldi has sought to show that all six were named after places. The tribes concerned border in general on the *pomerium*, and they seem to be contained within a circle of about five miles radius, perhaps corresponding to the sanctified limits of the *ager Romanus antiquus*; that was where the festival of the Ambarvalia took place, at the fifth milestone on the via Campana, and the Terminalia at the sixth milestone on the via Laurentina. The tribes with gentile names, on the other hand, are scattered over greater distances from Rome. Everything is consistent with the notion that only the former go back to the reign of Servius Tullius, when the modest acquisitions of territory were the anonymous achievement of the state, while the latter belong to the time when the patrician gentes were predominant, their ambition having free scope under the oligarchic régime of the first half of the fifth century.

Chapter Five
The Roman Republic

A The founding of the Roman republic and the genesis of its institutions (509-367)

According to Roman tradition and to a good many modern historians, the crisis of 509 that banished the kings and ushered in the republic was an event belonging purely to internal politics. The corruption of the monarchy had led, via a palace revolution triggered off by abuses, to a change of régime which came about in forms that were previously foreseen and to some degree constitutional. The election of the first pair of consuls took place at the comitia centuriata, as prescribed by Servius Tullius in his *Commentaries*.[1] 'The appearance of the consulate', wrote de Sanctis, 'was not the consequence, but the immediate cause of the fall of the monarchy.'[2] Everything was explained by an inevitable and domestic development of institutions, carried out as if *in vacuo*, without any external attack upon the sovereignty of the Roman people.

But we now begin to see more and more clearly that the international situation of Rome at the end of the sixth century was not one conducive to long and mature deliberation, and that the fall of the kings was initially one episode in the vast conflict waged by rival military coalitions in Latium.[3] The opposing forces can be seen the more easily because here, for the first time in Rome's history—and it becomes real history from this fact—we have a Greek source to support and correct the witness of the annalists.[4]

The story went that the exiled Tarquins appealed to Porsenna, king of Clusium, to restore them, and that he laid siege to Rome in 508.[5] The exploits of Horatius Cocles, Mucius Scaevola and Cloelia unnerved him and made him offer peace. It is a patriotic fiction to conceal his real victory. No one now doubts that Porsenna captured Rome.[6]

It was further related that, to keep his troops occupied, he despatched his son Arruns to attack Aricia in the Alban hills. At first victorious,

Arruns was later cut to pieces by Aristodemus of Cumae, whom the Latins had called to their aid.[7] In 506 Tarquinius Superbus took refuge with his son-in-law Maxilius Octavius at Tusculum.[8] Subsequently he went in voluntary exile to Aristodemus, and died at Cumae in 495.[9]

The date and general outline of these events are in large measure confirmed by a chapter of Hyperochus of Cumae,[10] a writer of the third century, but with local sources to rely on, who related the life of Aristodemus and touched incidentally on his expedition against Aricia in 504—the slight disagreement in date proves the independence of the two accounts and the correctness of the facts within a variation of four years: an alliance between Tarquin, the Latins and Aristodemus, hostility between Aristodemus and Porsenna.

It is in this context that we must see the dedication of the sacred grove of Diana at Nemi, near Aricia, which is cited (though incompletely) by Priscian, quoting the elder Cato.[11] It was made by the *dicator* (*dictator*) of the Latin League, Egerius Baebius of Tusculum, in the presence of the delegates of eight Latin peoples—those of Tusculum, Aricia, Lanuvium, etc. Priscian goes no further than the eighth name, which has a morphological peculiarity which was the motive for his citing the passage. The list should have included the thirty peoples of the League; since its order is neither alphabetical nor geographical we do not know whether it went on to mention Rome or not. However, Dionysius of Halicarnassus, in a similar list, gives 29 names of peoples, and Rome is not there.[12] We may suppose that the document illustrates a meeting of the Latin League in one of its new federal sanctuaries, that of Diana at Nemi.[13] The annalists assure us that Servius Tullius had built a temple of Diana on the Aventine, and that the assemblies of the League (already under Roman domination) had been transferred thither; the grove of Nemi was a mere daughter foundation.[14] That it was in fact the older is clearly shown by the patent antiquity and rich variety of its rites (the *rex Nemorensis*).[15] The Aventine temple was not founded until much later. At all events, it is no accident that Porsenna turned his arms against Aricia and that Aristodemus of Cumae, the friend of Tarquin, came to its help; the target of their operations was the centre of the Latin League.

The sequence of events can then be restored as follows: Porsenna, king of Clusium, represents the last of the waves of invasion which had before come from Tarquinii, then from Vulci, and descended on Latium. Despite the distortions of tradition, it was Porsenna who put the Tarquins to flight;

Rome, which he occupied, was his base for operations against the Latin League, which was then under the influence of Tusculum (held by the émigré king) and Aricia, the federal sanctuary in defence of which Aristodemus hastened from Cumae, where Tarquinius Superbus ended his days. Such are the external events which we must bear in mind if we are to understand the birth of the Roman republic.

When was the republic founded?

Before beginning the story of the new institutions that Rome made for herself on the fall of the kings, we have to say a few words on a question recently raised—namely whether the republic was indeed founded in 509, as the traditional accounts unanimously assure us. This is the year when the lists of the eponymous consuls begin; events henceforth will be dated *post reges exactos* or *post primos consules*. For some time there has been a tendency in several quarters to dispute this date and to bring the advent of the new régime down to 25 or 50 years later.[16]

It must be admitted that the year 509 seems in the common tradition to be implausibly laden with events: the expulsion of the kings and election of the first consuls, the consecration of the temple of Jupiter Capitolinus, the voting of the law that permitted appeal to the people (*provocatio*), and the signing of the first treaty between Rome and Carthage. It is obvious that this crowding of major events into the first year of the republic results not so much from genuine coincidence as from deliberate manipulation by annalists who wanted to concentrate every important 'first' upon this great climacteric of history. One is therefore justified in trying to unload 509 and redistribute its burdens; the problem is to decide over what lapse of time.

One point may be reckoned solid—the expulsion of the Tarquins at a date varying by perhaps a few years at the end of the sixth century, but a date confirmed, as we have seen, by the external evidence of the Cumaean chronicles. Some of the arguments against this date have been easily refuted. We find, it is said, no break of continuity in the course of Roman civilization about the year 509; Attic pots are imported in just as great a volume; religious and civic activity, as shown in the building of a series of temples decorated by Greek artists, continues with increasing brilliance. But it would be arbitrary to infer from this continuity in the cultural progress of Rome that the 'Etruscan leaders' did not leave around 509.[17]

The phenomena of civilization do not trot so obediently at the heels of political events. In the last quarter of the sixth century and the first quarter of the fifth, Latium shared in a *koiné* of culture[18] which transcends the frontiers of states and ties her closely to Campania and Etruria herself; this is the phase which art-historians term 'archaic': it is characterized by a uniform style in (e.g.) the architectural adornment of temples in Capua, Satricum, Veii, Caere, Falerii.[19] In the second quarter of the fifth century a general decline in production and importation affected all the centres of this common culture alike, Etruria as much as Latium. Pallottino pleasantly remarks that this recession in Etruria can hardly mean that the Etruscan leaders had then decamped from their own cities. Is it necessary to add that in Etruria also, during the fifth century, the monarchies were giving place to republics?[20] But the falls of dynasties and the changes of constitutions are not necessarily synchronized in different places.

At Rome, when the Tarquins left, Porsenna arrived. He was master of Rome for some time; no one has ever claimed that he was king. It was under his 'protectorate' (probably a short one) that the republic was born. The consular fasti of the first years of the republic contain various names, such as the Larcii in 506, 498 and 490, a T. Herminius in 506, a C. Aquilius Tuscus in 487, which show that there were still in Rome noble Etruscan families associated with the new form of government.

For the same reasons we must reject the argument of those who put the fall of the Tarquins and the advent of the republic about 473–471,[21] as an immediate consequence of the naval defeat of the Etruscans off Cumae in 474—a defeat which dealt indeed a mortal blow to their power and ruined their empire in Campania. This is too systematic a synchronization of two defeats, and it forgets that duration is one of the categories of history. Etruscan communications with Campania were made less secure by the liberation of Rome in 509, but the via Latina and the sea were capable of maintaining the contact for thirty years. It has even been proposed that the founding of Capua should be dated in 471, as an Etruscan attempt to strengthen their hand in the interior after their naval defeat in 474.[22]

To fix the date when the republic was set up, the Romans had used two methods of computation which should be regarded as distinct, despite possible mutual interference. After the dedication of the temple of Jupiter Capitolinus, it had been laid down that a nail was to be driven every year on the anniversary of the dedication (13 September) into the wall of the *cella* of Minerva.[23] In 304 the aedile Cn. Flavius had counted 204 nails *post*

Capitolinam (aedem) dedicatam. The Capitoline era thus established went back to 508, one year after the expulsion of the kings, according to Livy, but in fact the same Olympiadic year 67,4, i.e. 509–508, since the Roman and Olympiadic years were not in step.

In parallel with this Capitoline chronology the Romans had lists of eponymous magistrates. This was a practice very early attested in Greece and the east, and must have spread to Rome at an early date.[24] At first transmitted orally and in writing, perhaps partly reconstituted or completed after the sack of 390,[25] they nevertheless constitute—saving a few interpolations here and there—an authentic document, 'the first and most important document of Roman history'.[26] These lists began in 509–508.

In his brilliant book *Das altrömische eponyme Amt*, K. Hanell tried to show that the introduction of eponymous magistrates in Rome, bound up with reform of the calendar and the dedication of the temple of Jupiter Capitolinus, was only later assimilated to the advent of the republic, while in fact it did not coincide at all with a change of state, the eponymous magistrates having been until *c.*450 only ministers of the kings. Only later did the annalists thrown the end of the monarchy further back and identify the Capitoline era with the republic era. This is a bold theory, and Gjerstad's conclusions have been greatly influenced by it, but there are grave objections: we have already seen that the late sixth-century date for the expulsion of the Tarquins is confirmed by the agreement between Roman tradition and Greek sources.

Beside his main theory Hanell maintained (without convincing reasons) that Cn. Flavius had arrived at 509–508 as the Capitoline era by counting the pairs of consuls in the lists of eponyms, not by counting the nails, the ritual insertion of these having lapsed during the fourth century.[27] A more plausible suggestion is that of Alföldi.[28] It is generally agreed that the consular lists have some authority, except for the first *collegia* which consist of personages drawn from the legend of the fall of the Tarquins— Brutus, Tarquinius Collatinus, Sp. Lucretius, etc., with the no less legendary figure of P. Valerius Publicola among them. It is only about 503 that the Fasti become trustworthy. It may well be that the number of nails and the number of collegia of consuls, when counted in 304, did not agree, and that the eponymic lists only had some 200 sets of consuls for 204 years. Alföldi thinks that in 509–508, when M. Horatius consecrated the first nail, Tarquin was still on the throne; the republic and the lists of eponyms did not begin until 504—the year assigned by the Cumaean chronicles to the battle of Aricia.

Institution of the consulate

It is clear at all events that the republican constitution did not spring fully armed from the head of Jove, and that the expulsion of the Tarquins— brought about, as we have seen, as much by the arms of Porsenna as by forces of liberation within—was not immediately followed by two consuls entering at once upon their duties. After the collapse of the monarchy, there followed, as in all revolutions, 'an uncertain and fluid situation'[29] in which new institutions gradually took shape.

At the very beginning of the republic, power seems to have been in the hands of a *praetor maximus*:[30] in 509–508 this was M. Horatius, the only one of the six 'consuls' given for that year in the Fasti who is thought to be an historical personage. He it was who dedicated the temple of Jupiter Capitolinus, and his title is attested by the inscription enjoining the driving of a nail each year. It is an exceptional title, only explicable if we remember that in early Latin *praetor* is a generic term meaning 'magistrate' and that the superlative *maximus* implies a number of praetors greater than two. The departure of the Tarquins left in charge of affairs several of these assistants or ministers to whom the kings had delegated some part of their duties; they made up a rather ill-organized body of *praetores*, analogous to those that we find functioning in the Etruscan republics. There the government was carried on by collegia of *zilath* (in Latin *praetores*), presided over by a *zilath purthne*, the president or *prytanis*. This title corresponds exactly to *praetor maximus*. It is hardly surprising that Rome, subject to Etruscan ascendancy in the past, under the Tarquins, and the present, under Porsenna, should have borrowed from them its college of *praetors* together with its president.

In this way one of the conditions of liberty was realized: instead of monarchs for life there were annual magistrates, comparable with the Athenian archons. But the Roman republic took quite a different form: its distinguishing feature was an innovation seemingly without precedent, which Mommsen hailed as a creation out of nothing, most fully expressive of the genius of the people who invented it: not merely *annua imperia*,[31] but *bini imperatores*[32]—two consuls. The consular government in the classical period rests on the collegial principle and on *intercessio*. The two consuls share power equally (*pari potestate*), and each can oppose the action of the other.

The prototype of this sharing of sovereignty between two has been sought unsuccessfully in the Spartan double monarchy,[33] in the twin kingship of Romulus and Tatius when Romans and Sabines joined into one,[34] and in a supposed double dictatorship of the Latin League,[35] which is only perceptible occasionally in the fourth century in the double mediciate of the Oscans and Volscians,[36] where it is probably no more than an imitation of the Roman consulate.

If the latter was really invented, as it appears, at the beginning of the republic, one would like to know exactly how the idea arose. One attempted explanation, which has found much favour, is that the pairs of magistrates listed in the Fasti for the first half of the fifth century are in fact dictators with their *magistri equitum*.[37] We have seen that a *dictator* was the president of the Latin League and the supreme magistrate of several cities, e.g. Alba and Lanuvium. Rome made the dictatorship an extraordinary magistracy, one to which recourse was had only in the greatest danger, when for a limited time it suspended the exercise of all others; the dictator, once chosen by the consul, chose the master of the horse. According to this theory, the Romans, after the expulsion of the kings, followed the example of the Latins and set up a regular annual dictatorship, in which the dictator would have been associated with his *magister equitum* as an unequal colleague. Only at a later period, by a development of the relations between the two colleagues, would they have become coequal. Thus dictator and magister equitum would become consul and consul, the dictatorship being reserved then only for exceptional circumstances or for special tasks.

However attractive this theory, which has the authority of Beloch to vouch for it, it is liable to grave objections. For instance, each of the consuls had received the twelve lictors that belonged to the king; the dictator had 24: now if he had been the direct successor of the king, he would have had but 12. 'The dictatorship at Rome, as the supreme magistracy, is certainly later than the double magistracy of the consuls.'[38] Furthermore, the dictators and magistri equitum are not the same individuals as the consular pairs: the oldest authorities, says Livy,[39] call T. Larcius a dictator, whom the Fasti name as consul in 501, but that tradition assigns to him Sp. Cassius as magister equitum, not Post. Cominius whom the Fasti represent as his consular colleague.

In addition, there is good reason to think that the consuls anciently bore a different name—not *dictator*, but *praetor*.[40] In connection with this name (explained, according to a doubtful etymology, as *prae-itor*, 'he who goes in front [of the army]') two other solutions have been put forward. G. de Sanctis, reckoning the Roman army as comprising only three legions at the outset of the republic, supposed that it was commanded by three praetors (in reality the military tribunes), that these three praetors survived the fall of the monarchy, and that the one who stayed in Rome to administer justice was soon outclassed by the other two, who with their military responsibilities assumed a leading position.[41] Others suppose that before the end of the monarchy this army, whether of 3000 men or (as Fraccaro has shown) of 6000 hoplites, already showed signs of a binary division (e.g. the doubling of the three equestrian centuries into the sex suffragia, the two centuries each of engineers and musicians), and that it was commanded by two praetors.[42] At the siege of Ardea, Dionysius of Halicarnassus,[43] on the authority of some unknown source, says that the Roman soldiers were under the orders of two of Tarquin's lieutenants, M. Horatius and T. Herminius, who appear again as consuls, the former in 509 and 507, the latter in 506. These are the two royal praetors who remained in charge after the revolution and bestowed on the infant republic its dual supreme magistracy.

These methods of interpretation do justice to the empirical element in the rise of institutions, and certainly in the circumstances which we have described Rome was in no position to work out in the abstract the best possible form of government; but one would accept them more readily if they rested on less fragile foundations. One fact in particular seems to oppose them—that there was in 509–508 a *praetor maximus* presiding over a plurity of *praetors*.

If we examine these words more closely, they can throw light on our problem. We have seen that Livy, Zonaras (= Dio Cassius) and Festus testify to the consuls' having been formerly called praetors. The change of name seems to have come only after the decemvirate, in 449.

Etymologically *praetor* implies nothing more than pre-eminence: its military overtones come only from the fact that in primitive society warfare is the principal occupation of the leader. *Praetores, magistratus, principes* are almost interchangeable terms in Livy.[44]

Consul still remains unexplained. The old etymology *a consulendo* ('he who consults the people and senate')[45] is entirely given up. Some have proposed to interpret *consules* as *consodes*, from *sedeo*, i.e. 'those who sit together'.[46] A more probable, though still obscure, connection is with *praesul*,[47] which in the Salian ritual meant the chorus-leader, 'he who dances first', the other priests doing no more than follow and repeat his movements. *Praesul* in religious language may correspond to *praetor* in ordinary language, and *consul* may have been modelled upon *praesul*, since *praetor* could not so easily be modified by changing the prefix. The transition from *prae-* (*praesul*, *praetor*) to *cum-* (*consul*) illustrates two stages of constitutional development. But whichever of the etymologies we accept, *cum* certainly stressed the joint exercise of power.

The replacement of the name *praetor* by that of *consul*, whether gradually sanctioned by usage or prescribed by legislation (e.g. by the decemvirs), is therefore a fact full of meaning for history. One might suppose that it marked nothing more nor less than the creation of the consular régime; that formerly Rome was governed by a *praetor maximus*, and that only then, in 449, was the single supreme magistracy replaced by a dual magistracy. But we should not so hastily throw the Fasti out of the window. Let us rather say that the adoption of a new title reveals a growing consciousness of what was implied in a de facto colleague-ship, the consequences of which had not all been foreseen. So when, in the years immediately after the fall of the kings, the Romans set up two *praetores majores* and no longer a *praetor maximus* over all the other magistrates, it is sufficiently explained as an improved measure under the stress of events; time would clarify the relations between the two colleagues, regulate the right of *intercessio*, and reconcile the *par potestas* with the necessity of the *imperium majus*. Only then would the twin supreme magistrates deserve the name of *consules*.

Such a dual magistracy need imply no dichotomy in the society that created it. Its purpose is to permit contrary political forces and conflicting interests to have balanced representation and some check upon each other.[48] Disunity must have been the keynote of Rome on the morrow of the revolution. One glimpses a bunch of antagonisms which were not automatically reconciled: a pro-Etruscan party, an independence party, a party favouring the Tarquins, another favouring Porsenna, one for the Latin League, another for Roman autonomy, and in each party some extremists and some moderates. Above all, if the expulsion of the kings resulted not so much in the liberation of the people as in the victory of the patricians, resistance from the plebs would not be long in showing itself. In such a confused situation one supposes that certain rival tendencies, faced by a threat which they recognized as more grave, came to a compromise by which power was delegated to two of their representatives: to face the external danger, a national coalition of patricians and plebeians; against the plebeian threat an alliance of patricians and Etruscans; to meet the patrician offensive a league between plebeians and some Etruscans of the *minores gentes*. A priori the composition of the earliest consular *collegia* ought to retain some traces of such coalitions by preserving the names of office-holders of different ethnic or social origins. Unhappily, for many of the personages of the time, that remains obscure; but we should note that the lists of eponyms (assuming with Fraccaro[49] that they are trustworthy after 503) show in 502, 501 and 500 a patrician consul—Opiter Verginius, T. Larcius and Ser. Sulpicius (the first two of Etruscan stock)—and a plebeian consul, Sp. Cassius, Post. Cominius and Manius Tullius. Of the three formulae considered, the decisive one is likely to have been the third—an alliance between plebeians and some of the Etruscans.

The closing of the patriciate

The Fasti of the nascent republic show that at first nothing prevented a plebeian from becoming consul. This conclusion has only recently been reached, but it is based on facts which had long been behind a smokescreen of prejudice and were recovered by the systematic approach from Mommsen to Beloch. The witness of the Fasti, although they were reckoned basically authentic, was subordinated to the artificial interpretation of the annalists, for whom 'democratization' must needs have pursued a straight and steady path. At first, it was thought, the plebeians could vote but not be voted for; magistracies were open only to patricians; the consulate was thrown open to the plebs only by the Licinian laws in 367—a year which the annalists, from Fabius Pictor to Licinius Macer, had hailed as a turning-point in that great progress.[50] Henceforth one at least of the two consuls must be a plebeian (Diodorus assigns a similar law to 449).[51] But in fact, after 367, we find in the Fasti for 335—321 ten exclusively patrician pairs; and before 367, especially in the first half of the fifth century, plebeian names bob up here and there—a scandalous intrusion which modern historians have in-geniously explained away by supposing these to be the names of patrician gentes which subsequently died out and only reappeared later as plebeians—or alternatively that they are crude interpolations.

It is a better method, and at the same time more instructive, to study the Fasti without preconceptions, since their overall veracity and unique importance has not been denied even by their most violent detractors.[52]

From 509 to 486 they reveal twelve plebeian consuls. The time was one of intense political agitation, with the secession of the plebs and institution of tribunes in 494. One of these plebeian consuls, Sp. Cassius, consul in 502, 493 and 486, lived on in tradition—a highly romanticized tradition—as a demagogue; he was supposed anachronistically to have proposed the first agrarian law, and was accused of aiming at a *tyrannis*. His condemnation for *perduellio* and his execution on laying down office mark the end of a first period in the Fasti.

From 485 to 470 there is not one plebeian consul. Etruscan names also wholly disappear. On the other hand, a patrician gens scarcely known before, the Fabii, obtains the consulate and holds it for seven years on end, with various colleagues, also patricians. The mere perusal of the Fasti shows clearly that this was the time when there occurred what de Sanctis has called *la serrata del patriziato*,[53] a de facto prohibition on plebeians reaching the supreme magistracy and thus consecrating the triumph of the oligarchs. The Fabii engaged in warfare with Veii, which probably bordered on their tribal territories,[54] were wiped out in the battle of the Cremera in 477, and did not reappear in the consulate until 467. But the ban persisted, though with no law to sanction it, being only inscribed ever deeper in what was to be for posterity the *mos majorum*, a customary law stronger than the written one.

Except for T. Numicius or Minucius, consul in 469, no plebeian was able to get himself elected for 25 years. Then begins a third period: the consulate is open to P. Volumnius in 461, to two Minucii in 458 and 457, while in 454 both consuls are plebeians. 452 sees T. Genucius consul designate. But here we come to the decemvirate, which marks a new turning-point. It is noteworthy that 461 sees also a reappearance of Etruscan names.

The tribunes of the plebs

The Fasti then by themselves, stripped of the often anachronistic constructions put upon them by the annalists, make the origins of the conflict between patricians and plebeians appear in a wholly different light. It is highly unlikely that the problems dominating political life in the early fifth century were the same as those posed for the contemporaries of the Gracchi by the increasing agitation of an urban proletariat.[55] The opposing forces were rather those of rival clans, whose ambitions had been kept in check by the monarchy; when that was gone, some of them leagued together to grab power. The dualism of the ruling classes does not go back to the beginnings of the republic: it was a divorce which almost split the Roman people in two. Beside the patrician state a plebeian state arose, with its own magistrates, the tribunes and aediles of the plebs, its own gods, Ceres, Liber and Libera, its own political and administrative centre, the Aventine, its own assembly, the *concilium plebis*.

Here again the dates and circumstances are disputed.[56] The traditional tale is that in 494 the plebs, still mobilized from a campaign and kept under arms for fear of disorders, withdrew to the Mons Sacer (or the Aventine) in a First Secession (the second came in 449). But the eloquence of Menenius Agrippa, the plebeian consul (be it noted) of 503, recalled then to a sense of their duty. The senate, in a spirit of conciliation, agreed 'to grant the plebs special and inviolable magistrates, charged with defending it against the consuls, and to exclude all patricians from this office'.[57] The next year (493) the consul Sp. Cassius dedicated a temple to Ceres, Liber and Libera at the foot of the Aventine; this remained the recognized sanctuary of the plebs.

We may disregard the sugar coating of this anecdote, which seeks to dissemble the naked force of the manoeuvre which wrung the tribunate out of the senate. The facts themselves, despite the scepticism with which they have often been treated, are confirmed when we study more deeply the notion of a *lex sacrata*.

F. Altheim[58] has reminded us that it was customary among the Italic peoples, when levying troops, to compel the recruits to swear an oath— Livy describes its impressive ritual and accompaniments[59]—which delivered them over to the vengeance of Jupiter if they should disobey. This was a *lex sacrata*; the words continued in use to describe a law in which those voting for it invoked a curse on themselves if they broke it, or upon its transgressors in general.[60] The law setting up tribunes was a law of this kind;[61] and one cannot but be struck by the similarity between the examples given among the Volscians or the Samnites and the case of the Roman plebs, seceding *under arms*. Being unable to make good its claims by legal methods, it created a new law, binding at first only upon the plebs itself, while waiting for official recognition. It administered a military oath declaring sacer any member of the plebs (ultimately of the whole Roman people) who should violate the sanctity of its tribunes. This is the best explanation of the title given to the defenders of the plebs: the first *tribuni plebis* had been military tribunes.[62]

They were certainly two in number at first, as Piso and Cicero tell us:[63] the numbers five or four preferred by some other authors arose merely from the wish to relate the tribunate to the five centuriate classes or the four urban tribes.[64] In reality the two tribunes had been set up *contra consulare imperium*[65]—in opposition to the two consuls. Their rôle was defined by the words *auxilium* and *intercessio*: they came to rescue the plebeian who was threatened by decisions of the consuls; by their veto they intervened between the plebeian and the lictors.[66] One cannot fail to notice that this intercessio was the external counterpart of that which existed inside the consular collegium. If a plebeian consul had been able to intercede against a patrician consul on behalf of one of his own order, the plebs would have had no need of tribunes.

The first secession, the lex sacrata, the plebs' creation of its own magistrates (*suos magistratus*), was a reaction of despair. One might be tempted a priori to place it after the *serrata del patriziato* which for many years destroyed any chance the plebeians had of finding their defenders among the consuls. The annalists put it back to 494. For three years then there had been not one plebeian consul. But the following years (two plebeian consuls in 493, one each in 492 and 491) ought to have appeased the plebs somewhat. Did they despair too soon? It is better not to build too much on the chronology of the early tribunate:[67] the very names of the tribunes were for long excluded from the official lists of magistrates, and the names of the first have been supplied by guesswork.[68]

At all events, the founding of the temple of Ceres, Liber and Libera[69] is contemporary with the creation of the tribunate. The tradition dating it to 493 is confirmed 'within a few years' by archaeological findings. It was built in imitation of the temple of the Capitoline trinity, in honour of a plebeian trinity itself modelled on the latter, and it unfurled the religious banners of the seceding community in a spirit of defiance. The sanctuary was the repository of the plebeian archives, the treasury of the plebeians and the centre of grain-distribution to the plebs. Its ministers, the *aediles* (from *aedes*),[70] no less inviolable than the tribunes in terms of the *lex sacrata*, naturally became the magistrates charged with policing the city and supervising the markets in the vicinity of the harbour of Rome (arising naturally from their responsibility for grain-supply) and its public places. Where exactly the temple was is disputed: perhaps in the Forum Boarium itself (S. Maria-in-Cosmedin), perhaps at the foot of the Aventine[71]—at all events outside the *pomerium*.

The Aventine itself, which according to Piso was the scene of the first secession[72] and was certainly that of the later secession of 449, was to become the acropolis of the plebs. A *lex Icilia* in 456 *de Aventino publicando* is supposed to have placed some land there at the disposal of the plebeians.[73] It was there, perhaps, that they met as a *concilium plebis*, the legal existence of which was later recognized; it transformed itself into the *comitia tributa*.[74] At first, making decisions which bound only the plebs, it showed that spirit of aggressive isolationism in which the plebs, shut out from the consulate, aimed at being a state within the state. By its separatism and by its tribunate which was (in Mommsen's words) the instrument of a permanent revolution, it had forged itself irresistible weapons. In legalizing them, the patricians would do all they could to blunt their edge.

The decemvirate

The middle of the fifth century marks a vital stage in the history of Roman institutions and civilization. In 451 and 450 the *Fasti consulares* interrupt their list to record the advent of *decemviri* armed with consular powers and charged with drawing up laws. Cicero[75] tells us that the tribunes of the plebs abdicated together with the consuls to give place to the decemvirs. The latter, concentrating all the magistracies in their own hands, administered the republic to general satisfaction for their first year. Their legislative work being not yet complete, a second collegium was chosen in 450; but it ruled tyrannically and in 449 tried to make its powers permanent. Military defeat, the scandal over Virginia, and a second secession of the plebs brought the 'ten Tarquins' down, and the consular régime was restored.

Despite the romantic embellishments tacked on by the annalists, the historicity of the decemvirs and the authenticity of their work is now generally admitted.[76] The Law of the Twelve Tables, set up in the Forum on twelve tablets probably of bronze, was considered the fountain of all law both public and private;[77] it was learned by heart in the schools, often cited by writers: now it is known to us only in fragments, yet this mutilation does not prevent us from forming a fairly accurate notion of its qualities.[78]

What purpose did the lawgivers have in mind? Was it, as they proclaim in Livy,[79] to make all citizens equal before the law—*aequare leges omnibus*? One may retort that they did their job very poorly, since the only article of the law which speaks of patricians and plebeians is that which forbids intermarriage between them.[80] Here again it seems that the annalists saw the historical tradition through the political spectacles of their own day. Their task was rather (as the jurists or antiquity understood it[81] and as is shown by their very title, *decemviri legibus scribundis*) to substitute written law for customary law. Some statutes, no doubt, from the kingly period onwards, had been written and published—witness the Lapis Niger in the Forum. But laws in general were only inscribed in the *mos majorum* and applied in virtue of a procedure whose secrets were known only to the pontiffs and magistrates: in this sense the codifying and publishing of the law was a way of making it equal for all.[82] But above all else, it appears that the decemvirs were not content with fixing custom by writing, settling a few vexed points, innovating only in detail. The principal 'actions of law', i.e. the general modes of pleading (*sacramentum, manus injectio*, etc.) and the oldest forms of action in civil law (*usucapio, mancipatio* etc.), although the Twelve Tables are credited with inventing them, undoubtedly existed long before; but the spirit in which they were treated and codified set aside the religious motivations which had informed them to make them instead the expression of human will. The secularization of the law, the renunciation of *fas* in favour of *ius*—that was the great contribution of the decemvirs.[83]

The episode of Virginia has of course been decked with all the flowers of drama and pathos by the annalists.[84] It is worth noting, however, that basically it presents the appearance of a legal *exemplum* (the historians of law find in it the outline of a *vindicatio in libertatem*) 'destined to present a particularly striking example of the tendencies of the new legislation'.[85]

The ancients postulated Greek influence on the Twelve Tables. No one now believes in the supposed Roman embassy to Athens to study the laws of Solon,[86] but certain similarities between those laws and several articles of the Tenth Table, aimed at restricting lavish expenditure on funerals, are hard to explain.[87] Magna Graecia may have been the intermediary, or may have provided the examples of her own lawgivers, e.g. Zaleucus or Charondas. An émigré Greek, Hermodorus of Ephesus, had his statue in the Forum, and was supposed to have given advice to the decemvirs. The word *poena*[88] is borrowed from Dorian, and may point to influence from that quarter.

The legislative achievement of the decemvirs, as redactors of a code which was to determine the whole course of Roman legal history, indeed as creators of the idea of *ius* in the sense which P. Noailles has defined,[89] is very considerable; their political importance is no less. In the laborious building-up of republican institutions their part was epoch-making. Polybius thought that after them the Roman constitution only needed to be perfected in detail, and this was the point at which (as Cicero was to do in the *De republica*) he ended his account of the primitive stage in Roman history.[90] Their administration from 451–449 had been a passing attempt to create a new régime[91] which should substitute a multiple *collegium* for two consuls who were not able by their unaided strength to resolve the open conflict between patricians and plebs. What we in fact see here is a rejection—often to be repeated under different guises—of the dual magistrature and an attempt to return to the plurality of praetors or archons which had existed in the first days of the republic.[92] A *lex Terentilia* is said to have been proposed in 462 and urged indefatigably in the years that followed, tending to establish *quinqueviri* 'to regulate the consular power'.[93] The plebs, having given themselves two tribunes at first, now claimed ten; these were set up in 457 or 449.[94] We shall see that after the fall of the decemvirs, for threequarters of a century until the consulate was re-established in 367, boards of magistrates becoming ever greater in number —the 'military tribunes with consular power'—were substituted for the two consuls.

The decemvirs were set up to put an end to long-lasting troubles: that is how the annalists characterize the years 461–452 when the plebeians re-appear in the Fasti. If one believed the angry harangues which Livy puts into the mouths of the tribunes,[95] one would suppose that the consuls of 451 and 450 were exclusively patrician. But the names show one plebeian, T. Genucius, in 451; the year 450, in which Dionysius[96] reckons three (Q. Poetelius, K. Duillius and Sp. Oppius) had perhaps three more, T. Antonius, Manius Rabuleius and L. Minucius. The presidency was exercised masterfully by the patrician Appius Claudius—the first of the Claudii (unless the annalists have modelled his character on the best known of his descendants)[97] to follow that species of revolutionary conservatism by which the Sabine gens with its *insita superbia* tried to obtain plebeian support while pursuing the uncompromising ideals of its caste.[98]

The constitutional character of the Twelve Tables is still disputed. Tradition, perhaps by an anachronism, represents them as having been submitted to the vote of the people—a *lex rogata*.[99] But were they not rather a *lex data*—simply decreed by the decemvirs by virtue of their extraordinary powers? The latter seems the more likely.[100]

One of the articles (found in the Eleventh Table) forbade mixed marriages between patricians and plebeians. It set the annalists in a rage, and they penned impassioned speeches for the tribune C. Canuleius urging the abrogation of this *lex inhumanissima* (445 and after).[101] For a long time modern writers saw this in the perspective of a natural antagonism between the two orders and interpreted it as an abominable return to an obsolete taboo, only excusable (if then) as a survival from the past or as the recognition of a fact that could not be changed.[102] Last has shown that the ancient accounts agree in seeing it as an innovation consonant with the increasing desire of the patriciate to form a closed caste, by reserving for its own members the privilege of marriage by *confarreatio* and of *iustae nuptiae*.[103] The claim was swimming against the stream of history and had very soon to be given up; but that makes it none the less significant for our better understanding of the political struggles of the fifth century.

The judgement of history on the decemvirs must be complex. The movement which brought them to power and kept them there, and the legislative work which they accomplished and which survived their fall, comprise so many disparate elements that one hesitates to say what political ends, in the last analysis, they helped to forward. But we must distinguish the intentions from the results. Their advent obviously corresponds to the wish of the patricians to found their oligarchy more solidly, to keep plebeians out of the consulate, to slip out of the shackles of provocatio and shun the contamination of mixed marriage: on all these heads they signally failed. But on the other hand, their codifying, secularizing and publishing the laws in the Twelve Tables was a decisive factor in unifying the city. It would be too much to say (as some have done) that the principle of *aequatio legum omnibus* was proclaimed.[104] There was no distinction made of *gens*, except in the forbidding of mixed marriages. But the legal inequality of the census classes was reaffirmed in an article of the law which provided that the defence at law of a rich man (*assiduus*) should be guaranteed by an *assiduus*, while for that of a proletarian any citizen would suffice.[105]

The restoration of the republic in 449 brought with it two consuls, L. Valerius and M. Horatius, to whom tradition ascribed three laws: the decisions of the *concilium plebis* were henceforth to bind the whole people assembled in the *comitia tributa*; inviolability of tribunes and aediles was reaffirmed; in the future it would be impossible to create a new magistrature without appeal.[106] The *leges Valeriae Horatiae* then gave official blessing to all the points gained by the plebs over half a century; these were the laws which Polybius had in mind when he dates the second founding of the Roman constitution to this epoch.[107]

The question of plebeian access to the supreme magistracy was left untouched. No law had ever forbidden it, and so no law was needed to authorize it. It was as if the republic after the fall of the 'ten Tarquins' was making a fresh start, as before the *serrata del patriziato*. The plebeians were satisfied to see the consulate re-established after the tyranny of the decemvirs, and were preparing to present their candidates within the framework of the new constitution.

The patrician barrier was more effective than ever. The Fasti from 449–446 attest purely patrician consuls; they do so again from 444–441 and from 437–435. In the intervals the plebeians had much ado to secure a M. Genucius and perhaps Agrippa Curtius in 445, T. Menenius in 440 and Agrippa Menenius in 439. Meanwhile, in 444 and 438, the Fasti list three military tribunes with consular powers (the election of 444 must have been annulled for some formal defect; hence the recourse to two *consules suffecti*):[108] these *tribuni militum consulari potestate* were to be the next expedient devised in order to elude an insoluble problem.

The military tribunes with consular powers

Exactly why and how the consular tribunate was set up is very hard to know.[109] The annalists tell us that in 445 the patricians, facing plebeian pressure (one, perhaps both, of that year's consuls were plebeian), 'authorized the creation of military tribunes with consular functions, taken without distinction from patricians and plebeians',[110] without any change being made in the elective status of the consuls. Thus, to ensure that the consulate, which they were keeping for themselves, retained unimpaired its character as a magistracy consecrated by auspices, the patricians were granting to the plebs a pro-magistracy invested for practical purposes with the same powers. Whether the consular tribunes had, as the texts declare, the consular imperium and not merely the potestas, as their official title states, is still a matter of dispute.[111] They had no right to a triumph nor to the privileges granted to ex-consuls on their resigning office—the title of *consularis*, a place of honour in the senate, the *ius imaginum*, the purple toga.

Other authors say that this change in the constitution was made for military reasons: three military tribunes armed with consular powers and insignia were better able than two consuls to carry on warfare on more and more different fronts.[112]

An initial attempt in 444 was annulled by the augurs. The experiment was repeated in 438, 437 and every year from 434–432. After 426 the military tribunate became more or less the rule, the consulate the exception. From 391 to 367 there were no consuls at all. But the authorities are not always in agreement on the nature of the collegium—consuls or tribunes—which exercised power in a given year.[113]

The records for 444 (of disputed authenticity) show one patrician and two plebeians; but plebeian representation in the following *collegia* down to the end of the century is very slight: we find only three plebeian names— Q. Antonius in 422, Agrippa Menenius in 419 and 417, Sp. Rutilius in 417. P. Licinius Calvus in 400 is hailed by Livy as the first plebeian to have been chosen for the office. The annalist Licinius Macer is suspected of having drawn attention to this supposed primacy,[114] especially as Livy immediately adds 'All the others elected were patricians,'—yet all are agreed that three at least were plebeians. However that may be, this year of 400 does mark the advent of a plebeian majority to the consular tribunate, as again in 399, 396 and yet again in 379. Beloch was too hasty[115] in rejecting these lists as interpolations; his view finds less and less support. It is more instructive to note that the names of these plebeians are for the most part quite new.[116]

The most interesting fact is the regular increase in the number of consular tribunes. From 444 to 432 they were chosen in threes, between 426 and 406 there are four (reduced to three in 422, 418 and 408); in 405 there are six, and this number will remain constant until the end of the tribunate. Diodorus and Livy are clearly the victims of some error (e.g. adding in the two censors) when they raise the number of tribunes to eight for two or three years.[117]

The long political failure of the consular tribunate makes it hard to believe that its object was to make it easier for plebeians to attain the supreme magistracy. It has been suggested that before 400 the plebs was not strongly enough organized to avail itself of the opportunities opened to it by getting its own candidates elected. An interesting but unprovable theory would have it that consuls and consular tribunes were elected at different assemblies: the tribunes, the successors (Bernardi thinks)[118] of the old *tribuni celerum*, still belonged to the system of three ethnic tribes and were chosen by the curiae; thus the plebs, ineffective in the centuriate assembly, would have built its hopes (soon to be disappointed) on the older comitia.

A political explanation is so hard to find that one more readily accepts the military one, especially if we grant that the rise in the number of consular tribunes, from three in 444 to six on the outbreak of war with Veii, seems to correspond to the evolution of the army: being involved in ever more serious wars it grew from 3000 to 6000 men and demanded a command structure more proportioned to its numbers. This view, put forward by de Sanctis,[119] is opposed of course by the supporters of Fraccaro's thesis[120] that the legion of 6000 hoplites goes back to Servius Tullius. For them the military tribunes will have composed a general staff of six officers detached from field service; from this general staff, existing since the end of the monarchy, certain tribunes will have been picked out from 444 onwards to discharge political as well as military duties. Efforts have been made to show that the years with tribunes were usually years of peace, those with consuls years of war.[121]

We have explained why we cannot believe that the true centuriate army was organized before the second half of the fifth century: this was when it became common to appeal to a committee of officers when the plebs was violently opposing the patricians. To call in the army when troubles start is an expedient known in all ages. It will be remarked that they can be used for political tasks all the more easily when there is no fighting for them. Furthermore, in the first century of the republic the army was an instrument of victory for democracy. Refusal to serve in the army was the most powerful form of pressure that the plebs could bring to bear in order to wring concessions from the patricians, and the recruitment was done by the military tribunes. The first secession in 494 had been an insurrection of the people in arms, and the *tribuni plebis* created on that occasion derived their name from the military tribunes. The second, in 449, was also a revolt of the army, which is said to have designated ten men 'to exercise supreme command with the title and rank of military tribunes'.[122] So, if we explain the consular tribunate mainly in military terms, we have the advantage not only of being able to explain the increase in the number of tribunes by the increase in the strength of the army, but also of understanding how its creation could have appeared as a compromise in the struggle between plebs and patriciate.

B The beginnings of Roman expansion in the fifth century and in the first half of the fourth

Rome and the Latins

It was long believed that the federal organization of the Latin peoples, while it may have formed the basis of their political and legal life in protohistoric times, later lived on only in religious observances. The recent work of A. Alföldi[123] has shown that the sovereignty (in theory at least) of the *concilium Latinorum* and the obligations of a *ius Latinum* regulating commerce, marriage and the freedom of individuals within the League did not cease to be binding on Rome herself in principle up to the middle of the fourth century. Antiquaries of the late republic knew, and the annalistic tradition sometimes lets it show through, that down to 340 'the Latin peoples were accustomed to meet at the aqua Ferentina and rule the empire by their common decisions'—*imperium communi consilio administrare*.[124] Furthermore, on the year when her turn came round—but in that year only—Rome used to send a general to command the federal army, this being done *iussu nominis Latini*, on the orders of the Latin nation.[125] Under these circumstances it would seem that what we call the Roman conquest ought to be called, during all the fifth and half the fourth centuries, the Latin conquest. And in fact we observe that all the colonies founded in the course of those 150 years (all founded by Rome, according to the annalists) fall within the category of Latin colonies and would always possess that especial status. The series of Roman colonies only begins about 335 with the founding of Ostia. The Latin colonies were at first federal colonies.[126] Their establishment at Cora, Norba, Setia, Satricum, Velitrae and Circei marks out a defensive line on the eastern borders of Latium and represents the effort of the Latin nation as a whole to break the coalition of the Aequi and Volsci, which was far more threatening to Tusculum, for example, than to Rome.[127] The annalists, who let slip now and then the mention of an 'allied army',[128] under the command of a Roman consul who was presumably no more than a *dictator Latinus*,[129] systematically transferred to Rome's account all the credit and all the direction of operations in which she had done no more than participate.

Now that we have said this and stressed the importance and persistence of the federal ties which bound Rome to the Latin League and limited her independence, it is important to say that these ties became gradually looser and left more and more room for Roman initiative. The confederated cities appear incessantly engaged in warfare one against another, interrupted only by the 'truce of God' of the *feriae Latinae*; they were free to conclude particular alliances among themselves or even with a neighbouring enemy people.[130] A similar disunity is apparent in the league of twelve Etruscan peoples. The future now did not lie with primitive racial confederacies, but with a new form of political organization that was declaring itself—the city, taking the word in the Greek sense of *polis*, the Roman sense of *urbs*: not an accidental agglomeration of buildings, but an entity at once physical and spiritual, embracing a body of citizens ruled by their own laws.[131] In central Italy the Etruscans, who were in touch with the Greeks, had made themselves the promoters of the urban idea, and there can be little doubt that their domination in Latium, for all their seeming respect for the existing federal organization, hastened the coming of the *polis*, especially at Rome. After their departure Rome lost no time in claiming her autonomy in face of the Latins.

The stages of her progress within and without the League are hard to trace because of the distortions and anachronisms of the annalists: they draw a crowded panorama of campaigns, truces and treaties with Tibur and Praeneste, Ardea and Lanuvium, tending gradually to establish a de facto preponderance for Rome, which her lawyers then busied themselves in transforming into a de jure supremacy.[132]

At all events, some acquisitions of this kind must have been made quite early. The founding of the federal sanctuary of Diana Aventinensis, assigned by tradition to Servius Tullius—*et erat confessio caput rerum Romam esse*[133]—does not perhaps go back to the sixth century, but it is hard to bring it lower than 456 and the *lex Icilia de Aventino publicando* which was to turn the Aventine (a suitable place for international meetings by its extra-territorial position) into the seat of plebeian administration.

Before this time tradition assigns to the Romans a victory over the Latins at lake Regillus (499 or 496) and the conclusion of a treaty of alliance in 493—the *foedus Cassianum*, from the name of the consul who signed it, Spurius Cassius. The story of the battle is a tissue of borrowed epic and mythological elements,[134] but the supernatural intervention of the Dioscuri which decided the issue now seems less of an anachronism than it did, since, apart from the marble statues in the Greek style of the first half of the fourth century found in excavating the *lacus Iuturnae* near the temple of Castor and Pollux,[135] a dedication to the Dioscuri recently discovered at

Lavinium has shown how highly revered they were in Latium and at Rome at an early date.[136] The text of the *foedus Cassianum* given in Dionysius[137] is obviously a résumé or a literary paraphrase, not to be taken literally; but Cicero remembered having seen it engraved at length on a column of bronze 'behind the rostra' before the great changes wrought by Sulla in that part of the Forum,[138] and Festus (following a late republican savant) quotes two passages from it which in substance and form seem of about the same date as the Twelve Tables;[139] they contain the word *pecunia*, but there is nothing suspicious in this: long before money was introduced at Rome it was the word denoting any kind of wealth in cattle or crops. Festus' quotation concerns such questions as distraint on goods (*pignoris captio*) and it proves, when taken together with the penultimate clause in Dionysius' version, that the treaty, while establishing perpetual peace between the parties and providing for mutual assistance in case of war, also covered private legal relations between Romans and Latins.

There was every reason for such a treaty (Festus calls it the *foedus Latinum*) in the first days of the republic. We saw that the expulsion of the Tarquins, thanks to Porsenna's army, had taken the form of a revolt on Rome's part against the Latins. At the battle of Lake Regillus 'the Tarquins are still in the Latin army' which is aiming at their restoration.[140] After the Roman victory, it was necessary to reintegrate Rome into the league of 30 peoples, in which her place had remained unfilled.[141] Then it was that the principles of public and private law by which the federal organization was governed had to be reaffirmed and codified, but under conditions which, instead of bringing Rome back to her subordinate role, one among thirty, permitted her to pose as a separate state, holding talks on her own behalf and on equal terms with the collective body of all the other Latin peoples. Her dissidence of 509 had been her first act of independence. One is loth to believe that it was stipulated from then on that Romans and Latins would share equally the booty of wars which they waged in common, but it is probable that the *foedus Cassianum* confirmed in the minds of the Romans their feeling of independence, led them to consider their membership of the Latin League as a fiction that became less and less binding, and made them look upon Latin resistance to their pretended supremacy as treachery and a plain violation of the treaty.

The Sabellian invasions

It would be vain to try to follow in detail the campaigns fought by Rome on this internal front while she was fighting, in concert with the Latins, on an external one; for an important new fact invests the Roman (or Latin) conquest with its peculiarly dramatic colours. It was not accomplished in the partial vacuum which had earlier allowed the Etruscans to occupy without difficulty all the plains of central Italy, but in a world that was suddenly over-populated, unstable and threatening: so much so that what looks to us like a voluntary expansion on the part of the Latins was instead, at first, a defensive reaction. From the end of the sixth century all the peoples of the Apennines begin to boil over, to press on the frontiers of peoples already settled, and to push down into the coastal regions. This is the period of a long and manifold *ver sacrum*,[142] to use the term that denoted the Sabine migrations. When an epidemic or a famine bore hard on their wretched grazing grounds they vowed to Mars the children who should be borne to them the next spring; then, when these children had reached man's estate, they sent them off to found a colony, following the tracks of some totem animal, such as the bull which led some of them to Bovianum, or the magpie which led others to Picenum. The Sabines to the north of Rome, on the left bank of the Tiber, along the salt route (*via salaria*), had long been known; the Samnites, who do not appear until the middle of the fifth century, when they invaded Campania, were closely akin to the Sabines, and the very name is no more than a variant of 'Sabine'.[143] But they had other kinsmen too—the Aequi, Hernici, Marsi, Volsci, and in the southern end of Italy, the Lucanians. They are all embraced under the name of Sabellian peoples.

Now all these, the older and more settled being driven on by newcomers, began to move almost at once. In 504, according to tradition, the Sabine chief Atta Clausus (the ancestor of the Claudia gens) came down upon the Latin plain at the head of his tribe and won from Rome a grant of lands and citizenship.[144] At the same moment the Aequi, from the upper valley of the Anio, began to press upon the north of Latium, on Praeneste most of all.[145] As their allies they had the Hernici from the left bank of the Sacco,[146] and from its right bank the Volscians, whose progress is the easiest to trace on the ground.[147]

The Volscians

The Pontine plain, where to Hesiod's Greek sources only the Latins were visible to the north of M. Circeo,[148] where, in the sixth century, from

Latium to Campania, Etruscan civilization developed in those forms which one admires at Velitrae and Satricum,[149] was now wholly covered by these new conquerors: masters of Terracina, Pometia, Satricum, Velitrae, they keep up constant harrying attacks on the eastern frontiers of the Latins. To leave the horizon of the Romans, the invasions (or rather infiltrations) of the Samnites are not recorded until the second half of the fifth century, when they came down into Campania about 438, took Capua from the Etruscans in 423 and Cumae from the Chalcidians in 421.[150] At the same time the Lucanians, of whom the Bruttians were an offshoot, overran all the Calabrian isthmus as far as Sybaris on the Ionian sea, where the first colonists of Thurii came up against them.[151] On the Tyrrhenian coast the *periplus* of Pseudo-Scylax (mid-fourth century) knows only the Lucanians from Posidonia (now Paestum) onwards, apart from a Greek enclave at Velia. Nor had the Adriatic slopes escaped the attentions of the hardy mountaineers: they became the home of Paelignians, Frentanians and Peucetians, whose occupation of the plain of Apulia had pushed back the Iapygians on Tarentum and shaken the power of the Dorian colony for a time after 473.[152]

It is against the background of this unstable world, with Latium in constant danger of being overrun, that we must see those battles of which Livy has given such a splendid and uncertain narrative in books II—VI. The Hernici, caught between the Aequi and Volsci, were the first—after 486, we are told—to join with the Latins.[153] The Sabine invasions were repeated: a band led by Ap. Herdonius in 460 is said to have gained possession of the Capitol, which was liberated by a Tusculan dictator;[154] there will be no more talk of the Sabines after 448—not until the conquest of their territory in the third century. But the most inveterate foes were the Aequi and Volsci; defeated a hundred times, they re-formed again and again, and were not finally reduced until the beginning of the fourth century. History and legend long remembered the Volscian raid, led by the traitor Coriolanus, up to the very gates of Rome in 491, as also the victories won at the pass of the Mons Algidus, behind the Alban hills, where the Volsci and Aequi joined forces to fall upon Tusculum—victories won by Cincinnatus in 458 and by A. Postumius in 431 on 19 June, a day forever marked in the Fasti.[155]

Rome and Veii

At the same time Rome was engaged in a war that concerned her more directly, against Veii, the most southerly of the Etruscan mother-cities, ten miles north of Rome on the right bank of the Tiber.[156] The annalists, with their habitual anachronisms, make the beginnings of this inexpiable hostility go back to Romulus and Ancus Marcius,[157] but in fact Rome and Veii had a good understanding with each other in the kingly period. Their interests only came into conflict in the early days of the republic, when both wanted to exploit the saltings to the north of the mouth of the Tiber[158] and disputed possession of the right bank (*ripa Veiens*) of the 'Etruscan river' (*Tuscus amnis*),[159] which marked the frontier of Etruria. There lay the *silva Mecia*, whose timber went into building ships for Caere, and the Seven Cantons (*Septem pagi*), which were part of Veientine territory until Porsenna, as tradition has it,[160] handed them over to Rome. In fact Rome never established herself on this bank, in the *ager Vaticanus*, until the middle of the fifth century, with the creation of the *Romilia tribus*, named after T. Romilius Vaticanus, consul in 455. In the opposite direction, five miles upstream from Rome, there was a ferry of immemorial antiquity making it possible to take a route from Caere to Veii, and then on to Praeneste and Campania, without touching Rome.[161] Holding Fidenae, Veii controlled the salt trade along the via Salaria and could easily intercept grain supplies going down the river to feed Rome. To seize this bridging point and burst the shackle was one of the principal objectives in the war against Veii: it was only attained in 426.[162]

A half-century earlier, from 485–474, we find in the annalists a series of campaigns signalized by the loss of the 306 Fabii on the banks of the Cremera, a little watercourse that runs past Veii to join the Tiber near Fidenae: they had threaded their way thither through the woods to cut the road to Etruria.[163] The number of dead related in this legendary feat of arms reminds us of the 300 Spartans who fell at Thermopylae,[164] but its genuineness, behind the epic embellishments, can hardly be disputed: it provides, as a piece of sociology, a clear example of gens-warfare, in which a single, whole clan, independently of the state, took on the responsibility for a war. 'We propose', says their chief, 'to regard this war as a family affair and to pay its costs ourselves.'[165] And in fact the Fabia gens is usually located north-west of Rome in the direction of Veii: it was their own fief that the Fabii were proposing to defend—or to conquer.[166] One remarks also that after 487 the Etruscan names disappear from the Fasti at the moment when the Fabii make their appearance and follow each other uninterruptedly (485–479):[167] during those years, when Etruscan influence in domestic politics was eclipsed, and when the Fabia gens was all-powerful, the war against Veii was their private war.

But it was only after Fidenae was taken that Rome was able to aim the decisive blow at her rival; and then it was not easy. A ten-year war (406–396)—as long as the siege of Troy—which became loaded in the telling with prodigies and supernatural elements deriving ultimately from an Etruscan source,[168] culminated at last in the driving of a sap under the citadel, the capture of the city, and its political, if not physical, destruction. This time the Fabii took no part in events: the instrument of destiny, the *dux fatalis*, was M. Furius Camillus, dictator in 396. Camillus' gallantry and patriotism made him for the annalists the very model of Roman virtues.[169] He was exiled after his triumph; but Rome was soon to call him back.

The Gaulish invasions

The Roman capture of Veii was followed (in 390, says Livy: in 386, say the Greek chronologers) by the Gaulish capture of Rome. The ancients saw a religious significance in the juxtaposition of the two events.[170] We have seen[171] that the Gaulish expansion in Italy—caused by those internal movements in the Celtic world which about 560 had caused the La Tène culture to take over from the Hallstatt—had given rise in Italy, from the late sixth or early fifth century on, to a series of infiltrations that could be felt in Aemilia and the Romagna; the main violence of the invasion was to discharge itself in the early fourth century. A band of Gauls had crossed the Apennines and came up first against Clusium (Chiusi), demanding lands. Rome had been not unknown to the people of Clusium since Porsenna's day; indeed her grain was supplied from there. But it is very unlikely that they asked Rome for help. The story (from Etruscan sources) that the Senones were brought into their lands by a treaty means perhaps that in the faction-ridden city one political party had had recourse to Gaulish mercenaries, whose embarrassing presence had later been got rid of by sending them off towards Rome.[172] The Roman version of the events, which is very unfavourable to the Fabii, is patently a product of later annalistic manipulation.

The column of barbarians coming down the Tiber along the via Salaria met the Roman army some ten miles from the city, on the banks of a little left-bank tributary, the Allia. The numbers on each side have been greatly exaggerated: they are estimated at 30,000 on the Gaulish side, 15,000 on the Roman.[173] Among the latter Polybius mentions the Latin contingents,[174] although the annalists assure us that Rome was left in the lurch by her allies. The military tribune Q. Sulpicius, on whom the command devolved, had concentrated his reserves on a hill to the right, planning to hold the enemy centre and then make a flank attack; but the Gaulish chief Brennus frustrated this manoeuvre, stormed the hill, and put the Roman army to flight.[175] The 18th of July, the day of the worst defeat that Rome had yet suffered, remained for ever an accursed day (*dies religiosus*).

We cannot delay here over the splendid story that the annalists tell of the occupation and deliverance of Rome: Livy tells it best.[176] To ensure that the national worship, at all events, should continue, the holy objects were covered up and conveyed by the vestals to Caere, under the leadership of L. Albinius, who is probably an historical personage.[177] The magistrates, loaded with years and honours, sat with their insignia of office in their meeting-place by the Forum and waited for death, having pronounced the formula of *devotio* which consigned themselves as well as the enemy to the powers of darkness. The young men had fallen back on the Capitol; while waiting for an army of liberation under Camillus to assemble at Ardea and Veii, they unflinchingly endured—thanks, inter alia, to the vigilance of M. Manlius Capitolinus—a siege from which at least the temples on the citadel and the city's archives emerged intact.

The event made a great noise in the Greek world: the historian Theopompus, writing about 350, mentions it;[178] Aristotle, long before any annalist, says that the city was 'saved'—a salvation which he attributes to one Lucius.[179] Now Camillus and Manlius Capitolinus were both called Marcus, and it has been suggested that this Lucius was the L. Albinius who saved what was essential by preventing the holy objects from being destroyed. As seen from Caere, Albinius may well have seemed the man of the moment, more than any other.

Rome and Caere

We can see more and more clearly nowadays that the capture of Rome by the Gauls, which naturally assumed an exclusive importance in Roman tradition, was no more than an incident in the great conflict then raging between the Sicilian Greeks and the Etruscans[180]—a conflict in which the Gaulish invasion furnished the former with unforeseen help which they were quick to exploit. The chronology is still disputed in detail; but some of the synchronisms beloved of the Greek and Roman historians have a real significance: the fall of Melpum (Milan?) in 388 must have been a heavy blow to Etruscan power in the plain of the Po,[181] occurring just at the moment when Dionysius of Syracuse, by capturing Rhegium, completed his conquest of Magna Graecia and launched his fleets upon the Adriatic. Founding Ancona and Adria on that coast, he was happy to see his enemy's power weakened.[182] Justin, in his abridgement of the Gaulish historian Trogus Pompeius, tells us that about 386 Dionysius received a proposal for an alliance from some Gaulish ambassadors: 'Situated in the midst of his enemies, they could do him signal service by attacking them in the rear.'[183] Brennus' bands appear in fact to have pushed down into Iapygia; returning thence they fell into an ambuscade north of Rome and were massacred by the troops of Caere.[184] At very nearly this time (384–383) the Syracusan fleet descended on Pyrgi, the harbour of Caere, to make a punitive demonstration.[185] It all fits together, and when seen from this angle, the movements of the Gauls seem less fortuitous; they seem indeed the actions of mercenaries under remote control from their Syracusan paymaster. If Rome now appeared upon the Greek horizon, it was in the context of this war between Syracuse and Caere, which had as its historian Philistus, a contemporary and friend of the tyrant. The historicity of the facts is guaranteed.

It is interesting to see how close relations now become between Rome and Caere. The annexation of the territory of Veii had made them neighbours; the hospitality which the Caeritans extended towards the vestals and other Roman refugees; the recovery, thanks to Caere, of the spoils of Rome that the Gauls were carrying with them—all this laid the foundation of a real alliance. Rome granted to the Caeritans the right of public hospitality (*hospitium publicum*), which was the original and highly honourable form of *civitas sine suffragio*.[186] The merchants and craftsmen of Caere who dwelt in Rome received from the state full legal warranty for the exercise of their callings; although they were exempt from any military or fiscal obligations resting upon full citizens, and although they were excluded from the political responsibilities proper to the others, they were enrolled individually on the census registers, after the full citizens, on special tablets called the *tabulae Caeritum*. Later the grant of full citizenship gave these tables a degrading character, betokening deprivation of the rights of citizens; but at first they expressed a privilege instead.

Roman naval expansion

The causes and results of this rapprochement between Rome and Caere are highly significant. It was at first the counterpart of the disagreement between Rome and the Latins which arose shortly after the defeat:[187] it was the Etruscans who lent the moral and material support that allowed her to rise again, rebuild her walls and to resume with new vigour her political life. The 1000 acres enclosed by her walls—as rebuilt from 378 on—made her the biggest city in Italy: Caere was of only 370 acres. We must suppose that Rome lent considerable human resources to her Etruscan ally, already far gone towards decadence. It is now thought that the Latin forests supplied the timber from which the Caeretan fleets were built. It is hard to believe, but we have it on good authority, that Rome at this time began colonial enterprises overseas.[188] Theophrastus in the late fourth century knew of a colony which she had tried to found at some unspecified date ('formerly') in Corsica with 25 ships,[189] and this early witness strengthens Diodorus' statement that about 377 she sent 500 colonists to Sardinia.[190] As a maritime colony it was exempt from military service, which sufficiently disposes of the emendations *Satricum* or *Sutrium*, both of which were inland.[191] We must just accept the evidence of the texts and admit that Rome was then acting in concert with Caere—or rather, was making use of her ships, at all events her harbours, to take up the Etruscan colonial tradition in an area which Dionysius of Syracuse was trying to bring under his control. It seems, then, that from the first half of the century onwards Rome had begun to tread the stage of Mediterranean politics, claiming the attention of Sicilian historians and earning the right to be called (as Heraclides Ponticus called her) *polis hellenis*).[192] Even such a thing as the treaty of alliance between Rome and Marseille, which Justin makes as early as 386,[193] acquires some degree of credibility in this context.

Throughout the first half of the fourth century, and even later, we can see the ties between Rome and the Etruscan cities, cemented by common dangers and common interests, tightening or slackening as the threefold danger (Latin, Gaulish or Syracusan) approached or receded. The 'defection' of the Latins and the Hernici, attributed by the annalists to 389, was to be marked for thirty years by federal anarchy and individual ambition, particularly on the part of Praeneste and Tibur, which aimed at reestablishing the League on a new basis or at regaining control of it, and in so doing often enlisted the support of the Volscian or Gaulish enemy. The

G

memory of these conflicts is preserved in the Fasti, which record, for example, in 360 a triumph *de Galleis et Tiburtibus*. The former would have been armed bands based in Apulia, in contact with the Syracusan establishments there.

In the following years, between 358 and 354, Rome succeeded in obtaining the submission of the recalcitrant Latin cities, the pacification of Volscian territory, the capitulation of Tibur, and a cessation of hostilities with Praeneste. But just when the Latin League was restored, and when anarchy in Sicily ended the Syracusan threat to the west coast, relations with southern Etruria worsened. Caere was accused of having given free passage to forces of Tarquinii to ravage Roman territory, and the treaty with her was denounced. This is the date commonly assigned (probably by anticipation) to Caere's reduction to the status of a Roman *municipium*. But the same causes which had brought the two peoples together were soon to produce the same effects again : a third Gaulish invasion (350–349) occupied the Alban Hills, while a Syracusan fleet was debarking its forces at Antium. It became apparent that Rome, while burdening herself with the enormous military effort of mobilizing ten legions, could not avoid the necessities which made her follow in Etruscan footsteps : she concluded a treaty with Carthage in 348.[194]

C Roman political institutions in the fourth century

Statutory sharing of the consulate between patricians and plebeians

A decisive step in the development of Roman political institutions was taken about 367 with the re-establishment of the twin consulship, one of the two consuls being thenceforth compulsorily a plebeian. At the same time an urban praetor was set up underneath them to relieve them from civil jurisdiction, while two curule aediles were added to the existing plebeian aediles, sharing with them the tasks of police, sanitation, food supply, etc.[195]

The consular tribunate seems to have gone down about 376 or 375 amid anarchy deplored by Diodorus[196] and described by Livy as having lasted five years, during which it was impossible to elect any curule magistrate (*solitudo magistratuum*).[197] Two tribunes of the plebs, C. Licinius and L. Sextius, their mandate renewed ten times, kept up the struggle against the patricians and compelled the senate in the end, by their paralysing vetoes and the threat of civil strife, to agree to a plebiscite of three articles. What came to be known as the *leges Licinae Sextiae* comprised a law on debts, an agrarian law, and a law doing away with the consular tribunate and restoring the consulate, on condition that one of the consuls henceforth should always be a plebeian—*consulum . . .utique alter ex plebe crearetur.*[198]

With these events to inspire them, the annalists evolved a romantic tale in which the parts played by trivial causes in shaping great events, and by a woman's injured feelings in bringing about a revolution show the influence of Hellenistic tricks in writing history.[199] The law against usury may reflect a real 'pre-monetary' economic crisis caused by the rebuilding of Rome after the Gaulish invasion,[200] but the clauses limiting the extent of rural holdings to 500 jugera are an anticipation of the agrarian policy of the Gracchi. The picture drawn of political methods—tribunes obstructing the election of magistrates, even some tribunes within the collegium being won over to the senate and interceding against the rogations of their colleagues[201] —is equally an anachronism, reflecting the parliamentary struggles of the late republic. The striking delineation of the character of C. Licinius Stolo, always in the thick of things and reducing his colleague Sextius to a cipher (yet Sextius became the first plebeian consul of the new regime in 366!) shows the favouritism of Licinius Macer in manipulating the data supplied by tradition.

There can be no doubt, however, that what seems to us the essence of the thing, the law governing plebeian participation in the consulate, together with the interpretation that became canonical, namely that no plebeian had been consul before, was already found in the *Annales Latini* of Fabius Pictor: *quapropter tum primum ex plebe alter consul factus est, duoetvicesimo anno quo Romam Galli ceperunt.*[202]

The same interpretation, regarding as non-persons all the plebeian consuls of the first years of the republic, occurs also in the *Fasti Capitolini* for 367: [*consules e pl]ebe primum creari coepti sunt.* It was dictated by that philosophy of history which saw the progress of the plebs within the Roman state as a difficult but straight-line progression starting from zero. It has been adopted by a good many modern historians, some great names among them. We have already explained why we are more convinced by the modern tendency to regard the *serrata del patriziato* as having arisen from accidental causes about 25 years after the republic was set up, and to see the political struggles that later arose as having been caused by the patricians' desire to brand as their own property magistracies which had at first been open to both parties, and the plebeians' desire to win them back.

Against this background the law of 367 recovers its meaning and value. Plebeian access to the consulate had never been regulated by enactment. From 509 to 486 there are 12 plebeian consulates in the Fasti,[203] and there was no problem. The hardening of the patriciate did not prevent there being six more down to the decemvirate and one as late as 445, just before the consular tribunate was created. But this gradual elimination of the plebs arose from a de facto privilege that had no law to sanction it. The consular tribunate, which the annalists hold up as a compromise solution, only grudgingly made room for plebeian ambition:[204] the later collegia had no plebeians. Under these circumstances it was quite natural that C. Licinius and L. Sextius should demand that political rights which had not yet been defined, and for that very reason had been constantly encroached on for a century, should be defined and regulated by statute. The victory won by the plebs in 367 consisted not in being admitted in principle, if and when it pleased their opponents, to the consulship, but in sharing the supreme magistracy equally every year.

Here again is a difficulty (a lesser one, we think) in that the Fasti do not wholly bear out the promise of the Licinian laws.[205] For the first eleven collegia (366–356) the law is rigorously applied: the patrician L. Aemilius and the plebeian L. Sextius are colleagues, then Q. Servilius and the plebeian L. Genucius, etc. But the years 355–333 bring back the patrician monopoly;[206] so do the years 351, 349, 345, 343. It is only from 342 onward that the law is strictly observed.

We have already referred several times to the article by K. von Fritz which has decisively illuminated the reorganization of Roman government in 367: must we conclude with him that the *lex Licinia-Sextia* made no provision for the regular sharing of the consulate,[207] that it was content to stipulate that the patricians should allow a plebeian consul to be elected simply for the year 366, and that the rule did not become obligatory until 343 with the passing of the *plebeiscita* of L. Genucius?[208] We may indeed be surprised that a law passed in 367 should have been repeatedly ignored between 355 and 343; but indisputably for the years 366 to 356 it was in use for such a length of time that we cannot reduce it to a directive applicable to 366 alone. It is better to regard the seven illegal elections as the last dying kicks of patrician resistance. In any case, at that period the conditions of political life at Rome were undergoing a profound change:

the simple opposition of patricians and plebeians was now being overlaid by a rivalry between various groups, which was based, over and above the split between the orders, on alliances between families and individuals. This transformation of Roman society about the middle of the fourth century is probably even more important than the constitutional reform which reflects it and which it made possible.

Advent of a new nobilitas

It was the signal achievement of F. Münzer, in his *Römische Adelsparteien und Adelsfamilien*,[209] that he drew attention to a certain crumbling and disintegration of the patriciate that one sees beginning at this time, and to the appearance of what was more and more to become a new upper class—the *nobilitas*, comprising without distinction patricians and plebeians whose ancestors had held curule magistracies. Henceforth the conflict over principles would gradually give place to struggles between the ambitions of individuals.

Livy's delightful anecdote, in which a woman's wounded sensibilities determine the career of the tribune C. Licinius Stolo, is fairly sure not to be true.[210] It is still a fact that Licinius, 'a well-known figure despite his being plebeian', was the son-in-law of M. Fabius Ambustus; some other Licinii of that time—P. Licinius Calvus, consular tribune in 400, C. Licinius Calvus, magister equitum in 368—could also boast of close family ties with the Cornelii and Manlii.[211] Certainly the ban on marriages between patricians and plebeians pronounced in the Twelve Tables, and abolished by the *lex Canuleia* of 445, was now quite obsolete. The Fabii did not shrink from admitting into their gens, on an equal footing with a Sulpicius, one Licinius, a great landowner who had already earned the cognomen *Dives*: a branch of his family later, after 150 years of obscurity, was to bear the name in token of its proverbial wealth.[212] The political recognition of the plebs was the result of its economic rise, and was favoured by the liberal policy of some great patrician families. Among them were the Fabii, who, when threatened with extinction after the battle of the Cremera, found in alliances with successful plebeians and with the Italic nobility the strength which enabled them, from the beginning of the fourth century, triumphantly to reassert their position.[213]

In this way there came to be a centre party (*Mittelpartei*) in Rome, whose action made possible the compromise of 367. A group then emerged composed of 'new men' not associated with the anarchic struggles of earlier years—a group of moderates made up of patricians of the second rank (an Aemilius, a Sulpicius, a Servilius) and plebeians of the first (a Sextius, two Genucii, two Licinii). Accepted by the exhausted extremists on either flank, this party was to assure the peaceable operation of the recent laws from 366 to 361. The succession, indeed the continuance, in office of the same political figures for six years on end was ensured by the preponderating influence normally exerted by the consul presiding at the comitia over the election of his successors. But the year 360 brought a new alignment into power; with a Fabius and a Manlius at its head, it excluded all the members of the party of 366 from the consulate, with the exception of C. Sulpicius, and took on as partners some plebeians hitherto unknown and hence no doubt more amenable; sometimes indeed it was able to procure the election of two patricians, as we have seen. But from 342 the Aemilii and Servilii, after an eighteen-year eclipse, tread the stage again, with the Plautii now as their plebeian colleagues. For two very important periods, from 342 to 339 and from 330 to 328 the same stars grace the consular firmament and impress their stamp upon politics both foreign and domestic.[214] Thus, in a quarter of a century that seems to mark a new era, political activity in Rome ceased to be dominated by the antagonism of two castes which had formerly been invincibly opposed to each other and were now beginning to mingle, and was ruled more by the complex interplay of family alliances among plebeians and patricians, grouped about some outstanding personalities whose ideas, interests and careers they forwarded.

Other magistracies open to plebeians

The consulate once conquered, the other magistracies and even priesthoods were opened to the plebs after only a slight delay. To begin with the sacerdotal colleges of 367, the leges Liciniae-Sextiae had increased the importance of the college *sacris faciundis*[215]—whose relative acquiescence in plebeian claims has been remarked[216]—by increasing its numbers. The duumviri now became *decemviri sacris faciundis*, and the college acquired its character as the progressive wing of Roman religious organizations by the stipulation that five of the ten were to be plebeians. But the conservative strongholds of *jus sacrum*, the pontificate and augurate, were to hold out until 300.

Not long after it was set up in 367, the curule aedileship found room for at least one plebeian in the person of M. Popilius Laenas,[217] who was to reach the consulate four times, thanks to the alliance of the Fabii and Manlii. But it is in the history of the highest magistracies that we can clearly see that the promotion of the plebs from now on consists essentially in the rise of a small number of individual illustrious plebeians, enjoying the support of the patriciate. The dictatorship, it is said, was opened to plebeians from 356, the censorship from 351, the praetorship from 332. What we see here is in fact the success of two quite atypical individual careers: the same C. Marcius Rutilus had the honour of being the first plebeian dictator and the first plebeian censor, while the same Q. Publilius Philo was successively the second plebeian dictator, the second plebeian censor, and the first plebeian praetor.

It may seem surprising that the dictatorship, an extraordinary magistracy and a peculiarly archaic one, should have been so soon let go by the patricians (a plebeian, moreover, had been magister equitum in 368—C. Licinius Calvus). But they did not grant it to the first plebeian they met. C. Marcius Rutilus, even if the tradition connecting his family with Ancus Marcius and Coriolanus (Cn. Marcius Coriolanus) did not take shape until the second century,[218] was one of those new nobles to whom the patricians extended their patronage.[219] Raised to the consulate in 357 by the influence of the Fabii and Manlii, he had had a triumph over the Etruscans and Faliscans, and it was by one of the two consuls of 356, M. Fabius Ambustus or M. Popilius Laenas, that (according to the unchanging procedure) he was directly named (*dictus*) dictator. The censorship, which he likewise attained five years later, had been set up in 443, according to the traditional account, so as not to betray into the hands of the consular tribunes, who might in theory be plebeians, one of the firmest bastions of patrician society.[220] Now in the fourth century the censorship was certainly not that crown of a politician's career that it was in the second.[221] To have been consul was not a prerequisite, as we can still see in the cases of P. Cornelius Scipio (340) and Ap. Claudius Caecus (312). In the cursus honorum it ranked below the praetorship, and above the offices of curule aedile and magister equitum. To all appearance it was simply an office job, without imperium—'a slight thing' says Livy. But the working of the census implied the recording of individual wealth, military recruitment, drawing-up of senatorial lists (*lectio senatus*), which implied a moral jurisdiction (*cura morum*) that made the censor's authority dreaded. Long before Cato's day, Appius Claudius had shown what power a censor from a noble family could wield.

Such was the magistracy to which the plebeian C. Marcius Rutilus had raised himself in 351 by his merit alone. It was a personal concession: the law extending the benefit of it to his whole class came only later. In 339, in the period when the party of the Servilii and Aemilii had returned to power, another plebeian of genius, Q. Publilius Philo, being then consul, was named dictator by his colleague Ti. Aemilius Mamercinus.[222] Among the laws that bear his name is one providing that one of the two censors should always be a plebeian.[223] The next census-taking, in fact, which occurred after the longish interval of eight years in 332, fell to Spurius Postumius Albinus and Q. Publilius Philo, and thenceforth the principle of sharing it between the orders was rigorously observed.[224]

Meanwhile, from 336, the same Publilius had been praetor without any opposition from the Senate, says Livy.[225] No law was to sanction this new plebeian conquest: the praetorian lists (which are full of gaps)[226] show plebeian praetors in 322 (a Plautius!), 293, 283 (plus a *praetor suffectus*), and 280.

Thus the progress made by the plebs in the fourth century towards the great magistracies is at first the achievement of a very few—C. Licinius Stolo, C. Marcius Rutilus, Q. Publilius Philo, with the more or less open assistance of some patrician gentes, the Fabii, Manlii, Aemilii, Servilii, who made use of the new forces offered by these rich and energetic plebeians in their struggle for power. But at the same time they sought to reinforce the new ruling class by invoking the resources available to them from their external conquests: thanks to their support, many representatives of Italic nobility became integrated into Roman life and at once vied for honours.[227] Such were the Campanian P. Decimus Mus, consul in 340, the Tusculan L. Fulvius Curvus, consul in 322, the Etruscan L. Volumnius Flamma, consul in 307, the Praenestine Q. Anicius, curule aedile in 304, and from Tusculum again the Mamilii, who held several consulates starting from 265. The Fabian gens showed itself especially active in this policy of acceptance and assimilation: at the beginning of the century M. Fabius Ambustus had given one of his daughters in marriage to the plebeian C. Licinius Stolo; during the second Samnite war, Q. Fabius Rullianus married his daughter to Atilius of Caiatia; while the third was going on, M. Fabius Buteo became father-in-law of an Otacilia from Beneventum. A M. Otacilius held the consulship in 263, an Atilius Caiatinus in 255, two Fabii Buteones in 247 and 245; but this admixture of foreign blood enabled the gens, which was suddenly almost extinguished just before the first Punic war, to survive and keep in power through collateral lines until the trunk put out leaves again with Q. Fabius, who was to be called Cunctator, consul in 233.

It need not be stressed that this mixed nobility, combining the inheritance of a true-blue patriciate with a contribution from the élite of the plebeians and the Italian aristocracy, was very soon resolute to defend its newly-won privileges. The political problem of magistracies was solved; the economic and social problems remained. Chief of these was how the urban proletariat and freedmen should be represented in the assemblies. Roman politics had to work hard for another fifty years to solve this problem. This was the time above all when the comitia tributa took up its rôle and played it forcefully.

Comitia centuriata, comitia tributa

We have seen how the assemblies of the monarchy and republic had taken shape. We may forget the comitia curiata, which, even though they went on being summoned to confer imperium on magistrates[228] or to determine the legitimacy of an adoption, were no longer concerned with the living interests of the city. Of the various Roman assemblies the most important were the comitia centuriata, already described as *comitiatus maximus* in the Twelve Tables;[229] in a primitive form they had been set up by Servius Tullius, being based not on blood or dwelling-place, but on wealth, and comprising at first only one class of citizens, the *classis* properly so called, which furnished the contingent of hoplites. The rest of the population, the *proletarii* or *infra classem*, were shut out alike from army and assembly. The natural links between the political and the military aspects of the centuriate constitution—the comitia being always an assembly of the people in arms, conveyed on the Campus Martius outside the pomerium—made the two develop side by side; and it was at this time seemingly, the latter half of the fifth century, during the consular tribunate, that the number of effectives went up, and other classes variously distinguished were added to the primordial classis. More we cannot say, knowing what stumbling-blocks one meets in trying to apply the classical centuriate division to Rome before a money economy was brought in.

For a long time the decisions, either electoral or legislative, of the comitia centuriata were subject to the ratification of the Senate (*patrum auctoritas*): in *auctoritas* we may see a religious term, closely related to *augurium*, expressing the 'consecration' whereby the senate gave real force to the decisions of the assembly. In 339 the dictator Q. Publilius Philo sought to free the comitia from their nonage by making the senate confer a 'blanket' ratification before seeing the proposals: *ut legum, quae comitiis centuriatis ferrentur, ante initum suffragium patres auctores fierent.*[230]

The comitia centuriata were the assembly of the people (*populus*) without distinction of caste. The *comitia tributa* were the particular assembly of the plebeians (*concilium plebis*), going back to the time when the plebs, become aware of its rights which the patricians were denying, set itself up as a state within the state.[231] The special magistrates of the plebs, the tribunes, had the responsibility of convening it, by tribes, to submit to its vote resolutions which in principle affected the plebs and the plebs alone—*leges sacratae* incorporating a curse upon their transgressors, and more generally *plebei scita* or plebiscites. But the interests of the plebs could only be defended within the context of the whole people; thus the plebiscite of C. Canuleius in 445, abolishing the ban on marriage between patricians and plebeians, did not bind the plebs alone. It was the constant endeavour of the plebs, over more than 150 years, to have its plebiscites recognized as laws (leges) binding on the whole city. The story of this long struggle is not easy to follow, and it is made harder to study by the ambiguities of the annalists, who do not always distinguish clearly between the two terms. All that is certain is that it ended with the *lex Hortensia* in 287, providing that *quod plebs iussisset, omnes Quirites teneret*, that 'what the plebs should command was to bind the whole body of citizens'.[232] But tradition speaks of two previous pieces of legislation as having made the resolutions of the comitia tributa binding on the whole people—the *leges Valeriae-Horatiae* of 449 and a law proposed by Q. Publilius Philo in 339. Instead of treating these as mere anticipations, without any real basis, one tends nowadays to regard them as stages in a long process; we are forming a clearer conception of what plebiscites were like in the fifth and fourth centuries, in the process of changing from *leges sacratae* to simple *leges*.[233] Most of them were preceded by direct action which takes on the mythical aspect of a secession of the armed plebs to the Aventine, while in reality it was more probably a political strike, boycotting the elections and plunging the state into anarchy, as in 375. The *plebiscita* may be compared to resolutions of a powerful modern trade union: they acquainted the government with the wishes of the plebs, which then used various forms of pressure to force it to give them consideration—i.e. to put them to the vote of the comitia centuriata.[234]

Probably the first stage (after 449 perhaps) was the admission that the plebiscites to which the senate had willingly or perforce given its auctoritas were to become *leges populi* by the vote of the centuries.[235] Another restriction, possibly the *auctoritas patrum*, may have been removed in 339. At all events, after 287 the decisions of the comitia tributa and centuriata were absolutely equivalent, and in consequence the former, attended by all the citizens, presided over if required by the consuls, with less archaic and more expeditious procedure, acquired a monopoly of legislative procedure, while the election of curule magistrates, except quaestors, remained the business of the comitia centuriata.

The latter were also to take over and maintain permanently the function of a supreme appellate court, defined by the *lex Valeria de provocatione*. *Provocatio ad populum*, appeal to the people, was the last resort of the Roman citizen threatened with death or scourging with rods by a magistrate in cases where the intercessio of a tribune would have been inoperative: from then on a vote of the comitia centuriata was required. The establishment of this right, as fundamental in Rome as habeas corpus in England, is ascribed by the annalists to two earlier *leges Valeriae*, the first passed at the founding of the republic in 509, the latter forming part of the *leges Valeriae-Horatiae* of 449. There seems to be general agreement now that the only authentic *lex Valeria de provocatione* is that of the consul M. Valerius Corvus in 300.[236]

The independence of the popular assemblies, or rather the ever clearer preponderance of the comitia tributa over the centuriata, was able, however, to take on its true democratic sense only if the lower classes of the population could make their presence felt, especially in the former. This problem raised its head in a peculiarly urgent form in the closing years of the fourth century; and it well expresses the needs of the age and of its great social changes that the moving spirit should have been not a consul, but a censor, Appius Claudius Caecus.

Policies of Appius Claudius

He is a very great figure, of varied gifts and wide culture; his *Sententiae* in Saturnian metre, admired by Panaetius and by Cicero, made him the founder of Latin literature[237]—they were supposed to show Orphic leanings—and he was also an orator and jurist. The censorship—his first public office (312)—he took as the opportunity for epoch-making reforms and innovations;[238] being in charge of the public purse, he could take the initiative in religious concerns, as the taking-over by the state of the private cult of Hercules at the Ara Maxima[239] and in great public works which continued to bear his name—the aqua Appia, the earliest of the city's aqueducts, and the via Appia from Rome to Capua, connecting the two capitals of the Romano-Campanian world. In the work of the census itself, he was not content with modernizing the spelling of proper names, like the good grammarian he was, but he attempted a really revolutionary move in allowing every man to enter himself in the tribe of his own choice. The effect of this was to distribute the *humiles*, the people of low birth, throughout the existing four urban and 27 rustic tribes, and risked delivering the comitia tributa into their hands. After a struggle lasting several years, Q. Fabius Rullianus, censor in 304, parried the threat by confining all the *humiles* to the urban tribes; thus, whatever their numbers, they could carry only four tribes out of 31. In another area, the recent *lex Ovinia*[240] having transferred from the consuls to the censors the preparation of the senatorial lists (*lectio senatus*), Appius Claudius admitted for the first time the sons of freedmen, and in 304 (for example) a scribe, Cn. Flavius, became curule aedile.

On this second plank in his platform—the admission of *libertini* to the senate—the texts are tolerably clear; but on the first the notice in Diodorus is too brief, and that in Livy too confused:[241] none of the proposed interpretations is wholly satisfactory. In the method of recruiting the tribes there was something that Ap. Claudius wanted to change—but what?[242] What social category is concealed under Livy's anachronistic use of *humiles*? Mommsen's theory was long accepted, that the censor for the first time took account in his records of personal, not landed, property, and thereby 'corrupted' at once the *forum* (i.e. the comitia tributa) and the *campus* (i.e. the *comitia centuriata*):[243] but there is not a word of this in the texts, and Latin usage will not permit *humiles* to mean 'capitalists', even if the capital was not in land. P. Fraccaro,[244] in the study in which he demolished Mommsen's theory, claims that Ap. Claudius was trying to decant the urban proletariat into the rustic tribes, which would reduce his action to a demagogic manoeuvre to secure a majority for his policies in the comitia tributa. This is the light in which Livy saw it,[245] but the *turba forensis* is not the urban proletariat, and it is hard to see what interest a *humilis* from the Vicus Tuscus in Rome could have had in enrolling himself in (e.g.) the tribus Stellatina that was set up in 387 after annexation of the lands of Capena. This is what makes the theory of Lily Ross Taylor attractive[246]—she adopts in essentials the theory of Fraccaro, but sees the *humiles* as having been essentially made up of freedmen. They might have been former Roman citizens enslaved for debt and now set free by the abolition of the *nexum*, foreign immigrants, either workmen or intellectuals (the latter class coming mostly from Etruria), but also, and on Ross Taylor's theory especially, they were freedmen domiciled in the rustic tribes which had been created in the vicinity of Rome by the recent extensions of the ager Romanus. In these places there would have been a native population partly of servile origin, who, before they could become Roman citizens, had to be emancipated by the praetor (*manumissio per vindictam*) or by the censor (*manumissio censu*). We may suppose that previous censors had enrolled these new citizens in the urban tribes, since the emancipation took place at Rome. Appius Claudius allowed them to be enrolled in the tribe where they lived: this was logical enough, but it could not fail to alarm the Roman landlords of the estates where they worked. However that may be, it is in the four urban tribes that we find the mass of the *libertini* (under their own name this time) at the beginning of the second century, while the rustic tribes were traditionally regarded as the preserve of free men.[247]

These pressures exerted by a servile or half-servile plebs on the Roman constitution should be seen as related to the social troubles that were plaguing Etruria at the same time: at Volsinii and Oenarea the slaves, given their freedom in large numbers, entered the senate of these towns and took over the government.[248]

In Rome these pressures, finally contained by the counter-measures of Q. Fabius Rullianus, and perhaps previously weakened by the wise concessions of Ap. Claudius, brought no such grave consequences. We can see how far his policy of favouring freedmen went in the individual instance of Cn. Flavius. He was a freedman's son, perhaps of Etruscan origins: Appius Claudius made his fortune. During his curule aedileship, Flavius published the formulae of the civil law (*legis actiones*)[249] and had the calendar posted up in the Forum, i.e. he made known the distinction between *dies fasti* and *nefasti*, so that the plebs could thenceforth know how and when it could stand up for its legal rights. It is interesting to note that this same Flavius, when civil tension was running very high, dedicated in the Forum a brazen *aedicula* to the goddess Concordia. Under the Greek name of *Homonoea* this was to be one of the great political conceptions of the

Hellenistic world, but even from the middle of the fourth century we find Homonoea depicted on coins of Metapontum[250] and her praises sung by the Pythagorean Archytas, the strategus of Tarentum.[251] The Greek Homonoea cannot be simply equated with Cicero's slogan *concordia ordinum*: as a philosophical ideal it principally implied mutual help in society, assistance given to the poor by the rich.[252] In this sense Ap. Claudius might well put Concordia on his banners, although his policies had so gravely offended the nobility. At all events, we may see here Greek, perhaps Pythagorean, influence at work in shaping his ideals.

The character of Appius Claudius is hard to grasp. It is full of contradictions, which are all the harder to untangle because the annalists cast him in the image of the later historical Claudii with all the *insita superbia* that distinguished the gens.[253] As an aristocratic demagogue he had tried to hand over the comitia to the *humiles*; yet on occasion he could show himself the most uncompromising of patricians. He violated the Licinio-Sextian laws by refusing, as interrex, to let a plebeian be a candidate for the consulship;[254] he fought against the admission of plebeians to priesthoods;[255] he prolonged his censorship beyond the legal term.[256] He had some of the qualities of the Sicilian tyrants: at Forum Appi, on the Appian way, he had a statue of himself set up with a royal diadem;[257] his enemies accused him of planning to rule all Italy through his numberless *clientelae*, recruited mainly among freedmen.

It is certain that he reacted vigorously against the moderate policy of welcoming noble plebeians which had been championed by the Fabii. One of his latest biographers, a pupil of Münzer's, relates him to the clan-rivalries that raged in the Rome of 312, and regards him as an opportunist who was out to steal the popularity of Q. Publilius Philo.[258] It is possible that he sought the support of the masses as an instrument to reinstate the patricians in their privileges.[259] It seems more likely, however, that his policies, open as they were to Greek, Campanian and Etruscan influences, were the antithesis of a blinkered conservatism, and were extremely well adapted to the problems of the day.[260] E. S. Staveley regards him as the leader of a group which was tending to transform the agrarian economy of Rome by strengthening the industrial factors in the city.[261] This is still uncertain, but Mommsen saw clearly enough when he compared him with Cleisthenes and Pericles.[262]

D The conquest of Italy

At the same period when the birth (or rebirth) of Roman maritime ambitions was signalized by the alliance with Carthage, an equally important widening of her horizons on land led her there also to transcend the boundaries within which her part had hitherto been played, namely Latium, Etruria and the Volscian country. Around 340,[263] after a rapid sequence of battles and negotiations, she succeeded in establishing her rule over Latium and in breaking once and for all the resistance of the Latin League, while at the same time she involved herself in the series of three Samnite wars which were to end, after 66 years, in the conquest of all southern Italy down to Tarentum.

These are confused happenings, worked up by the annalists into an edifying story in which the guiding principles of Roman policy are the 'just war' and loyalty to allies. However biased their account, it would be wrong to deny that the indisputable imperialism of Rome from that time on shows a feeling that self-justification is needed, together with a consciousness of a rather demanding *fides Romana*.[264] What makes it harder than ever to understand the events is that they took place both at home and abroad, in Rome, in Capua, in Samnite country, and that the economic and social forces whose workings we have just studied keep making themselves felt amid the contradictions of diplomacy and the deep moving impulses behind the outbreaks of violence.

The deditio of Capua

In 438 and 423 some Samnites had formed themselves into a Campanian state with Capua as its capital.[265] But their kinsmen of the mountains had still kept up the pressure on the inhabitants of the coveted plains. In 354 Rome (or the Latin League) had concluded a treaty of alliance and friendship with them.[266] When, about 343, the Samnites threatened the Sidicini of Teanum (Teano), where the Latin Way debouches into Campania, the latter appealed to the Campanians, who in turn asked the Romans for help. To appease the Romans' scruples, they gave themselves over, persons and possessions, into the power of Rome by pronouncing the formula of *deditio*;[267] thus, in virtue of an obligation transcending their bond with the Samnites, Rome could defend them legitimately as an act of self-defence. So runs the tale: very likely the deditio of 343 is a mere anticipation of the deditio or capitulation of 211, when the Capuans were to be severely punished for their defection. At all events, Rome, in the midst of great social disorder, did not hesitate then to intervene on the Campanian side: this was the First Samnite War (343, or more likely 341).[268] But not long after, the pro-Samnite party in Rome came to the top again, compelled the renewal of the alliance, the abandonment of the Sidicini—which gravely prejudiced the commercial interests of the Latins—and a complete reversal of the situation. From 340–338 a decisive struggle took place between Romans and Samnites on one side, Latins, Campanians and Sidicini on the other. This was the Latin War.

Dissolution of the Latin League

One of the most important results of this war (which the Romans considered a provocative defection of the Latins) was the dissolution of their league.[269] This period saw an official end to the age-old custom, till then more or less kept up in theory, whereby 'the Empire was administered by common decisions'.[270] The status of each people was decided individually, by *senatusconsulta* which cut to pieces the organic unity of the *nomen Latinum*.[271] All now lost the advantages which they had hitherto enjoyed from having a federal law which, from Aricia to Tibur, did such things as guaranteeing marriages, commercial transactions, transfers of property, etc.[272] Some received the doubtful privilege of gaining (as Lanuvium, Aricia, Nomentum and Pedum did) or retaining (like Tusculum) the *civitas sine suffragio*, or citizenship without voting rights. Others, like Tibur and Praeneste, remained allied cities (*civitates foederatae*), which gave them some degree of autonomy, but they were shorn of some of their lands. Velitrae (Velletri) was destroyed and its inhabitants deported to Rome on the right bank of the Tiber. New colonists were sent to Antium, where the harbour was confiscated; the native dwellers were given citizen-rights and permitted to enroll themselves among the colonists. All the other Latins (they are not specified) were simply deprived of the right of marriage, trade, and assembly. But even those most favoured, and those to whom Rome had condescended to grant her *civitas*, speedily perceived that in giving up the advantages of the old federal organization—since all their private and public interests were now cognizable by Roman magistrates—the principal obligation that they had contracted was that of being entered on the census rolls and of serving in the legions. Thus Latium was unified with Rome

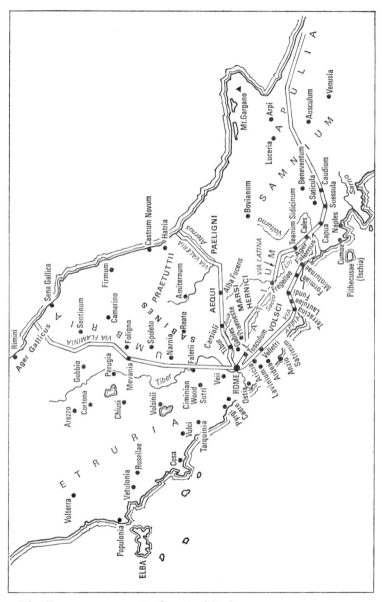

5 The Roman conquest of central Italy

as the capital, and Rome's military manpower was thereby vastly increased.

Annexation of Campania

At the same time the Romans consolidated their expansion into Campania. They first assured their control of the coastal highway (the future Appian Way) that led there by granting civitas sine suffragio to Formiae and Fundi. Also, the territory of Falernum (*ager Falernus*) was taken away from Capua to punish that city's alleged defection.[273] At Capua itself, as in the neighbouring Cumae and Suessula, a significant distinction was made: the Campanian knights, who had not defected, received the honours of civitas, and an inscription set up at Rome in the temple of Castor laid down that the 1600 knights of Capua should receive a grant of 450 drachmae per annum from the Roman people.[274]

By thus sparing and protecting their Capuan counterparts, the Roman knights were carrying out a policy which Rome can be seen practising throughout her conquest, namely of relying on the local nobility: the deditio of Capua must have been in reality an agreement between two groups of aristocrats who were worried at the progress of the lower orders. In Capua the steady infiltration of Samnites tended to enlarge the plebs and thus to create an imbalance which the knights had thought to redress by appealing to certain factions at Rome. It has been suggested that one of the consuls of 340, P. Decius Mus, a Campanian by extraction as his name shows, had made himself the most active champion of the rapprochement.[275] In Rome, however, it appears that this tendency, represented by the Fabii, had fallen foul of the policy of a party that was at once democratic and favourable to the Samnites, its principal leaders being the Aemilii Mamercini and the Plautii.

However that may be, the oldest and least manipulated account of relations between Rome and Capua presents a fairly rapid evolution in three stages: *foedere primum, deinde conubio atque cognationibus, postremo civitate.*[276] In the beginning we can detect the existence of a treaty of alliance, possibly on the lines of a Greek *isopoliteia*, assuring equal conditions to both parties.[277] These political ties will have been strengthened by marriages between members of the two ruling castes. The loyalty of the Campanian knights during the Latin War gained for them the right of Roman citizenship, which a few years later (334) was extended to the entire people of Capua, but *sine suffragio*.

The resulting symbiosis has caused some writers to talk of a Romano-Campanian state, bringing under one rule the lands from the Tiber to the Volturnus.[278] These are in fact the boundaries of the kingdom of Aeneas as promised by Cassandra in those enigmatic verses in which Lycophron (*c.* 275) shadows forth the views of Timaeus the historian.[279] But the Romano-Campanian state was never (or only for the briefest time) the amphisbaenic affair that this view would suggest. It had but the one head, and Capua, despite the fool's bargain made by her knights, was soon no more than a federated township, that is to say, a city which, while bene-fitting from the prestige and perhaps a few immunities derived from the original treaty (*foedus*), was none the less subject to the burdens (*munera*) laid on the *municipia*.[280] From 334, when *civitas Romana* was conferred, to 216, when Hannibal's victories gave her the hope of recovering her liberty, she lived in the condition, at once protected and dependent, of a city exempt from direct political responsibilities, although some of her natives were able, in settling at Rome, to become full citizens and to exert their influence on common concerns. The Campanians, in their capacity as Roman citizens, served in great numbers in the Roman legions; but this did not prevent the Romans from using on occasion an irregular corps of mercenaries which turns up under the name of *legio Campana*, or from employing the valuable help of the Campanian cavalry in special units—the *alae equitum Campanorum*.[281] The Campanians, as citizens of Rome, had no right to strike money; the ascription to Capua of the first Roman didrachms, from 340 onwards, under the name of Romano-Campanian coinage, rests only on a hypothesis of Mommsen's which has been disposed of by modern critics, and the only money of her own struck by Capua dates from the revolt (216–211); throughout the remainder of the third century she only uses coins put out under the name of Rome.[282] Lastly, it is wrong to say, as Livy does,[283] that after 318 Capua was reduced to the status of a pre-fecture, *praefecti Capuam* being sent out each year from Rome to administer justice in place of the suspended local magistrates. Very likely there were at Capua, in the latter half of the fourth century, social disorders, in connection with the democratic agitation building up at Rome, and express-ing a still lively dissatisfaction. But the creation of the *praefecti Capuam* is no earlier than the capitulation of 211: down to that date Capua kept a large measure of administrative and juridicial autonomy; the Oscan language remained the official one, and inscriptions of the third century attest the continuance of her municipal magistracies—among others there is a *meddix tuticus* at the head of a college of *meddices*. Although we are still uncertain about some aspects of the institutions in force, and although factual reality seldom meets all the demands of an abstract definition, Capua is the clearest example of a city of half-citizens, as defined by Mommsen.[284]

Alliance with Naples

By setting foot in Campania, Rome had entered into immediate contact with Magna Graecia. Cumae indeed, for the last three-quarters of a century, had been little more than a half-barbarous Oscan village. Naples,[285] however, founded by Cumae in the seventh century on the hill of Pizzo-falcone (Parthenope, Palaeopolis), and reconstructed further east in more open country about 470 with the help of the Athenians and the Syracusans of Pithecusae, had been able until then almost completely to resist the invasion and infiltration of the Samnites—not quite completely, for her Fasti were already tainted with Oscan names.[286] Here again the aristocracy, Greek in their origins, chose rather to ally themselves with Rome, while the plebs joined the Samnites and seceded to Palaeopolis. After a short military action, Q. Publilius Philo won a triumph over the *Samnites Palaeopolitani* (326). But Rome was then starting on a philhellene policy, and granted Naples an alliance on privileged terms, allowing her to keep her own magistrates, worship, language and coinage.[287] Her obligations were limited to lending the help of her fleet in war, and she did not fail to do so in the First Punic War. Her loyalty during the war with Pyrrhus and later became proverbial, and at the same time she remained a living centre of Hellenism within the Roman world. It was from Naples in the third century that Rome borrowed the purely Greek cult—one quite independent of the old Roman Ceres—of the *sacra Cereris Matris*, its priestesses being drawn from the noble families of Naples and Velia.[288] Naples of course was only one of the cities of Magna Graecia with which Rome was to establish bonds during this latter half of the fourth century: Tarentum also was shortly to appear on the horizon.

The Samnite Wars

The Samnite Wars (we have already mentioned the first in 343 or 341; there still remain the second from 326–304 and third from 298–290) show in fifty years a prodigious expansion of Roman conquest. Bloody, confused, interminable,[289] they appear in the annalistic tradition (which is often suspect) as a continuous series of victories and defeats up and down Italy—distant expeditions into Apulia and Umbria, sudden threats to communications at the very gates of Rome; the theatre of operations constantly changes; for a long time the Romans do not attack the fortress of Samnium itself, but devote their military and political efforts to reducing the area of Samnite influence and cutting them off from their potential allies. This has the agonizing result that when hostilities start again, all the previous conquests, even of the Hernici and Aequi, are called in question again, and that at the last the conflagration spreads to all the peninsula, leaguing together the Samnites of course, but also the Etruscans, Umbrians and Gauls against Rome. When the smoke had cleared away, it was acknowledged that Rome was the mistress of the native part of Italy, and that only the Greek part remained to be conquered.

The Samnite confederacy

The Samnites made up a confederacy of several tribes, which showed a seemingly unflinching coherence under the command of common magistrates.[289] Their power was at first a function of their multitude: a constant excess of population, ill fed in their native Abruzzi, and partly absorbed in later times by mercenary armies and gladiatorial schools, was always on hand to fill the gaps in their ranks; they were also animated by a kind of martial mystique which sanctified their penchant for brigandage. We have already mentioned their legendary practice of the *ver sacrum*;[290] their general levy was attended by the most appalling religious ceremonies—a *legio linteata* was formed, so named from the linen tent in which the recruits from the nobility had to pronounce a most blood-curdling oath upon pain of death, in front of an altar dripping with blood.[291] The Samnites also had very efficient armament, and the Romans speedily imitated them in replacing the lance by javelins (*pila*) and adopting the general use of the oblong leather buckler (*scutum*).[292] They manoeuvred in open formations, as being better suited to mountain warfare: again it was their influence that made the Romans adopt manipular tactics.[293]

For all the Romans might say,[294] it was not simply the desire to protect Campania against Samnite aggression that led them into this struggle to the death. Certainly the foundation of the colonies of Cales and Fregellae (334,

328) show that they wanted to fortify the via Latina, which the Samnites (taking over from the Volscians) were threatening to cut, and in the sequal did.[295] But it is commonly agreed that from the first Rome had more distant ends in view, and that, as soon as the affair of Naples was over, she set her sights on Apulia; the annalists indeed, by a pleasing anachronism, bring in Tarentum at the beginning of a conflict which, to their eyes, did not end until her fall in 272. It is in fact quite likely that Tarentine influence had penetrated deeply into Samnium, although few will be ready to accept the all too pretty story of the talks held at Tarentum between Archytas, Plato and the Samnite leader, Herennius Pontius.[296] But it is hard to believe that Tarentum, constantly at war with her Lucanian and Messapian neighbours, and having to invoke against them such foreign mercenaries as Alexander the Molossian,[297] should have been driven by the fear of Rome to cement an alliance for their benefit between the Lucanians and the Samnites. Rome was called into northern Apulia (among the Daunians, to be precise) by Luceria and Arpi, which Tarentum, too remote and too much occupied, was ill able to protect against Samnite depredations.[298] The Samnites, according to an inspired guess of A. Grenier's, were trying to obtain summer pastures in the plain for the seasonal movements of their herds.[299] At the same time, Rome would be taking her enemy in the rear.

This explains the first rather surprising manifestations of Roman strategy, namely the ravaging of the territory of the Vestini (at the mouth of the Aternus, modern Pescara, on the Adriatic coast), who were accused of making common cause with the Samnites (325). The object was to establish regular communications with Apulia by going round north of Samnium through the lands of the Aequi, Marsi, Paeligni and Marrucini—this was a route not long afterwards to be taken by the via Valeria built by M. Valerius Maximus, censor in 307—, and then along the coast towards Monte Gargano.[300] The foundation of several colonies after the second and third Samnite wars were over—Alba Fucens (303), Carsioli (298), Hatria, Castrum Novum, Sena Gallica (283) and Firmum as late as 264—attests the importance that Rome still attached, even after her victory, to this route and to her expansion on the Adriatic.

The pax Caudina

In 321, however, growing weary of this long detour,[301] and urgently summoned to the assistance of Luceria, the two consuls T. Veturius

Calvinus and Sp. Postumius Albinus tried to force a passage straight through the heart of Samnium—as the prolongation of the via Appia, also called via Traiana, was to do in classical times. At Caudium, between Capua and Beneventum, they committed themselves to the double defile of the Caudine Forks, and found themselves trapped. The consuls had to accept disgraceful terms of surrender, and the whole army was sent under the yoke. Rome was obliged to evacuate her colonies, Fregellae among them, and all the valley of the Liris (the route of the via Latina) came under Samnite control.[302]

At this point, according to the annalists, the senate at once disowned the compact; hostilities were resumed, and revenge assured by some speedy victories. That the latter were invented holus bolus to wash away the disgrace of the Caudine Forks is now not seriously disputed. A question of public law remains: If Rome had subscribed to a genuine peace treaty, how could she take up arms again? The debates held in the senate on the occasion let it appear that the agreement concluded by the consuls was not a *foedus* in the strict sense, sanctioned by the fetials and thus binding on the Roman people, but a *sponsio* which was personally binding only on the magistrates who had taken the initiative.[303] By handing over the latter to the enemy—in Livy's moving narrative it is the consuls themselves who first demand such a measure—Rome regained her freedom of action. Doubts have often been felt as to the historicity of this way of interpreting the *pax Caudina*,[304] and the annalists have been thought to have modelled it on the more recent *pax Mancina*: in 137 the consul C. Hostilius Mancinus had to capitulate before Numantia; the senate disowned the sponsio and handed the *sponsor* over to the enemy. But the justice of the parallel has been disputed, and it has been shown that this kind of sponsio is in fact very old.[305] In fact the annalists seem to have been elaborating on a genuine occurrence, which illustrates the sense of rigorous legality which made Rome, in the heat of this merciless conflict, feel in some measure tied by her conception of a just war.

The following years give us glimpses of a confused mêlée: more allies fall away, the fabric of Roman conquest seems to be cracked; not only the via Latina, but the coastal highway, the later via Appia, is no longer safely under control; there is fighting at Satricum, at Lautulae between Terracina and Fundi, at Ausona, Minturnae, Vescia; the infection even spreads for a moment to Capua itself. But Rome clings to her purpose, animated by a great military leader, L. Papirius Cursor—the same who, by Livy's account, would have been a match for Alexander had the latter turned his arms westward; she fights back blow for blow, attacks the Samnite strong-holds of Saticula and Bovianum, and at last clears the road to Luceria, where in 314 she founds a colony which will henceforth contain the Samnite threat to Apulia.

The war, which Livy[306] speaks of as virtually over, went on for ten more years. After Rome had resolved to invade Samnium and had taken by storm one of her capital cities, Bovianum, Samnite resistance seemed broken: the old alliance was renewed (304), but it was to be no more than a five-year armistice. The last years of this war, however, begin to assume the character of the third, which saw the general coalition of the Italic peoples against Roman supremacy: hostilities with the Etruscans begin in 311, and with the Umbrians shortly after.[307]

Etruria, the seat of an ancient civilization, with its treasures still virtually intact, provided Roman imperialism with a temptation which it could not resist in the thick of the Samnite war, although it meant conflict with a considerable population (*multitudo hominum*)[308] and great economic resources (*pecunia*).[309] In southern Etruria, Rome had already destroyed Veii, annexed Caere, conquered Tarquinii; it was in central Etruria that she was now to commit her forces, starting from Sutri, the key to Etruria, and following the future via Cassia. In this conquest the most important initiatives were taken by the Fabii, and the province became virtually a fief of theirs. Thus Q. Fabius Maximus Rullianus, five times consul from 322 to 295, opened up the impenetrable Ciminian forest to Roman arms (310), and emerged in sight of the rich corn-lands of the upper Tiber valley. Livy makes him push as far as the *Camertes* of Camerinum (Camerino) in Umbria; but this is plainly a confusion with the *Camertes* of Clusium (Chiusi), of which the Etruscan name was *Camars*.[310] Clusium, with which the Romans had kept up friendly relations since the days of Porsenna and the Gaulish invasion, was one of the bases for Roman penetration as far as Perugia, Cortona and Arezzo. In the last-named city the Romans supported the princely family of the Cilnii, from which Maecenas derived his ancestry, against a democratic threat to their power. But Volsinii (Bolsena) the religious and federal metropolis of Etruria, remained impregnable, and the pacification of the country was constantly being challenged, while on the right bank of the Tiber the Umbrians of Mevania and Narnia had taken up arms and were drawing upon themselves military operations that trod out the line of the future via Flaminia.

The Third Samnite War

But in 298 Roman attention was drawn to the south, where the Third Samnite War blazed up again; further afield, Lucania, which the Romans claimed to be defending against the Samnites, was conquered by P. Cornelius Scipio Barbatus. Apulia also began to boil over. This was the Third Samnite War, to be waged at first on two fronts; then, after the victories in 296 of the proconsul Decius Mus, who ravaged Samnium, drove out the Samnite army and made it retire into Etruria, it was in the north that Rome would have to face her united foes—the Etruscans almost to a man, the Samnites now by their side and urging them to battle, the peoples of Umbria, the Gauls, mainly Senones, who were to serve at first as mercenaries for Etruscan gold until they finally threw their whole weight into the scale. All Italy was in arms against 'a tyranny not to be born'.[311] Events are still further complicated by the rivalry of the Fabii and Claudii: Q. Fabius Rullianus, with P. Decius Mus as his regular fellow-consul (308, 297, 295), and Ap. Claudius Caecus, whose colleague with equal regularity is L. Volumnius (307, 296), an Etruscan who had become a Roman citizen. The wrangles between the generals, dramatically coloured by the annalists and family pride, were all the more frequent since the enlargement of the theatre of operations and the increase in number of the legions compelled them to retain as pro-magistrates the consuls of the preceding years.

In 295, at Sentinum in northern Umbria, a great battle took place between the Gauls and Samnites and the Romans under Fabius and Decius, while the Etruscans were kept at home by a clever diversionary move and while Volumnius was operating in Samnium, where fighting had broken out again. An imprudent attack by Decius came to grief before the Gaulish cavalry and chariots; to avert defeat he devoted himself and the enemy to the Manes and the goddess Tellus. On the right wing Fabius, biding his time like his famous descendant in the Hannibalic War, threw back the Samnites, took the Gauls in the rear, and won total victory.

The bloody struggle of Sentinum made a great stir in the world and soon acquired the trappings of legend, particularly where the *devotio* of Decius was concerned. A contemporary Greek historian, Duris of Samos, set the number of Samnite and Gaulish dead at 100,000; Livy was to bring it down to 25,000. But the consequences of the triumph won by Fabius *de Samnitibus et Etrusceis, Galleis* were decisive for all the northern front. The Senones were thrown back to the sea and lost a part of their territory, and the foundation of the colonies of Sena Gallica (289) and of Ariminum (Rimini) in 268 set the seal on the Romanization of the *ager Gallicus*. Umbria was subdued by the incorporation of Spoleto and Foligno into Roman territory and by the granting of treaties of alliance to Camerino and Iguvium (Gubbio). In Etruria the campaign was prolonged by raids across the territory of Rusellae and Vulsinii, until the Etruscan metropolis—the consul M. Atilius Regulus held a triumph over the Volsones in 294— associated itself with the request for peace presented by Perugia and Arezzo.[312] Nearer Rome, a revolt of the Falisci in 293 was easily put down.

Conquest of Etruria

Sentinum had shattered the coalition between the peoples of the north and south; but the war was not yet over. On the Etruscan front, fighting broke out again around Vulsinii, where resistance was to last for another thirty years. The loss of Livy's second decade conceals from us the details of the struggle, but the *Fasti triumphales* preserve the essentials—a triumph of Ti. Coruncanius in 280 *de Volsiniensibus et Vulcientibus*, of M. Fulvius Flaccus in 265 *de Vulsiniensibus*. In these last struggles one can clearly see an element of social repression amid the operations of war. Etruria was the scene at that time of democratic agitations which the local aristocracies sought to repress with the help of Roman arms. At the siege of Troilum (a city otherwise unknown), Sp. Carvilius permitted the richest citizens to leave, on payment of ransom, before reducing the plebs to surrender.[313] At Vulsinii, as at Oinarea, the freedmen had seized power and were oppressing the former ruling class;[314] the nobles conspired to invoke the aid of Rome; the Romans came and re-established them, and that was the end of Vulsinii's independence. The Etruscan towns were deprived of much of their territory and, with the exception of Caere (*civitas sine suffragio*) and the colonies (Cosa was founded in 273) possessed the status of allied cities (*urbes foederatae*).[315]

At the same period (290) the Sabines of the central region from Amiternum to Reate, who had taken no part in the Samnite wars, tried to burst the vice which was closing on them: a lightning campaign led by Manius Curius took them in the rear and brought their attack to nothing.[316] In 268 they were granted *civitas sine suffragio*. We have mentioned earlier the implausible theory of Mommsen's, which still finds its supporters, that the myth of a Romano-Sabine synoecism under Romulus and Tatius was concocted on the occasion of these events.[317]

In the south, Sentinum had not prevented the Samnites from making their seasonal raids into Campania and on the Latin Way. They could still put into the field levies of 40,000 men,[318] and although the Fasti proclaim triumphs *de Samnitibus* every year, tradition preserved the memory of some sharp defeats for the Romans. But in the end the Samnites, exhausted, sued for peace. It had been necessary, however, to wage war also against the Lucanians and Apulians: the latter were devastating the territory of Luceria, and several expeditions going round by the Adriatic coast had to be mounted to overcome their resistance. Their submission was marked in 291 by the founding of the colony of Venusia. The Sabines and the Praetuttii were still in arms; the capture of Amiternum and the founding of Hatria (289) finally took care of them.

Tarentum

Relations between Rome and Tarentum had gradually become tense. It was not that war between them was natural or inevitable: they had the same enemies—Samnites, Lucanians and Bruttians, and Tarentum, which for fifty years had been calling in Spartan or Epirot mercenaries to contain them (Archidamus from 343 to 338, Alexander the Molossian from 336 to 333 or 331, and Cleonymus in 303–302), must have been at first very happy to see the Romans fall on the rear of her barbarians. Alexander indeed concluded an alliance with them. But the hegemony which Tarentum had assumed over the Italiot confederation in the days of Archytas (390–350) was now threatened from without and shaken from within, and she beheld with uneasy jealousy the protectorate which Rome was beginning to exercise in her stead over the Apulians and Lucanians. The foreign princes also, whom she invoked in order to restore the situation, whose principal object was to build a personal empire in the west, could clearly see what an obstacle Roman imperialism was to their ambitions.

By the end of the fourth century, Rome's political horizon had greatly enlarged. Contemporary Greek sources seem to attest the presence of a Roman delegation among the embassies sent to Alexander the Great in 323 by the Etruscans, Lucanians and Bruttians.[319] The renewal of the Carthaginian alliance in 348, the activities of the pirates of Antium, continuing after that town had been reduced to a Roman municipium in 338,[320] and the foundation of the port of Ostia about 335,[321] all show that the destiny of Rome was to lie in future as much at sea as on land. The development of her naval interests around 306–302 is attested by several important diplomatic events: this is the period from which Polybius dates the friendship between Rome and Rhodes, although there was no treaty to formalize it;[322] but the third treaty concluded with Carthage in 306 (which must be the one whose clauses are preserved for us by the Sicilian Philinus in the third century) defines the zones of influence of the two powers, excluding Rome from Sicily and Carthage from Italy.[323] Thus Rome seems to have made Carthage accept 'a kind of Italian Monroe doctrine',[324] reserving for her own enterprises Italy in the old sense of the word, i.e. the peninsula of Bruttium; the boundary-line was fixed through an islet in the Lipari archipelago.[325] This interpretation of Philinus' treaty is confirmed by the agreement reached shortly afterwards (about 302) between Rome and Tarentum (the latter under Cleonymus): Rome undertook not to send her fleet north of the Lacinian promontory, or of Croton.[326] It seems then that there was a triple entente between Rome, Carthage and Tarentum to pursue a common policy against Syracuse under Agathocles.

Among the factors that determined this irresistible southward movement we must assign a large part to the pressure of Oscan elements which Rome had absorbed by annexing Capua and with whose interests she had charged herself. Capua's role in her independence had been as a funnel through which the surplus of a population which was perpetually swollen by Samnite infiltration was poured into southern Italy and Sicily. From the end of the fifth century we find that the Siciliots and Carthaginians have at their service, wandering about the island, bands of Campanian mercenaries.[327] As soon as Rome bore the responsibility for Campanian politics she had necessarily to take over the control of these irregular military units, sometimes secretly encouraging their natural indiscipline. The cape of Bruttium was the assembly point of the Mamertines, who camped there before launching their attack on Messina, where they founded a state (288).[328] But in 282 the garrison set up by Rome at Rhegium bore the name of *legio Campana*;[329] it was not a proper legion, but a sort of free company commanded by a Campanian *condotto*. In 280 it mutinied, massacred the citizens and took over the city which it was supposed to protect, entered into the most friendly relations with the Mamertines of Messina, and in the end was severely punished—although not until 270, having actually received some reinforcements in 278. Nothing could better illustrate the mixture of connivance and disclaimer, planning and laissez-faire that marked Roman imperialism of that period, constantly dragged forward by the machinery of its conquests.

Roman expansion in Magna Graecia is also to be explained by the opportunities afforded by intestine struggles in the cities. In Thurii and Tarentum, as formerly in Capua and Naples, the local aristocracies encouraged Roman intervention not merely to meet the barbarian threat, but to put down democratic movements.[330]

The *casus belli* arose in 282,[331] when Thurii appealed for help not to Tarentum, in whose sphere of influence she was, but to Rome. The Romans freed her from Lucanian pressure, and set up a Roman garrison in the city. Hipponium, Rhegium, Locri and Croton received Roman garrisons about the same time. A fleet of six warships came cruising north of the Lacinian cape, contrary to the agreement of 302, and essayed a demonstration in the gulf of Tarentum. They were given a smart drubbing, some of the ships were sunk, Thurii was retaken and the nobles expelled. Rome now tried to negotiate, but the democrats in Tarentum appealed to Pyrrhus, king of Epirus.

Pyrrhus

Pyrrhus was the last of the mercenary captains to whom Tarentum entrusted her fate.[332] But to the meteor of Epirus himself the dream which he had of uniting under his sceptre the Greek cities and barbarian tribes of southern Italy was only one adventure among many. It consoled him for the loss of Macedonia and was a prelude to his recovery of it; and the careless strokes that staggered the western world were less important in his eyes than those which he dealt to his rivals in Greece proper while pursuing mirages that constantly formed anew. His heroic adventures in Italy have reached us only through a distorting medium in which Ennius and the annalistic tradition have played some part: his elephants may have frightened the legions, but his bravura and his generous chivalry laid their charm on posterity. But his western campaigns ended after six years (280–275) in failure; distracted by too many irreconcilable projects, ill supported by the Italiots, 'sapped by centuries of prosperity' as Lévêque describes them,[333] disheartened by the resistance of the Romans, who pooled all their energies and mobilized their proletariat for the first time, he became in truth the man of 'Pyrrhic victories', victories that were never turned to advantage.

Having landed at Tarentum in May 280 with an expeditionary force including contingents from the Diadochi, he won his first victory in July 280, near Heraclea at the mouth of the Sinni: the legions of the consul P. Valerius Laevinus stood up to the shock of the phalanx, but gave way before the charge of the elephants, and were cut to pieces by the cavalry. Pyrrhus then proposed to march on Rome, following the via Latina as far as Anagni, or perhaps Praeneste. But he went no further: Rome's allies were more loyal than he expected, and his rear was in danger. Also, the conditions of peace which he had put up to the senate through his ambassador Cineas had been rejected.[334] His terms were harsh: in return for freeing his prisoners without ransom, he proposed a treaty of alliance, but demanded restoration of lands annexed from the Samnites, Daunians, Lucanians and Bruttians. This would have put a complete stop to Roman expansion in the south, and would have made all southern Italy a confederation with Tarentum as capital. In the traditional tale, Appius Claudius, old and blind, emerges from his long retirement to carry the rejection of these terms. Pyrrhus withdrew into Campania.

The campaign of 279 was played out in northern Apulia, in Daunia, which Pyrrhus tried to detach from the Roman alliance by besieging the colony of Venusia. A great battle, with even more troops engaged than before, was fought in the summer on the banks of the Aufidus, at Ausculum. It lasted two days, and although the Romans had devised chariots armed with scythes to use against the elephants, in the end they were defeated, but not routed. Later annalists made it an indecisive battle, or even a Roman victory, and concocted the story that one of the consuls, P. Decius Mus, imitated the *devotio* of his father at Sentinum.

After Ausculum Pyrrhus remained quiet for over a year. Various anecdotes claim to fill in this empty period: e.g. the tale of his physician who suggested to the Romans that he poison him—a proposal rejected by C. Fabricius Luscinus (cos. 278) with all the indignation of an antique Roman. A more credible story is that Cineas went as ambassador again with the same terms, and that his diplomacy was as fruitless as the year before. This time it was Carthage that intervened; with 120 Punic keels riding in the harbour of Ostia, Mago persuaded the senate not to make a separate peace. This was the fourth treaty between Rome and Carthage: by it the two cities undertook not to make a written agreement with Pyrrhus other than jointly, and Carthage promised Rome ships and money. She was trying to keep Pyrrhus in Italy, having already got wind of his plans for a Sicilian campaign.

The two years (September 278 to the autumn of 276) which Pyrrhus spent in the island began, as before, with brilliant promise that was after-wards bitterly disappointed. The Campanians of Rhegium and the Mamer-tines of Messina, standing for Roman interests in the Narrows, opposed his landing; he outflanked them by sailing for Taormina. His mere arrival made the Carthaginian fleet raise the siege of Syracuse; the normally squabbling Siciliots hailed him as king and formed a holy alliance. In 277 he took a triumphal promenade, easily freeing the Greek cities and conquering the Carthaginian province. The Carthaginians—without a thought apparently for their Roman allies—sued for peace: they would pay a war indemnity, provide ships to take the expeditionary force home, but would keep Lilybaeum, the only stronghold that had not been reduced. Pyrrhus refused, but gave up his design on Lilybaeum after a siege of two months (autumn 277).

The next year he withdrew to Syracuse and indulged himself in the dream of carrying the war into Africa, as Agathocles had done. The preparations for this new adventure, the need to commandeer equipment, and the steps that he took to overcome Siciliot resistance won him the name of tyrant. He left Sicily in the autumn of 276, suffered a naval defeat in the straits, where the Syracusan fleet was sunk, and landed at Locri, where he plundered the temple of Persephone. Meantime an attempt upon the Campanians of Rhegium reinforced by the Mamertines of Messina had cost him heavy losses.

Rome had spent the two years principally in rebuilding her armies. In 275 Pyrrhus re-opened hostilities: coming up from Apulia through Samnium, along what was to be the prolongation of the via Appia, he gave battle to the consul Manius Curius Dentatus in mountainous country, terrain in which he could not deploy his heavy armaments, and this caused his defeat. Curius held a triumph *de Samnitibus et rege Pyrrho*. A second battle, in which the other consul, L. Cornelius Lentulus, won the day, beating the Samnites and Lucanians, was fought in the *Campi Arusini*, which some place in Lucania, some near Beneventum. In autumn of the same year Pyrrhus left for Epirus, whither a new destiny summoned him; but he did not wholly abandon Italy: he left at Tarentum his son Helenus and his principal lieutenant Milo.

The Romans, unlike the Italiot Greeks, who lacked moral fibre, had shown an unflinching tenacity, mounted a superhuman war effort, learned from their foe the means to defeat him, adopted his camps as the model for their own, invented chariots to fight against his elephants. When the trial was over, Magna Graecia was to be once and for all subject to Rome.

A recent discovery[335] lets us see how one of her cities, Locri, was affected. The victory of Heraclea had driven out the Roman garrison from Locri, as from all the Ionian coast. Since the archives of the temple of Zeus were found, we know 27 bronze tablets which register year by year the loans approved by the temple to the city to meet expenses incurred in the public cause, inter alia the expense of the war-levy imposed by Pyrrhus during the six years of his occupation (280–275). We recall that on his return from Sicily in the autumn of 276 he laid violent hands on the treasures of the temple of Persephone. Pyrrhus' departure was the sign for a request to the Romans to return: numismatics here offers a valuable testimony in the form of a silver stater representing Rome seated, crowned by Pistis. Now Pistis here is not a Greek divinity, but the translation of the Roman *fides*, faithfulness. Whether spontaneous or dictated, this tribute in any case shows that Rome sought to place her conquest in a context of ethical ideals.

After Locri and the other cities of Magna Graecia had fallen, Tarentum fell too in her turn, defended to the last by Milo against the Romans in concert with the Tarentine aristocrats who were established around the city. In 273 came a triumph over the Lucanians, Samnites and Bruttians: in this year the Latin colony of Paestum (Posidonia) was founded. In 272 came a double triumph over the barbarians, with the Tarentines now added. Tarentum was accorded the status of *civitas foederata*, kept its administrative autonomy, but lost its political independence, and was obliged, like Naples, to furnish Rome with ships and equipment in time of war.[336]

Rome a Mediterranean power

By defeating Pyrrhus the Romans made a great impression throughout the Greek world; there is no reason to doubt the truth of the story that in 273 Ptolemy Philadelphus, an ally of Pyrrhus, sent ambassadors laden with gifts to Rome: he sent such embassies even to Hindu princes.[337] This fact-finding mission, even if it did not lead to the signing of any actual treaty, as Livy says it did,[338] shows astonishment and curiosity at the progress of this new power. At the same time Lycophron, librarian to Ptolemy and the adoptive son of Lycus of Rhegium, made his Cassandra prophesy the supremacy of Rome by land and sea after the war with Pyrrhus was over.[339] Still more significant, however, is the interest taken in the rising star by the Sicilian Timaeus of Tauromenium: he, from his exile in Athens, was the first to turn his attention determinedly to the political forces that were arising in the west and to seek detailed information on Roman civilization.[340] He knew the tradition of the Trojan origin of the Romans, mentioned the ritual of the October Horse, and described the Penates of Lavinium. Above all, he was aware of this great historical fact, until then seen by no one, that by her victory over Pyrrhus Rome was going to take the place of the Greeks in the struggles which they had kept up against Carthage for three centuries over his native Sicily. With this in mind he put forward a significant synchronism between the foundation dates of the two cities, and declared (Heaven knows by what reckoning, says Dionysius of Halicarnassus)[341] that Rome was founded in the same year as Carthage, in 814; to his big *History of Sicily* he added a monograph on *The War with Pyrrhus*, which he carried down to 264, the year when the First Punic War broke out.[342]

Livy in his turn was to observe[343] that a series of chain-reactions, starting from Roman intervention in Capua, led successively to the Samnite wars, the war with Pyrrhus, and the Punic wars. We have already said that Rome, in taking over responsibility for governing Campania, was insensibly led to realize those ambitions which were driving her new subjects to expand into southern Italy and Sicily. We have seen what part the Campanians of Rhegium and the Mamertines of Messina played in the war against Pyrrhus: the former were made use of for a dozen years, and finally called sharply to order in 270; it was in defence of the latter, threatened by Syracuse and defended by Carthage, that Rome sent forces into Sicily in 264, in defiance of the treaty of 306. The truth is that the Oscan nobility, allied with the declining Roman families, was wielding an increasing power in the senate and tending to Italianize Roman policy more and more.[344] At the moment when the First Punic War was about to flare up, the Fasti show a sudden eclipse of the Fabii, whose faces had always been turned towards Etruria, and the rise of gentes coming originally from Campania, especially the Atilii with their cognomina Caleni, Caiatini, Serrani or Sarani, showing that they came from Cales, Caiatia and the Sarno valley. The Atilii held the consulate seven times between 267 and 245 and three years running from 258 to 256. The First Punic War was to be their war; and once engaged against Carthage in Sicily, they could not help taking up again, under C. Atilius Regulus, consul in 257, the plan conceived in 310 by Agathocles,

H

tyrant of Syracuse and toyed with in 276 by Pyrrhus, 'king of Sicily'—namely to carry the war to Africa. Regulus' expedition in 265–255, carried through in the teeth of conservative opinion, miscarried. But Scipio Africanus was to renew it successfully in 205, despite all the protests of a Fabius Cunctator, and thus realize the dream long dreamed by Sicilians and Campanians.

E   Conclusion: Rome at the beginning of the third century

The first three decades of the third century, a period when from Sentinum to Tarentum through the Pyrrhic war all the nation's energies were flung into a purely military effort, see no addition—except the *lex Hortensia de plebiscitis* of 287[345]—to the previous advances of democracy. All magistracies were now accessible to plebeians. The political problem might be reckoned as solved, even if the social problem, raised by the proposals of Appius Claudius, remained blocked by the reaction of Q. Fabius Rullianus which stuffed all the freedmen and *humiles* into the four urban tribes.[346] The Fabii Maximi, in full command of the senate, ensured by their repeated consulates the success of their liberal-conservative policy:[347] Q. Fabius Maximus Rullianus was consul again in 297 and 295, his son Q. Fabius Maximus Gurges in 292, 276, 265; this last was the first of 62 years that Q. Fabius Maximus Verrucosus was to pass as augur—the future Fabius Cunctator of the Hannibalic war. What they stood for was the unfailing hegemony of the *nobilitas*.[348] Under their patronage 'new men' made their way into the ruling class, often hailing from Italian towns which were being assimilated—Sabines like Manius Curius Dentatus, Campanians like the Atilii, coming after the Decii Mures, Etruscans like the Volumnii and Ogulnii.[349]

Roman civilization, thus suddenly pushed into a wider world, underwent a revival of Greek influence and a profound enrichment of art and religion. The ideology of Victory,[350] which had been spread throughout the Hellenistic world by the deification of the invincible Alexander, took possession of Rome at the moment when she devoted herself to the tasks of conquest: a temple was vowed to Bellona Victrix in 296, to Jupiter Victor in 295, to Victoria on the Palatine in 294. The Hercules of travellers and tradesmen became the *Hercules Magnus*, *Hercules Victor* of the triumphant generals.

In this transformation of religion Etruria seems to have been an especially important intermediary, as she had been in the sixth century—witness the part played by the brothers Q. and Cn. Ogulnius, who probably came from Clusium.[351] As tribunes of the plebs in 300 they had carried a law that threw open the conservative priesthoods—the pontificate and augurate— to plebeians; in each college, previously consisting of four members, they set up new posts (four in one, five in the other) reserved for plebeians.[352] Roman religion now accepted more readily foreign, even exotic, divinities. In 292 Q. Ogulnius went to Epidaurus heading a ten-man legation to bring back the serpent of Aesculapius; the god then had a sanctuary on the *insula Tiberina* where incubation was practised: its priests were Rome's first physicians.[353] In 273 Ogulnius was sent on an embassy with Q. Fabius Gurges to the court of Ptolemy Philadelphus in Alexandria. Ultimately he was to attain the highest magistracies—the consulate in 269 and dictatorship for the celebration of the *feriae Latinae* in 257.

From the time when they were aediles together in 296, the Ogulnii had had occasion to beautify the city in ways which show the spirit that animated Rome at the moment when, even in the conflict, she could see wider horizons opening:[354] they did not merely restore and embellish the Capitol, with a bronze doorsill, silver vases adorning three consecrated tables in the *cella*, and a terracotta acroterion representing Jupiter in a quadriga, replacing the one which Tarquinius Superbus had put on top of the pediment; not only did they pave the via Appia (recently laid out by Ap. Claudius) and provide it with sidewalks where it left the porta Capena; above all these they set up in the Forum, near the Ruminal figtree, a bronze group representing the she-wolf and the twins.[355] This is not the celebrated Capitoline wolf that one can admire today in the Palazzo dei Conservatori: that is the work of a sculptor from Vulci in the first half of the fifth century.[356] The reproduction of it in a new style which was made in 296 showed a Rome at once looking back to her Etruscan past and becoming aware of her new greatness. There is a representation of it on the reverse of a didrachm struck in 269, while Q. Ogulnius himself was consul: this is the first truly Roman coin to issue from the mints which had recently been set up.

It is in fact to this period—the first thirty years of the third century— that we must assign the beginnings of Roman coinage. The creation of a currency in itself shows the accelerating economic development of Rome, the complexity of the interests in which she was involved, and her closer and closer contacts with the world of Magna Graecia, Carthage, and Ptolemaic Egypt.

The history of Roman coinage was brought in ancient times within a systematic chronology, set out most fully in Pliny:[357] he sets out its successive stages across the centuries—at first values were reckoned in heads of cattle (*pecunia*), and the only form of money known was crude ingots of bronze (*aes rude*). Servius Tullius was the first to put a mark on them, e.g. a representation of an ox, recalling the first meaning of *pecunia*: this was *aes signatum*. The first silver coinage was not struck until the consulate of Q. Ogulnius and C. Fabius (269) and was in the shape of a denarius worth ten asses of bronze.

From 1860 onwards a hypothesis of Mommsen's was accepted as proven truth:[358] it accepted the date 269 for the introduction of the denarius, but admitted that 70 years earlier, about 340, Rome had called on Campanian mints to issue the didrachms bearing the legend *Romano* (= *Romanom*, i.e. *Romanorum*), later *Roma*, and at the same time some heavy bronze pieces (*aes grave*).

In our time this theory has been vigorously criticized: H. Mattingley and his fellow workers at the British Museum since 1924 have been bold enough to reject the Plinian date for the denarius;[359] the latest arguments point to its being a creation of the Second Punic War (214).[360] At the same time it was shown that the previous didrachms and aes grave, with a similar scaling-down of the chronology, only came out in the war with Pyrrhus.

This new dating, as now established in R. Thomsen's synthesis,[361] does not rest only on the establishment of the *triumviri monetales* in 289,[362] nor on the new purpose to which the temple of Juno Moneta seems to have been put during the Pyrrhic war,[363] but on a full and careful examination of weights and types: the first issue of didrachms, with a horse's head on the reverse in imitation of Carthaginian money, and with the head of Mars on the obverse, inspired by that of Metapontum, must be contemporary with the treaty of 279 between Rome and Carthage. This piece was widely imitated by the Latin colonies, notably by Cosa after its foundation in 273.[364] The third issue, with Hercules and the wolf suckling the twins, comes from the consulate of Q. Ogulnius in 269.[365] The fourth, with the head of Rome as a goddess and with Victory crowning a palm, about 264, shows alphabetical markings which relate it to the coinage of Arsinoe in Egypt.[366] It is also a considerable advance in scholarship to have proved that the aes grave, which begins with a Janus-Mercury series and continues with Apollo and the Dioscuri, and even the *aes signatum*, the symbols on which are also of Hellenistic style, were contemporary with the first Roman didrachms.[367] As for the latter, we can no longer doubt that it was the financial problems posed by the war with Pyrrhus that made the Romans first strike coins in silver; it was the influence of Magna Graecia that made Rome mint another metal than bronze; and it was her alliance with Carthage, and probably the supply by her ally of the metal needed, that decided the choice of her most significant reverse types. But the end of the Tarentine war in 272 did not end a process which was henceforth irreversible. The limits of this study do not allow us to trace the sequel: it is not until about 235 that we see appearing, on the reverse of the *as*, the prow which symbolizes Roman mastery of the seas.[368] But the issues from 289 to 264 already show her decisive steps forward, her increasing consciousness of her own ambitions, her definitive achievement of great-power status in the Mediterranean, and her complete transformation from the little farming town that she had long been into a city of capitalists open to every current of Hellenistic economics.

Part Two

Research: Its Problems and Directions

1 'Anti-Invasionism' and its Limits

It is a very good thing that the scholarship of our day, in reconstructing the way in which civilization arose in Italy, emancipated itself from 'Kossinna's Law', which proclaimed as recently as 1928 that 'any distinct cultural province, no matter how limited, bears witness to a distinct race',[1] which can be identified each time with a people whose name history has preserved. A principle much more comfortable to the nature of things is that laid down by V. Gordon Childe, that 'culture and race do not coincide'[2]— we should perhaps add: 'not necessarily'. This view gives some explanation of the endless and inextricable complexity of the archaeological and linguistic data from which we start in our desperate struggles to retrace the way in which Italy was peopled.

It was also a good thing to protest against the extremism of those nineteenth-century myths, haunted by the romantic dream of the *Völkerwanderungen*,[3] which were fain to represent the peopling of Italy as a series of great invasions, in which a flood of blond barbarians, attracted by the South, poured in and submerged the shores of the Mediterranean. 'Those who lived through the dark days of invasion,' writes C. Courtois, 'in the early years of the fifth century—the invasion of 406 and the Gothic invasion—felt as if something monstrous were happening which confounded them by its very dimensions. They spoke in terms of flood or fire.'[4] Until very recently there was a tendency to paint the arrival of the Indo-Europeans in these apocalyptic colours, like a tidal wave striking again and again.

The reaction came about principally in Italy, between the two wars, when prehistorians and archaeologists like U. Rellini and G. Patroni began to claim that indigenous peoples had played, in the rise of the cultures of Italy, a part which had not been adequately recognized, and to reduce to a minimum the part played by intervention from outside, finally denying that there had been any. Their first attack was on the sacred dogma announced by L. Pigorini, that all Italian protohistory was to be explained by the invasion of the terramara peoples and their successors from one end of Italy to the other. U. Rellini in 1929 had already rejected the theory except for supposing that '*small nuclei* arrived, bringing with them the practice of cremation and the elements of the Indo-European language: a human yeast, which modified the evolution of native culture *in the Po valley* and explains the rise of a new civilization'.[5] But against this narrowly regional phenomenon, he reported a number of bronze-age settlements from Basilicata to the Salerno region, the Abruzzi, the Marches and the Campagna, forming an unbroken and flourishing chain; these settlements he would only venture to describe as *extra-terramaricole*,[6] but for all that they were to take the foreground in the reconstruction of Italian origins. Shortly afterwards, as Pigorini's theory crumbled and the complexity of the problems became more apparent, G. Patroni went to extremes in his rejection of 'invasionism' in all its forms. It was in this spirit that he wrote in 1939, analysing the Indo-Europeanizing of Italy: 'The spread of Indo-European languages in central and southern Italy came about not through invasion by peoples with their political institutions already formed, but through exchange and imitation and by slow but very long infiltration of individuals—among these, I think, we may count women especially, since pottery, which is a female art, attests the introduction of new elements.'[7]

Patroni went on to say: 'The Indo-Europeanizing of Italy goes back to the late neolithic; it took place across the Adriatic (never in history has there been so much sailing as then from one shore of the Adriatic to the other). One of the vehicles of such a change of language must have been the arrival of women from the other shore, fetched over by the Italic peoples possibly as slaves, more likely as wives, for their proficiency in domestic skills: in prehistory and among savage peoples the making of pots is a task for women, and in fact the neolithic pottery of central Italy is marked by themes and techniques which have their centre of diffusion in the Balkan and neighbouring Aegean areas.'[8]

Finally, to define more closely the manner of diffusion (drop by drop, as it were) of Indo-European languages in the very bosom of the native peoples of Italy, he had recourse to an idea which found much acceptance, that of 'linguistic leavens': 'Where the Romance languages are concerned, there is one fact that the linguistic atlases teach us—that the language of a region is always the language of its most important place. Language is not inherited by blood; it is a social phenomenon, arising from exchanges and contacts which give rise to imitation by others of those speakers of the language who enjoy the greatest prestige . . . But I attach extreme importance (much more than to those just named) to persons who are striving to accomplish projects of their own: we may assert that the linguistic leaven works most strongly in those whose own interest is most concerned . . . The market that sprang up around a ship putting in to our Adriatic coast (and there were ships landing every day for thousands of years) was one of these key areas. We certainly had ships going to the other shore, but there must have been fewer of them, and contacts of this sort were not so effective linguistically.'[9]

It was in this peaceful, almost idyllic, atmosphere (for such a picture as this cannot but call to mind the 'noble savage' of the eighteenth century and Chateaubriand's Natchez Indians) that the Indo-Europeanizing of Italy took place over long centuries: all violence is ruled out; so is all entry on the scene (even in amity) of any passably well equipped ethnic group. And one must not suppose that this view appealed to the fancy only of Patroni himself. It turns up in different forms at the basis of the thinking of most of the linguists and prehistorians of our day: witness E. Pulgram, who in 1958 saw the arrival of the peoples (or rather individuals) who brought the Indo-European languages into Italy as resembling the peopling of the United States in the nineteenth century: 'The movement which then took place may be compared to the displacement of European emigrants (as individuals or as national groups) in the settlements of the New World. The first comers did not instal themselves solidly on the Atlantic coast, to be followed by ever new arrivals going ever farther west, as in a kind of leapfrog. Nor is it correct to say that the first emigrants, although they naturally settled on the eastern seaboard, were gradually pushed further and further west by later arrivals from Europe: such would be a migration by sustained frontal pressure. These two main types of movement did take place separately, but more often simultaneously in a bewildering variety of mixtures and complications. In sum, any given individual or group of individuals in the U.S.A. cannot be assigned to a particular period or type of emigration if we only base ourselves on his final domicile. In the same way it might happen that the direct descendant of a citizen of Homer's Troy could find himself set up as a master blacksmith in a Villanovan village on what was to be the Palatine at Rome. But another dweller on the same site, sharing the same culture, might look to southern Austria or to Villanovan Bologna for his fore-elders. A third might be a direct descendant of neolithic natives. The fact that all three were members of the same cultural group and spoke the same language at a given period (e.g. 700 B.C.) does not mean that they had a common ethnic origin.'[10]

It fell to M. Pallottino, in the report that he presented to the International Congress of Historical Sciences in 1955, under the title *The historical origins of the Italic peoples*, to sum up the new trends in a formula giving exactly their meaning and application. Taking care to avoid the over-simplification into which 'invasionists' and 'indigenists' were alike hurried by their passionate polemic,[11] and seeing how the notion of race had become atomized, and how the all too rigid systems which had previously been advanced in order to explain a people's present by its past had hopelessly foundered, he concluded that it was more profitable to study how peoples had achieved their unity, starting from heterogeneous elements. This reversal of viewpoint made the *ethnos* appear as a phenomenon of long and slow working-out, in which individuals or groups of individuals, coming from different places, had progressively crystallized around urban centres and organizations that bound them together. Nationhood was something after arrival, not before departure. In sum, it was a matter of replacing, where the psychology and methodology of research were involved, 'an abstract concept of *derivation* by a concrete concept of *formation*'.[12]

As we said at the outset, it was salutary to react against the excesses of 'invasionism'—not only against the general notion of human avalanches overwhelming all in their path, but especially against the illusion that invading peoples came in readymade, with ways of thought that could not be effaced, with a baggage-train of language and culture not to be altered, with politics and religion fully fledged. The new approach now opened to researchers was fertile in other ways too, for it obliged them to take account of characters acquired on the spot, of the changes due to the dwelling-place itself, to the neighbourhood, to the accidental and unforeseen development, through the environment, of one or other inherited quality. Our ideas were vastly enriched by the views already advanced by Patroni (trading ships as key points) and steadily maintained by Pallottino concerning the attraction exerted on emigrants by regions either more developed economically or more civilized politically (e.g. under Hellenic influence)—regions into which we still find them coalescing in the historical period (the Campanians, Lucanians, etc.).[13] This being granted, it is still true that, looking now only to the factors of *formation*, if we want to hold both ends of the chain, we shall speedily have occasion to ask whether we can wholly break with the factors of *derivation*.

It is obvious to start with that the idyllic pictures formerly beloved of indigenists have to be taken with a grain of salt. The modern anti-invasionists suppose that Italian culture began with a kind of golden age like that of the fable, where people in general were settled, peacefully exchanging the products of their industry, welcoming their guests from abroad as benignly as Evander welcomed Aeneas when he landed on the bank of the Tiber. Now in fact, when the fogs of prehistory or protohistory begin to thin out, what we descry in the half-light of the sixth, fifth and fourth centuries is not indeed the destructive onrush of Huns or Vandals, but movements (still disquieting enough) of bands in search of their place in the sun; and instead of being a novelty, such movements seem to have been rather the tail end of interminable marching columns moving from time immemorial. The Roman annalists represent the Sabine Atta Clausus (the ancestor of the Claudii) as coming down in the late sixth century from his native hills with 5000 men of military age to demand from Rome lands and admission to the senate.[14] Less than a century later, some Samnites turned up in the Campanian plain, offering their muscles as tillers of the soil to the Etruscans of Capua; then they infiltrated gradually into the northern part of the city and won citizens' rights: all this took place slowly, without fuss, by negotiations and agreements that seemed to have been freely concluded, but were in fact caused by irresistible pressure.[15] The new colonists, as Livy calls them, were happier if everything went off without a blow being struck; they did not enjoy violence for its own sake, and only had recourse to it as late as possible, in a night of massacre whose horrors were repeated in the end in all the towns where their countrymen took over similarly—Cumae, Naples, Paestum, Messina, Rhegium.[16] Their conscience already felt the need of some moral justification: the Mamertines who attacked Messina in 288 pretended to have come of their own free will to help the city free itself from the foreign yoke. In general they tied up their projects of conquest with a religious rite that covered up the sordid reality: when labouring under famine or pestilence, their forebears had conceived themselves instructed by an oracle to dedicate to Mars and drive out the youth of their tribe (*ver sacrum*); these, following in the footsteps of a bull, went off into the unknown to look for a new country.[17] We may be sure that there were plenty of these 'sacred springs' in Italy's immemorial past before they reached the pages of history, and to exclude them from our picture of prehistory or protohistory would be even more of a misrepresentation than to deny the peaceable contacts, the trading, the fairs and markets, and the ships that sailed peaceably to and fro across the Adriatic.

The fact is that the indigenist position is untenable, and those who are ever tempted to adopt it nearly always depart from it in the end.[18] The problem is a quantitative one: somewhere between invasions en masse and individual immigration we should like to be able to estimate the effective numbers in those 'small nuclei' that contemporary historians descry stirring and moving about in Italy from neolithic times onward. We may recall, as some indication, that in the historical period the Sabines under Atta Clausus numbered 5000 men in the traditional account,[19] and that the so-called legio Campana that seized Rhegium in 280 amounted to 1200.[20] Above all it would be valuable to know how far these groups, amid all their travels and vicissitudes, were capable of remaining faithful to any very ancient traditions.

I suppose that everyone will readily accept the picture that P. de Francisci draws of these obscure movements in his admirable book *Primordia Civitatis*: 'For at least forty centuries the peninsula witnessed a constant arrival and intermingling of currents of immigration which we should not envisage (as has long been the custom) as mass invasions by peoples who already had a rudimentary organization, but rather as successive and gradual displacements of groups infiltrating where the land was empty or sparsely populated, establishing themselves next door to the local people and being absorbed into them wholly or partly, sometimes adopting the local civilization, sometimes imposing their own, in a continuous action and reaction which gave rise (Latium is a typical example) to marginal civilization which not only in language, but in culture and above all in religion, bear the marks of a long and complex evolution. The population-groups representing these marginal composite civilizations are found, when the protohistoric period begins, still in a fluid state; so much so that (taking Rome as an illustration) right up to the fifth century we witness a continuous arrival of new elements—new both demographically and culturally.'[21]

Making use of recent archaeological discoveries together with the concepts of primitive Roman law, de Francisci has claimed that in the hut-villages of the Palatine, which have only lately been brought to light, we possess the habitat of some of these groups which had come to the end of their wanderings, and at the same time the concrete expression of those primary social formations which gradually, by a sort of coagulative process, gave rise to the Roman state—namely, the families.

Each of the huts on the General and Palatine is a *domus*, the seat of the basic family group; a collection of them makes a *vicus*, a village or hamlet; the *pagus* is the zone 'where the pastoral or agricultural work of the *vicus* is done'.

De Francisci has also given us a very strict definition of the *familia*, based on the concept of *parentes*:[22] legal and inscriptional texts prove that the worship of the latter (*parentatio*) which was celebrated by the *paterfamilias* within the house was limited to three generations—the father, grandfather, and great-grandfather. This view is strengthened by the extent of the group of *agnates*, which in ancient usage went no further in the collateral line than the sixth degree, embracing the *consobrini* (cousins in the fourth degree) and *sobrini* (cousins in the sixth degree).

A family of this type, with at its head the *proavus* exercising the *patria potestas* in its well-known rigour on three generations, was the basic unit of the village and the building block of future political organizations. It is obvious that the notion held by the Italian jurist approaches closely to that of the American linguistic scholar E. Pulgram, when he represented a family from Troy, another from central Europe, and a third that had always dwelt in the same place, living together as neighbours on the Palatine.

But the consequences to which we are led if we have to accept this view are equally obvious. 'On the death of the *proavus*, the original group splits up into as many families as there were sons, and each of these duly takes up the functions of a *paterfamilias*.'[23] Now since the cult of the *parentes* does not go back beyond the great-grandfather (*habeas propitios deos tuos tres*, says a colourful epitaph in CIL IV, 1679), it follows that the *memory* of a family, being constantly borne away in an ever-flowing stream of evolution, could last only three generations, after which its traditions sank irrecoverably into the dark—unless there was a wider organization than the family to keep these traditions alive.

This wider organization was, above all things, the *gens*. It has to be agreed that in a view that is too much open to 'factors of formation', like that of de Francisci, the gens is an entity beset with confusion and contradiction.[24] On the one hand it arises from the solidarity created between family groups who get their living from the same pagus; under the pressure of the same economic realities these groups undergo a sort of natural 'polymerization' and give rise to a group of higher order; but on the other hand it arises from a community of name (the *gentilicium*), which presupposes descent from the same remote *princeps gentis*,[25] and from common participation in various *sacra gentilicia*,[26] as for example the worship of the Sun in the Aurelia gens, and in certain specific mores, like that which forbade the women of the Quintia gens to wear articles of gold.[27] Now all this shows ties which could not have been formed on the spot by mere coexistence but go back to a more ancient heritage. Thus, going back on his previous denials, de Francisci is compelled to admit some element of kinship at the origin of the gens, or even, with F. de Martino, the working of the racial factor:[28] 'The formation of the *gentes* cannot be reckoned as a phenomenon that took place on the soil of Rome, but rather as the end of a process which went on in the phases during which the groups were still in movement, during the periods when they stayed in one place.'[29]

In this same chapter of *Primordia Civitatis* some especially remarkable pages are devoted to the break-up of gentes like the Mamilii and Julii, which in the full light of history show a tendency to fragmentation and diaspora. But this break-up had begun long before those who were ultimately to settle at Rome had reached their goal. The immigrating peoples had made various halts on their way, in hut villages 'where naturally they ordered themselves in families, groups of families, and what we call *gentes*'. Then, when the time came to move again, 'the *gentes* were not always able to maintain their unity, and it might come about that they broke up into smaller groups'.[30] In certain cases this might take on the aspect of a *ver sacrum*.

We have analysed de Francisci's theories in detail, because they show how a study deliberately turned towards 'the concrete concept of formation' is always at some point compelled to turn back towards elements of tradition at least, if not of derivation. The gens that he claims to have defined is a Janus-like figure, with one face turned backwards towards the past.

This conception is in some respects akin to that which many jurists, both ancient and modern, had sustained under the name of the 'patriarchal theory'—among others F. de Martino, who at the outset of his *Storia della Costituzione Romana* does not shrink from writing: 'The popular community from which Rome took its origins derived from that branch of the Indo-Europeans which . . .' How *derived*? Via a great many contacts, with much crossing and overlaying of influences which presumably altered it profoundly, but still leaving the possibility—this being the point that we wished to arrive at—of some very ancient inheritances. For my part, I suspect that this transmission took place within the gentes: de Martino has very well observed how their decay, which went on steadily throughout the Etruscan kingdom and the republic,[31] conferred on the familiae powers which the gentes had perforce to abandon. 'In the historical period the gens was' [we may say, 'was already'] 'only a wreck of what it had once been.'[32]

I also believe that these *gentes*, the inhabitants of the *vici*, were further mutually connected into larger ethnic units, like those of which coherent vestiges have been pointed out in Rome's first beginnings by B. Paradisi[33] and U. Coli.[34] One is surprised to find de Francisci, in his determination to deny all importance and even existence to what he contemptuously labels 'conglomerates', resorting to rather feeble arguments: the *populi Albenses* who met yearly at Monte Cavo to celebrate the festival which was to be the *Feriae Latinae* throughout Rome's history, were in his view 'neither states nor federations of states, but religious associations with worship as their sole end'.[35] It was only later, he declares, that political ties were added to religious ones. But one cannot suppose that religious ties—for example that one which gave the right of *carnem petere* at a common sacrifice only to the members of the Latin League[36]—were not even more deeply inscribed than those of politics in the decrees of a past which admitted neither improvisation nor innovation. Here is what seemed to me necessary to underline. We have here religious bonds of unity, and political bonds: the former are 'elements of derivation', or at all events, of tradition, the latter 'elements of formation', and a complete picture of the origins dare not omit either the former or the latter. Rome recreated her destiny on the seven hills, but it is possible, indeed necessary to affirm that on her way thither she had not wholly dissipated her Indo-European inheritance.

2 The Problem of Etruscan Origins

The problem of Etruscan origins is today still unsolved; that is why I have taken it out from the general body of the work to present it here as precisely as possible, tracing the lines along which it seems to be approaching a solution. We are now past the stage of diametrically opposed assertions, irreconcilable statements of opposites. On the one hand it is admitted that if there was some immigration from the east, it was the work only of a dynamic minority destined to work like yeast in raising the dough of the indigenous cultures; on the other, one has to recognize that the western Mediterranean, from the Mycenaean period on, was constantly furrowed by ships bearing traders and, if necessary, colonists. The question is one of quantity; the essential fact is that in the iron age, between the Tiber and Arno, there was an intimate mingling of peoples of various provenances, their interpenetration producing the Etruscans of history.

Much more categorical positions were taken up by the ancients and, until quite recently, by modern writers. Herodotus tells us that in the thirteenth century before our era some Lydians led by a son of Atys called Tyrrhenos or Tyrsenos—*Tyrrhenoi* or *Tyrsenoi* is the Greek for 'Etruscans'— emigrated to Italy, where they founded their cities.[37] Contrariwise, Dionysius of Halicarnassus avers that the Etruscans, resembling no other people either in language or in manners, were the aboriginal inhabitants.[38]

The theory that the Etruscans came from the east has been the ruling one in our day, and has been sustained with great vigour by P. Ducati, among others, in his *Le problème Etrusque*.[39] And all the cultural facts, culled mainly from archaeology and the history of religion, have been assembled and analysed by A. Piganiol in an essay under the significant title, *Les Étrusques, peuple d'Orient*.[40] 'If we were only permitted one phrase,' says Piganiol, 'in which to describe Etruria, we should have to content ourselves with saying that it is like a fragment of Babylonia in Italy.' And indeed no one will deny that from 700 onwards, when the Etruscans take on a form and figure, their civilization appears strikingly oriental. Their affinities with the east have long been underlined by various features, among them divination by hepatoscopy (examination of the livers of victims) practised both by them and by the Babylonians: the bronze liver found at Piacenza, in some respects similar to the terracotta livers of Marisur on the Euphrates and of Ugarit in Syria is the best-known indication.[41] Modern excavation has continued to suggest further parallels. At Gordion in Phrygia large cauldrons of bronze have been found, which have around their wide opening appliqués representing Sirens, manufactured in Armenia in the kingdom of Urartu; other examples are known from Praeneste and Vetulonia.[42] A synagogue has been found at Sardis in Lydia, dating from the third century of our era, which shows the re-use of bas-reliefs which once decorated an archaic altar of Cybele, in a style reminiscent of the bronze plaques of the chariot from Castel San Marino or those of the Loeb tripod.[43] Along the Arno, notably at Quinto Fiorentino, tombs have been excavated with a tholos and approach-corridor recalling those of Mycenae.[44] In a different intellectual context we may recall, as one of the major arguments for the eastern origin of the Etruscans, the inscription found in 1885 on Lemnos in the northern Aegean, which, if it is not Etruscan, is at all events the most closely resembling Etruscan of anything that has been found outside Italy.[45]

If asked to define more closely the dates and circumstances of the migration, the partisans of this theory place it in the early seventh century and connect it with the changes of state in Asia Minor produced by the invasion of the Cimmerians and Scythians;[46] they see it as analogous to the Norman invasions.[47] But they do not exclude the possibility that the trail may have been blazed by earlier waves of migration—the Pelasgi in the eighth century and, yet earlier, some of the people called *Tursha* (Tyrsenoi?), who figure along with the *Shardana* (Sardinians?) among the 'peoples of the sea' in Egyptian records.

By way of reaction against the excesses of the traditional theory of an eastern origin, the indigenist theory has been vigorously supported since the war in some of the works of M. Pallottino, especially in a book entitled *L'origine degli Etruschi*[48] which undertakes a methodical refutation of the arguments brought forward. Furthermore—here he soon received the support of F. Altheim in his *Der Ursprung der Etrusker*,[49]—Pallottino thought that it was high time that historians abandoned the sterile search for 'factors of derivation', and set about the more fruitful pursuit of 'factors of formation'.[50] The Etruscans, whatever may have been the various racial elements in their composition as a people, had no true historical existence except in Etruria, where those elements, grappling in a new geographical location with new social and economic problems, created together a political entity radically different from any of the ingredients, of whatever place or time. 'Culture and race do not coincide.' The cultural facts which seem to indicate the effective identity of the Etruscans with some eastern peoples are to be accounted for by commercial imports and the prestige which a higher culture exercised over a lower, causing imitation and assimilation. Could we not show by similar arguments that Roman civilization results from an invasion of Italy by the Greeks? For Pallottino the decisive argument is the unbroken continuity by which, in Etruria, we pass from the earliest Villanovan culture to the full flower of Etruscan civilization in the same cities and the same cemeteries. These same Villanovans, established from the tenth century in sites where the Etruscans were to have their classical metropolitan centres—Veii, Tarquinia, Vetulonia, Volsinii, or at least important towns such as Bisenzio and Marsiliana, were to transform themselves in the seventh century, by a native development not implying any massive influx of foreigners, into the Etruscans of the orientalizing phase. The Villanovans are no more than proto-Etruscans, the Etruscans no more than civilized Villanovans. The rise of Etruscan power will then have been only the result of their growing suddenly and prodigiously rich by the vigorous commercial exploitation of the copper and iron mines of Elba and the opposite coast. These riches came to light very abruptly, and the lure of them explains to some degree the outburst of Greek colonizing activity at that time, if it is true that the motive which led the Chalcidians about 770 to settle on Ischia and a little later at Cumae was the hunt for metals.[51] Now it is precisely at this period that we find the first Villanovan cemeteries at Capua: Capua was to become an Etruscan city, but the three phases which the excavators have distinguished have an unbroken development from the middle of the eighth to the end of the sixth century, from Villanovan to Etruscan properly so called.[52] In Campania, just as in Etruria, the cultural continuity leads us to the same conclusion.

Nevertheless, the latest indications are that the unabashed enunciation of opposites is no longer felt by all to be the best way of dealing with the impasse, and that a new and more qualified examination of the data seems to be under way in several areas of research; it does not hope at once to achieve a definitive solution—this it leaves for a future less cluttered with conjectures—but allows us perhaps to see in what sense the question can be more clearly apprehended.

We must say at once that these studies (among which the contributions of H. Hencken[53] must be mentioned) do not exclude the possibility of external intervention. We are too well aware nowadays that the western Mediterranean around 1000 B.C. was not a *mare clausum* to reject a priori the tradition that easterners had come to the Etruscan shores. This tradition is not to be reduced to the tale told by Herodotus; it turns up under various, often more credible aspects, and since J. Bérard's book one tends to believe that the stories of the wanderings of Ulysses, Diomedes and Aeneas in the west are not to be rejected as pure fables, but to be accepted as the reflection in legendary form of real historical movements. And above all, even if we say nothing of the affinities that scholars have detected between Etruscan and the languages of Asia, the Etruscoid stele from Lemnos cannot be explained on a purely indigenist theory.

This being premised, two facts seem firmly established:

1. Any Etruscan migration must have taken place before Greek colonization started. It is hard to believe that the Greeks vigilantly watching the Sicilian narrows from 650 onwards would not have recorded (if nothing more) the passage of the Tyrrhenian fleet, and that Greek historians would have no tradition of it save as something that happened long, long ago.[54]

Also, if the Chalcidians, as is generally allowed, were animated by the need for raw materials—specifically the ores of Elba—it is hard to explain why they did not push their trading-posts forward into Etruria itself, unless they had found that it was private fishing.

2. Every known Etruscan city is preceded by a Villanovan settlement on the same site. This makes it impossible to accept Herodotus' statement that the Etruscans 'founded in Italy the cities where they presently dwell', unless we identify them with the Villanovans.[55] About Caere (Cerveteri) we go by imperceptible transitions from the Villanovan necropolis of Sorbo, dominated by the Regolini-Galassi tomb, to the Etruscan cemeteries of Banditaccia and Abetone.

Now the establishment of this latter fact, which bids us seek the origins of Etruscan culture in the Villanovan, compels us to reopen the question of Villanovan civilization itself.

We have seen[56] that in the early iron age it covered a great part of peninsular Etruria, where it occupied three provinces, Aemilia, Etruria and the later addition of Campania and the Salerno region. It shows in these places specific traits subject to local variation caused by contiguity: thus the last phases of Villanovan at Bologna show close connections (long-footed fibulae, situlae) with the Venetic culture at Este; the Villanovan of southern Etruria is connected with the culture of Latium by the presence in graves of those hut-urns which imitated the huts in which the living dwelt; we can also see (e.g. in the settlements of the Salerno region) that the earlier population put up a prompt and decisive resistance.

But although our knowledge of these general or particular aspects has been pushed by archaeology as far as it can go, we still cannot answer the question, 'What people (or peoples) were the bearers of this culture?' Some incline to think that Villanovan civilization, in the zones where it appears, only marks a stage in Italian civilization. Others cannot be content without asking (as they will about the Etruscans) who the Villanovans were. Here again we must not forget that they must have taken shape in Italy out of heterogeneous contingents who had converged from different directions.

The spread of the Urnenfelder culture had been associated with population movements which can be tied up with the first Celtic migrations. Both the Hallstatt and the Villanovan cultures seem to be the direct result of this expansion; and it is apparent that the diffusion of the Villanovan ossuary (fairly close copies of it have been found in Hungary, Rumania and Yugoslavia) did not take place in the way of peaceful trade. The situla of La Certosa would be bought, the crested helmets and cross-hilted swords would be bought if necessary, or else imitated; but no one would buy or imitate a Villanovan ossuary if he had no organic reason to set store by it. At least one element in the Villanovan amalgam came originally from the Balkans.[57]

Two tendencies have recently displayed themselves which, while still uncertain, may be blazing the trail towards a better understanding of the way in which Italy was peopled in the period of transition between the bronze and iron ages. One, represented by Pallottino,[58] alters the traditional north-to-south direction assigned to the movement, and proposes that historians should turn it through 90 degrees: either a full-scale invasion or an infiltration, he suggests, an invisible conquest, now military, now economic, had its starting-point not in the north, from the Alps, but in the east, from the Aegean. The other suggestion[59] is that the Villanovans, reckoned as an urnfield people, had set themselves up principally in three maritime regions of Italy—on the south coast of Etruria, near the mouths of the Po at Spina, and to the south of Naples, which would seem to imply that they came by sea.

However that may be, future scholars will presumably connect the movements of peoples which then took place with the outward drive of Balkan peoples which had its effects (in very confused conditions, of course) on Greece and the Aegean (the Dorian invasion), the Adriatic, and Italy. It is conceivable that in the complicated general post that was caused by these multiple pressures a group of Aegean navigators may have been dragged along on the skirts of the main drive towards Italy: the *Tyrsenoi* and a people inseparable from the Etruscans in tradition, the Pelasgi.

Concurrently with these archaeological interpretations, a new look at the texts has shown how fragile is the testimony assigned to Herodotus on the Lydian oʌigin of the Etruscans. Herodotus himself only tells the story as a local variant (φασὶ δὲ αὐτοὶ Λυδοί),[60] while several chapters earlier[61] he mentions a different version which he declares to be historical. The Lydian source which he was following in 1,94 gave only a particular application of a general tradition that we shall discuss later. It is not easy to guess the author of it: certainly not Xanthus of Lydia, whose *Lydiaca* was used by Herodotus, for he said that Atys had two sons, Lydos and Torebos, neither of whom emigrated.[62] We may suspect that the story by which

Lydia claimed bonds of kinship with the Etruscans arose when Etruscan power was at its zenith (sixth century), independently of Xanthus and before his time, and that the slight resemblance between Torebos and Tyrsenos set the fiction going.

Nevertheless, before Herodotus, the *Tyrsenoi* had been equated by Hellanicus of Lesbos with the Pelasgi,[63] a partly mythical people whom ancient writers amused themselves with discovering everywhere before the arrival of the Greeks. Considered, however, as an historical people, they seem, rolling stones though they were,[64] to have special associations with Thessaly and the Hellespont, and with Imbros and Lemnos in the northern Aegean:[65] now Hellanicus' identification is the only way of accounting for the existence in Lemnos of the Etruscoid inscription of the sixth century; it shows that there was in this island, up to the Athenian colonization, a nucleus of population related to the Etruscans. But precisely that legendary tradition which, as Bérard has shown,[66] contains an element of truth, tells of the Pelasgian migration to Italy, where they mingled with the Aborigines and pushed the Siculi back from the peninsula into Sicily; and archaeology confirms at Lipari and Milazzo the arrival of the Siculi at the end of the second millennium. Better still, Hellanicus, followed by Herodotus, told how the Pelasgians had landed in the Adriatic at the Po delta, at Spina, crossed the Apennines and founded Cortona inland.[67] Of course the colonization of Spina by the Pelasgians, affirmed by Hellanicus at the very moment when that Graeco-Etruscan port was at the peak of its prosperity, may be a flattering invention. But it remains true that the solution of the problem of Etruscan origins, if indeed they came into Italy to be absorbed and yet make themselves felt in the Villanovan culture, must henceforth be tied up with the problem of the Pelasgians.

3 Chronology of Greek Colonization and Pottery Chronology

The chronology of Greek colonization in Italy and Sicily seemed for a long time to rest primarily on the testimony of ancient authors, especially of Thucydides. In an early chapter[68] of his sixth book he lists the Sicilian colonies in chronological order of their foundation, dating them before or after the founding of Syracuse: thus Hyblaean Megara was colonized five years after Syracuse, Acrae 70 years after. Now Megara lasted for 245 years before being taken by Gelo of Syracuse at a recent and well-established date, viz. 483; thus Syracuse must have been founded in $(483 + 245 + 5) = 733$. It is generally admitted that Thucydides took these figures from the Syracusan historian Antiochus, who wrote about 450 and made the foundation of his native city the starting-point of his sums. Other writers in other cities came to slightly different conclusions: Ephorus, for example, instead of the sequence Naxos—Syracuse—Leontini—Megara, proposed Naxos—Megara, Syracuse—Leontini.[69] Their dates are preserved for us by Pindar and his scholiasts, by Diodorus and Strabo, by Eusebius in the Armenian version of his chronicle and in the Latin translation made by Jerome; they are over-shadowed by the authority of Thucydides where Sicily is concerned, but for Magna Graecia we have no other sources. Such are the literary sources of information; they provide a general framework in which details might be disputed, but which as a whole was for a long time not seriously questioned. It may be found, in the shape of a synoptic table, in Bérard's book.[70]

But there is also another available method of dating, based on the development of archaic Greek pottery, especially that of Corinth. It is a fact that, almost every time, the earliest pottery found in the Greek colonies in Italy and Sicily belongs to the first phase of proto-Corinthian, called proto-Corinthian geometric.[71] In only a very few cases we find earlier material, showing, for example that the island of Pithecusae (Ischia) was occupied before the colonists installed themselves on the mainland at Cumae (this is one of the most important gains of recent research).[72] The successive developments of proto-Corinthian in the orientalizing period—through a first and then a second black-figure style, then after a transitional period to the formation of Early, Middle and Late Corinthian—provide a relative chronology which it would be desirable to turn into an absolute one; and to this end attempts have been made to tie it in as accurately as possible with the foundation-dates of the Sicilian colonies.

Thus the primitive sanctuary of Selinus, dedicated to Demeter Malophoros, shows a great many shards of Early Corinthian, with some bits here and there of proto-Corinthian and Transitional; it has been inferred that the beginnings of Early Corinthian coincide with the foundation of Selinus, dated by Thucydides in 628–627.[73] Likewise the spherical aryballoi which are typical of early proto-Corinthian are common in the necropolis of Fusco at Syracuse; and since Syracuse was founded, according to Thucydides, in 733, we must make proto-Corinthian begin between 750 and 700, perhaps c.740.[74] Consequently Pithecusae, where older types of cups and skyphoi have been found, must be dated around 770;[75] and indeed the texts confirm that it was very early. Sometimes the progress of archaeology enables us to correct the Thucydidean tradition. Excavations at Megara have brought to light proto-Corinthian cups of a very archaic type not found at Syracuse, and it has been concluded that Megara, said by Thucydides to have been founded in 728–727, must have been occupied from 750 on, and that the priority assigned to Syracuse was a patriotic falsehood assignable to Antiochus, Ephorus having preserved a juster understanding of the historical sequence.[76]

It need hardly be said that the historians and archaeologists of the last half-century who have followed Schweizer,[77] Johansen[78] and Payne[79] in studying the problems of the chronology of Greek colonization in relation to pottery typology have never closed their eyes to the imperfections of their method. 'It is very risky,' wrote F. Villard in 1948,[80] 'to hang the dating of proto-Corinthian on such a shaky peg' as the chronological data provided by Thucydides, Diodorus, Eusebius and Jerome. J. Bérard inveighed against the vicious circle involved in 'dating eighth-century pottery finds absolutely with the help of dates given by ancient tradition, then appealing to the pottery chronology thus established as supporting the ancient tradition'.[81] The archaeologists did not fail to realize that the dates given by Thucydides and Ephorus might have been arrived at by a reckoning in generations which was open to all kinds of mistakes—although J. Bérard and T. J. Dunbabin strove to exorcize this spectre by supposing that each colony must have kept written documents which were dated *ab urbe condita*:[82] does not a fragment of Callimachus' *Aitia* confirm that in Zancle and other Sicilian colonies the anniversary of the founding was regularly celebrated by a banquet to which the shades of the oecists were invited and called upon by name?[83]

This construction, built by rule of thumb, but on the whole standing up well and agreeing with what we thought we knew of the major forces at work in the eighth and seventh centuries, was vigorously assailed in a book by R. van Compernolle which came out in 1959 under the title *Étude de chronologie et d'historiographie siciliotes*.[84] The author had the courage to face the hypothesis of genealogical chronology and to examine it thoroughly. The dates given by Thucydides, he thinks, are an artificially coherent construction based on a reckoning in generations of 35 years each (not of 30, 33⅓ or 40 years as in other reckonings equally well attested). He has found traces of this 'modulus' of 35 years elsewhere, in the chronology of the Mermnads of Lydia, in the date of the foundation of Carthage, and in those of the founding and overthrow of Sybaris; but with Thucydides it is quite apparent in the 70 years (35 x 2) which separate the founding of Carthage from that of Acrae, in the 245 years (35 x 7) of Megara's existence, and in the 105 years (35 x 3) that elapsed between the founding of Syracuse and that of Selinus—five years between Syracuse and Megara plus 100 between Megara and Selinus. All the other figures can be reduced to the same common denominator, although a little subtlety is sometimes required. But did a fifth-century historian like Antiochus, who was Thucydides' source, possess genealogical lists on which he could base his calculations? Van Compernolle proves that he did by tracing out those of the Dinomenids of Gela and the Emmenids of Agrigentum: Antiochus set the founding of Agrigentum in 581–580, three 35-year generations before the victory gained by Theron (fourth of the dynasty) at the Olympics of 476–475. Furthermore, the adoption of a modulus of 35 years for the length of one generation seems to have been supported by the pseudo-Hippocratic theory of hebdomads and by Pythagorean notions on the significance of numbers.[85]

Van Compernolle reckons that the chance of his theory's being wrong is one in 8,796,388,244. His demonstration is sometimes too systematic, but it is powerful and eloquent and carries conviction. One cannot escape his conclusion: the duration of one generation cannot be set at 35 years (nor yet 30 or $33\frac{1}{3}$) except by a false and misleading convention. A dynasty of three rulers might have reigned longer in a city than one of four or five rulers in another. Starting from certain basic dates in the first half of the fifth century, different for different cities, the seven Syracusan generations take us back quite artificially to 733, as six generations at Gela take us back to 689. This genealogical chronology only marks the ignorance that necessarily beset an historian like Antiochus, if in fact he had only oral traditions on which to base himself.

Several critics in reviews and articles have not shrunk from drawing such conclusions as these: 'Mr van Compernolle's conclusions (it is no use to deny it) throw whole stretches of archaic history into complete disarray—all those parts, that is, which had been built on the Thucydidean chronology, touched up here and there, and which the passage of Mr van Compernolle has left in total ruin . . . This certainly calls into question archaeological chronology, especially that of proto-Corinthian and Corinthian.'[86] 'The essential service rendered by Mr van Compernolle is to have made us admit that the dates of colonies in Sicily in the eighth and seventh centuries cannot be historical, and that all the systems of chronology are artificial constructions going no further back than the fifth century . . . All that lasted was oral traditions preserving the memory of the order in which they were founded; what interested each city was not to know in what year it was founded, but whether it was founded before or after its neighbours. When at a later date men began to take an interest in the chronology of the archaic period, they had only two things at their disposal—this order of founding, more or less distorted by propaganda from this or that quarter, and a computation of the time that had elapsed based upon the genealogies of noble families.'[87]

We are still waiting for the historians and pottery-experts to get their breath again after Van Compernolle's bombshell; but in the meanwhile we may try to get our bearings. Now that the smoke has cleared a little, the devastation appears less widespread than it did at first. After this it will presumably be impossible ever to believe in the Thucydidean account again, and it will probably drag down in its fall the other chronologies from Ephorus to Eusebius, unless (as is not inconceivable) the theory of a time-reckoning by Olympiads, by eponymous magistrates or *ab urbe condita* (cf. the fragment of Callimachus previously mentioned: unless I am much mistaken, Van Compernolle has not considered the significance of this) should again gain ground. It is agreed, however, that the fifth century might still have remembered the relative order of founding:[88] the tradition that made Cumae the oldest of the Italian and Sicilian colonies[89] and accorded Naxos, despite Syracusan pretensions, the primacy among those of Sicily[90] remains consequently intact; and the pioneering part which was always assigned to the Syracusans in the Greek colonizing movement is still firmly established. In general outline, the relative chronology of the colonization remains unshaken.

We should further notice that the chronologoy f proto-Corinthian and Corinthian pottery, which as a relative chronology is unassailable, comes through the test fairly well, even in the form where it was bidding fair to become absolute. The fact is, as we said earlier, that the men who were busy working it out in detail were not so naive as some have thought; they had taken their precautions. It is rather careless to say that the chronology of Corinthian ceramic rests only on the foundation date of Selinus, and that from Thucydides' date of 628–627 pottery-dating simply plods on from style to style, 25 years for each, until the beginning of proto-Corinthian.[91]

Payne's successors in fact spared no effort to cross-check at every step, to make sure of contacts with other series of documents—orientalizing tombs in Etruria, Egyptian or Egyptian-inspired material, the archaeology of Cyprus, the archaic coinage of Athens, the founding of Marseilles around 600[92]—so that when their task was completed, one could look on the traditional foundation-dates simply as a temporary scaffolding used to help build a structure which in the end was strong enough to stand without it. Thus F. Villard, when he presented in 1948 his chronological table of proto-Corinthian, spoke of it as 'a middle term, perhaps a rather lame conclusion, certainly inaccurate despite its appearance of precision', yet with dates which 'seem to flow directly from the facts'.[93]

We may suppose that the chronologies that will be built on the bomb-site of the Thucydidean chronology will bear out what T. J. Dunbabin wrote in a posthumous article: 'Payne's chronology is exact relatively . . . But it has no absolute value unless we allow 25 years tolerance in either direction.'[94] And none other than J. Ducat recently, having roundly rejected all the earlier chronologies, has tried to find a new datum-line in the destruction of Smyrna. He has concluded from this that the transition from Early to Middle Corinthian can be set at 585–580: Payne's date was 600.[95] A variation of this order is important to the experts on pottery, but to the general historian it hardly threatens any fatal consequences.

Hence it is now the archaeological chronology that enables us (without getting, in the strict sense, into Bérard's vicious circle) to construct a chronology of Greek colonizing activity. It is an approximate chronology, in which the pre-Compernollian dates, so to speak, of *c.*770 for Pithecusae and *c.*740 for Cumae may be used to anchor our ideas and mark the stages of an evolution which would certainly lose none of its significance if one had to move it up or down a quarter of a century. This is why in our narrative section the Thucydidean dates were not used; but for the rest no change was made in the traditional chronology.

4 Note on the Sources for Early Roman History: From Hypercriticism to the Rehabilitation of the Tradition

It is customary for every introduction to early Roman history to begin with a recommendation to caution in the use of the ancient sources. There is every justification for stressing how few authentic texts can go back to so remote a period or—and here is the main reason why a scholar like Ettore Pais is so sceptical—can have survived the burning of Rome by the Gauls in 390.[96] One recalls that on the admission of Cicero himself the vainglory of noble families had often falsified the Fasti, putting in *falsi triumphi*, *plures consulatus* to glorify fictitious ancestors.[97] Finally it is usual to attack the methods of the Latin annalists, who were less concerned, it is thought, with consulting original documents than with copying stories from one writer into another and heightening their dramatic effect.

We should note that in the last fifty years or so these warnings have been becoming less gloomy, and have been accompanied by warnings against another danger, which has been christened *hypercriticism*. The word itself is no vulgar newcomer: as an epithet, it was applied to Scaliger. But as a substantive it has come in our days to have a pejorative colouring in the reaction which has followed the too negative and destructive attitude found in the early works of Pais—*Storia della Sicilia e della Magna Grecia* (1894) and *Storia di Roma* (1898–9)—a reaction which first set in with the learned and judicious *Storia dei Romani* of G. de Sanctis (1907 onwards). Pais himself was affected by it in his later years: I do not know whether it was he or his excellent translator and adapter J. Bayet who wrote in 1926 in the first volume of *Histoire romaine* in Glotz's *Histoire Générale*: 'Between a blind credulity that uncritically swallows the tradition whole, and an arrogant hypercriticism which denies everything, there is a middle way which can lead to the truth.'[98] It is true that so happy and unlooked-for an issue then seemed only possible 'by building on the results of the comparative history of other peoples'. About the same time, first in his *Conquête romaine*, then in his *Histoire de Rome*,[99] A. Piganiol similarly protested against the hypercriticism of Pais and his followers. He also remarked that 'a reaction can be detected today in favour of the annalistic sources which have ordinarily been despised'.[100]

This was only a beginning. What we see today is a full-scale rehabilitation (more or less explicit) of the literary tradition; in some writers this goes so far as to believe its literal truth and to treat it as so authoritative that the slightest doubt about there having been seven kings or about their order of succession becomes rank blasphemy. Now this reversal of the former situation is not a mere quirk of fashion. It has been engendered in large part, no doubt, by the weariness and discouragement with which one saw so many systematic and conflicting reconstructions rise up on the ruins of the tradition, only to collapse one after another. Confronted by the failure of these sometimes forced theories, of which it has been said that 'they testify to their authors' imagination more than they can be considered as the natural fruit of historical research',[101] hypercriticism has been driven to self-criticism. Historians have been forced to admit that the satisfaction with which they viewed the creations of their intellect, creations so ingenious and satisfying in their handling of fragmentary and uncertain data, was merely a way of preferring themselves to the truth. Nowadays it is almost true that an excessively brilliant hypothesis, claiming to explain everything, wins only a tired smile. A return to the sources has gradually forced itself upon us, as a return to a basic collection of data which deserves more credit than all the structures that we might build on its ruins.

The truth is that a series of considerable discoveries in recent years has tended strongly to buttress the tradition and strikingly to discredit hypercriticism. The discovery of Mycenaean imports on every shore of Italy and Sicily has made the fabled voyages of Ulysses and Diomedes in the west more credible.[102] Excavations on the Palatine have revealed an eighth-century village of huts near where the ancients revered the *casa Romuli*, thus agreeing with the traditional date for the founding of Rome.[103] The Villanovan finds at Capua support the witness of those who place the beginnings of the city about 800.[104] The Etruscan epigraphers have reported from Rome inscriptions of the sixth and even the seventh century, adding new arguments to those already derived from archaeology to verify the overlordship of the Tarquins.[105] A dedication to Castor and Pollux, found at Lavinium and dating from the sixth to fifth centuries, shows that the worship of the Dioscuri had already been imported from Magna Graecia into Latium before the fabulous battle of Lake Regillus where they supposedly came in on the Roman side against the Latins;[106] and terracotta figurines showing Aeneas carrying his father Anchises, attest the presence of Rome's national hero at Veii in the first half of the fifth century.[107] Thus, in places where we could not venture to believe that things were as old as tradition made them, archaeology confirms the early dating; and it is hard to find any instance where the progress of the ancillary historical sciences has convicted the tradition of falsehood. With these developments in view, one is sometimes tempted to accept the tradition en bloc, and when hypercritics deny and critics have their doubts, to declare: 'It was useless for you to prove by what seemed cogent arguments that Livy had no possibility of telling the truth, had no right to tell it. The fact is that he did tell the truth.'

Here are two opposite dangers—hypercriticism and what one might call hypocriticism—and one would like briefly to describe the present situation of research into early Roman history with one of them on either hand.

The historical outlook will, first of all, be marked by a feeling of modesty where sources are concerned. A new respect, engendered by something of an uneasy conscience, has replaced the inquisitorial rigour with which one used to interrogate the witnesses. For a long time it had seemed that, when faced with any statement by a Roman historian, sound method demanded that one should a priori reckon it false, work out in what circumstances it had been invented, of what later events it was a deliberate anticipation, and what public or private interest it was intended to serve. The elaboration of data referring to Rome's earliest history was always reckoned to be very late, and a decisive role in it was assigned to the propaganda of glib and mendacious *Graeculi* who made it their business, by delusive etymologies and ingenious twisting of the facts, to flatter the pride and ambition of the new masters of the world. This suspicious attitude is now on the retreat, as regards both the peoples themselves and those who wrote their history: for instance, it took all the lucid common sense of F. Altheim to make it once more apparent that the acceptance of the Greek gods by the peoples of Italy could be explained, quite apart from all constraint, quite apart from all economic circumstances which spread knowledge of them, by the simple and profound fact that they presented themselves to the Italian consciousness as being truer and greater divinities.[108] It is also being admitted that the tradition does not set systematically about leading us into error, and that the motives which inspired it in its effort to trace the first beginnings were not basically dishonest: are not the first words of caution uttered by Cicero and Livy?

Nevertheless, one will not place a blind confidence in the tradition. Ancient historians often made mistakes, just as modern ones do. Like the latter, they were too intelligent, and they strove to retrace the sequence of events in remote ages with a disinterested desire to understand, which still let some of their contemporary prejudices filter through. Their narrative was inevitably interpretation.

The annalists have long been blamed for letting themselves be dominated, in their representation of the patrician-plebeian conflicts of the fifth century, by their own experience of the agrarian struggles in the times of the Gracchi and of Sulla.[109] More recently A. Alföldi has drawn attention to the distortions which had even earlier crept into the image of relations between early Rome and the Latins arising from Rome's later sovereignty over them.[110] In such conditions the task of the modern historian is to remove the parasite growth of interpretation in the hope of separating out the facts on which it has battened.

In this connection, one of the most subtle hallucinogenic forces against which we have to be on guard is that which tempts us to regard the history of states as following a uniform course of greatness and decline. The Roman poets of the Augustan age dwelt in wonder on the humble origins of the city: 'This Rome, now so great, was once no more than a grassy hill.'[111] Livy himself feels that Roman power had had a long infancy, had grown up, displayed the powers of its maturity, and thereafter was declining.[112] All our classical notions are also dominated by the conception of a slow growth *ex nihilo*, in a steady and linear progression: one climbs a steep slope, one reaches the top; one goes down the other side. Yet we know very well that things were not so simple: after the golden age of the Antonines, the third century may have been given up to military anarchy, but the fourth was another golden age. The beginnings of Roman civilization should equally be regarded not as a straight line leading steadily upward, but as a sine curve with peaks and troughs. This new attitude helps us to see more clearly the part played by the Etruscans in the seventh and sixth centuries as a cultural leaven in Italy, and as the agency through which Rome reached a grandeur which she never forgot and never looked back to but with nostalgia. Then came a decline—the 'middle ages', the 'night', the 'hiatus' of the fifth century[113]—and after that the climb up again. One can find here something of the distinction made by Pallottino between 'elements of formation' and 'elements of derivation': every moment in history is only to a certain degree determined by the past; it opens up creative possibilities; nothing is wholly foreseen. In Roman history we shall be on guard against the illusion of continuity.

Her basic documents, which claim our undivided allegiance, are above all those provided by archaeology: all that we can learn of archaic Italy from the stratigraphy of the cemeteries, the finds of native and imported pottery, the remains of architectural decoration, paintings and bronzes, intaglios and coins, is of inestimable value. These data are almost the sole basis of the reconstruction of primitive Rome offered by Alföldi, who tends to go even too far in rejecting all the annalistic accounts traceable to Fabius Pictor. To these we must add the contribution (surely no less important) of epigraphy—Latin, Greek, Etruscan, Oscan, Umbrian, down indeed to the most inconsiderable dialects of Italy. Finally, we should not overlook the results of linguistic research: the history of words is one of the most faithful reflections of cultural history, and the study of it contributes valuably to general history. The names of Ernout, Devoto and Dumézil are enough to remind us how usefully one may cross from the one discipline to the other.

But what about the literary sources? The 'interpretations' that we have spoken of overlie a great number of facts which are only accessible through those interpretations. These facts are essentially the texts of treaties, legal formulae, and the Fasti. When Dionysius tells us that in his day there was a bronze stele in the temple of Diana on the Aventine, bearing the decree, complete with the names of the peoples taking part, which in Servius Tullius' day had made that temple into the federal sanctuary of the Latins,[114] we will not at once give him the lie. The obsession with forgeries is now past. The discovery of contemporary inscriptions, such as the treaty between Sybaris and the Serdaioi,[115] or the dedications of Thefarie Velianas at Pyrgi,[116] strengthen the authenticity of the *lex vetusta* of the *praetor maximus* that L. Cincius had deciphered on the Capitol.[117] Many of the fragments of the Twelve Tables which have come down to us deserve the most complete acceptance.[118] Lastly, the consular Fasti, which used to be suspected of frequent interpolations, are nowadays reckoned, except for the very first years of the republic, as 'the first and most important document of Roman history'.[119] Instead of arbitrarily deleting the plebeian names, as Mommsen and Beloch did, sound method seems rather to require that we admit them as such, and revise instead the interpretation which made plebeians originally ineligible for the consulate.[120] Naturally discussion is still open on each individual case. It is also open on the question of the total or partial disappearance of public and private archives in the fire of 390: 'most of them perished', says Livy,[121] and the Romans, one supposes, set about reconstituting them immediately after. But Livy is mistaken in thinking of these archives as being like the *commentarii pontificum*, written on perishable materials; we should think not of masses of annals that could have been destroyed in the fire, but of a few inscriptions on stone or bronze, which might have survived as the Lapis Niger inscription has survived. In any case, if they were made up again, to reconstruct a hundred years is not beyond the powers of memory of a primitive people that was accustomed to transmit its history by word of mouth.[122] When Timaeus, about 300, consulted the priests at Lavinium, it is hard to say of what remote past they may not have been the faithful depositaries.

I

Such is the mood of restrained confidence, of cautious acceptance, in which the historian of the ancient world will examine the events related for his attention—events which are not necessarily true, nor yet necessarily false, but of which the real worth may be established in each case by individual examination. Very often, rather than replace them by an overambitious theory, he will resign himself to remaining in ignorance.

5 The Treaties between Rome and Carthage

The problem of dating the treaties between Rome and Carthage is one of the apples of discord of modern historiography. Out of the four diplomatic instruments which defined the relations of the two powers before they entered in to armed conflict in 264, the oldest is referred by Polybius, no trifling authority, to the year when the republic was founded, 509. It is necessary to say that his thesis, having been long disputed and considered (not without solid reasons) as an anticipation and to be rejected, is nowadays gaining ground. The most recent bibliographies show that it commands a large majority.[123] But it is not a problem to be resolved by the counting of votes.

As concerns the literary sources, it can be posed as follows: Polybius[124] dates in 509 a first treaty, written in an archaic Latin which even the experts of his day found very hard to interpret. He goes on to mention two others, preserved, like the first, in the Capitol near the temple of Jupiter, but he makes no such remarks concerning them; the second he does not date, but the third is contemporary with Pyrrhus' operations in Italy and is confounded with the one which Livy dates to 279.

Diodorus,[125] on the other hand, when he comes to the year 348, says that the first treaty between Rome and Carthage was concluded in that year.

In that same year of 348, Livy mentions a treaty but does not say that it was the first.[126] He says that it was renewed for the third time in 306,[127] and for the fourth in 279.[128] Now in 343 he mentions the arrival of a Carthaginian embassy to congratulate the Romans on their victory over the Samnites:[129] it is not impossible that on this occasion the treaty of 348 was renewed for the second time.

These facts can be summed up in the following table:

	Polybius	Diodorus	Livy
509	I		
348		I	a treaty
306			III
279	III		IV

The interesting feature of Polybius's testimony, apart from the early date assigned to the first treaty, is that he alone reproduces the texts and gives a commentary on them.

His treaty of 509 sets up an alliance between Rome and Carthage. The first stipulated condition forbids the Romans and their allies to sail beyond the Fair Promontory—that is, says Polybius, to visit the *emporia* of Byzacena and Little Syrtis. The name *Promontorium Pulchri* is applied by Livy to what is now Cap Farina, northwest of Carthage,[130] and in consequence, in Polybius' interpretation, access to Carthage itself would be interdicted to the Romans. Meltzer, followed by Gsell and de Sanctis, has concluded (wrongly, I think) that Polybius was mistaken:[131] the forbidden zone, he thinks, would have extended west from Cap Farina, and Carthage was trying to protect her establishments in Mauretania and her stage-points towards Tartessus. The clauses that follow admit and regulate, under the surveillance of public functionaries, Roman trade in Africa and Sardinia and give it special privileges in the Punic part of Sicily.

The restrictions thus imposed on Roman movements on the Carthaginian coasts have as their counterpart as undertaking by Carthage to respect Roman sovereignty in Latium, to do no harm to the Latin *subjects* of Rome, among others the peoples of Ardea, Antium, Laurentum, Circeii and Terracina; not to attack the towns of those who were not her subjects; and, if they should happen to take one, to hand it back intact to the Romans.

The second of Polybius' treaties (which apparently his contemporaries found no harder to understand than the third, dated 279) had differences from and similarities with the first which are difficult to evaluate. It insisted on the reciprocal nature of the various clauses that follow to safe-guard the interests of the two parties: 'And that the Romans shall do likewise.—And that the Carthaginians shall do likewise.'

This time we find the peoples of Tyre and of Utica expressly mentioned by name alongside the allies of the Carthaginians. The zone in which Roman piracy, trade and colonization is forbidden is delimited now not only by the Fair Promontory to the east, but by a town of southern Spain, Mastia

Tarseion (i.e. probably Cartagena in the land of the Tartessians) to the west. Henceforth the Romans are forbidden to trade in Sardinia and Africa, except at Carthage; they keep the *ius commercii* in the Punic parts of Sicily.

On the Latin side there is no more talk of subjects, although Polybius in his commentary seems to think that Ardea, Antium, Circeii and Terracina (the Laurentines are left out), which were listed in the first treaty, were also the subjects of protective clauses in the second. Perhaps he did not trouble to repeat the clauses which were re-enacted unchanged. The peoples expressly aimed at are the non-subjects: in this connection a precise modification is brought in: if the Carthaginians take a Latin town which is not subject to Rome, they will keep the property and the people, and hand back the town to the Romans; if Carthaginian pirates capture the nationals of a town allied with Rome they are not obliged to take them to *the ports* of Rome, where they would be freed.

We will not delay over the third treaty: it reaffirmed all the other clauses of the previous agreements, only adding some articles about the relations of the two parties in the event that one of them should conclude an alliance with Pyrrhus. Let us also leave aside for the moment the treaty which was perhaps concluded towards the end of the previous century (306), which served the Sicilian Philinus as one of the texts for his anti-Roman propaganda, but which Polybius considered not to be genuine.[132] Let us merely remember at the end of this preliminary exposition that the three treaties gave rise, as Polybius tells us, to the taking of oaths: for the first, the Romans invoked Jupiter Lapis, according to ancient usage; for the latter two Mars and Quirinus. This raises many questions, but it does confirm the peculiar and archaic nature of the first.

In the most recent phases of the long controversy over the first treaty, two arguments among those that can be brought to bear against Polybius' dating present themselves with great force. Alföldi has sought to show that in the late sixth century Rome was cut off from the mouths of the Tiber by the territories of Veii (the *ripa Veiens*) and Lavinium, and was thus unable to cherish maritime ambitions.[133] On the other hand A. Aymard, in an incisive study of the second treaty,[134] has persuaded himself that it was no more than 'a collection of amendments' to the first, 'keeping in force all those clauses of it . . . which it did not modify'; hence he concluded that there could not have been 'too long a lapse of time between them' (alluding to the 160 years between 509 and 348), and inclined to date them close together in the mid-fourth century.[135] At all events it seems that we need a *terminus ante quem* in 340, since there is no allusion to the dissolution of the Latin League, nor yet to the establishment of a Romano-Campanian state, which would have extended Rome's responsibilities southwards far beyond the frontiers of Latium. In Alföldi's view the first treaty was concluded in 348, the second in 343, both reflecting the 'extreme tension' then prevalent in Latium.[136]

Nevertheless, Aymard's conclusions, founded on the close interdependence that he describes between a 'basic document' and a 'collection of amendments', quite apart from their taking no account of Polybius' clear statement that the first treaty was written in a very archaic Latin and sanctioned by a very ancient form of oath—which might suggest that 'a long enough period of time' had in fact elapsed between the first and the second —have the drawback that they bear only on those clauses which refer to the safeguarding of Roman rights in Latium: the clauses dealing with the protection of Carthaginian interests in Africa[137] indicate that her empire had developed considerably in the interval.

Now it is to be seen that the first treaty is concerned only with the Carthaginians and their allies, while the second is concluded in the name of the three peoples of Carthage, Utica and Tyre, with their respective allies, Carthage taking precedence and being mentioned alone, to the exclusion of her cosignatories, after the preamble. It has also been noted that the first treaty assigns only a starting-point (the Fair Promontory) to Punic westward expansion, while the second gives it a finishing-point in the land of the Tartessians. And certainly the mention of Tyre and Utica (not as allies of Carthage, as has mistakenly been said[138] but as powers theoretically coming in on the same footing as herself) does not provide a clear chronological indication for each of them. It seems to correspond to a moment when Carthage sets herself up as the heir of Tyre, her now fallen metropolis, and of Utica, the oldest Phoenician colony in Africa, declaring her ability now to take over and carry on their imperial policies in the Mediterranean. The decline of Tyre, under ceaseless attack from Assurbanipal and Nebuchadnezzar, from the Persians in the second half of the sixth century, and finally from Alexander, who 'destroyed' the city in 332, did not prevent her from rising each time from her ashes:[139] as late as 310 Carthage continued to send her the tithe of her revenues.[140] But this unquenchable vitality did not enable Tyre any longer to carry out distant enterprises in a western world where the new colonizing forces of Greeks and Etruscans had begun to play a part; and at a certain point Carthage became her successor. At the beginning of the fifth century Carthage seems to have been little more than an outpost of the Phoenician empire, but during that century the new policies seem to have achieved self-awareness: the great exploring voyage of Hanno beyond the Pillars of Hercules took place about 450.[141] It was at this same time that Utica, which figures in the periplus of the Pseudo-Scylax (*c.*350) as one of a list of Carthaginian dependencies, must have become subject to Carthage at the moment when the latter had built up in Africa a territory big enough to serve as the basis of her imperial ambitions;[142] but Utica, we must say again, is not mentioned in this treaty as an ally or a subject; more precisely, she is mentioned beside the metropolis as the elder sister, and Carthage shows respect for her title at the very moment when she is taking over the inheritance of both.

We may leave on one side another difference—no negligible one— between the two treaties. In the first, permission is granted to trade in Africa and Sardinia under certain conditions: in the second, such trade is wholly forbidden. This hardening of policy, which may be explained by an increasingly protective attitude in Punic colonialism, in Sardinia especially, cannot in itself be dated with accuracy, but there is nothing in it that conflicts with the conclusions that seem to be forced on us when we examine the Punic parts of the treaties. If we consider only that side, we can only subscribe to Polybius' chronology and admit with him that it will have taken not less than a century—the fifth century, full of revolution, reform and new ventures—for the Carthage of the first treaty, reduced to her own resources and scarcely looking beyond the Fair Promontory, to transform herself into an imperial metropolis which had set out to tread the path of Utica and Tyre, and at the moment when the second treaty was signed, had appropriated their possessions in Africa, Sardinia and Spain.

If now, with the understanding gained from this aspect of the facts, we return to what is said about the relations of Rome with her subjects and allies, Aymard's proposed interpretation of the second treaty, in which he sees no more than a 'collection of amendments' agreed to not long after the drawing up of the 'basic document', will no longer seem so persuasive. It is certainly hard to estimate how long a development in public and private law had taken place between the first and the second: the procedure of manumission, presumably *per vindictam*, which is referred to is in fact ageless, although its legal expression (*manus iniectio*) may reflect a state to which legal formulae did not develop until the time of the Twelve Tables.[143] But particularly the mention, together with the subject and non-subject Latins, of peoples who have contracted an alliance (literally a 'written peace') with Rome, brings in a new kind of relation between state and state. Among these allied cities we find Tibur and Praeneste, which became *civitates foederatae* in 358 and 354: it would be surprising indeed if they were omitted from the articles of the first treaty, supposing that to have been signed in 348.

Now if we decide to make the first treaty older than 348, it is clearly impossible to stop halfway. Apart from the archaism of the language in which it was couched, it must have been earlier than the descent of the Volscians into the Ponptine marshes (between 495 and 491), when Rome and the Latins lost for a century the harbours of Terracina, Circeii and Antium. The Greeks of the sixth century knew that all the land to the north of the Circeian promontory belonged to the Etruscans, who had not failed to secure their lines of communication with their Campanian province.[144] The occupation of the plain by the Volscians in the early fifth century coincided with the weakening of Etruscan power, and involved the Latins, now left on their own, in a century-long series of bloody conflicts which only began to hold out hopes of a reconquest when they entered Terracina again in 406, forced the Volscians to capitulate in 389, founded a colony at Circeii in 393, and saw the submission of Antium to Rome in 377—yet even so it was 358 before the country was completely reduced, when the tribes *Pomptina* and *Poblilia* were created.[145] In other words, as it was in our analysis of the Carthaginian clauses, so it is with the Latin: the whole fifth century needs to be reckoned between the first treaty and the second.

It goes without saying that the date 509 should not be taken literally: it is a palpable artifice to allot an event so pregnant with consequences to the first year of the republic. The inscription was no more likely to give the name of the king or magistrates responsible than have the inscriptions of archaic treaties found at Olympia (alliances between Elis and Heraea, between the Anaitoi and Metapioi, between Sybaris and the Serdaioi);[146] and this will have enabled Polybius' informants to assign it to the legendary Lucius Brutus. But they will hardly have been far astray in assigning it to the latter half of the sixth century, and the age of the Tarquins is in fact that which suits both form and content best.

It fitted 'perfectly into a wider context of contemporary diplomatic instruments'.[147] Let us remember how active Carthage was in this connection throughout the western Mediterranean—the treaties that she signed with Caere, which in 535 or so pitted the joint Punic and Etruscan navies against the colonizing efforts of the Phocaeans. The inscriptions lately found at Pyrgi have shown that her religious and political ascendency over her ally had not declined at the outset of the fifth century; and now that the archives of the Etruscan cities have begun to be opened up, we may expect that further finds will confirm the closeness of the bonds between them. But when the Tarquins were lords of Rome, it is natural that they should have cherished the same ambitions as a Thefarie Velianas, that they should not have narrowed their horizon to the seven hills and abruptly renounced the maritime calling of their people, and that they should have proposed to make use of their new harbours (Terracina, Circeii, Antium, possibly the mouths of the Tiber) and to protect the coasts of Latium and what was to be Volscian territory.

Now if we declare Polybius the winner, this means that we must considerably revise our notions of the power of Rome under the Etruscan kings and of the nature of their power in Latium. The petty Rome in thrall to the Latin League, and only little by little asserting her sovereignty, that Alföldi has depicted in his recent book, is in fact only the Rome of the fifth century, entangled in the difficulties of the 'dark age' into which the withdrawal of the Etruscans had thrown it. We have already seen that the conception which we form of the origins of Roman power—the classic image of a slow growth from nothing, a straight-line graph trending steadily upward, has to give way to the image of a sine curve with peaks and troughs. Seen in this light, the first treaty between Rome and Carthage, restored to the sixth century, is a document whose authority transcends all the constructions of hypercriticism.

Of course it is true that many individual problems still have to be faced if we want to see the concrete details of events. Perhaps future research will throw light on them. In what language was the treaty written? How did it survive until it was renewed in the middle of the fourth century? How could it be deciphered by the contemporaries of Polybius? It is likely that the language used was Latin, not Etruscan: the Lapis Niger inscription, mentioning the rex, shows that Latin then was different from the Latin of the second century, but also shows its syntactical capabilities. I agree with Alföldi[148] that the Etruscans had tried 'to establish a symbiosis' with the people they had conquered, and consequently did not make the use of Etruscan official in Rome. Engraved on tablets of bronze, as the most common practice was, and preserved in a shrine on the Capitol near the temple of Jupiter Optimus Maximus—which perhaps was not yet built— the treaty is exempt from the suspicions attaching to the survival of other inscriptions written on more perishable materials and exposed to the burning of the lower city by the Gauls. It was normal that the Roman diplomats who proposed to renew it in 348 should have consulted the old text; the language did not present to them the difficulties which it was to give two centuries later, and they will have striven to reproduce its tenor and formulae as faithfully as possible, except for 'amendments'. Renewals of this sort after a long interval of time are not unexampled in international relations in the ancient world: the *foedus Gaditanum*, originally concluded in 206, was renewed in 78.[149] We may also mention the *decretum Etruriae* which spoke of the inhabitants of Sardes as 'brothers' (*consanguinei*), and which was invoked by the Sardian delegates when they claimed in A.D. 26 the honour of erecting a temple to Tiberius:[150] the alliance in question presumably went back only to the war against Antiochus of Syria, c.189, but after a lapse of two centuries it had not disappeared from the Lydian archives.

Part Three

Instruments of Research: Bibliography

1 General Bibliography

A General histories

In the *Histoire générale* edited by G. Glotz the works principally consulted will be:

1 A. MORET, *Histoire de l'Orient, t.II: IIe et Ie millénaires, Les empires: rivalités des Égyptiens, Sémites, Indo-Européens.*

2 G. GLOTZ, R. COHEN, *Histoire grecque, t.I: Des origines aux guerres médiques; t.II: La Gréce au Ve siecle; t.III: Le IVe siècle: la lutte pour l'hégémonie.*

3 E. PAIS, J. BAYET, *Histoire romaine, t.I: Des origines à l'achèvement de la conquête.*

4 G. BLOCH, J. CARCOPINO, *Histoire romaine, t.II: La république romaine de 133 avant J.-C. à la mort de César.*

In the series 'Peuples et civilisations':

5 A. PIGANIOL, *La conquête romaine*, 5th ed., Paris 1967.

In the 'Clio' series:

6 A. PIGANIOL, *Histoire de Rome*, 5th ed., Paris 1962.

In addition:

7 F. ALTHEIM, *Römische Geschichte*, 2 vols, Frankfurt 1951–3.

8 J. BELOCH, *Griechische Geschichte*, 8 vols, Strasburg 1893–1904; 2nd ed., 1912–27.

9 Id., *Römische Geschichte bis zum Beginn der punischen Kriege*, Berlin 1926.

10 G. DE SANCTIS, *Storia dei Romani*, vols 1–2: *La conquista del primato in Italia*, 2nd ed., Florence 1956–60.

11 L. PARETI, *Storia di Roma*, vol. 1, Turin 1951.

12 H. H. SCULLARD, *A History of the Roman World* (753–146 B.C.), 3rd ed., London 1961.

B History of religion

13 G. WISSOWA, *Religion und Kultus der Römer* (*Handbuch der Altertumswissenschaft*, V, to be consulted in the second edition, Munich 1912) is still fundamental; sets out the data very clearly.

14 K. LATTE, *Römische Religionsgeschichte*, which replaced the former work in the same collection in 1960, has not the same value as a reference-book, but has many valuable suggestions.

15 A. GRENIER, *Les religions étrusque et romaine*, Paris 1948, is valuable for its attempt (as the title claims) to do justice to the Etruscan heritage, by its careful reproduction of the texts, and by the accuracy of its references.

The history of Roman religion has received new life since 1930 from F. ALTHEIM, who has paid particular attention to relations with Greece in the archaic period and to the Italian context:

16 F. ALTHEIM, 'Griechische Götter im alten Rom', *Religionsgeschichtliche Versuche und Vorarbeiten*, 22, 1, Giessen 1931.

17 Id., 'Terra Mater', *RGVV* 22, 2, Giessen 1931.

18 Id., *Römische Religionsgeschichte*, 3 vols, Berlin (Göschen) 1931; 2nd ed., 1956. The first volume has been translated into English:

19 Id., *A History of Roman Religion*, tr. H. Mattingly, London 1938.

20 Id., *Römische Religionsgeschichte*, 2 vols, Baden-Baden 1951.

To other important works should also be mentioned:

21 J. BAYET, *Histoire psychologique et politique de la religion romaine*, Paris 1957, with a remarkable analysis of Roman religious mentality.

22 G. DUMÉZIL, *La religion romaine archaïque*, Paris 1966, in which the author makes a synthesis of his studies into comparative mythology and traces Indo-European survivals in Roman religious sentiment and ritual.

We may further add:

23 A. PIGANIOL, *Recherches sur les jeux romains*, Strasburg 1923.

24 H. WAGENVOORT, *Roman Dynamism, Studies in ancient Roman thought, language and custom*, Oxford 1947 (studies the irrational elements in Roman religion).

See also [744] and [753]—[765].

C Geography and topography

The student needs above all the two great atlases:

M. BARATTA, P. FRACCARO, L. VISINTIN, *Atlante storico*, Novara 1954.

H. BENGTSON, V. MILOJCIC, *Grosser historischer Weltatlas*, I: *Vorgeschichte und Altertum*, 3rd ed., Munich 1953, with index.

We may particularly recommend the pocket atlas of J. PERTHES, *Atlas antiquus*, with index, several editions, Gotha.

For the topography of Rome:

25 G. LUGLI, *Roma antica. Il centro monumentale*, Rome 1946.

26 Id., *Monumenti minori del Foro romano*, Rome 1947.

27 Id., *Fontes ad topographiam veteris Urbis Romae pertinentes*, Rome 1952–65. The six volumes so far cover I. General topography of Rome; II. The Tiber and the springs; III, IV, VI—VIII. The regions of Rome. Published separately: *Mons Palatinus*, 1960.

28 S. B. PLATNER, T. ASHBY, *A topographical dictionary of ancient Rome*, London 1929; repr. 1966.

To these may be added:

29 J. LE GALL, *Le Tibre, fleuve de Rome dans l'Antiquité*, Paris 1952 Problems of living in cities in Greece, Etruria, Italy, Rome are discussed by:

30 P. LAVEDAN, J. HUGUENEY, *Histoire de l'urbanisme (Antiquité)*, 2nd ed., Paris 1966.

31 F. CASTAGNOLI, *Ippodamo di Mileto e l'urbanistica e pianta ortogonale*, Rome 1956.

32 R. MARTIN, *L'urbanisme dans la Grèce antique*, Paris 1956.

D Epigraphical sources

(i) Greek (Sicily and Magna Graecia)

The inscriptions of Sicily and Italy are collected by G. Kaibel (1890) in vol. 14 of *Inscriptiones Graecae (IGSI)*. The most important are reproduced in W. Dittenberger, *Sylloge Inscriptionum Graecarum*, 3rd ed., 1915–24 (*SIG³*).

For archaic inscriptions one may consult:

33 L. H. JEFFERY, *The local scripts of archaic Greece*, Oxford 1961.

On the dialects of Magna Graecia:

34 A. PAGLIARO, 'Il problema linguistico', *Atti del III. Convegno sulla Magna Grecia*, 1963, 87–111.

(ii) *Pre-Italic epigraphical sources*

35 R. S. CONWAY, S. E. JOHNSON, J. WHATMOUGH, *The Prae-Italic Dialects of Italy*, London 1933; repr. 1968.
36 V. PISANI, *Le lingue dell' Italia oltre il latino*, Turin 1953. As its title suggests, this collection includes all languages spoken in Italy apart from Latin, i.e. the 'Italic dialects' (Indo-European) as well as Ligurian and Messapian.
37 O. PARLANGELI, *Studi Messapici*, Milan 1960.

On the substrata:

38 C. BATTISTI, *Sostratti e parastratti nell' Italia preistorica*, Florence 1959.

(iii) *Italic epigraphical sources*

39 E. VETTER, *Handbuch der italischen Dialekte. I: Texte mit Erklärung, Glossen, Wörterverzeichnis*, Heidelberg 1953.
40 A. DE FRANCISCIS, O. PARLANGELI, *Gli Italici del Bruzio nei documenti epigrafici*, Naples 1960.
40b M. LEJEUNE, 'Phonologie osque et graphie grecque', *REA*, 72, 1970, 271–316 (collection and philological study of Oscan inscriptions in the Greek alphabet in southern Italy).
41 M. DURANTE, 'Il siculo e la sua documentazioné, *Kokalos* 10–11, 1964–5, 417–50.
42 G. GIACOMELLI, *La lingua falisca*, Florence 1963.

On the Tabulae Iguvinae:

43 G. DEVOTO, *Tabulae Iguvinae*, 3rd ed., Rome 1962.
44 A. ERNOUT, *Le dialecte ombrien*, Paris 1961.
45 H. W. POULTNEY, *The bronze tablets of Iguvium*, Baltimore 1959.

On Venetian, now connected with the Italic languages:

46 M. LEJEUNE, *Les inscriptions vénètes*. Publications of the University of Trieste, Istituto di Glottologia, 1965, 185–206.

There are numerous articles by the same author, inter alia:

47 M. LEJEUNE, 'Problèmes de philologie vénète', *RPh* 25, 1951, 202–35; 1952, 192–218.

48 Id., 'Stèles votives d'Este', *SE* 21, 1950–51, 215–27.

49 Id., 'Les bronzes votifs de Lagole', *REA* 54, 1952, 51–82.

50 Id., 'Notes de linguistique italique', *REL* 31, 1953, 117–74; 32, 1954, 120–38; 38, 1960, 132–50.

51 Id., 'Venetica', *Latomus* 12, 1953, 385–401; 13, 1954, 9–24, 117–28; 25, 1966, 7–27, 381–413, 677–88.

52 Id., 'Contribution à l'histoire des alphabets vénètes', *RPh* 31, 1957, 169–82.

52b Id., *Lepontica*, Paris 1971.

53 G. PELLEGRINI, *Le iscrizioni venetiche*, Pisa 1955.

54 G. PELLEGRINI, A. L. PROSDOCIMI, *La lingua venetica: I. Le iscrizioni*, Padua 1967.

55 M. G. DELFINO, *Il problema dei rapporti linguistici tra l'osco e il latino*, Genoa 1958.

56 G. DEVOTO, *Scritti minori*, 2 vols, Florence 1958–67 (brings together many earlier articles, a good part of them concerned with the Italic languages).

(iv) Etruscan epigraphical sources

The *Corpus Inscriptionum Etruscarum* (*CIE*) published by C. PAULI, O. A. DANIELSON, G. HERBIG, B. NOGARA and E. SITTIG, still only runs to six fascicules and a supplement:

I, 1893–1902: Fiesole, Volterra, Siena, Arezzo, Cortona, Chiusi, Perugia.

II, 1, 1907: Orvieto.

   2, 1923: Populonia, Vetulonia, Vulci.

   3, 1936: Tarquinii.

   4, 1970: Ager Volsiniensis, Ager Tarquiniensis, Caere.

III, 1, 1912: Ager Faliscus.

Suppl. 1, 1911: Liber linteus (the Zagreb mummy-wrappings).

The volume on the *Instrumentum* is in preparation.

A. FABRETTI, *Corpus Inscriptionum Italicarum* (*CII*), Turin 1967, with three volumes of supplements and an appendix (1880), and to various separate publications. A *Rivista di Epigrafia Etrusca* is published every year by *Studi Etruschi*. A very valuable selection of Etruscan inscriptions has been published by:

M. PALLOTTINO, *Testimonia Linguae Etruscae* (*TLE*), Florence 1954, with index; 2nd ed., 1968.

We should mention finally:

M. FOWLER, H. G. WOLFE, *Materials for the study of the Etruscan language* (University of Wisconsin Press 1965), produced by computer methods and containing a Corpus (texts in *CIE*, *TLE* and other epigraphic fragments), an index of words according to frequency, a reverse index, and an alphabetical index of all words in their contexts.

The study of these inscriptions is made easier by:

57 G. BUONAMICI, *Epigrafia etrusca*, modelled on the course in Latin epigraphy published by R. Cagnat, Florence 1932.

58 M. PALLOTTINO, *Elementi di lingua Etrusca*, Florence 1936.

58b A. J. PFIFFIG, *Die Etruskische*, Graz, 1969.

58c C. DE SIMONE, *Die griechischen Entlehnungen im Etruskischen*, 2 vols, Wiesbaden 1968–70.

On the most important Etruscan inscriptions:

59 K. OLZSCHA, *Zur Interpretation der Agramer Mumienbinde*, *Klio*, Beiheft, 20, 1939.

60 Id., 'Die Kalendardaten der Agramerbinden', *Aegyptus* 1959, 339–55.

61 A. J. PFIFFIG, 'Studien zu den Agramer Mumienbinde: Der Etruskische Liber Linteus', *Denkschr. Oesterr. Akad. d. Wiss.* 81, Vienna 1963.

62 J. HEURGON, 'Influences grecques sur la religion étrusque', (*TLE* 131), *REL* 35, 1957, 106–26.

63 A. J. PFIFFIG, 'Untersuchungen zum Cippus Perusinus', *SE*, 29, 1961, 111–14.

64 M. PALLOTTINO, 'Sulla lettura e sul contenuto della grande iscrizione di Capua', *SE*, 20, 1949, 159–96.

65 M. PALLOTTINO and others, 'Scavi nel santuario di Pyrgi e scoperta di tre lamine d'oro iscritte in etrusco e in punico', *AClass*, 17, 1964, 39–117.

66 A. J. PFIFFIG, 'Uni-Hera-Astarte, Studien zu den Goldblechen von S. Severa-Pyrgi mit etruskischer und punischer Inschrift', *Denkschr. Österr. Akad. d. Wiss*, 88, 2, Vienna, 1965.

67 J. HEURGON, 'The Inscriptions of Pyrgi', *JRS*, 56, 1966, 1–15.

68 G. COLONNA, M. CRISTOFANI, G. GARBINI, 'Bibliografia delle pubblicazioni piu recenti sulle scoperte di Pyrgi', *AClass*, 18, 1966, 279–82.

On the origin and diffusion of the Etruscan alphabet in Italy:

69 J. A. BUNDGÅRD, 'Why did the art of writing spread to the West? Reflexions on the alphabet of Marsiliana', *Analecta Romana Instituti Danici*, 3, 1965, 11–72.

70 A. GRENIER, 'L'alphabet de Marsiliana et les origines de l'écriture à Rome', *MEFR*, 41, 1924, 3–41.

71 J. HEURGON, 'Note sur la lettre *Λ* dans les inscriptions étrusques', *Studi in onore di L. Banti*, Florence 1965, 177–9.

72 M. LEJEUNE, Observations sur l'alphabet étrusque, dans *Tyrrhenica*, Milan 1957, 158–69.

73 Id., 'Notes de linguistique italique, 13 : Sur les adaptations de l'alphabet étrusque aux langues indo-européennes d'Italie', *REL*, 35, 1957, 88–105.

74 F. SLOTTY, *Studien zur Etruskologie. I. Silbenpunktierung und Silbenbildung im Altetruskischen*, Heidelberg 1952.

On Etruscan proper names:

75 H. RIX, *Das etruskische Cognomen*, Wiesbaden 1965.

76 W. SCHULZE, 'Zur Geschichte der lateinischen Eigennamen', *Abhandl. d. königl. Gesellschaft d. Wissenschaften zu Göttingen*, Phil. Hist. Kl., N.F. 5, 5, 1904; 2nd ed., 1966.

On the supposed relation between Etruscan and Hittite:

77 V. GEORGIEV, *Hethitisch und Etruskisch: Die Hethitische Herkunft der etruskischen Sprache*, Académie bulgare des Sciences, Linguistique balkanique, 5, 1, Sofia, 1962.

(v) Latin epigraphical sources

The archaic Latin inscriptions, up to the death of Caesar, are given in the first volume of the *Corpus Inscriptionum Latinarum* (*CIL*) published by Mommsen in 1863. They should be consulted in the second edition (*CIL* I²), by TH. MOMMSEN, H. HENZEN and C. HUELSEN (*Pars prior*) and E. LOMMATZSCH (*Pars posterior*, fasc. I, 1918; fasc. II, 1931; fasc. III, 1943). The student will also consult the thirteenth volume of the *Inscriptiones Italiae, Fasti et Elogia*, by A. DEGRASSI:

XIII, 1 : *Fasti consulares et triumphales*, Rome 1947;

XIII, 2: *Fasti anni Numani et Iuliani*, Rome 1963, an edition with commentary on the Roman calendars;

XIII, 3: *Elogia*, Rome 1937.

Photographs of some of the principal republican inscriptions can be found in the same author's *Imagines*, Berlin 1965.

Under the title *Inscriptiones Latinae liberae reipublicae* (*ILLRP*), I, 1957; II, 1963, A. Degrassi has presented the essentials of *CIL* I², adding all the recently discovered inscriptions of that class.

A. Degrassi has also made a separate small edition of the *Fasti Capitolini*, out of *Inscriptiones Italiae* XIII, 1, which is very useful (Paravia series, 1954).

The prosopographical data of the *Fasti* have been assembled by:

78 T. R. S. BROUGHTON, *The Magistrates of the Roman Republic* (*MRR*), 2 vols and a volume of supplements, New York 1952.

For a judicious appraisal of the value of the *Fasti*, see:

78b P. FRACCARO, *La storia romana arcaica*, in his *Opuscula*, I, Pavia 1956.

The early Latin inscriptions are studied linguistically in:

79 A. ERNOUT, *Recueil de textes latins archaïques*, Paris 1916, often reprinted. See also:

80 A. ERNOUT, 'Le parler de Préneste d'après les inscriptions', *Mél. de la Soc. de Linguistique* 13, 1905–6, 293–349.

Some admirable studies, under a misleading title, in:

81 F. ALTHEIM, *Geschichte der lateinischen Sprache*, Frankfurt 1951.

E Literary sources

There is no point in listing the various authors, who are accessible in good critical editions, as the Budé series, the Teubner library, the Bibliotheca Oxoniensis, the Paravia series and the Loeb Classical Library.

We must stress the importance of the collections of fragments of Greek and Roman historians:

The *Fragmenta Historicorum Graecorum* (*FHG*) edited by C. MÜLLER, 5 vols, 1841–1870, is now almost wholly superseded by F. Jacoby, *Die Fragmente der griechischen Historiker*, Berlin and Leyden, 1926–58 (*F. Gr. Hist.*). It comprises three parts, with volumes of commentary and notes:

I, *Alte Genealogie*, e.g. Hecataeus of Miletus;

II, *Universalgeschichte und Hellenica*, e.g. Posidonius;

III, *Geschichte von Städte und Völkern*; in this part, section B ('Autoren über einzelne Städte und Länder') brings together, from p. 540 on, those authors who wrote on Sicily and Magna Graecia—Antiochus of Syracuse (no. 555), Philistus (556), Timaeus (566); section C assembles the historians, either Greek or writing in Greek, who dealt with Rome and Italy.

The fragments of the Latin historians are edited by H. PETER, *Historicorum Romanorum Reliquiae (HRR)*, 2 vols, 1870; 2nd ed., 1906–14; a new edition is forthcoming. The first volume contains all the annalists, with a valuable introduction on each.

As an excellent introduction to the study of the sources of Roman history, we may cite:

82 A. ROSENBERG, *Einleitung zur römischen Geschichte*, Berlin 1921.

Among the recent publications dealing either with individual authors or with ancient historiography in general, we may mention:

83 E. GABBA, 'Studi su Diogini da Alicarnasso', *Athenaeum*, 38, 1960, 175–225; 39, 1961, 98–121.

84 Id., 'Considerazioni sulla tradizione letteraria sulle origini della Repubblica', *Entretiens XIII*, Fondation Hardt, Vandœuvres-Geneva 1966, 135–69.

85 K. HANELL, 'Zur Problematik der älteren römischen Geschichtsschreibung', *Entretiens IV*, Fondation Hardt, Vandœuvres-Geneva 1956, 148–84.

86 P. LÉVEQUE, 'Lycophronica', *REA*, 57, 1955, 36–56.

87 S. MAZZARINO, *Il pensiero storico antico*, 3 vols, Bari 1966.

88 A. MOMIGLIANO, 'Perizonius, Niebuhr and the Character of early Roman Tradition', *JRS*, 47, 1957, 104–14.

89 Id., 'Atene nel III secolo e la scoperta di Roma nella storia di Timeo di Tauromenium', *RSI*, 71, 1959, 529–56 = *Terzo Contributo alla storia degli studi classici e del mondo antico*, Rome 1966, I, 23–53.

90 Id., 'Linee per una valutazione di Fabio Pittore', *RAL* 15, 1960, 310–20 = *Terzo Contributo . . .* I, 55–68.

91 P. PEDECH, *La méthode historique de Polybe*, Paris 1954.

Finally, the invaluable commentary on Polybius:

92 F. W. WALBANK, *A historical commentary on Polybius*, I (Books I–VI), Oxford 1957; II (Books VII–XVIII), 1967.

F Sources on Roman law

The texts are found in:

93 C. G. BRUNS, *Fontes iuris Romani Antiqui*, 7th ed., Tübingen 1909.

94 P. F. GIRARD, *Textes de droit romain*, 6th ed., Paris 1937.

95 S. RICCOBONO, J. BAVIERA, V. ARANGIO-RUIZ, *Fontes iuris romani anteiustiniani (FIRA)*, 3 vols, Florence 1941–3.

On public law there is still no substitute for:

96 TH. MOMMSEN, *Römisches Staatsrecht*, 3 vols, Berlin 1874–87.

An excellent collection of Roman legislation is found in:

97 G. ROTONDI, *Leges publicae populi Romani*, Milan 1922, reprinted 1966.

This is supplemented by:

98 G. BARBIERI—G. TIBILETTI, art. 'Lex' in the *Dizionario epigrafico di antichita romana* of E. de Ruggiero, IV 22–5, Rome 1957, 3–94.
See further [624–628], [721], [727].

G Sources on numismatics

A manual that has not been superseded is:

99 B. V. HEAD, *Historia numorum, a manual of Greek numismatics*, Oxford, 2nd ed., 1911; reprinted 1963.

For Italian coinages (Etruria, Umbria, Picenum, Samnium, Campania) one still has recourse to:

100 A. SAMBON, *Les monnaies antiques de l'Italie*, I, Paris 1903.

And for Roman coinage to:

101 J. BABELON, *Description historique et chronologique des monnaies de la République romaine*, 2 vols, Paris 1885–6, reprinted 1963.

A better book now is:

102 E. A. SYDENHAM, *The coinage of the Roman republic*, London 1952.

There are many new ideas and facts in:

103 L. BREGLIA, 'Le antiche rotte del Mediterraneo documentate da monete e pesi', *RAAN* 1955, 7–122.

104 Id., *Numismatica antica, storia e methodologia*, Milan 1964.
See also [512–514]; [767–772].

H Dictionaries of antiquities

CH. DAREMBERG, E. SAGLIO, E. POTTIER, *Dictionnaire des antiquités grecques et romaines*, Paris 1877–1918, 9 vols (in many parts now antiquated).

A. PAULY, G. WISSOWA, *Real-Encyclopädie der classischen Altertumswissenschaft*, Stuttgart 1893 etc., 76 vols, now almost complete. First part (I et seq., from A to Quorenus); second part (IA et seq., from R. to Zenius); ten volumes of supplement.

P. LAVEDAN, *Dictionnaire illustré de la mythologie et des antiquités grecques et romaines*, Paris 1926—a one-volume abridgement and modernization of Daremberg and Saglio, but without references.

2 Specialized Bibliography

A The original population

(i) *The problems posed*

105 E. DEMOUGEOT, 'Variations climatiques et invasions', *RH* 233, 1965, 1–22.

106 V. GORDON CHILDE, *Prehistoric Migrations in Europe*, Oslo 1950.

107 H. HENCKEN, 'Indoeuropean languages and archaeology', *American Anthropological Association*, 84, 1955.

108 G. KOSSINNA, *Ursprung und Verbreitung der Germanen in Vor- und Frühgeschichtlicher Zeit*, Leipzig 1928; 2nd ed., 1934.

109 M. LEJEUNE, 'La position du latin sur le domaine indo-européen', *Mémorial des Études latines*, Paris 1943, 7–31.

110 M. PALLOTTINO, 'Le origini storiche dei popoli italici', *Atti del X. Cong. intern. di Scienze storiche*, Rome 1955, II, 1–60.

111 G. PATRONI, 'La preistoria', *Storia politica d'Italia*, Milan 1937; 2nd ed., 1951.

112 Id., 'L'indoeuropeanizzazione dell' Italia', *Athenaeum* 17, 1939, 213–26.

113 E. PULGRAM, *The Tongues of Italy: prehistory and history*, Cambridge, U.S.A. 1958

a THE INDO-EUROPEANS

114 P. BOSCH-GIMPERA, *Les Indo-Européens, problèmes archéologiques*, tr. R. LANTIER, Paris 1961.

115 J. LOICQ, 'Les Indo-Européens et l'archéologie préhistorique d'après P. Bosch-Gimpera', *RBPh*, 41, 1963, 112–34.

116 G. DEVOTO, *Origini indoeuropee*, Florence 1962.

b THE PEOPLING OF ITALY; HISTORICAL PEOPLES OF ITALY

117 G. DEVOTO, *Gli antichi Italici*, Florence 1929; 3rd ed., 1968.
118 H. NISSEN, *Italische Landeskunde:* 1. *Land und Leute:* 2. *Die Staedte*, Berlin 1883–1902.
119 M. PALLOTTINO, 'Popolazioni storiche dell'Italia antica', *Guida allo Studio della civiltà romana antica*, Naples-Rome-Milan, 1952, 71–90. On individual problems:
120 L. A. HOLLAND, 'The Faliscans in prehistoric times', *PAAR*, 5, 1925.
121 N. LAMBOGLIA, *Liguria Romana, studi storico-topografici*, 1, Rome 1939.
122 E. T. SALMON, *Samnium and the Samnites*, Cambridge 1967.

c MODERN WORKS OF SYNTHESIS

123 L. HOMO, *L'Italie primitive et les débuts de l'impérialisme romain*, Paris 1925.
124 D. RANDALL MACIVER, *Italy before the Romans*, Oxford 1928.
125 J. WHATMOUGH, *The Foundations of Roman Italy*, London 1937.

d ARCHAEOLOGICAL MATERIAL

126 M. EBERT, *Reallexikon der Vorgeschichte*, 15 vols, Berlin 1924–32.
127 G. A. MANSUELLI, *Les civilisations de l'Europe ancienne*, Paris 1967.
128 R. PITTIONI, 'Italien, Urgeschichtliche Kulturen', *RE*, suppl. 9, 1962, 105–371.
129 J. SUNDWALL, *Die älteren italischen Fibeln*, Berlin 1943.
130 F. VON DUHN, F. MESSERSCHMIDT, *Italische Gräberkunde*, 2 vols, Heidelberg 1924–39.

e STRATIGRAPHY OF LIPARI

131 L. BERNABÒ BREA, *Sicily before the Greeks*, London 1957.
132 M. CAVALIER, 'Civilisations préhistoriques des îles Éoliennes et du territoire de Milazzo', *RA*, 50, 1957, 123–47.
133 Id., 'Les cultures préhistoriques des îles Éoliennes et leur rapport avec le monde égéen', *BCH*, 84, 1960, 319–46.
134 Id., 'La grotte de Zinzulusa (terre d'Otrante) et la stratigraphie de Lipari', *MEFR*, 72, 1960, 7–34.

f CHALCOLITHIC AGE

135 L . BERNABÒ BREA, 'Il neolitico e la prima civiltà dei metalli', *Atti del I. Convegno sulla Magna Grecia*, Taranto 1961 (Naples 1962), 61–97.

136 F . RITTATORE, 'Necropoli eneolitica presso il ponte S. Pietro nel Viterbese', *SE*, 16, 1942, 557–62.

137 F . RITTATORE, 'Scoperte di età eneolitica e del Bronzo nella Maremma Tosco-Laziale', *Rivista di Scienze preistoriche*, 6, 1951, 3–33.

138 P . C . SESTIERI, 'Primi risultati degli scavi nella necropoli di Paestum', *RAAN*, n.s., 23, 1947–8, 251–308.

139 Id., 'La necropoli preistorica di Paestum', *Atti del I. Convegno intern. di Preistoria e Protostoria mediterranea*, Florence 1950, 195–200.

140 Id., 'Paestum', *Itinerari dei Musei e Monumenti d'Italia*, Rome, 3rd ed., 1954.

141 F . VON DUHN, 'Remedello', *Reallexikon der Vorgeschichte*, 11, 122.

g BRONZE AGE

142 W . HELBIG, *Die Italiker in der Po-Ebene*, Leipzig 1879.

143 C . E . ÖSTENBERG, *Luni sul Mignone e problemi della preistoria d'Italia*, Lund 1967.

144 T . S . PEET, *The Stone and Bronze Ages in Italy*, Oxford 1909.

145 R . PERONI, 'Per una definizione dell'aspetto culturale 'subapenninico' come fase culturale a se stante', *Mem. Linc.*, series 8, 9, 1960, 4–253.

146 L . PIGORINI, 'Le più antiche civiltà dell'Italia', *BPI*, from 1883 to 1908.

147 S . M . PUGLISI, *La civiltà appenninica*, Florence 1959.

148 U . RELLINI, *Le origini della civiltà italica*, Rome 1929.

149 Id., 'Le stazioni enee delle Marche di fase seriore e la civiltà italica', *Mon. Ant. Linc.*, 34, 1931, 129–280.

150 Id., 'La civiltà enea in Italia', *BPI*, 53, 1933, 63–96.

151 G . SÄFLUND, *Le terremare della provincia di Modena, Reggio, Emilia, Palma, Piacenza*, Lund-Leipzig 1939.

h URNFIELD AND VILLANOVAN CULTURES

152 G . ANNIBALDI, 'I rapporti culturali tra le Marche e l'Umbria nell'età del ferro', *Atti del I. Convegno di Studi Umbri*, Gubbio 1963 (1964), 91–8.

153 Id., 'Rinvenimenti villanoviani a Fermo', *BPI*, 10, 1956, 229–35.

154 *Civiltà del Ferro*, studi pubblicati nella ricorrenza centenaria della scoperta di Villanova (important articles by L. LAURENZI, G. A. MANSUELLI, R. PERONI, etc.), Bologna, 1960.

155 P. DUCATI, *Storia di Bologna*. I: *I tempi antichi*, Bologna, 1928.

156 W. DUMITRESCU, *La civiltà del ferro nel Piceno*, Bucharest 1930.

157 A. GRENIER, *Bologne villanovienne et étrusque*, Paris 1912.

158 K. KRÖMER and others, *Das Gräberfeld von Hallstatt*, 2 vols, Florence 1959.

159 L. LAURENZI, 'La civiltà villanoviana e la civiltà del ferro dell'Italia settentrionale e dell'Europa centrale', *Civiltà del Ferro*, 3–71.

160 P. LAVIOSA-ZAMBOTTI, 'Le Origini della civiltà di Villanova', *Civiltà del Ferro*, 73–98.

161 *Mostra dell'arte delle situle dal Po al Danubio*, Padua 1961.

162 H. MÜLLER-KARPE, *Beiträge zur Chronologie der Urnenfelderzeit nördlich und südlich der Alpen*, Berlin 1959.

163 M. PALLOTTINO, 'Sulle facies culturali arcaiche dell'Etruria', *SE*, 13, 1939, 85–129.

164 Id., 'Sulla chronologia dell'età del bronzo finale e dell'età del ferro in Italia', *SE*, 28, 1960, 11–47.

165 D. RANDALL MACIVER, *Villanovan and Early Etruscans*, Oxford 1924.

166 Id., *The Iron Age in Italy*, Oxford 1927.

167 U. RELLINI, 'Sull'origine della civiltà del ferro in Italia', *SE*, 12, 1938, 9–16.

168 G. SÄFLUND, 'Bemerkungen zur Vorgeschichte Etruriens', *SE*, 12, 1938, 17–55.

169 R. SCARANI, 'Repertorio di scavi e scoperte dell'Emilia e Romagna', *Preistoria dell'Emilia e Romagna*, II, Bologna 1963.

i THE IRON AGE IN SOUTHERN ITALY

170 E. GABRICI. 'Cuma', *Mon. Ant. Linc.*, 22, 1913, 5–872.

171 W. JOHANNOWSKY, 'Gli Etruschi in Campania', *Klearchos*, 19, 1963, 62–75.

172 Id., on the Villanovan discoveries at Capua, *Atti del III. Convegno sulla Magna Grecia*, Taranto 1963, 261–3.

173 K. KILIAN, 'Untersuchungen zu früheisenzeitlichen Gräbern aus dem Vallo di Diano', *MDAI (R)*, Erg. Heft, 10, 1964.

174 J. DE LA GENIÈRE, 'Note sur la chronologie des nécropoles de Torre Galli et Canale-Janchina', *MEFR*, 76, 1964, 7–23.

175 Id., *Recherches sue les cultures indigènes et la pénétration grecque en Italie méridionale: Sala Consilina*, Naples 1968.

176 M. MAYER, *Apulien vor und während der Hellenisierung*, Leipzig-Berlin 1914.

177 J. MERTENS, *Ordona*: I. *Rapport provisoire sur les travaux de la mission belge en 1962–1963 et 1963–1964*, Brussels-Rome 1965.

178 M. NAPOLI, V. PANEBIANCO, B. D'AGOSTINO, *Mostra della Preistoria e della Protostoria nel Salernitano*, Salerno 1962.

179 P. ORSI, 'Le necropoli preelleniche calabresi di Torre Galli e di Canale, Ianchina, Patariti', *Mon. Ant. Linc.*, 31, 1926, 5–276.

180 Q. QUAGLIATI, 'Necropoli arcaica ad incinerazione presso Timmari nel Materano, *Mon, Ant. Linc.*, 16, 1906, 5–166.

181 P. SESTIERI, 'Necropoli villanoviane in provincia di Salerno', *SE*, 28, 1960, 73–107.

182 G. SÄFLUND, 'Eine vorgriechische Siedlung bei Tarent', *Dragma Martino P. Nilsson*, Lund-Leipzig 1939, 453–90.

j THE CULTURE OF LATIUM

183 T. ASHBY, 'Alba Longa', *JPh*, 27, 1901, 37–50.

184 D. BRUSADIN, 'Su un'urna a capanna di Campo Reatino', *BPI*, n.s., 10, 1956, 449–54.

185 W. R. BRYAN, 'Italic Hut Urns and Hut Urns Cemeteries', *Papers and Monographs of the American Academy in Rome*, 4, 1925.

186 D. FACCENNA, 'Rinvenimento di una necropoli dell'età del ferro in Tivoli', *BPI*, n.s., 9, 1954–5, 413–26.

187 P. G. GIEROW, *The Iron Age Culture of Latium*: I. *Classification and Analysis*, Lund, 1966; II. *Excavations and Finds*: 1. *The Alban Hills*, Lund 1964.

188 G. LUGLI, 'Dove sorgeva Alba Longa?', *NAnt*, 64, 1929, 522–8.

189 R. PERONI, 'Tradizione subappeninica nella decorazione ceramica della cultura laziale', *AClass*, 10, 1958, 243–54.

190 G. PINZA, 'Monumenti primitivi di Roma e del Lazio antico', *Mon. Ant. Linc.*, 15, 1905, 5–844.

k THE ORIGINS OF ROME: ARCHAEOLOGICAL DATA

191 A. M. COLINI, 'Storia e Topografia del Celio nell'antichità', *Memorie della Pontef. Acc.*, 7, 1944.

192 E. GJERSTAD, *Early Rome*: I. *Stratigraphical Researches in the Forum Romanum and along the Sacra Via* (1953); II. *The Tombs* (1956); III. *Fortifications, Domestic Architecture, Sanctuaries, Stratigraphical Excavations* (1960); IV. *Synthesis of archaeological Evidence* (1966), Lund.

193 Id., 'Discussions concerning Early Rome', 2, *Opuscula Romana*, V, 1965, 1–74.

194 H. MÜLLER-KARPE, 'Vom Anfang Roms', *MDAI* (R), Erg. Heft, 5, 1959.

195 Id., 'Zur Stadtwerdung Roms', *MDAI(R)*, Erg. Heft, 8, 1963.

196 M. PALLOTTINO, 'Le origini di Roma', *AClass*, 12, 1960, 1–36.

197 R. PERONI, 'Per una nuova cronologia del sepolcreto arcaico del Foro: sequenza culturale e significato storico', *Civiltà del Ferro*, 461–99.

198 Id., 'S. Omobono: materiali del età del bronzo e degli inizi dell'età del ferro', *BCAR*, 77, 1959–1960 (1962), 3–28.

199 S. M. PUGLISI, 'Nuovi resti sepolcrali nella valle del Foro Romano', *BPI*, n.s., 8, 1951 (1952, 45–9).

200 Id., 'Gli abitatori primitivi del Palatino attraverso le testimonianze archeologiche e le nuove indagini stratifiche sul Germalo', *Mon. Ant. Linc.*, 41, 1951, 1–138.

201 P. ROMANELLI, 'Problemi archeologici del Foro Romano e del Palatino', *StudRom*, 1, 1953, 3–12.

202 P. ROMANELLI, G. CARETTONI, E. GJERSTAD, S. M. PUGLISI, 'Nuove indagini su Roma antichissima', *BPI*, n.s., 9, 1954–5, 257–322.

203 P. ROMANELLI, 'Nuovi dati archeologici sulla storia primitiva di Roma', *Bull. de la Fac. des Lettres de Strasbourg*, 1960, 235–43.

204 Id., 'Certezze e ipotesi sulle origini di Roma', *StudRom*, 13, 1965, 5–18.

(ii) *The peopling of France in prehistory*

a THE CELTS IN GENERAL

205 P. BOSCH-GIMPERA, 'Les mouvements celtiques, *EC*, 5, 2, 1950–51, 352–400; 6, 1, 1952, 71–126; 6, 2, 1953–4, 328–55; 7, 1, 1955, 146–84.

206 P.-M. DUVAL, 'Contribution des fouilles de France (1941–1955), à l'histoire de la Gaule', *Historia*, 5, 1956, 238–53.

207 J. FILIP, *Keltové ve Středni Europě*, Prague 1956 (summary in German: *Die Kelten in Mitteleuropa*).

208 C. F. C. HAWKES, 'The Celts: Report on the study of their culture and their Mediterranean relations', *Actes du VIIIe Congr. intern. d'Archéologie classique*, Paris 1963, 61–79.

b COLLECTIONS AND TOOLS OF RESEARCH

209 J. DÉCHELETTE, *Manuel d'archéologie préhistorique, celtique et gallo-romaine*, still indispensable, 4 vols., Paris, 1908–15.

210 P.-M. DUVAL, 'Chronique gallo-romaine,' *REA*, fasc. 2 of every year since 1953.

c MODERN WORKS OF SYNTHESIS

211 A. GRENIER, *La Gaule celtique*, Paris 1945.

212 Id., *Les Gaulois*, Paris 1945.

213 H. HUBERT, *Les Celtes et l'expansion celtique jusqu'à l'époque de la Tène*, Paris 1932.

214 Id., *Les Celtes depuis l'époque de la Tène et la civilisation celtique*, Paris 1932; revised ed. 1950.

215 P. JACOBSTAHL, *Early Celtic Art*, Oxford 1944.

216 C. JULLIAN, *Histoire de la Gaule*. The first two volumes (I. *Les invasions gauloises et la colonisation grecque*; II. *La Gaule indépendente*) are more particularly germane to our period. Paris 1908.

d THE TUMULUS CIVILIZATION

217 G. FABRE, *Les civilisations protohistoriques de l'Aquitaine*, Paris 1952.

218 F. HENRY, *Les tumulus du département de la Côte-d'Or*, Paris 1933.

219 P. A. SCHAEFFER, *Les tertres funéraires préhistoriques dans la forêt de Haguenau*, 2 vols., Haguenau 1926–30.

e THE URNFIELDS

220 W. KIMMIG, 'Où en est la civilisation des champs d'urnes en France, principalement dans l'Est?', *RAE*, 2, 1951, 65–81; 3, 1952, 7–19; 137–72; 5, 1954, 7–28; 209–29.

221 M. E. MARIÉN, 'Où en est la question des champs d'urnes?', *AC*, 17, 1948, 413–44.

222 H. RIX, 'Zur Verbreitung und Chronologie einiger keltischer Ortsnamentypen', *Festschrift für P. Goessler*, Stuttgart, 1954, 99–107.

f HALLSTATT CULTURE; VIX

223 A. BRISSON, J.-J. HATT, 'Les nécropoles hallstattiennes d'Aulnay-aux-Planches (Marne)', *RAE*, 4, 1953, 193–233.
224 A. BRISSON, J.-J. HATT, 'Fonds de cabanes de l'age du bronze final et du premier âge du fer en Champagne', *RAE*, 17, 1966, 165–97.
225 J. CARCOPINO, *Promenades historiques aux pays de la Dame de Vix*, Paris 1957.
226 R. JOFFROY, 'La tombe de Vix', *MMAI*, 48, 1, 1954.
227 Id., *Les sépultures à char du premier âge du fer en France*, Dijon 1958.
228 Id., *L'oppidum de Vix et la civilisation hallstattienne finale dans l'est de la France*, Dijon 1960.
229 Id., *Le trésor de Vix, histoire et portée d'une grande découverte*, Paris 1962.

g LA TÈNE I

230 D. BRETZ-MAHLER, *La civilisation de La Tène I en Champagne: le faciès marnien*, doctoral thesis, Paris (Sorbonne) 1965.
231 P.-M. FAVRET, 'Les nécropoles des Jogasses à Chouilly (Marne)', *Préhistoire*, 5, 1936, 24–119.
232 G. GOURY, *L'enceinte d'Haulzy et sa nécropole*, Nancy 1908.
233 J.-J. HATT, 'Fouilles du Pègue et de Malpas, et leur signification pour la chronologie des invasions celtiques', *CRAI*, 1959, 86–91.

h ENSÉRUNE

234 J. JANNORAY, *Ensérune, contribution à l'étude des civilisations pré-romaines de la Gaule méridionale*, Paris 1955.
235 Id., 'La poterie ibérique et l'expansion des Ibères en Gaule méridionale', *Mél. Charles Picard*, 1948, 448–62.

i THE CELTS IN GREECE AND ITALY

236 P. BIENKOWSKI, *Die Darstellungen der Gallier in der hellenistischen Kunst*, Vienna 1908.
237 R. CHEVALLIER, 'La Celtique du Pô, position des problèmes', *Latomus*, 21, 1962, 366–70.

238 J.-J. HATT, 'Sur les traces des invasions celtiques en Italie du Nord', *RES*, 38, 1960, 69–70.

239 G. A. MANSUELLI, 'Problemi storici della Civiltà gallica in Italia', *Hommages à A. Grenier*, 1962, 1067–93.

240 C. PEYRE, 'L'armement défensif des Gaulois en Émilie et en Romagne, perspectives historiques', *Studi Romagnoli*, 14, 1963, 255–77.

(iii) *The peopling of Spain in the early historic period*

241 P. BOSCH-GIMPERA, 'Two Celtic waves in Spain, *PBA*', 26, 1939.

242 Id., 'Les Celtes et la civilisation des urnes en Espagne', *Préhistoire*, 8, 1941, 121–57.

243 Id., *El pobliamento antiguo y la formación de los pueblos de España*, Mexico, 1945.

244 Id., 'Los Iberos', *Cuadernos de Historia de España*, 9, Buenos Aires 1948.

245 Id., 'La formazione dei popoli della Spagna', *PP*, 11, 1949, 97–129.

246 R. ÉTIENNE, *Le culte impérial dans la péninsule ibérique*, ethnological introduction, 28–48 with maps 5 and 6, Paris 1958.

247 M. GÓMEZ-MORENO, *Misceláneas (Historia Arte Arqueologia), La Antigüedad* series, Madrid 1949.

248 F. PALLARES SALVADOR, *El poblado ibérico de San Antonio de Calaceite*, Bordighera-Barcelone 1965.

249 L. PERICOT-GARCIA, *L'Espagne avant la conquête romaine*, tr. R. LANTIER, Paris 1952.

250 A. TOVAR, 'Le substrat prélatin de la péninsule ibérique, *Actes du Ier Congr. de la Fédération intern. des Associations d'Études classiques*, Paris 1951, 49–60.

B The Etruscans

a THE PROBLEM OF THEIR ORIGIN

A colloquium on this subject was held in London in 1958: *A Ciba Foundation Symposium in Medical Biology and Etruscan Origins*, London 1959, with contributions by H. HENCKEN, R. BLOCH, A. PIGANIOL, L. BANTI, J. B. WARD PERKINS and others.

251 F. ALTHEIM, *Der Ursprung der Etrusker*, Baden-Baden 1950.

252 P. BOSCH-GIMPERA, 'Réflexions sur le problème des Étrusques', *Mélanges A. Piganiol*, Paris 1966, 637–43.
253 G. DEVOTO, 'Gli Etruschi nel quadro dei popoli italici antichi', *Historia*, 6, 1957, 23–33.
254 P. DUCATI, *Le problème étrusque*, Paris 1938.
255 H. HENCKEN, 'Archaeological Evidence for the Origin of the Etruscans', *A Ciba Symposium*, 29–49.
256 Id., 'A View of Etruscan Origins', *Antiquity*, 40, 1966, 205–211.
257 Id., *Tarquinia, Villanovans and early Etruscans*, Cambridge, U.S.A., 2 vols., 1968.
258 M. PALLOTTINO, *L'Origine degli Etruschi*, Rome 1947.
259 Id., 'Erodoto autoctonista', *SE*, 20, 1949, 11–16.
260 Id., 'Nuovi studi sul problema delle origini etrusche (bilancio critico)', *SE*, 29, 1961, 3–30.
261 L. PARETI, *Le Origini etrusche*, Florence 1926.
262 A. PIGANIOL, 'Les Étrusques, peuple d'Orient', *Cahiers d'Histoire mondiale*, 1, 1953, 328–52.
263 G. SÄFLUND, 'Über den Ursprung der Etrusker', *Historia*, 6, 1957, 10–22.
264 F. SCHACHERMEYR, *Etruskische Frühgeschichte*, Berlin 1929.
265 H. H. SCULLARD, 'Two Halicarnassians and a Lydian, a Note on Etruscan Origins', *Studies presented to V. Ehrenberg*, London 1966, 225–31.
266 J. B. WARD PERKINS, 'The Problem of Etruscan Origins', *HSCP*, 64, 1959, 1–26.

b ETRUSCAN CIVILIZATION : GENERAL WORKS

The classic treatise of
267 K. O. MÜLLER, W. DEECKE, *Die Etrusker*, 2 vols., Stuttgart 1877, has been reprinted with introduction and bibliography by A. J. Pfiffig, Graz 1965.
268 L. BANTI, *Il mondo degli Etruschi*, Rome, 2nd ed., 1960.
269 R. BLOCH, *Le mystère étrusque*, Paris 1956.
270 A. BOËTHIUS, 'The Etruscan centuries in Italy', *Etruscan Culture, Land and People, Archaeological Research and Studies . . . by the Swedish Institute in Rome*, Malmö 1962, 1–126.
271 P. DUCATI, *Etruria antica*, 2 vols., Turin 1927.
272 J. HEURGON, *La vie quotidienne chez les Étrusques*, Paris 1961.

K

273 A. HUS, *Les Étrusques, peuple secret*, Paris 1957.

274 A. NEPPI MODONA, *A Guide to Etruscan Antiquities*, Florence, 5th ed., 1963.

275 M. RENARD, *Initiation à l'étruscologie*, Bruxelles 1941.

276 E. RICHARDSON, *The Etruscans, their Art and Civilization*, Chicago-London 1964.

277 H. H. SCULLARD, *The Etruscan Cities and Rome*, London 1967.

278 M. PALLOTTINO, *Etruscologia*, Milan, 5th ed. 1968 (cf. *La civilisation étrusque*, translation of the 2nd ed. by R. BLOCH, Paris 1949).

279 O. W. VON VACANO, *Die Etrusker: Werden und geistige Welt*, Stuttgart 1955.

C ETRUSCAN CEMETERIES AND TOMBS

280 Å. ÅKERSTRÖM, *Studien über die etruskischen Gräbern, unter besonderer Berücksichtigung der Entwicklung des Kammergrabes*, Lund-Leipzig 1934.

281 M. BIZZARRI, 'La necropoli di Crocefisso del Tufo in Orvieto', *SE*, 30, 1962, 1–154.

282 G. CAPUTO, 'La Montagnola di Quinto Fiorentino, l'orientalizzante e le tholoi dell'Arno', *BA*, 47, 1962, 115–52.

283 C. DENSMORE CURTIS, 'The Bernardini Tomb (Praeneste)', *MAAR*, 3, 1919.

284 Id., 'The Barberini Tomb (Praeneste)', *MAAR*, 5, 1925.

285 J. FALCHI, *Vetulonia e la sua necropoli antichissima*, Florence 1891.

286 S. GSELL, *Fouilles dans la nécropole de Vulci*, Paris 1891.

287 J. HEURGON, 'Valeurs féminines et masculines dans la civilisation étrusque', *MEFR*, 73, 1961, 139–60.

288 R. MENGARELLI, 'Caere e le recenti scoperte', *SE*, 1, 1927, 145–71.

289 Id., 'Le necropoli di Caere. Nuove osservazioni su speciali usi e riti funerari', *SE*, 11, 1937, 77–93.

290 M. MORETTI, 'Caere: La necropoli della zona B detta della tegola dipinta', *Mon. Ant. Lince*, 42, 1955, 1049–1135.

291 L. PARETI, *La tomba Regolini-Galassi del Museo Gregoriano Etrusco e la civiltà nell'Italia centrale nel sec. VII a.C.*, Rome 1947.

292 R. RICCI, 'Caere: La necropoli della zona A detta del Recinto', *Mon. Ant. Linc.*, 42, 1955, 201–1048.

293 G. ROSI, 'Sepulchral architecture as illustrated by the rock façades of central Etruria', *JHS*, 15, 1925, 1–59; 17, 1927, 59–96.

3b E. and G. COLONNA, Castel d'Asso: necropoli rupestri d'Etruria, 2 vols., Rome 1970.

94 R. VIGHI, 'Caere: Il sepolcreto arcaico del Sorbo', *Mon. Ant. Linc.*, 42, 1955, 24–199.
See also [640]; [643]; [648].

d EXCAVATIONS IN ETRUSCAN CITIES

95 R. BARTOCCINI, 'Tre anni di scavi a Vulci (1956–1958)', *Atti del VII. Congr. intern. di Archeologia classica*, Rome, II, 1961, 257–81.

96 R. BLOCH, 'Volsinies étrusque: essai historique et topographique', *MEFR*, 59, 1947, 9–39.

97 Id., 'Gli Scavi della Scuola francese a Bolsena', *SE*, 31, 1963, 399–424.

98 F. E. BROWN, 'Cosa: I. History and Topography', *MAAR*, 20, 1951.

99 Id., 'Cosa: II. The Temples and the Arx', *MAAR*, 26, 1960.

00 G. D'ACHIARDI, 'L'industria metallurgica a Populonia', *SE*, 3, 1929, 397–404.

01 A. DE AGOSTINO, 'Nuovi contributi all'archeologia di Populonia', *SE*, 24, 1955–1956, 255–68.

02 Id., 'La cinta fortificata di Populonia', *SE*, 30, 1962, 3–9.

03 F. DE RUYT, 'Nouvelles oeuvres d'art étrusque découvertes à Castro (prov. de Viterbe)', *CRAI*, 1967, 150–68.

3b G. CAMPOREALE, *La Tombe del Duce* (Vetulonia), Florence 1967.

04 G. FOTI, 'The principal cities of southern Etruria and their special characteristics', *A Ciba Symposium*, 12–23.

4b K. HANELL and others, 'The excavations of the Swedish Institute in Rome in San-Giovenale and its environs', *Etruscan Culture, Land and People*, Malmö, 1962, 277–358.

05 C. LAVIOSA, 'Rusellae', *SE*, 27, 1959, 2–40; 28, 1960, 289–337; 29, 1961, 31–45; 31, 1963, 39–65; 33, 1965, 49–106.

06 A. NEPPI MODONA, *Cortona etrusca e romana nella storia e nell'arte*, Florence 1925.

07 M. PALLOTTINO, 'Tarquinia', *Mon. Ant. Linc.*, 36, 1937.

08 P. ROMANELLI, 'Tarquinia: Scavi e ricerche nell'area della città', *Not. Sc.*, 1948, 193–270.

09 J. B. WARD PERKINS, 'Veii: The historical Topography of the ancient City', *PBSR*, 39, 1961, 1–123.

e THE CISALPINE AND CAMPANIAN PROVINCES

310 N. ALFIERI, P. E. ARIAS, H. HIRMER, *Spina*, Munich 1958.
311 A. MAIURI, 'Greci ed Etruschi a Pompei', *Saggi di varia antichità*, Venice, 1954, 241–74.
312 G. A. MANSUELLI, 'La terza Bologna', *SE*, 25, 1957, 13–30.
313 Id., *Marzabotto, Guida alla Città e al Museo Etrusco*, Bologna 1966.
314 'Spina e l'Etruria Padana', *Atti del I. Convegno di Studi Etruschi*, Florence 1959.
315 M. PALLOTTINO, 'Gli Etruschi nell'Italia del Nord', *Hommages à A. Grenier*, Brussels 1962, 1207–16.
316 M. ZUFFA, 'La questione etrusca in Felsina', *Civiltà del Ferro*, Bologna 1960, 119–30.

f ETRUSCAN SOCIETY AND INSTITUTIONS

317 T. FRANKFORT, 'Les classes serviles en Étrurie', *Latomus*, 18, 1959, 3–22.
318 J. HEURGON, 'Les pénestes étrusques chez Denys d'Halicarnasse (IX, 5, 4)', *Latomus*, 18, 1959, 713–23.
319 Id., 'L'État étrusque', *Historia*, 6, 1957, 63–97.
320 R. LAMBRECHTS, *Essai sur les magistratures des républiques étrusques*, Brussels–Rome 1959.
321 S. MAZZARINO, 'Sociologia del mondo etrusco e problemi della tarda etruscità', *Historia*, 6, 1957, 98–122.

g ETRUSCAN RELIGION

322 J. M. BLÁZQUEZ, 'La tomba del Cardinale y la influencia orfico-pitagórica en las creencias etruscas de ultratumba', *Latomus*, 24, 1965, 3–39.
323 C. CLEMEN, *Die Religion der Etrusker*, Bonn 1936.
324 F. DE RUYT, *Charun, démon étrusque de la mort*, Brussels 1934.
325 G. FURLANI, 'Mantica babilonese e mantica etrusca', *Tyrrhenica, Saggi di Studi etruschi*, Milan, 1957, 61–76.
326 G. HERBIG, 'Zur religion und Religiosität der Etrusker', *Historia*, 6, 1957, 123–32.
327 J. HEURGON, 'The date of Vegoia's Prophecy', *JRS*, 49, 1959, 41–5.
328 J. NOUGAYROL, 'Les rapports des haruspicines étrusque et assyro-babylonienne et le foile d'argile de Falerii Veteres (Villa Giulia), *CRAI*, 1955, 509–19.

29 M. PALLOTTINO, 'Deorum sedes', *Studi in onore di A. Calderini e R. Paribeni*, Milan 1956, III, 223–4.

30 A. PIGANIOL, 'Sur le calendrier brontoscopique de Nigidius Figulus', *Studies presented to A. C. Johnson*, Princeton 1951, 79–87.

31 C. O. THULIN, *Die Etruskische Disciplin*, 3 vols., Göteborg 1906–9.

32 C. C. VAN ESSEN, *Did Orphic Influences on Etruscan Tomb Painting Exist?*, Amsterdam 1927.

33 S. WEINSTOCK, 'Martianus Capella and the Cosmic System of the Etruscans', *JRS*, 36, 1946, 101–29.

34 Id., ' "Libri fulgurales" ', *PBSR*, 19, 1951, 122–53.

h ETRUSCAN ART

35 P. AMANDRY, 'Objets orientaux en Grèce et en Italie aux viiie et viie siècles av. J.-C.', *Syria*, 35, 1958, 73–109.

36 A. ANDRÉN, *Architectural Terracottas from Etrusco-Italic Temples*, Lund 1940.

37 J. BAYET, 'Position historique et technique de l'art étrusque', *R. Arts*, 5, 1955, 130–38.

38 J. D. BEAZLEY, *Etruscan Vase-Painting*, Oxford 1947.

39 R. BLOCH, 'L'art étrusque et son arrière-plan historique', *Historia*, 6, 1957, 53–62.

40 E. COCHE DE LA FERTÉ, *Les bijoux antiques*, Paris 1956.

41 T. DOHRN, *Die schwarzfigurigen etruskischen Vasen aus der zweiten Hälfte des 6. Jhs*, Diss. Cologne 1937.

42 G. Q. GIGLIOLI, *L'Arte etrusca*, Milan 1935.

43 G. M. A. HANFMANN, *Altetruskische Plastik: I, Die menschliche Gestalt in der Rundplastik bis zum Ausgang der orientalisierenden Kunst*, Diss. Würzburg 1936.

44 Id., Greece and Lydia; the Impact of Hellenic Culture, *Actes du VIIIe Congrès intern. d'Archéologie classique*, Paris 1963, 491–9.

45 Y. HULS, *Ivoires d'Étrurie*, Brussels-Rome 1957.

46 A. HUS, *Recherches sur la statuaire de pierre étrusque archaïque*, Paris 1961.

47 Id., 'Quelques cas de rapports directs entre Étrurie, Cappadoce et Syrie du Nord vers 600 av. J.-C.', *MEFR*, 71, 1959, 7–42.

48 Id., 'Sculpture étrusque (1945–1964)', *Lustrum*, 1966-II, 145–72.

49 R. MAXWELL HYSLOP, 'Urartian Bronzes in Etruscan Tombs', *Iraq*, 18, 1956, 150–67.

350 M. MORETTI, *Nuovi Monumenti della pittura etrusca*, Milan 1966.

351 K. A. NEUGEBAUER, 'Archaische Vulcenter Bronzen', *AA*, 38–9, 1923–4, 302–26.

352 M. PALLOTTINO, *La peinture étrusque*, Geneva 1952.

353 Id., *La sculo di Vulca*, Rome, 2nd ed., 1948.

354 Id., 'Gli Scavi di Karmer Blur in Armenia e il problema delle connessioni tra l'Urartu, la Grecia e l'Etruria', *AClass*, 7, 1955, 109–23.

355 R. REBUFFAT, 'Une pyxis d'ivoire perdue de la tombe Regolini-Galassi', *MEFR*, 75, 1963, 369–431.

356 P. J. RUS, *Tyrrhenica: an archaeological Study of Etruscan Sculpture in the archaic and classical periods*, Copenhagen 1941.

357 Id., *An Introduction to Etruscan Art*, Copenhagen 1953.

358 Id., 'Art in Etruria and Latium during the first half of the Vth century B.C.', *Entretiens XIII*, Fondation Hardt, 1966, Vandoeuvres-Geneva, 65–96.

C External influences on civilization in Italy

(i) *Mycenaean influences*

359 F. BIANCOFIORE, 'La ceramica micenea dello Scoglio del Tonno e la civiltà del bronzo tardo nell'Italia meridionale', *RIA*, 7, 1958, 5–44.

360 Id., *La civiltà micenea nell'Italia meridionale: I. La ceramica*, Rome 1963.

361 A. FURUMARK, *The Mycenaean Pottery, Analysis and Classification*, Stockholm 1940–41.

362 Id., *The Chronology of Mycenaean Pottery*, Stockholm 1941.

363 S. MARINATOS, 'The Minoan and Mycenaean Civilization and its Influence on the Mediterranean and on Europe', *Atti del VI. Congr. intern. delle Scienze preistor. e protostoriche*, Rome 1962, I, 161–76.

364 G. PUGLIESE CARRATELLI, 'Prima fasi della colonizzazione greca in Italia', *Atti del I. Convegno di Studi sulla Magna Grecia*, Taranto 1961 (Naples 1962), 137–49.

365 Id., 'Per la storia delle relazioni micenee con l'Italia', *PP*, 13, 1958, 205–20.

366 W. TAYLOUR, *Mycenaean Pottery in Italy and Adjacent Areas*, Cambridge 1958.
Cf. [131].

(ii) *Phoenician colonization in the west*

a ON THE PHOENICIANS IN GENERAL the latest books are:

67 D. HARDEN, *The Phoenicians*, London 1962.

7b S. MOSCATI, *Il mondo dei Fenici*, Milan 1966.

On individual points:

68 W. F. ALBRIGHT, 'The Eastern Mediterranean about 1060', *Studies presented to D. M. Robinson*, Saint Louis, I, 1951, 223–31.

69 J. DAUVILLIER, 'Le droit maritime phénicien', *RIDA*, 6, 1959, 33–63.

70 J.-G. FÉVRIER, 'L'ancienne marine phénicienne et les découvertes récentes', *NClio*, 1/2, 1949–50, 128–43.

71 P. MONTET, *La nécropole royale de Tanit*, Paris 1947.

b HISTORY AND PRESENT STATE OF THE PROBLEM

72 J. BELOCH, 'Die Phoeniker im aegeischen Meer', *RhM*, 49, 1894, 111–32.

73 V. BÉRARD, *Les Phéniciens et l'Odyssée*, Paris 1903; revised ed. with new material, 2 vols, 1927.

74 Id., *La résurrection d'Homère*, Paris 1930.

75 R. CARPENTER, Phoenicians in the West, *AJA*, 62, 1958, 35–53.

76 G. GARBINI, 'L'espansione fenicia nel Mediterraneo', *Cultura e scuola*, 1963, 92–7.

77 Id., 'I Fenici in Occidente', *SE*, 34, 1966, 111–47.

78 S. MOSCATI, 'Rapporti tra Greci, Fenici, Etrusci ed altre popolazioni alla luce delle nuove scoperte', *Quaderni Acc. Linc.*, 87, 1966, 3–9.

c THE PROBLEM OF TARSHISH

79 W. F. ALBRIGHT, 'New light on the early history of Phoenician Colonization', *BASO*, 83, Oct. 1941, 14–22.

80 R. DION, 'Tartessos, l'Océan homérique et les travaux d'Hercule', *RH*, 224, 1960, 27–44.

81 P. CINTAS, 'Tarsis, Tartessos, Gadès', *Semitica*, 16, 1966, 5–37.

82 J. M. SOLÁ SOLÉ, 'Tarshish y los comienzos de la colonizacion fenicia en Occidente', *Sefarad*, 17, 1957, 23–35.

83 U. TÄCKHOLM, 'Tartessos und die Saülen des Herakles', *Opuscula Romana*, V, Lund 1965, 143–200.

d THE PHOENICIANS IN CYPRUS

384 E. GJERSTAD, *The Swedish Cyprus Expedition*, IV. 2: *The Cypro-geometric, Cypro-archaic and Cypro-classical periods*, Stockholm 1948.

e IN MALTA

385 S. MOSCATI and others, *Missione archeologica italiana a Malta:*
— 'Rapporto preliminare della campagna di 1963', Rome 1964;
— 'Rapporto preliminare della campagna di 1964', Rome 1965;
— 'Rapporto preliminare della campagna di 1965', Rome 1966.
Notices are published every year in *Oriens Antiquus*, Rome.

f IN SICILY

386 S. CHIAPPISI, *Il Melqart di Sciacca e la questione fenicia in Sicilia*, Rome 1961.

387 P. CINTAS, 'La céramique de Motyé et le problème de la date de la fondation de Carthage', *BCTH*, 1963–4 (1966), 107–15.

388 B. J. S. ISSERLIN, 'The Oxford University archaeological trial excavations at the Phoenician site of Motya near Marsala (Sicily)', *Atti del VII. Congr. intern. di Archeologia classica*, Rome, II, 1961, 41–3.

389 V. TUSA and others: *Mozia*, I: *Rapporto preliminare della campagna di scavi*, 1964; *Mozia*, II: 1965; *Mozia*, III: 1966; *Mozia*, IV: 1967.

390 J. I. S. WHITAKER, *Motya, a Phoenician colony in Sicily*, London 1921.

g IN SARDINIA

391 F. BARRECA, G. PESCE, *Mostra della Civiltà punica in Sardegna*, Cagliari 1959.

392 F. BARRECA and others, *Monte Sirai*, I: *Rapporto preliminare della Missione archeologica dell'Università di Roma e della Soprintendenza alle Antichità di Cagliari*, Rome 1964; *Monte Sirai*, II: *Rapporto preliminare . . .*, Rome 1965; *Monte Sirai*, III: *Rapporto preliminare . . .*, Rome 1966.

393 A. DUPONT-SOMMER, 'Nouvelle lecture d'une inscription phénicienne archaïque de Nora, en Sardaigne (CIS, 1, 144)', *CRAI*, 1948, 12–22.

394 J.-G. FÉVRIER, 'L'inscription archaïque de Nora', *Rev. d'Assyriologie*, 44, 1950, 123–6.

395 G. LILLIU, 'Rapporti fra la civiltà nuragica e la civiltà fenicio punica in Sardegna', *SE*, 18, 1944, 323–70.

396 Id., 'Le stele puniche di Sulcis', *Mon. Ant. Linc.*, 40, 1944.

397 G. PATRONI, 'Nora, colonia fenicia in Sardegna', *Mon. Ant. Linc.*, 14, 1904, 109–268.

398 G. PESCE, *Sardegna punica*, Cagliari 1960.

399 Id., *Tharros*, Cagliari 1966.

400 A. TARAMELLI, 'Nuove ricerche nel santuario nuragico di Santa Vittoria di Serri', *Mon. Ant. Linc.*, 34, 1931, 6–122.

h IN AFRICA: I — CARTHAGE

401 E. BOUCHER, 'Céramique archaïque d'importation au Musée Lavigerie de Carthage', *Byrsa*, 19, 1953, 11–38.

01b P. CINTAS, 'Un sanctuaire précarthaginois sur la grève de Salammbô', *Rev. Tun.*, 3rd series, 1, 1948, 1–31.

402 Id., *Céramique punique*, Paris 1950.

403 Id., 'Laurentianus, LXIX, 22 ou la torture d'un texte', *Mélanges A. Piganiol*, Paris 1966, 1681–92.

03b Id., *Manuel d'archéologie punique*, I, Paris 1970.

404 P. DEMARGNE, 'La céramique punique', *RA*, 38, 1951, 44–52.

405 E. O. FORRER, 'Karthago wurde erst 673–663 v. Chr. begründet', *Festschrift F. Dornseiff*, Leipzig 1953, 85–93.

406 E. FRÉZOULS, 'Une nouvelle hypothèse sur la fondation de Carthage', *BCH*, 79, 1955, 153–76.

407 P. GAUCKLER, *Les nécropoles antiques de Carthage*, 2 vols., Paris 1915.

408 S. GSELL, *Histoire ancienne de l'Afrique du Nord* (the first four volumes), Paris 1914–20.

409 D. HARDEN, 'The Pottery from the precinct of Tanit at Salammbo, Carthage', *Iraq*, 4, 1937, 59–89.

410 C. PICARD, *Carthage*, Paris 1951.

10b G.-CH. PICARD, 'Le sanctuaire dit de Tanit à Carthage', *CRAI*, 1945, 443–52.

411 Id., *Les religions de l'Afrique antique*, Paris 1954.

412 Id., *Le monde de Carthage*, Paris 1956.

413 J. VERCOUTTER, *Les objets égyptiens et égyptisants du mobilier funéraire carthaginois*, Paris 1945.

i AT VARIOUS PLACES IN NORTH AFRICA

414 P. CINTAS, 'Deux campagnes de fouilles à Utique', *Karthago*, 2, 1951, 1–88; 5, 1954, 89–154.

415 L. FOUCHER, *Hadrumetum*, Tunis 1964.

416 P. CINTAS, 'Fouilles puniques à Tipasa', *RAfr*, 92, 1948, 263-330.

417 G. VUILLEMOT, *Reconnaissances aux échelles puniques d'Oranie*, Autun 1965.

j IN MOROCCO

418 J. CARCOPINO, *Le Maroc antique*, Paris 1943.

419 P. CINTAS, *Contribution à l'étude de l'expansion carthaginoise au Maroc*, Publications de l'Institut des Hautes Études marocaines, 56, 1954.

420 M. EUZENNAT, 'Rapport sur l'archéologie marocaine en 1957 et 1958', *BCTH*, 1959–60 (1962), 45–59.

421 A. JODIN, 'Note préliminaire sur l'établissement préromain de Mogador', *BAM*, 2, 1957, 9–40.

422 Id., 'Statuettes de tradition phénicienne trouvées au Maroc', *BAM*, 4, 1960, 427–35.

423 Id., *Mogador, comptoir phénicien du Maroc atlantique*, Rabat 1966.

424 M. TARADELL, 'Nota acerca de la prima epoca de los Fenicios en Marruecos', *Tamuda*, 1, 1958, 71–88.

425 F. VILLARD, 'Céramique grecque du Maroc', *BAM*, 4, 1960, 1–26.

k IN SPAIN

426 M. ASTRUC, *La necropoli de Villaricos*, Madrid 1951.

427 P. BOSCH-GIMPERA, 'Phéniciens et Grecs dans l'Extrême-Occident', *NClio*, 3, 1951, 269–96.

428 G. BONSOR, 'Les colonies agricoles préromaines de la vallée du Baetis', *RA*, 35, 1899, 126–159; 232–325; 376–91.

429 R. DION, 'Le problème des Cassitérides', *Latomus*, 11, 1952, 306–14.

430 A. GARCIA Y BELLIDO, 'El Mundo de las Colonizaciones' (*Historia de Espana*, I, 2, by D. R. MENÉNDEZ PIDAL, Madrid 1952).

431 H. G. NIEMEYER, 'Feldbegehung bei Torre del Mar', *MDAI(M)*, 3, 1962, 38–44.

432 M. PELLICER, 'Excavaciones en la necropolis punica "Laurita" del Cerro de San Cristobal (Almuñécar, Granada)', Madrid 1962 (cf. 'Ein altpunisches Gräberfeld bei Almuñécar, prov. Granada: *MDAI(M)*', 4, 1963, 9–38.

433 M. PELLICER, H. G. NIEMEYER, H. SCHUBART, 'Eine altpunische Kolonie an der Mündung des Rio Velez', *AA*, 1964, 476–93.

433b H. G. NIEMEYER, H. SCHUBART, 'Toscanos und Trayamar', *MDAI(M)*, 9, 1968, 76–105.

433c Id., 'Tartessos y sus problemas', *V. Symposium internacional de Prehistoria Peninsular*, Barcelona 1969.

434 A. SCHULTEN, *Tartessos*, Hambourg, 2nd ed., 1950.

435 D. VAN BERCHEM, 'Sanctuaires d'Hercule-Melqart: contribution à l'étude de l'expansion phénicienne en Méditerranée', *Syria*, 44, 1967, 73–109; 307–38.

l IN ITALY

436 U. KAHRSTEDT, 'Phoenikische Handel an der Italienischen Küste', *Klio*, 12, 1912, 461–73.

437 A. PIGANIOL, 'Les origines d'Hercule', *Hommages à A. Grenier*, Brussels 1962, 1261–4.

438 R. REBUFFAT, 'Les Phéniciens à Rome', *MEFR*, 78, 1966, 7–48.

439 B. SEGALL, 'Some Syrian and Syro-Hittite elements in the Art of the West', *AJA*, 60, 1956, 165–170.

440 D. VAN BERCHEM, 'Hercule-Melqart à l'Ara Maxima', *RPAA*, 32, 1959–60, 61–8; cf. [435].

(iii)—1. *Greek colonization in southern Italy and Sicily*

Since 1961 Taranto has witnessed every year a 'Convegno di Studi sulla Magna Grecia': nine volumes of *Atti* have been published:

I. *Greci e Italici in Magna Grecia*, 1961, Naples 1962;

II. *Vie di Magna Grecia*, 1962, Naples 1963;

III. *Metropoli e Colonie*, 1963, Naples 1964;

IV. *Santuari di Magna Grecia*, 1964, Naples 1965;

V. *Filosofia e Scienze in Magna Grecia*, 1965, Naples 1966;

VI. *Letteratura e Arte figurata nella Magna Grecia*, 1966, Naples 1967;

VII. *La Città e il suo Territorio*, 1967, Naples 1968;

VIII. *La Magna Grecia e Roma nell'età arcaica*, 1968, Naples 1969;

IX. *La Magna Grecia nel Mondo ellenistico*, 1969, Naples 1970.

In each of these Convegni the superintendants of Campania, Lucania, Calabria and Apulia review the results of the latest archaeological work. The Istituto di Storia antica of the University of Palermo has been publishing the periodical *Kôkalos* since 1955. The fourth volume (1958) was devoted to Timoleon, the eighth to the influence of colonization on the native peoples.

a TWO GENERAL WORKS ARE INDISPENSABLE

441 J. BÉRARD, *La colonisation grecque de l'Italie méridionale et de la Sicile dans l'Antiquité: l'histoire et la légende*, Paris 1941; 2nd ed., 1957.

442 T. J. DUNBABIN, *The Western Greeks: the history of Sicily and South Italy from the foundation of the Greek colonies to 480 B.C.*, Oxford 1948; important analysis by:

443 J. BÉRARD, 'L'hellénisation de la Grande-Grèce', *RA*, 35, 1950, 182–8.

b FOR BIBLIOGRAPHY ON GREEK COLONIZATION IN THE WEST WE ARE INDEBTED TO:

444 J. BÉRARD, *Bibliographie topographique des principales cités grecques de l'Italie méridionale et de la Sicile dans l'Antiquité*, Paris 1941.

c OTHER WORKS OF SYNTHESIS

445 J. BAYET, *La Sicile grecque*, Paris 1930.

446 E. CIACERI, *Storia della Magna Grecia*, 3 vols., Milan-Genoa-Rome 1927.

447 F. LENORMANT, *La Grande-Grèce*, 2 vols., Paris 1881.

448 B. PACE, *Arte e Civiltà della Sicilia antica*, 4 vols., Milan-Genoa-Rome-Naples 1935.

449 E. PAIS, *Storia della Sicilia e della Magna Grecia*, Turin 1894.

450 A. SCHENK VON STAFFENBERG, *Trinkakria: Sizilien und Grossgriechenland*, Munich-Vienna 1963.

The following are also concerned with colonization in the west:

451 E. BELIN DE BALLU, *L'histoire des colonies grecques du littoral nord de la mer Noire*, annotated bibliography of books and articles published in the U.S.S.R. 1940–62, Leyden 1965.

452 K. SCHEFOLD, 'Die Grabungen in Eretria im Herbst 1964 und 1965', *AK*, 9, 1966, 106–24; 11, 1968, 91–109; 12, 1969, 72–87.

453 E. WILL, *Korinthiaka: recherches sur l'histoire et la civilisation de Corinthe des origines aux guerres médiques*, Paris 1955.

d CHRONOLOGY OF COLONIZATION, ESPECIALLY ON POTTERY-DATINGS

454 J. DUCAT, 'L'archaïsme à la recherche de points de repère chronologiques, *BCH*, 86, 1962, 165–84.

455 F. JOHANSEN, *Les vases sicyoniens*, Paris 1923.

456 H. PAYNE, *Necrocorinthia, a Study of Corinthian art in the archaic period*, Oxford 1931.

457 Id., *Protokorintische Vasenmalerei*, Berlin 1933.

458 B. SCHWEIZER, 'Untersuchungen zur Chronologie und Geschichte der geometrischen Stile in Griechenland', *MJDI (A)*, 33, 1918, 1–152.

459 G. VALLET, F. VILLARD, 'Céramique et histoire grecque', *RH*, 225, 1961, 295–318.

460 R. VAN COMPERNOLLE, *Étude de chronologie et d'historiographie siciliotes: recherches sur le système chronologique des sources de Thucydide concernant la fondation des colonies siciliotes*, Brussels-Rome 1959.

461 F. VILLARD, 'La chronologie de la céramique protocorinthienne', *MEFR*, 60, 1948, 7–34.

462 Id., *Les Vases grecs*, Paris 1958.

e ISCHIA AND CHALCIDIAN COLONIZATION

463 G. BUCHNER, 'Nota preliminare sulle ricerche preistoriche nell'Isola d'Ischia', *BPI*, n.s., 1, 1936–7, 65–93.

464 Id., *Origine e passato dell'Isola d'Ischia*, Naples 1948.

465 Id., 'Scavi nella necropoli di Pithecusa', *ASMG*, n.s., 1, 1954, 11–19.

466 Id., C. F. RUSSO, 'La coppa di Nestore e un'iscrizione metrica di Pitecusa dell'VIII. secolo av. Cr.', *RAL*, 10, 1955, 215–34.

467 Id., 'Lo scavo della necropoli di Pitecusa', *Atti del III. Convegno sulla Magna Grecia*, 1963, 263–74.

468 H. METZGER, 'Sur la date du graffite de la "coupe de Nestor"', *REA*, 67, 1965, 301–5.

469 G. VALLET, *Rhegion et Zancle*, Paris 1958.

470 Id., 'La colonisation chalcidienne et l'hellénisation de la Sicile orientale', *Kôkaslos*, 8, 1962, 30–51.

f MEGARIAN AND DORIAN COLONIES IN SICILY:
HYBLAEAN MEGARA

471 G. VALLET, F. VILLARD, 'Les dates de fondation de Mégara Hyblaea et de Syracuse', *BCH*, 76, 1952, 289–346.
472 Id., *Mégara Hyblaea: 2. La céramique archaïque*, Paris 1964.
473 Id., 'Le repeuplement de Mégara Hyblaea à l'époque de Timoléon, *Kôkalos*, 4, 1958, 100–106.
473b F. VILLARD, 'Mégara Hyblaea', *MEFR*, 63, 1951, 7–52.

g GELA AND AGRIGENTUM

474 D. ADAMESTEANU, 'Nouvelles fouilles à Géla et dans l'arrière-pays', *RA*, 49, 1957, 20–46; 147–180.
475 Id., 'Rapporti tra Greci ed indigeni nella luce delle nuove scoperte in Italia', *Atti del VII. Congr. intern. di Archeologia classica*, Rome 1961, II, 45–52.
476 Id., 'L'ellenizzazione della Sicilia ed il momento di Ducezio', *Kôkalos*, 8, 1962, 199–209.
477 E. DE MIRO, 'La fondazione di Agrigento e l'ellenizzazione del territorio fra il Salso e il Platani', *Kôkalos*, 8, 1962, 122–52.
478 T. J. DUNBABIN, 'Minos and Daedalos in Sicily', *PBSR*, 16, 1948, 1–18.
479 P. GRIFFO, L. VON MATT, *Géla: destin d'une cité grecque de Sicile*, Paris 1964.

h COLONIZATION IN OTHER AREAS OF SICILY

480 A. DI VITA, 'La penetrazione siracusana nella Sicilia sud-orientale alla luce delle più recenti scoperte archeologiche', *Kôkalos*, 2, 1956, 177–205.
481 Id., 'Camarina e Scornavacche in età Timolontea', *Kôkalos*, 4, 1958, 83–99.
482 V. TUSA, 'L'irradiazione della civiltà greca nella Sicilia occidentale', *Kôkalos*, 8, 1962, 52–68.

i COLONIZATION IN MAGNA GRAECIA

483 L. VON MATT, U. ZANOTTI-BIANCO, *La Magna Grecia*, Genoa 1961.

j VARIOUS COLONIES, FROM WEST TO EAST

484 P. ORSI, 'Caulonia', *Mon. Ant. Linc.*, 23, 1914, 685–947.

485 G. SCHMIEDT, R. CHEVALLIER, *Caulonia e Metaponto:* applicazioni della *fotografia aerea in ricerche di topografia antica nella Magna Grecia*, Florence 1959.

486 J. S. CALLAWAY, *Sybaris*, Baltimore 1950.

487 V. EHRENBERG, 'The foundation of Thurii', *AJPh*, 69, 1948, 149–170 (= *Polis und Imperium*, Zurich-Stuttgart 1964, 298–315).

488 L. PONNELLE, 'Le commerce de la première Sybaris', *MEFR*, 27, 1907, 243–76.

489 F. SARTORI, 'Il problema storico di Sibari', *AR*, n.s., 5, 1960, 145–163 (= 'Sybaris: das historische Problem und die neuesten archäeologischen Entdeckungen', *Die Welt als Geschichte*, 21, 1961, 195–210).

490 P. ZANCANI-MONTUORO, 'Sibariti e Serdei', *RAL*, series 18, 17, 1962, 1–9.

491 J. PERRET, *Siris: recherches critiques sur l'histoire de la Siritide avant 453–452*, Paris 1941

492 P. ZANCANI-MONTUORO, 'Siris-Sironi-Pixunte', *ASCL*, 18, 1949, 1–20.

493 D. ADAMESTEANU, 'Problèmes de la zone archéologique de Métaponte', *RA*, n.s., 1967, 3–38.

494 F. G. LO PORTO, 'Ceramica arcaica della necropoli di Taranto', *ASAA*, 37–8, 1959–60, 7–230.

495 Id., 'Gli scavi sull'acropoli di Satyrion', *BA*, 49, 1964, 67–80.

496 P. WUILLEUMIER, *Tarente des origines à la conquête romaine*, Paris 1939.

497 J. BÉRARD, 'Les origines historiques et légendaires de Posidonia à la lumière des récentes fouilles archéologiques', *MEFR*, 57, 1940, 7–31.

498 Id., 'A l'Héraion du Silaris, près de Paestum', *RA*, 40, 1952, 12–22; 45, 1955, 121–140.

498b A. MAIURI, 'Origine e decadenza di Paestum', *Saggi di varia antichità*, Venice 1954, 79–96.

499 P. SESTIERI, 'Le origini di Posidonia alla luce delle recenti scoperte di Palinuro', *AClass*, 2, 1950, 180–86.

500 P. ZANCANI-MONTUORO, *Sibari, Poseidonia e lo Heraion*, ASCL 19, 1950, 65–84.

501 Id., U. ZANOTTI-BIANCO, F. KRAUSS, *Heraion alla foce del Sele:* 1. *Il santuario, il tempio della dea, rilievi figurati varii*, Rome, 1951; 2. *Il primo thesauros*, Rome 1954.

502 A. GITTI, 'Sulla colonizzazione greca nell'alto e medio Adriatico', *PP*, 24, 1952, 161–91.

503 G. VALLET, 'Athènes et l'Adriatique', *MEFR*, 42, 1950, 33–52.

k TRADE-ROUTES IN MAGNA GRAECIA:
THE 'ISTHMUS ROUTES'

504 E. KIRSTEN, 'Viaggiatori e vie in epoca greca e romana', *Atti del II. Convegno sulla Magna Grecia*, 1962, 137–58.

505 A. MAIURI, 'Vie di Magna Grecia', *Atti del II. Convegno sulla Magna Grecia*, 1962, 61–70.

506 E. LEPORE, 'Vie di Magna Grecia: incontri di economia e di civiltà', *Atti del II. Convegno sulla Magna Grecia*, 1962, 197–221.

507 G. VALLET, 'Les routes maritimes de la Grande-Grèce', *Att del II. Convegno sulla Magna Grecia*, 1962, 117–135.

l RELATIONS WITH MOTHER-CITIES; POLITICAL INSTITUTIONS

508 S. MAZZARINO, 'Metropoli e colonie', *Atti del III. Convegno sulla Magna Grecia*, 1963, 51–85.

509 F. SARTORI, *Problemi di storia constituzionale italiota*, Rome 1953.

510 J. SEIBERT, *Metropolis und Apoikie*, Diss. Wurzburg 1963.

511 G. VALLET, 'Métropoles et colonies, leurs rapports jusque vers la fin du VI*e* siècle', *Atti del III. Convegno sulla Magna Grecia*, 1963, 209–29.

m COINAGE

512 L. BREGLIA, 'Problemi della più antica monetazione in Magna Grecia', *AIIN*, 1954, 11–20.

513 Id., 'La coniazione incusa di Magna Grecia', *AIIN*, 1956, 23–37.

514 A. STAZIO, 'Metropoli e colonie: la documentazione numismatica', *Atti del III. Convegno sulla Magna Grecia*, 1963, 113–32.

n ART IN MAGNA GRAECIA

515 E. LANGLOTZ, M. HIRMER, *Die Kunst der Westgriechen in Sizilien und Unteritalien*, Munich 1963.

516 S. MOLLARD-BESQUES, *Les terres cuites grecques*, Paris 1963.

517 E. D. VAN BUREN, *Archaic fictile revetments in Sicily and Magna Graecia*, London 1923.

518 G. VALLET, F. VILLARD, 'Un atelier de bronziers: sur l'école du cratère de Vix', *BCH*, 79, 1955, 50–74.

519 P. WUILLEUMIER, *Le trésor de Tarente*, Paris 1930.

O CULTURE AND RELIGION

520 M. BIEBER, *The history of the Greek and Roman theater*, Princeton 1939.

521 P. BOYANCÉ, 'L'influence pythagoricienne sur Platon', *Atti del V. Convegno sulla Magna Grecia*, 1965, 73–113.

522 D. COMPARETTI, *Laminette orfiche*, Florence 1910.

523 A. DELATTE, *Essai sur la politique pythagoricienne*, Liège-Paris 1922.

524 A. FRASSINETTI, *Fabula Atellana*, Pavia 1953.

525 G. GIANNELLI, *Culti e miti della Magna Grecia: contributo alla storia più antica delle colonie greche in Occidente*, Florence 1922; 2nd ed., Naples 1963.

526 M. P. LOICQ-BERGER, *Syracuse, histoire culturelle d'une cité grecque*, Brussels 1967.

527 A. OLIVIERI, *Frammenti della commedia greca e del mimo nella Sicilia e nella Magna Grecia*, Naples, 2nd ed., 1947.

528 G. PUGLIESE CARRATELLI, 'Culti e dottrine religiose in Magna Grecia', *Atti del IV Convegno sulla Magna Grecia*, 1964, 19–45.

P POLITICAL HISTORY

529 H. BERVE, *Die Herrschaft des Agathokles*, Munich 1953.

530 M. J. FONTANA, Fortuna di Timoleonte, *Kôkalos*, 4, 1958, 3–23.

531 P. ORLANDINI, 'La rinascità della Sicilia nell'età di Timoleonte alla luce delle nuove scoperte archeologiche', *Kôkalos*, 4, 1958, 24–30.

532 M. SORDI, *Timoleonte*, Palermo 1951.

533 K. F. STROHEKER, *Dionysios: I. Gestalt und Geschichte des Tyran von Syrakus*, Wiesbaden 1958.

(iii)—2. *Greek colonization in Gaul and Spain*

a ON PHOCAEAN COLONIZATION the problems are admirably stated by:

534 J.-P. MOREL, 'Les Phocéens en Occident; certitudes et hypothèses', *PP*, 108–110, 1966, 378–420.

534b Id., 'Les Phocéens dans l'Extrême-Occident, vas depuis Tartessos', *PP*, 130–33, 1970, 285–9.

   See also:

535 J. CARCOPINO, 'Les leçons d'Aléria', *Rev. de Paris*, Oct. 1962, 1–15.

536 M. GIGANTE, 'Il logos erodoteo sulle origini di Elea', *PP*, 108–110, 1966, 295–310.

537 J. JEHASSE, 'La "victoire à la cadméenne" d'Hérodote (I, 166) et la Corse dans les courants d'expansion grecque', *REA*, 64, 1962, 241–86.

538 S. MAZZARINO, *Introduzione alle guerre puniche*, Catania 1947.

539 M. NAPOLI, 'La ricerca archeologica di Velia', *PP*, 108–110, 1966, 190–226.

540 G. NENCI, 'Le relazioni con Marsiglia nella politica estera Romana', *RSL*, 24, 1958, 24–97.

541 G. VALLET, F. VILLARD, 'Les Phocéens en Méditerranée occidentale et la fondation de Hyélè', *PP*, 108–110, 1966, 166–190.

   A conference was organized in April 1969 by the Centre Jean Bérard at the Institut Français in Naples. The reports and papers were published in a special number of *La Parola del Passato*: Nuovi Studi su Velia, (130–33, 1970).

b FOUNDING OF MARSEILLES AND HELLENIZING OF SOUTHERN FRANCE

542 F. BENOIT, *Recherches sur l'hellénisation du midi de la Gaule*, Aix-en-Provence 1965.

543 Id., Épaves de la côte de Provence', *Gallia*, 14, 1956, 23–34.

544 J. BRUNEL, 'Étienne de Byzance et le domaine marseillais', *REA*, 47, 1945, 122–33.

545 Id., 'Marseille et les fugitifs de Phocée, *REA*, 50, 1948, 5–26.

546 G. DAUX, 'Le trésor de Marseille', *BCH*, 82, 1958, 360–64.

547 H. GALLET DE SANTERRE, 'A propos de la céramique grecque de Marseille: questions d'archéologie languedocienne', *REA*, 64, 1962, 378–88.

548 P. JACOBSTAHL, J. NEUFFER,' Gallia Graeca: recherches sur l'hellénisation de la Provence', *Préhistoire*, 2, 1933, 1–64.

549 H. ROLLAND, 'A propos des fouilles de Saint-Blaise: la colonisation préphocéenne; les Étrusques; le domaine de Marseille', *REA*, 51, 1949, 83–99.

550 Id., *Fouilles de Saint-Blaise (Bouches-du-Rhône)*, Paris 1951.
551 Id., *Fouilles de Saint-Blaise (1951–1956)*, Paris 1956.
552 F. VILLARD, *La céramique grecque de Marseille*, Paris 1960.
553 Id., 'Les canthares de bucchero et la chronologie du commerce étrusque d'importation', *Hommages à A. Grenier*, Brussels, 1962, 1625–35.

C MASSILIOT EXPANSION ON THE MAINLAND, AND GREEK TRADE-ROUTES IN GAUL (A colloquium on this topic was held in Dijon in 1958)

554 A. ALFÖLDI, 'La corporation des Transalpini et Cisalpini à Avenches', *Ur-Schweiz*, 16, 1952, 3–9.
555 F. BENOIT, 'Observations sur les routes du commerce gréco-étrusque', *Actes du Colloque de Dijon*, 15–20.
556 H. A. CAHN, 'Le vase de bronze de Graechwil et autres importations méridionales en Suisse avant les Romains', *Actes du Colloque de Dijon*, 21–30.
557 W. DEHN, 'Die Befestigung der Heuneburg (Per. IV) und die griechische Mittelmeerwelt', *Actes du Colloque de Dijon*, 55–62.
558 P.-M. DUVAL, 'Les inscriptions gallo-grecques, trouvées en France', *Actes du Colloque de Dijon*, 63–70.
559 J.-J. HATT, 'Commerce grec du VIe siècle et commerce italo-grec du Ve', *RAE*, 6, 1955, 150–52.
560 Id., A. PERRAUD, CH. LAGRAND, 'Le Pègue, habitat hallstattien et comptoir ionien en Haute-Provence', *Atti del VII. Congr. intern. di Archeologia classica*, Rome 1956, III, 177–86.
561 P. JACOBSTHAL, 'Rhodische Bronzekannen aus Hallstatt-Gräbern', *JDAI*, 44, 1929, 198–200.
562 W. KIMMIG, 'Kulturbeziehungen zwischen der nord-westalpinen Hall-stattkultur und der mediterranen Welt', *Actes du Colloque de Dijon*, 75–87.
563 L. LERAT, 'L'amphore de bronze de Conliège (Jura)', *Actes du Colloque de Dijon*, 89–98.
564 CH. PICARD, 'Les voies terrestres du commerce hallstattien', *Latomus*, 19, 1960, 409–28.
565 D. VAN BERCHEM, 'Du portage au péage: le rôle des cols transalpins dans l'histoire du Valais antique', *MH*, 13, 1956, 199–208.

D Rome under the kings

a THE ORIGINS OF ROME

566 A. ALFÖLDI, *Early Rome and the Latins*, Ann Arbor 1964.

567 R. BLOCH, *Tite-Live et les premiers siècles de Rome*, Paris 1965.

567b Id., *Les Origines de Rome*, Paris 1959, 2nd ed., 1968.

568 E. CIACERI, *Le Origini di Roma*, Milan 1937.

569 F. CORNELIUS, *Untersuchungen zur frühen römischen Geschichte*, Munich 1940.

570 P. DE FRANCISCI, *Primordia Ciuitatis*, Rome 1959.

571 F. DE MARTINO, *Storia della Costituzione Romana*, I, 2nd ed., Naples 1958.

572 E. GJERSTAD, *Legends and Facts concerning early Roman History*, Lund 1962.

573 E. MEYER, *Römischer Staat und Staatsgedanke*, 2nd ed., Zürich-Stuttgart 1961.

574 A. MOMIGLIANO, 'An Interim Report on the Origins of Rome', *JRS*, 53, 1963, 95–121 = *Terzo Contributo* . . ., Rome 1966, II, 545–98.

575 T. MOMMSEN, *Römische Forschungen*, 2 vols., Berlin 1864.

576 A. PIGANIOL, *Essai sur les origines de Rome*, Paris 1916.

b THE 'MONTES' AND 'COLLES'

577 P. GRIMAL, 'Le dieu Janus et les origines de Rome', *Lettres d'Humanité*, IV, 1945, 15–121.

578 T. HACKENS, 'Capitolium Vetus', *BIBR*, 33, 1961, 69–88.

579 L. A. HOLLAND, 'Septimontium or Saeptimontium', *TAPhA*, 84, 1953, 16–34.

580 Id., *Janus and the Bridge*, Rome 1961.

581 A. K. MICHELS, 'The Topography and Interpretation of the Lupercalia', *TAPhA*, 84, 1953, 35–59.

582 T. MOMMSEN, 'Tatiuslegende', *Gesammelte Schriften*, IV, 22–35.

583 J. POUCET, 'Le Septimontium et la Succusa chez Festus et Varron: un problème d'histoire et de topographie romaines', *BIBR*, 32, 1960, 25–73.

584 Id., 'Les origines mythiques des Sabins à travers l'oeuvre de Caton, de Cn. Gellius, de Varron, d'Hygin et de Strabon', *Études étrusco-italiques*, Recueils de travaux d'histoire et de philologie, 4th series, 31, Louvain 1963, 155–225.

585 Id., *Recherches sur la légende sabine des origines de Rome*, Louvain 1967.

586 Id., 'L'importance du terme "Collis" pour l'étude du développement urbain de la Rome archaïque', *AC*, 36, 1967, 99–115.

87 A. VON GERKAN, 'Zum Suburaproblem', *RhM*, 96, 1953, 20–30.

88 G. WISSOWA, 'Septimontium und Subura', *Gesammelte Abhandlungen zur römischen Religions- und Stadtsgeschichte*, 1904, 230–52.

C STRUCTURE OF PRIMITIVE ROMAN SOCIETY

89 F. R. ADRADOS, *El sistema gentilicio decimal de los indoeuropeos occidentales y los origenes de Roma*, Madrid 1948.

90 A. ALFÖLDI, *Der frührömische Reiteradel und seine Ehrenabzeichen*, Baden-Baden 1952.

91 E. BENVENISTE, 'Le nom de l'esclave à Rome', *REL*, 10, 1932, 429–40.

92 Id., '"Liber" et "Liberi"', *REL*, 14, 1936, 51–8.

2b Id., 'Le vocabulaire des institutions indo-européennes', 2 vols, Paris 1969.

93 J. BINDER, *Die Plebs, Studien zur römische Rechtsgeschichte*, Leipzig 1909.

94 G. BLOCH, 'La plèbe romaine', *RH*, 106, 1911, 241-75; 107, 1911, 1–42.

95 G. BONFANTE, 'The Origins of the Latin Name-System', *Mélanges J. Marouzeau*, Paris 1948, 43–59.

96 G. DEVOTO, 'Le origini tripartite di Roma', *Athenaeum*, 31, 1953, 335–43 (= *Scritti minori*, II, Florence 1967, 348–54).

97 G. DUMÉZIL, *Mitra-Varuna, essai sur deux représentations indo-européennes de la souveraineté*, Paris 1940; 2nd ed., 1948.

98 Id., *Jupiter, Mars, Quirinus, essai sur la conception indo-européenne de la société et sur les origines de Rome*, Paris 1941.

99 Id., *Horace et les Curiaces*, Paris 1942.

00 Id., *Tarpeia, cinq essais de philologie comparative indo-européenne*, Paris 1947.

01 Id., 'Remarques sur les dieux "Grabovio-" d'Iguvium', *RPh*, 28, 1954, 225–35.

02 Id., *Aspects de la fonction guerrière chez les Indo-Européens*, Paris 1956.

03 Id., *L'idéologie tripartite des Indo-Européens*, Paris 1958.

3b Id., *Mythe et Epopée: l'idéologie des trois fonctions dans les épopéas des peuples indo-européens*, Paris 1968.

3c Id., *Idées romaines*, Paris 1969.

3d Id., *Heur et Malheur du guerrier*, Paris 1969.

04 FUSTEL DE COULANGES, *La cité antique*, Paris 1864.

05 Id., *Les origines du système féodal, le bénéfice et le patronat pendant l'époque mérovingienne*, Paris 1890.

606 H. LÉVY-BRUHL, 'Esquisse d'une théorie sociologique de l'esclavage à Rome', *Revue générale du droit*, 1931, 1–19.

d THE KING: RELIGIOUS CONCEPTIONS

607 P. CATALANO, *Contributo allo studio del diritto augurale*, Turin, I, 1910.
608 G. DUMÉZIL, 'A propos du latin "ius"', *RHR*, 67, 1948, 95–112.
609 Id., 'Ordre, fantaisie, changement dans les pensées archaïques de l'Inde et de Rome (à propos du latin "mos")', *REL*, 32, 1954, 139–62.
610 Id., 'Remarques sur "augur", "augustus"', *REL*, 35, 1957, 126–51.
611 A. ERNOUT, 'Augur, Augustus', *Mém. de la Soc. de Linguistique*, 22, 1922, 234–8 (=*Philologica*, I, Paris 1946, 67–71).

e KINGSHIP AND ITS BADGES

612 U. COLI, *Regnum*, Rome 1951.
613 A. ALFÖLDI, 'Insignien und Tracht der römischen Kaiser', *MDAI(R)*, 50, 1935, 1–171.
614 Id., 'Hasta, Summa Imperii: the Spear as Embodiment of Sovereignty in Rome', *AJA*, 63, 1959, 1–27.

f THE REGIA

615 F. E. BROWN, 'New Soundings in the Regia', *Entretiens XIII*, Fondation Hardt, Vandoeuvres-Geneva 1966, 47–60.

g RELIGIOUS FUNCTIONS OF THE KING: THE CALENDAR

616 O. LEUZE, *Die römische Jahrzählung, ein Versuch ihre geschichtliche Entwicklung zu ermitteln*, Tübingen 1909.
617 A. K. MICHELS, 'The "Calendar of Numa" and the Pre-Julian Calendar', *TAPhA*, 80, 149, 320–46.
618 Id., *The Calendar of the Roman Republic*, Princeton 1967.
619 J. PAOLI, 'Les définitions varroniennes des jours fastes et néfastes', *RD*, 30, 1952, 294–327.
620 Id., 'La notion de temps faste et celle de temps comitial', *REA*, 56, 1954, 121–49.
621 M. RENARD, 'Iuno Covella', *Mél. H. Grégoire*, Brussels 1952, IV, 401–408.
622 H. J. ROSE, 'The pre-Caesarian Calendar', *CJ*, 40, 1944–4, 65–76.

h JUDICIAL FUNCTIONS OF THE KING

623 L. GERNET, 'Paricidas', *RPh*, 11, 1937, 13–29.

624 M. KASER, 'Das altrömische Ius', *Handbuch des Altertumswissenschaft*, 10, 3, 3, 1, Munich 1955.

625 H. LÉVY-BRUHL, *Quelques problèmes du très ancien droit romain*, Paris 1934.

626 Id., *Nouvelles études sur le très ancien droit romain*, Paris 1947.

627 P. NOAILLES, *Fas et Jus, études de droit romain*, Paris 1948.

628 Id., *Du droit sacré au droit civil*, Paris 1949.

i POLITICAL FUNCTIONS OF THE KING

629 G. BLOCH, *Les origines du sénat romain*, Paris 1883.

630 J. CARCOPINO, 'Les prétendues "lois royales"', *MEFR*, 54, 1937, 344–76.

631 A. MAGDELAIN, 'Auspicia ad patres redeunt', *Hommages à J. Bayet*, Brussels, 1964, 527–473.

632 J. PAOLI, 'Le "Ius Papirianum" et la loi Papiria', *RD*, 24, 1946–7, 157–200.

j THE TRADITIONAL ACCOUNT: THE TROJAN LEGEND

633 A. ALFÖLDI, *Die Troianischen Urahnen der Römer*, Basle 1957.

634 F. BÖMER, *Rom und Troia: Untersuchungen zur Frühgeschichte Roms*, Baden-Baden 1951.

635 J. HEURGON, '"Lars", "largus" et "Lare Aineia"', *Mél. A. Piganiol*, Paris 1966, 655–64.

636 J. PERRET, *Les origines de la légende troyenne de Rome*, Paris 1942.

k NUMA

637 J.-P. MOREL, 'Thèmes sabins et thèmes numaïques dans le monnayage de la République romaine', *MEFR*, 74, 1962, 7–59.

l THE ETRUSCANS IN ROME: THE TARQUINS

638 A. ALFÖLDI, 'Die Etrusker in Latium und Rom', *Gymnasium*, 70, 1963, 385–93.

639 A. BLAKEWAY, '"Demaratos": a study in some aspects of the earliest hellenisation of Latium and Etruria', *JRS*, 25, 1935, 129–49.

640 M. CRISTOFANI, *La tomba delle iscrizioni a Cerveteri*, Florence 1965.

641 J. HEURGON, 'Tite-Live et les Tarquins', *IL*, 7, 1955, 56–64.

642 M. PALLOTTINO, 'La iscrizione arcaica su vaso di bucchero rinvenuta ai piedi del Campidoglio', *BCAR*, 69, 1941, 101–107.

643 Id., 'La necropoli di Cerveteri', *Itinerari dei Musei e Monumenti d'Italia*, 3rd ed., 1944.

m SERVIUS-TULLIUS-MASTARNA; VULCI AND ROME

644 G. COLONNA, 'S. Omobono, la ceramica etrusca dipinta', *BCAR*, 87, 1959–60, 125–43.

645 Id., 'Il ciclo etrusco-corinzio dei Rosoni, contributo alla conoscenza della ceramica e del commercio vulcente', *SE*, 29, 1961, 47–88.

646 M. CRISTOFANI, 'Ricerche sulle pitture della tomba François à Vulci', *Dialoghi di Archeologia*, I, 1967, 186–219.

647 J. HEURGON, 'La coupe d'Aulus Vibenna', *Mél. J. Carcopino*, Paris 1966, 515–28.

648 F. MESSERSCHMIDT, 'Nekropolen von Vulci', *JDAI*, Erg. Heft, 12, Berlin 1930.

n SERVIUS TULLIUS: THE CENTURIATE CONSTITUTION

649 P. DE FRANCISCI, 'Per la storia dei comitia centuriata', *Studi V. Arangio-Ruiz*, Naples 1953, I, 1–32.

650 G. DE SANCTIS, 'Le origini dell'ordinamento centuriato', *RFIC*, 61, 1933, 289–98.

651 P. FRACCARO, 'La storia dell'antichissimo esercito romano e l'età dell'ordinamento centuriato', *Opuscula*, II, Pavia, 1957, 287–306.

652 R. FRIEZER, *De ordening van Servius Tullius*, Diss. Amsterdam 1957.

653 H. M. LAST, 'The Servian Reforms', *JRS*, 35, 1945, 30–48.

654 H. MATTINGLY, 'The property qualifications of the Roman classes', *JRS*, 27, 1937, 99–107.

655 A. MOMIGLIANO, 'Studi sugli ordinamenti centuriati', *SDHI*, 4, 1938, 509–20.

656 C. NICOLET, 'La réforme des comices de 179 av. J.-C.', *RD*, 39, 1961, 341–58.

657 M. P. NILSSON, 'The introduction of Hoplite Tactics at Rome', *JRS*, 19, 1929, 1–11.

658 A. PIGANIOL, 'Un document d'histoire sociale, la constitution servienne', *Annales d'histoire économique et sociale*, 5, 1933, 113–24.

659 E. SCHÖNBAUER, 'Die römische Centurien-Verfassung in neuer Quellenschau', *Historia*, 2, 1953, 21–49.

660 E. S. STAVELEY, 'The constitution of the Roman Republic: I. The origin and early development of the centuriate organization', *Historia*, 5, 1956, 74–122.

661 U. VON LÜBTOW, *Das römische Volk und sein Recht*, Frankfurt 1955.

O THE SANCTUARY OF DIANA ON THE AVENTINE

662 A. ALFÖLDI, 'Il santuario federale latino di Diana sull'Aventino e il tempio di Ceres', *SMSR*, 32, 1961, 21–39.

663 A. MOMIGLIANO, 'Sul "dies natalis" del santuario federale di Diana sul l'Aventino', *RAL*, 17, 1962, 387–92 (= *Terzo Contributo* . . ., II, 641–48).

P THE SERVIAN WALL AND THE FOUR URBAN TRIBES

664 F. CASTAGNOLI, 'Roma Quadrata', *Studies presented to D. M. Robinson*, Saint Louis 1951, I, 389–99.

665 G. LUGLI, 'Le mura di Servio Tullio e le cosi dette mura serviane', *Historia*, Rome, 7, 1933, 3–45.

666 P. QUONIAM, 'A propos du mur dit de Servius Tullius', *MEFR*, 59, 1947, 41–64.

667 G. SÄFLUND, *Le mura di Roma repubblicana*, Lund 1932.

Q THE EARLIEST RURAL TRIBES

668 A. ALFÖLDI, 'Ager Romanus antiquus', *Hermes*, 90, 1962, 187–213.

669 L. ROSS TAYLOR, *The voting Districts of the Roman Republic*, Rome 1960.

R AN INSCRIPTION OF THE KINGLY PERIOD

670 G. DUMÉZIL, 'Sur l'inscription du Lapis Niger', *Mél. J. Lebreton, Recherches de Sciences religieuses*, 39, 1952, 17–29 (= *REL*, 36, 1958, 109–111).

S THE FIRST TREATY BETWEEN ROME AND CARTHAGE

671 A. AYMARD, 'Les deux premiers traités entre Rome et Carthage', *REA*, 59, 1957, 277–93.

672 E. COLOZIER, 'Les Étrusques et Carthage', *MEFR*, 65, 1953, 63–98.

673 F. HAMPL, 'Das Problem der Datierung der ersten Verträge zwischen Rom und Karthago', *RhM*, 101, 1958, 58–75.

674 O. MELTZER, *Geschichte der Karthager*, 3 vols, Berlin 1879.

675 R. REBUFFAT, 'Hélène en Égypte et le Romain égaré (Hérodote, II, 115, et Polybe, III, 22–24)', *REA*, 58, 1966, 245–63.

E **The Roman republic**

a POLITICAL INSTITUTIONS; THEIR EVOLUTION; FOUNDING OF
THE REPUBLIC

676 A. ALFÖLDI, 'Die Herrschaft der Reiterei in Griechenland und Rom nach dem Sturz der Könige', *Festschrift K. Schefold, AK* 10, 1967, 4. Beiheft, 13–47.

677 Id., 'Zur Struktur des Römerstaates im 5. Jahrhundert v. Chr.' *Entretiens XIII*, Fondation Hardt, Vandoeuvres-Geneva, 1966, 225–90.

678 A. BERNARDI, 'Patrizi e plebei nella costituzione della primitiva reppublica romana', *RIL*, 79, 1945–6, 1–24.

679 Id., 'Dagli ausiliari del "Rex" ai magistrati della "Respublica",' *Athenaeum*, 30, 1952, 3–58.

680 R. BLOCH, 'Le départ des Étrusques de Rome selon l'annalistique et la dédicace du temple de Jupiter Capitolin', *RHR*, 149, 1961, 141–56.

681 Id., 'Rome de 509 à 475 environ av. J.-C.', *REL*, 37, 1959, 118–31.

682 K. HANELL, *Das altrömische eponyme Amt*, Lund 1946.

683 Id., 'Probleme der römischen Fasti', *Entretiens XIII*, Fondation Hardt, Vandoeuvres-Geneva, 1966, 177–96.

684 J. HEURGON, 'L. Cincius et la loi du "clauus annalis"', *Athenaeum*, 42, 1964, 432–41.

685 Id., 'Magistratures romaines et magistratures étrusques', *Entretiens XIII*, Fondation Hardt, Vandoeuvres-Geneva, 1966, 99–132.

686 A. MAGDELAIN, *Recherches sur l'imperium: la loi curiate et les auspices d'investiture*, Paris 1968.

686b Id., 'Procum Patricium', *Studi in onore di Ed. Volterra*, II, 1969, 247–66.

687 S. MAZZARINO, *Dalla Monarchia allo Stato Repubblicano, ricerche di storia romana arcaica*, Catania 1946.

688 E. MEYER, 'Zur Frühgeschichte Roms', *MH*, 9, 1952, 176–81.

689 A. MOMIGLIANO, 'Procum Patricium', *JRS*, 56, 1966, 16–24.

690 Id., 'Osservazioni sulla distinzioni fra patrizi e plebei', *Entretiens XIII*, Fondation Hardt, Vandoeuvres-Geneva, 1966, 199–221.

691 Id., 'Praetor Maximus e questioni affini', *Studi in onore di G. Grosso*, Turin 1968, 161–75.

692 M. PALLOTTINO, 'Il filoetruschismo di Aristodemo e la data della fondazione di Capua', *PP*, 47, 1956, 81–8.

693 Id., 'Fatti e Leggende (moderne) sulla più antica storia di Roma', *SE*, 31, 1963, 3–37.

694 R. WERNER, *Der Beginn der römischer Republik*, Munich-Vienna 1963.

b THE TRIBUNATE OF THE PLEBS

695 F. ALTHEIM, ' "Lex sacrata", Die Anfänge der plebeischen Organisation *Albae Vigiliae*', Amsterdam, I, 1940 (= *Römische Religionsgeschichte*, 1951, I, 221–51).

696 J. BAYET, 'L'organisation plébéienne et les "leges sacratae" ', Appendix V to: *Tite-Live*, III, 1942, 145–53.

697 A. MERLIN, *L'Aventin dans l'Antiquité*, Paris 1906.

698 G. NICCOLINI, *Il tribunato della plebe*, Milan 1932.

699 K. VON FRITZ, ' "Leges sacratae" et "plebei scita" ', *Studies presented to D. M. Robinson*, Saint Louis, II, 1953, 893–905.

c THE DECEMVIRS AND THE TWELVE TABLES

700 J. BAYET, 'Le problème du "conubium" entre le patriciat et la plèbe", Appendix II to: *Tite-Live*, IV, 1946, 126–32.

701 Id., 'La loi des Douze Tables, Appendix III to: *Tite-Live*, III, 1942, 129–33.

702 Id., 'Le procès de Virginie', Appendix IX: *Tite-Live*, III, 1942, 133–45.

703 F. WIEACKER, 'Die XII Tafeln in ihrem Jahrhundert', *Entretiens XIII*, Fondation Hardt, Vandoeuvres-Geneva, 1966, 293–362.

d THE MILITARY TRIBUNES WITH CONSULAR POWERS

704 J. BAYET, 'Origines et portée du tribunat consulaire', Appendix III to: *Tite-Live*, IV, 1946, 132-48.

705 E. S. STAVELEY, 'The significance of the consular tribunate', *JRS*, 43, 1953, 30–46.

e THE LICINIAN LAWS

706 K. VON FRITZ, 'The Reorganisation of the Roman Government in 366 B.C. and the so-called Licinio-Sextian Laws', *Historia*, I, 1950, 1-44.

707 J. SUOLAHTI, *The Roman Censors, a study of the social structure*, Helsinki 1963.

f THE REFORMS OF APPIUS CLAUDIUS

708 A. GARZETTI, 'Appio Claudio Cieco nella storia politica del suo tempo', *Athenaeum*, 25, 1947, 175-244.

708b P. FRACCARO '"Tribules" ed "Aerarii", una ricerca di diritto pubblico romano', *Opuscula*, II, Pavia, 1957, 149-70.

709 C. NICOLET, 'Appius Claudius et le double forum de Capoue', *Latomus*, 20, 1961, 683-720.

710 H. PALMER, 'The censors of 312 and the State religion', *Historia*, 14, 1961, 294-324.

711 E. S. STAVELEY, 'The political Aims of Ap. Claudius Caecus', *Historia*, 8, 1959, 410-33.

g FORMATION OF THE NOBILITAS

712 F. MÜNZER, *Römische Adelsparteien und Adelsfamilien*, Stuttgart 1920; 2nd ed., 1963.

713 F. CASSOLA, *I gruppi politici romani nel III secolo a.C.*, Trieste 1962.

h THE CONQUEST OF ITALY: THE CASUS BELLI

714 T. ASHBY, 'La rete stradale romana nell'Etruria meridionale in relazione a quella del periodo etrusco', *SE*, 3, 1929, 171-85.

715 A. GRENIER, 'La transhumance des troupeaux en Italie et son rôle dans l'histoire romaine', *MEFR*, 25, 1905, 293-328.

716 J. HEURGON, *Trois études sur le 'Ver sacrum'*, Brussels, 1957.

717 L. A. HOLLAND, 'Forerunners and Rivals of the primitive Roman Bridge', *TAPhA*, 80, 1949, 281-319.

i THE ARMY

718 P. COUISSIN, *Les armes romaines: essai sur les origines et l'évolution des armes individuelles du légionnaire romain*, Paris 1926.

719 J. HARMAND, *L'armée et le soldat à Rome de 107 à 50 av. notre ère*—much of the information is relevant to the earlier army—Paris 1967.

j LEGAL AND MORAL ASPECTS OF THE CONQUEST

720 D. ANZIANI, '"Caeritum Tabulae"', *MEFR*, 31, 1911, 435–56.

721 H. BENGTSON, *Die Staatverträge des Altertums:* II. *Die Verträge der griechischrömischen Welt von 700 bis 338 v. Chr.*, Munich-Berlin 1962.

722 P. BOYANCÉ, '*Fides Romana' et la vie internationale* (Annual public conference of the five Academies, 1962).

723 W. DAHLHEIM, '*Deditio' und 'Societas': Untersuchungen zur Entwicklung der römischen Aussenpolitik in der Blütezeit der Republik*, Diss. Munich 1965.

724 F. DE VISSCHER, 'La "deditio" internationale et l'affaire des Fourches Caudines', *CRAI*, 1946, 82–95.

725 E. KORNEMANN, '"Polis' und "Urbs"', *Klio*, 6, 1905, 72–93.

726 A. MAGDELAIN, *Essai sur les origines de la 'sponsio'*, Paris 1941.

727 A. N. SHERWIN-WHITE, *The Roman Citizenship*, Oxford 1939.

728 E. TAUBLER, 'Die Umbrish-sabellischen und die römische Tribus', *SHAW*, 1929–30., 4, 3–23.

729 L. ZANCAN, '*Ager publicus': ricerche di storia e di diritto romano*, Padua 1935.

k PROGRESS OF THE CONQUEST: RELATIONS WITH THE LATINS

730 A. PIGANIOL, 'Romains et Latins: I. La légende des Quinctii', *MEFR*, 38, 1920, 285–316.

731 E. T. SALMON, 'Rome and the Latins', *Phoenix*, 7, 1953, 93–104, 123–35.

732 Id., Roman Expansion and Roman Colonization in Italy, *Phoenix*, 9, 1955, 63–75.

l THE WAR WITH ARISTODEMUS OF CUMAE

733 B. COMBET-FARNOUX, 'Cumes, l'Étrurie et Rome à la fin du VIᵉ siècle et au début du Vᵉ siècle: un aspect des premiers contacts de Rome avec l'hellénisme', *MEFR*, 69, 1957, 7–44.

m ROME AND VEII

734 J. BAYET, 'Véies: réalités et légendes', Appendix III to: *Tite-Live*, V, 1954, 125–40.

735 J. HUBAUX, *Rome et Véies, recherches sur la chronologie légendaire du Moyen Age romain*, Lèige 1958.

n THE GAULISH INVASION

736 J. BAYET, 'L'invasion celtique et la catastrophe gauloise', Appendix V to: *Tite-Live*, V, 1954, 156–70.

737 Id., M. Furius Camillus, Appendix IV to: *Tite-Live*, V, 1954, 140-56.

738 A. MOMIGLIANO, 'Camillus and the Concord', *CQ*, 36, 1942, 111–20.

o STATE OF FORCES IN ITALY IN THE FOURTH CENTURY

739 M. SORDI, *I rapporti romano-ceriti e l'origine della 'ciuitas sine suffragio'*, Rome 1960.

p THE CONQUEST, STARTING FROM THE LATIN WAR

740 A. AFZELIUS, *Die römische Eroberung Italiens* (340–254 *v. Chr.*), Copenhagen 1942.

q IN CAMPANIA

741 J. HEURGON, *Recherches sur l'histoire, la religion et la civilisation de Capoue préromaine, des origines à 211 av. J.-C.*, Paris 1942.

742 M. NAPOLI, *Napoli greco-romana*, Naples 1959.

743 C. NICOLET, 'Les "Equites Campani" et leurs représentations figurées', *MEFR*, 74, 1962, 463–517.

r BEGINNINGS OF ROMAN POWER AT SEA

744 J. CARCOPINO, *Virgile et les origines d'Ostie*, Paris 1919.

745 A. MOMIGLIANO, 'Due punti di storia romana arcaica', *SDHI*, 2, 1936, 389–98.

S THE CONQUEST OF ETRURIA

746 A. J. PFIFFIG, *Die Ausbreitung des römischen Städtewesens in Etrurien und die Frage der Unterwerfung der Etrusker*, Florence 1966.

t PYRRHUS

747 J. CARCOPINO, 'Pyrrhus, conquérant ou aventurier?' in: *Profils de conquérants*, Paris 1961, 9–108.

748 A. DE FRANCISCIS, 'L'Archivio del tempio di Zeus a Locri', *Atti del Congr. intern. di Numismatica*, Rome, 1961 (1965), 117-29.

749 Id., 'L'Archivio del tempio di Zeus a Locri', *Klearchos*, 3, 1961, 17–41; 4, 1962, 66–83; 6, 1964, 73–95; 7, 1965, 21–36.

750 P. LÉVÊQUE, *Pyrrhos*, Paris 1957.

u ROME AND THE HELLENISTIC MONARCHIES

751 J. CARCOPINO, 'Les débuts de l'impérialisme romain', *JS*, 1923, 112–21; 173–81; 1924, 18–30 = *Les étapes de l'impérialisme romain*, Paris 1961, 68–105.

752 M. HOLLEAUX, *Rome, la Grèce et les monarchies hellénistiques au IIIe siècle av. J.-C.*, Paris 1921.

v PROGRESS OF ROMAN RELIGION

753 A. ALFÖLDI, 'Diana Nemorensis', *AJA*, 64, 1960, 137–44.

754 J. BAYET, *Les origines de l'Hercule romain*, Paris 1926.

755 R. BLOCH, 'L'origine du culte des Dioscures à Rome', *RPh*, 34, 1960, 182–94.

756 J. CARCOPINO, *La louve du Capitole*, Paris 1925.

757 Id., 'Les origines pythagoriciennes de l'Hercule romain', *Aspects mystiques de la Rome païenne*, Paris 1942, 173–206.

758 J. GAGÉ, *Apollon romain, essai sur le culte d'Hercule et le développement du 'ritus Graecus' à Rome des origines à Auguste*, Paris 1955.

759 Id., *Matronalia, essai sur les dévotions cultuelles des femmes dans l'ancienne Rome*, Brussels 1963.

760 H. LE BONNIEC, *Le culte de Cérès à Rome, des origines à la fin de la République*, Paris 1958.

761 G.-CH. PICARD, *Les trophées romains*, Paris 1957.

762 R. SCHILLING, *La religion de Vénus, depuis les origines jusqu'au temps d'Auguste*, Paris 1954.

763 Id., 'Une victime des vicissitudes politiques: la Diane latine', *Hommages à J. Bayet*, Brussels, 1964, 650–67.

764 S. WEINSTOCK, '"Victor" and "Invictus"', *HThR*, 1, 1957, 211–47.

765 Id., 'Two archaistic inscriptions from Latium' (dedication to the Dioscuri, the Lare Aineia inscription), *JRS*, 50, 1960, 112–18.

W ECONOMIC EFFECTS OF THE CONQUEST: ORIGINS OF ROMAN COINAGE

766 J. BAYET, 'Manlius et la "fides": problèmes économiques et prémonétaires', Appendix IV to: *Tite-Live*, VI, 1966, 120-26.

767 T. V. BUTTREY, 'The Morgantina Excavations and the date of the Roman denarius', *Atti del Congr. intern. di Numismatica*, Rome, 1961 (1965), 261–7.

768 J.-B. GIARD, 'La monnaie de Capoue et le problème de la datation du denier romain', *Atti del Congr. intern. di Numismatica*, Rome, 1961 (1965), 235–260.

769 H. MATTINGLY, 'The Romano-Campanian Coinage and the Pyrrhic War', *NC*, 4, 1924, 181–209.

770 Id., 'The first Age of the Roman Coinage', *JRS*, 19, 1929, 19–37.

771 S. P. NOE, 'Coinage of Metapontum', *Numismatic Notes and Monographs*, 47, New York 1931.

772 R. THOMSEN, *Early Roman Coinage*, 3 vols, Copenhagen 1957–61.

Notes

Figures in brackets refer to numbered entries in the bibliography.

Preface

1 Below, p. 378f.
2 E.g. the origins of coinage in Rome: below, p. 347f.
3 A. Momigliano, 'Osservazioni sulla distinzione fra patrizi e plebei'; A. Alföldi, 'Zur Struktur des Römerstaates im 5. Jahrhundert v. Chr.', both in *Entretiens XIII* of the Hardt Foundation. 1966.
4 Discovery of pre-Hellenic Phoenician settlements in southern Spain, see below,

p. 138f.; of eighth-century dwellings on the Palatine, see below, p. 62f.; of a sixth-century dedication to the Dioscuri at Lavinium, see below, p. 180; of Etrusco-Punic inscriptions at Pyrgi, see below, p. 110.
5 E.g. that the Alban cemeteries are no older than those of Rome, which cannot be an Alban colony, see below, p. 74f.

Part One   Present Knowledge

Chapter One

1 The Neolithic age in Mediterranean Europe forms the subject of a chapter by G. Bailloud in *La Préhistoire* (Nouvelle Clio) I, 184–7.
2 H. Nissen [118], 468f.; G. Devoto [117]; M. Pallottino [119].
3 E. Vetter [39], no. 149,2; no. 200, G, 2; G. Devoto [117], 113f.
4 Tab. Iguv. I, b, 17; VI, b, 58 etc.
5 E. Vetter [39].
6 A. Ernout [80].
7 G. Giacomelli [42].
8 M. Lejeune [46–52].
9 G. Devoto [43]; J. W. Poultney [45]; A. Ernout [44].
10 A. de Franciscis and O. Parlangèli [40].
11 E. Vetter [39], 359f.; M. Durante [41].
12 R. S. Conway, S. E. Johnson, J. Watmough [35].
13 O. Parlangèli [37].
14 F. Altheim [81], 180f.

15 V. Pisani [36], 303f.
16 F. Altheim [81], 92f.
17 M. Lejeune [109], 14.
18 M. Lejeune [109], 17.
19 G. Devoto [117], 49f.; M. Lejeune [109], 13f.
20 M. G. Delfino [55].
21 M. Lejeune [46], 188.
22 On Kossinna's law and its discussion by V. Gordon Childe, see below, p. 225f.
23 L. Bernabò Brea [131]; M. Cavalier [132–4].
24 L. Bernabò Brea [131], 61f.
25 F. von Duhn [141], II, 122; [130], I, 14f.
26 F. von Duhn [130], I, 27f.; F. Rittatore [136, 137].
27 P. C. Sestieri [138, 139], [140], 27f.
28 The best description is in T. E. Peet [144], 289f.
29 F. von Duhn [130], pl. 34, nos.

L

116–22; J. Sundwall [129], 66f.
30 L. Bernabò Brea [131], 60.
31 G. Mansuelli [127], 78 and 487f.
32 In the *Bullettino di Paletnologia italiana*
from 1883 to 1908 [146]; cf. F. von Duhn
[126], 13, 258f.; [130], 116f.
33 F. von Duhn [130], pl. 15, fig. 49;
L. Homo [123], 41, fig. 1; J. Whatmough
[125], 72.
34 G. Säflund [151].
35 G. Säflund [151], 224; S. M. Puglisi
[147], 74.
36 G. Säflund [151], 237; S. M. Puglisi
[147], 74.
37 M. Pallottino [164], 21.
38 U. Rellini [148, 150].
39 S. M. Puglisi [147].
40 G. Säflund [182].
41 See below, p. 24f.
42 L. Bernabò Brea [131], 103f.
43 M. Cavalier [132], 135.
44 L. Bernabò Brea [131], 129f.
45 L. Bernabò Brea [131], 122f.
46 L. Bernabò Brea [131], 125, fig. 23.
47 M. Cavalier [132], 141.
48 M. Pallottino [164].
49 Below, p. 34f.
50 G. Mansuelli [127], 481.
51 H. Müller-Karpe [162], 4f;
cf. M. Pallottino [164], 45.
52 F. von Duhn [130], 190f.
53 Q. Quagliati [180].
54 Above, p. 8.
55 Below, pp. 56, 86.
56 H. Müller-Karpe [162], 95f.,
pls. 86 and 87A.
57 H. Müller-Karpe [162], 95f.,
pl. 90–102.
58 H. Müller-Karpe [162], 77f.,
pl. 84 and 85A.
59 H. Müller-Karpe [162], 66.
60 H. Müller-Karpe [162], 67f.,
pl. 40–45 and 46A–E.
61 H. Müller-Karpe [162], 49f., pl. 25–6,
62 L. Bernabò Brea [131], 136f.
63 L. Bernabò Brea [131], 143f.
64 More recently, bearing in mind the
evolution leading from *pithoi* to situlae
(Lipari) and then to the bowl-lidded urns,
L. Bernabò Brea has come to disbelieve in
the arrival of a new people practising
cremation; he inclines now to think merely
of the diffusion of differing religious
notions, with ordinary domestic receptacles
being used first, then the specifically
cinerary urn.
65 G. Mansuelli [127], 117f.

66 K. Krömer [158].
67 A. Grenier [157]: the work has hardly
dated after fifty years, but it was not till
shortly after its appearance in 1913 that
the necropolis of S. Vitale was brought to
light; P. Ducati [155]; L. Laurenzi [159];
G. Mansuelli [127], 117f.
68 A. Grenier [157], 133.
69 H. Müller-Karpe [162], pl. 63, 79;
the author includes the first Villanova
phases in the urnfields culture.
70 P. Ducati [155]; H. Müller-Karpe
[162], pl. 57.
71 [161].
72 M. Pallottino [163, 307].
73 H. Hencken [255], 34f., fig. 4 and 6A.
74 D. Randall MacIver [124], 44.
75 G. Annibaldi [153].
76 P. C. Sestieri [181]; M. Napoli,
V. Panebianco, B. d'Agostino [178], 63f.,
fig. 18, 19, 21; K. Killian [173], 18, 30;
pl. 3, 1; 4, 1; J. de La Genière [175].
77 [177], 79f., fig. 23.
78 [177], 105f., fig. 33f.
79 W. Johannowsky [171, 172].
80 F. von Duhn [130], II, 161f.;
D. Randall-MacIver [166]; W. Dumitrescu
[156]; G. Annibaldi [152].
81 P. Romanelli, *Corpus Vasorum*, Italy IV,
Lecce I.
82 E. Gabrici [170]; F. von Duhn [130],
535f.; J. Heurgon [741], 32, 395.
83 P. Orsi [179]; J. de La Genière [174].
84 G. Säflund [182], 23f.
85 Until recently one had to rely on the
work of G. Pinza [190]; cf. F. von Duhn
[130], I, 391f. We now have the work of
P. G. Gierow [187]. H. Müller-Karpe [194]
should also be consulted.
86 T. Ashby [183]; G. Lugli [186].
87 M. Pallottino [196], 15;
P. G. Gierow [187], I, 451.
88 G. Säflund [168], 30f., P. G. Gierow
[187], I, 451.
89 M. Pallottino [196], 11f.
90 P. G. Gierow [187], I, 448.
91 H. Müller-Karpe [162], 43f.;
R. Peroni [197], 498; M. Pallottino
[196], 13. E. Gjerstad, since writing [193],
has replaced his earlier division into
I, IIA, IIB, III by a division into I, II,
III, IV.
92 R. Peroni [197], 496; cf. M. Pallottino
[196], 13.
93 E. Gjerstad, exceptionally, [572], 55,
makes it begin 530/525.
94 H. Müller-Karpe, R. Peroni.

95 P. G. Gierow [187], I, 498f., following E. Gjerstad.
96 See the table in P. Gierow [187], I, 373.
97 R. Peroni [197], 464.
98 E. Gjerstad [193], 1f.
99 P. G. Gierow [187], I, 503.
100 P. G. Gierow [187], I, 460f.
101 R. Peroni [197], 476 and 483.
102 P. G. Gierow [187], I, 484f., 502.
H. Müller-Karpe [194], 45f., pl. 19, oddly tries to find Aegean parallels. On the hut-urns of Germany, which are particularly frequent in the Elbe region, see H. Hencken [255], 35, fig. 5.
103 P. G. Gierow [187], I, 206f.; H. Müller-Karpe [194], 56f.
104 P. G. Gierow [187], I, 306f.
105 F. Bömer [634], 90f.
106 H. Müller-Karpe [194], 51f.; R. Pittioni [128], 264; P. G. Gierow [187], I, 77.
107 A. Alföldi [566], 246f.; P. G. Gierow [187], I, 449, n.3.
108 P. G. Gierow [187], I, 457.
109 P. G. Gierow [187], I, 476f.
110 P. G. Gierow [187], I, 458.
111 E. Gjerstad [192], III, 378f.; IV, 30f.; R. Peroni [198], 8f.; P. Romanelli [204], 6f.
112 A. K. Michels [581], 47.
113 L. A. Holland [580], 29f.
114 J. Le Gall [29], 28f.
115 Liv. I, 4, 3.
116 Tib. II, 5, 33; Prop. IV, 2, 7; 9, 5.
117 S. M. Puglisi [200]; P. Romanelli [203], 237f.; [204], 9f.; R. Bloch [567], 35f.
118 G. Carettoni [202], 261f.
119 E. Gjerstad [192], I, 86f.
120 E. Gjerstad [192], I, 29f., esp. 48f.
121 P. Romanelli [204], 7.
122 Varro, L.L., V, 157; G. Lugli [25], 578.
123 E. Gjerstad [192], II, 13f.
124 For example grave C, 52f., fig. 43–8.
125 For example grave HH, 44f., fig. 33–5.
126 E. Gjerstad [192], II, p. 14, fig. 1.
127 Grave U, 70f., fig. 69–70.
128 Grave PP, 46f., fig. 37.
129 S. M. Puglisi [199]. E. Gjerstad [192], II, 86f., fig. 84–5; 111f., fig. 109, 111; 113f.; fig. 109, 112; 116f., fig. 110, 113. Gjerstad assigns grave 1 to period II, and 2, 3 and 4 to period III. R. Peroni, however [197], 463f., dates them (correctly, it would seem) to period I— graves 1 and 2 to IA, 3 and 4 to IB;

cf. H. Müller-Karpe [194], 14–30; M. Pallottino [196] 13; P. Romanelli in *Gnomon* XXXI, 1959, 438f.
130 We may note especially the correspondence between grave I and that of S. Lorenzo Vecchio; H. Müller-Karpe [194], 45, pl. 22C and 23A.
131 E. Gjerstad [192], II, 17.
132 P. Romanelli [204], 7f.
133 E Gjerstad [192], III, 206; IV, 1, 38 and 52; opposed by H. Müller-Karpe [194], 39f.; M. Pallottino [196], 24.
134 A. M. Colini [191]; M. Pallottino [196], 27.
135 E. Gjerstad [192], II, 267f.; M. Pallottino [196], 32. The small number of finds is sufficiently explained by the history of the Quirinal: in the eighteenth century Urban VIII completely transformed its appearance by levelling two heights and filling a valley to produce the present plateau of the Quirinal gardens (T. Hackens [578], 78f.).
136 E. Gjerstad [192], II, 277f.
137 R. Peroni [197], 487f., 496; but Gjerstad [192], II, 269, makes one of them period I.
138 E. Gjerstad [192], II, 162f.; R. Peroni [197], 488f.
139 E. Gjerstad [192], II, 265.
140 E. Gjerstad [192], II, 165; H. Müller-Karpe [194], 137.
141 As P. G. Gierow seems to think, [187], I, 478.
142 Below, p. 32f.
143 The cremation grave at Rieti (hut-urn, biconic vase with single handle and wide mouth, v. D. Brusadin [184], 449) suggests rather to E. Gjerstad [192], IV, 1, 267 and 338, that a Latin group had arrived in this part of the Sabine area.
144 Graves a circolo: D. Faccenna [186]; S. M. Puglisi [147], 99. E. Gjerstad [192], IV, 255 observed the resemblances to the grave-furnishings of the Esquiline.
145 L. Homo [123], 96f.
146 On the economic advantages of the site by the Tiber, 'the town of the first bridge', see J. Le Gall [29], 42f.
147 This is the classic conception of *Roma Quadrata*: G. Lugli [27], I, 73f.; [25], 400f.; but see F. Castagnoli [664] and below.
148 L. A. Holland [580], 57, n.1.
149 E. Gjerstad [572], 15.
150 M. Pallottino [196], 27f.;

P. de Francisci [570], 131.
151 R. Peroni [197], 457f., 496, dates the tomb between the Palatine and Germal as period II A, and those of the temple of Caesar in the period I A and B; cf. P. Romanelli [204], 6 and 8. On the other hand, Gjerstad assigns the former to period I ([192], IV, 1, 53), and the latter in periods II and III ([192], III, 86, 111f.; IV, 1, 53, 57).
152 L. Homo [123], 105f. and fig. 4.
153 G. Wissowa [588]; A. von Gerkan [587]; E. Gjerstad [572], 23, n.2; [192], IV, 1, 42 and 339.
154 L. A. Holland [579]; J. Poucet [583].
155 L. A. Holland [580]; cf. also P. Grimal [577].
156 F. von Duhn [130], I, 431f.; R. Peroni [197], 487, 497; M. Pallottino [196], 25f.
157 T. Mommsen [582]; H. Müller-Karpe [194], 35f. The forming of the tradition has been studied by J. Poucet [584].
158 J. Poucet [586].
159 Varro, *L.L.* V, 52.
160 Varro, *L.L.* V, 51; J. Poucet [585] 11f.
161 Tacitus, *Ann.* I, 54, 1; J. Poucet [585], 391f.
162 Geiger in *RE* I, A 2, 1875f.
163 G. Wissowa [13], 483, n.1; but see K. Latte [14], 87, n.1.
164 Livy, I, 13, 4; 'geminata' *ib.* 13, 5. Cf. A. Piganiol [576] and A. Alföldi in his forthcoming *Lupercalia*.
165 G. Wissowa in *RE* IV, 1, 480f.
166 But not his interpretation or his chronology, which puts the end of the pre-urban era about 575 and the beginning of the Etruscan monarchy about 525.
167 E. Gjerstad [572], 40f.; cf. [192], IV, 1, 43.
168 Arbois de Jubainville, *Les premiers habitants de l'Europe*, 1889, I, 356f.; C. Jullian [216], I, 110f.
169 N. Lamboglia [121].
170 C. F. Hawkes [208].
171 G. Mansuelli [127], 83f.
172 G. Mansuelli [127], 54f.; 64f.; bibliography, 529.
173 G. Mansuelli [127], 77f.
174 G. Mansuelli [127], 72.
175 F. A. Schaeffer [219].
176 F. Henry [218], 26f.
177 W. Kimmig [220].
178 A. Grenier [212], 71.
179 A comparative table of chronologies

in W. Kimmig [220], II, 1951, 73.
180 A Brisson, J.-J. Hatt [223]; cf. [224].
181 J. Jannoray [234], 364f., 371f.
182 P. Bosch-Gimpera [114], 241f.; [241, 242].
183 M. E. Mertens [221], 443, n.1, draws attention to the disagreements on this point.
184 P. Bosch-Gimpera [114], 242: the European migrations that occurred successively from the mid-second to the first millennium B.C. are spoken of by the author as 'the Celtic movements'.
185 H. Rix [222] will not admit that there is any correspondence between the distribution of placenames in *-dunum*, *-briga*, *-magus* and the distribution of the cemeteries of the bronze and early iron ages.
186 A. Grenier [212], 71f.; cf. H. Hubert [213], 231f.
187 A. Grenier [212], 76.
188 W. Kimmig [220], III, 1952, 11f.; A. Brisson, J.-J. Hatt [223], 230f.
189 F. Henry [218], 29f.; R. Joffroy [228].
190 R. Joffroy [228], 145; J. Carcopino [225], 34f.
191 R. Joffroy [226].
192 About 525 B.C.; R. Joffroy [226; 229], and see below, p. 189.
193 They may have been set in motion by a sudden cooling of the climate and an increase in humidity, which caused them to migrate towards the south: E. Demougeot [105]; cf. P.-M. Duval [210], LXVII, 1965, 405.
194 H. Hubert [214], 2.
195 H. Hubert [213], 103f., 106f.; A. Grenier [212], 77f.; P.-M. Duval [210], LXII, 1960, 386f.
196 H. Hubert [214], 6.
197 Abbé Favret [231]; A. Grenier [211], 26.
198 H. Hubert [213], 2.
199 H. Hubert [213], 3.
200 G. Goury [232]; D. Bretz-Mahler [230], 308f.
201 Caesar, *B.G.* I, 2 and 3; R. Dion, *Ann. du Collège de France*, 63, 1963, 389f.; P.-M. Duval [210], 66, 1964, 358f.
202 J.-J. Hatt [233, 238].
203 C. Jullian [216], I, 254.
204 H. Hubert [214], 23.
205 J. Bayet [736], 156f.

206 A. Grenier [212], 112f.;
P. Bosch-Gimpera [205], VI, 1953–54,
345f.; G. Mansuelli [239].
207 G. Mansuelli [239]; R. Chevallier
[237]; C. Peyre [240].
208 A. Grenier [212], 120f.;
J. Filip [207]; cf. P.-M. Duval [210],
59, 1957, 333.
209 P.-M. Duval, REA, 63, 1961, 367.
210 P. Bienkowski [236].
211 A. Grenier [212], 89f.
212 P. Bosch-Gimpera [245];
L. Pericot-Garcia [249]; G. Mansuelli [127],
263–82. For a résumé of the data and the
problems see R. Etienne [246], 24–48,
with maps 5 and 6.
213 G. Mansuelli [127], 77f.
214 See below, pp. 57 and 67f.

215 P. Bosch-Gimpera [244].
216 Strabo III, 4, 19;
J. Jannoray [234], 383f., 413f.
217 M. Gómez-Moreno [247];
A. Tovar [250]; J.-G. Février, Histoire de
l'écriture, 2nd ed., Paris, 1959, 328–31.
218 See below, p. 252.
219 A. Grenier [212], 100f.;
P. Bosch-Gimpera [241, 242, 243];
G. Mansuelli [127], 267f.;
and see above, p. 39.
220 Herod. II, 33; IV, 49;
A. Grenier [212], 101f.
221 G. Mansuelli [127], 268, 274f., 437.
222 G. Mansuelli [127], 277f.
223 F. Pallarés Salvador [248];
G. Mansuelli [127], 274.
224 J. Jannoray [234], 465; [235].

Chapter Two

1 See below, p. 233f.
2 J. Heurgon [272], 16.
3 C. O. Thulin [331], III, 3f., with the
texts; P. Lavedan [30], 298f.
4 J. Heurgon [319], 86f.
5 F. de Ruyt [303].
6 K. Hanell [304b].
7 R. Vighi [294].
8 J. Bayet [337], 132.
9 J. Falchi [285]; Å. Åkerstrom [280], 124f.
10 G. Caputo [282].
11 G. Rosi [293].
12 R. Mengarelli [289]; M. Moretti [290];
J. Heurgon [287].
13 J. Heurgon [272], 196f.
14 J. Bayet [337], 132.
15 Livy XXII, 3, 3; J. Heurgon [272], 123f.
16 G. D'Achardi [300]; J. Heurgon
[272], 151f.
17 See below, p. 55.
18 See below, p. 76f.
19 J. Heurgon [319], 88f.
20 J. Heurgon [741], 77;
F. Altheim [251], 51, 60f.
21 Livy IV, 33, 5.
22 J. Heurgon [741], 59f.
23 TLE 2; M. Pallottino [64].
24 A. Maiuri [311], 241f.
25 See above, p. 19.
26 Timaeus, F. Gr. Hist. 566 F. 50,
and see below, p. 91f.
27 Hellanicus in Dion Hal. I, 18f., 26;
Herod. I, 57.
28 M. Zuffa [316]; M. Pallottino [315].
29 S. Mazzarino [321], 99f.

30 N. Alfieri, P. E. Arias, M. Hirmer [310].
31 G. A. Mansuelli [313].
32 G. Vallet [469], 43f.; this study of
course was not able to take into account the
recent discoveries at Spina.
33 M. Pallottino [278], 119f.
34 See below, p. 101.
35 See below, p. 183f.
36 On the Etruscan state see
J. Heurgon [319]; R. Lambrachts [320].
37 S. Mazzarino [687], 67, 95.
38 A. Alföldi [590].
39 T. Frankfort [317]; J. Heurgon
[272], 74, 318.
40 J. Heurgon [272], 81f.
41 J. Heurgon [272], 95f.; [287].
42 The Regolini-Galassi tomb at Caere is
described by L. Pareti [291]; the
Bernardini and Barberini tombs at Praeneste
by C. Densmore Curtis [283, 284].
43 D. Harden [367], 188; Y. Huls [345].
44 R. Maxwell Hyslop [349];
M. Pallottino [354]; P. Amandry [335].
45 E. Coche de la Ferté [340], 72f.
46 R. Rebuffat [355], 423f.
47 A. Hus [346], 126f., 338f.
48 G. Vallet [469], 156f.
49 For the tomb with the Greek pots see
M. Moretti [290], 241f.
50 F. Villard [462], 60.
51 T. Dohrn [341], 33f.;
J. D. Beazley [338], 1, 12f.
52 M. Pallottino [352]; M. Moretti [350].
The beginnings of Etruscan wall-painting,
under the influence of imported pottery,

are analysed in an article by J. M. Dentzer,
'Les systèmes décoratifs dans la peinture
murale italique', *MEFR*, 80, 1968, 85–141.
53 P. J. Riis [356]; K. A. Neugebauer [351].
54 A. Andrén [336].
55 M. Pallottino [353].
56 Pliny, *NH* XXXV, 157.
57 Reproduced countless times: among
others by C. Q. Giglioli [342],
pl. 189–96.
58 C. O. Thulin [331];
J. Heurgon [272], 283f.; [237].
59 Festus, p. 358 L.
60 S. Weinstock [334].
61 A. Piganiol [330].
62 C. O. Thulin [331], II, 24f. pl. 1;
A. Grenier [15], 34f.; S. Weinstock [333];
M. Pallottino [329].
63 J. Heurgon [71], 183f.
64 A. Grenier [15], 34f.
65 Varro *L.L.* V, 46.
66 M. Pallottino and others [65];

J. Heurgon [67].
67 F. de Ruyt [323].
68 On the Capuan tile (*TLE*, 2), see
M. Pallottino [64]; the mummy-windings
from Zagreb (*TLE* 1), are discussed by
K. Olzscha [59]; A. J. Pfiffig [61].
69 Livy VII, 2.
70 V. Georgiev [77].
71 W. Schulze [76]; H. Rix [75].
72 See above, p. 44.
73 *TLE*, 359.
74 *TLE*, 570; A. J. Pfiffig [63].
75 *TLE*, 131; J. Heurgon [62].
76 See above, p. 46.
77 M. Pallottino [278], 367f.
78 M. Pallottino [64].
79 K. Olzscha [60].
80 M. Pallottino [58].
81 M. Lejeune [72, 73].
82 A. Grenier [70]; J. A. Bundgård [69];
below, p. 74f.
83 F. Slotty [74].

Chapter Three

1 J. Berard [441]; G. Giannelli [525].
2 J. Bérard [441], 315.
3 The chronology of Mycenaean pottery,
established by A. Furumark [362],
comprises three periods. The third is
almost the only one which concerns export
to the west, and is subdivided into Myc.
III A (1425–1300), Myc. III B (1300–1230)
and Myc. III C (1230–1025).
4 W. Taylour [366].
5 L. Bernabò Brea [131], 108, 115,
125f., 131; [135], 92;
M. Cavalier [132], 133f.
6 G. Buchner [463], 79; [464], 36.
7 C. E. Östenberg [143], 128f.,
fig. 31 and 32,1.
8 G. Säflund [182], F. Biancofiore [359,
360]; N. Degrassi, *Atti del I Convegno di
Taranto*, 225f. Some Mycenaean finds in
other parts of Italy and the Mediterranean,
at Torcello, in Campania, Sardinia and
Spain, remain uncertain; W. Taylour
[366], 170f.
9 Sp. Marinatos [363], 161f.
10 G. Pugliese Carratelli [364, 365].
11 Strabo VI, 1,15, following Antiochus
of Syracuse, *F.Gr.Hist.*, 555 F.12.
12 Virgil *Aen.*, 10, 174.
13 Sp. Marinatos [363], 166.
14 L. Bernabò Brea [131], 102.
15 L. Bernabò Brea [131], 103.

16 F. Biancofiore [360], 104.
17 W. Taylour [366], 128.
18 F. Biancofiore [360], 101f.
19 E. Lepore [506], 215f.
20 Arist., *Pol.* VII, 9, 1329b 14–15,
following Antiochus of Syracuse,
F.Gr.Hist., 555 F.3.
21 N. Degrassi, *Atti del III Convegno di
Taranto*, 154f.
22 F. G. Lo Porto [495], 74f.
23 Strabo VI 3, 2 (279), following
Antiochus of Syracuse, *F.Gr.Hist.* 555 F.13;
J. Bérard [441], 165.
24 G. Picard, *Castellum Dimmidi*,
Algiers-Paris 1947, 36.
25 E. F. Gautier, *Le passé de l'Afrique du
Nord*, Paris, 1937, 155f., has pointed out
that 'in the western Mediterranean basin
the only two places outside Africa where
Moslem occupation became permanent
were Andalusia and Sicily', where
Phoenicians and Carthaginians had prepared
the way for Islam. In the following section
I use the term 'Punic' in the normal sense,
as opposed to Phoenician, to refer to
Carthaginian expansion and colonization.
26 R. Dion [380].
27 R. Dion [429].
28 J. Carcopino [418], 49f. ('Les
Phéniciens et les Grecs: histoire et
légendes') and 73f. ('Le Maroc marché

punique de l'or').
29 Texts in S. Gsell [408], I, 359f.
29a S. Gsell [408], I, 374f.
29b Thuc. VI, 2, 6.
29c Diod. V, 16.
30 V. Bérard [373]; cf. [374], 146.
31 J. Beloch [372].
32 V. Bérard [373], II, 15.
33 V. Bérard [373], I, 63f.
34 R. Carpenter [375].
35 L. Pareti [291], 483f.
36 G. Vallet [469], 182f.
37 P. Cintas [402], 480.
38 W. F. Albright [379]; D. Herden [367];
G. Garbini [376, 377]; R. Rebuffat [355],
409f.; S. Moscati [378].
39 The name was given to at least three
places: Kition in the island of Cyprus,
Carthage in Africa, and later to Cartagena
in Spain.
40 Od. XV, 415f.; cf. A. Moret [1],
II, 609; G. Germain, Essai sur les origines
de certains thèmes odysséens, Paris, 1954, 446.
41 Herod. IV, 126; J. Carcopino
[418], 107f.
42 Notably P. Cintas [416], 270f.;
cf. [414], 75.
43 L. Foucher [415], 27, n.35.
44 L. Bernabò Brea [131], 155f.
45 A. Garcia y Bellido [430], 484;
W. F. Albright [379] dates them in the
eighth century; D. Harden [367], 207, in
the sixth.
46 A. Taramelli [400], 314f.; the ninth
century according to P. Bosch-Gimpera
[427], 274, n.2.
47 S. Chiappisi [386]; D. Harden [367],
62 and pl. 93; F. Benoit [542], 31, n. 19.
Degenerate replicas of this type have been
found in Morocco: A. Jodin [422].
48 On relations between Ugarit and the
west see C. A. Schaeffer, Ugaritica, II,
Paris, 1949, 112f.
49 W. F. Albright [368] on the Unamon
papyrus; B. Bosch-Gimpera [427], 272.
50 P. Cintas [416], 264, n.7.
51 J. G. Février [370].
52 I Kings, 9, 26–8; II Chron., 7,8,17.
53 I Kings, 10,22; II Chron., 9,21.
54 A. Schulten [434]; J. M. Solá Solé [382]
reviews the earlier work up to 1957 and
puts forward an etymological interpretation.
See also the recent articles of U. Täckholm
[383] and P. Cintas [381]; the former
concludes in favour of the lower chronology,
the latter favours the higher.
55 I Kings, 22, 49.

56 H. L. Lorimer, Homer and the
Monuments, London 1950, 66, and
R. D. Barnett, JHS 70, 1950, 105,
quoted by F. Villard [425], 18 and n.5
on p. 17.
57 According to the Arabian historians
cited by P. Cintas [402], n.627.
58 Pol. III, 24, 5; F. W. Walbank [92],
I, 347; cf. below, p. 388.
59 Ezek. 27, 12.
60 R. Dion [380], 28f.
61 The supposed reference to an
expedition of Hiram I against Utica, in
two passages of Josephus, rests only on the
emendation of a corrupt ethnic name:
S. Gsell [408], I, 361 and n.7.
62 Thuc. VI, 2, 6; see the plans of Tyre,
Carthage, Motye, Mogador and Cadiz in
D. Harden [367], 28f.
63 P. Cintas [414], 19f.
64 C. Picard [410], 20f.; D. Harden 94f;
tophets at Motye, Nora, Tharros, Monte
Sirai, Hadrumetum and Carthage.
65 E. Gjerstad [384], IV, 2, 436f.
66 S. Moscati [378], 4f.; [385].
67 Cicero, Verr. II, 4,103.
68 J. I. S. Whitaker [390];
B. S. J. Isserlin [388]; V. Tusa [389].
Motye was destroyed in 397 by Dionysius of
Syracuse.
69 D. Harden [367], 37 and figs. 6–7.
70 J. I. S. Whitaker [390], fig. 72–3;
P. Cintas [402], 502, 584; dating
confirmed in the main by the excavations
of 1963–4: V. Tusa [379], I, 15.
71 P. Cintas [387], 115; [402], 479.
72 T. J. Dunbabin [442], 22, 327.
73 L. Foucher [415].
74 P. Cintas [414], 37f.
75 F. Barreca, G. Pesce [391];
G. Pesce [398].
76 G. Lilliu [396].
77 G. Lilliu [395].
78 CIS I, 144; W. F. Albright [379], 17;
A. Dupont-Sommer [393]; J. G. Février
[394]. Rhys Carpenter [375] would bring it
down to the end of the eighth century.
79 G. Patroni [397].
80 G. Pesce [399].
81 F. Barreca [392].
82 G. Vuillemot [417].
83 M. Taradell [424]; M. Euzennat
[420], 52f.
84 D. Harden [367], 36f., fig. 5;
P. Cintas [419], 35f.; A. Jodin [421, 423].
85 F. Villard [425].
86 D. Harden [367], 41, fig. 8;

D. van Berchem [435], 80–87.
87 G. Bonsor [428].
88 M. Astruc [426].
89 H. G. Niemeyer [431]; M. Pellicer, H. G. Niemeyer, H. Schubart [433]; see also H. Schubart [433b].
90 M. Pellicer [432]; cf. J. Leclant, *Orientalia* 33, 1964, 403–4.
91 There was a statue of Osorkon II at Byblos; P. Montet [371], I, 21f.
92 Strabo XV, 1,6, from Megasthenes; Josephus, *Ant*, X, 11, 1.
93 Strabo III, 5, 5.
94 R. Dion [380], 31.
95 Herod. IV, 152.
96 Herod. I, 163.
97 S. Gsell [408], I, 380 sq.
98 Josephus, *Ant*. VIII, 13,2.
99 *Pol*. XII, 28a 3.
100 Josephus, *c. Apion*. I, 17, 107–8; 18, 117–26; *Antiq*. VIII, 3, 1; on the last-named passage see P. Cintas [403], [403b].
101 Justin XVIII, 4–5.
102 E. O. Forrer [405]; E. Frézouls [406].
103 Virgil, *Aen*. I, 621; 729f.
104 P. Cintas [402], 11, n. 20 and 478.
105 P. Gauckler [407]. There is a good account of the excavations in the cemeteries of Carthage in J. Vercoutter [413], 16f.
106 E. Boucher [401], 12, 33, 37.
107 D. Harden [367], 95f.; [409].
108 P. Cintas [402], 490f.; P. Demargne [404], 49f.
109 G.-Ch. Picard [411], 28f.
110 P. Cintas [402], 480.
111 R. Rebuffat [355], 409f.
112 See above, p. 67.
113 Herod. IV, 42; S. Gsell [408], 230f.
114 *CIS* I, 5; D. Harden [367], 54 and 119.
115 Diod. 20, 14; S. Gsell [408], I, 395f.
116 S. Gsell [408], 421–2.
117 Polyb. III, 22, 5–9; 24, 1–3; 11–12. See below, p. 253.
118 J. Carcopino [418], 56.
119 P. Cintas [416], 270f.
120 J. Carcopino [418], 73f.; G. Ch. Picard [412], 45.
121 U. Kahrstedt [436]; B. Segall [439], 169.
122 *Il*. XXIII, 743f.
123 D. Harden [367], 188, fig. 54–5; 187, fig. 53 and pl. 46.
124 Y. Huls [345].
125 R. Rebuffat [355].
126 A. Hus [347].
127 A. Hus [346], 110, 368f.

128 F. Altheim [16], 206f.
129 *Od*. IV, 615f.
130 J. Bayet [754].
131 J. Bayet [754], 456.
132 A. Piganiol [437].
133 D. van Berchem [440]; [435], 307–38.
134 J. Carcopino [757], 199f.; see the same scholar's review of Bayet's thesis in *JS*, 1928, 157f., and 205f.
135 R. Rebuffat [438].
136 M. Lejeune [73].
137 G. Buchner, C. F. Russo [466]; L. H. Jeffery [33], 235f.; H. Metzger [468].
138 A. Grenier [70].
139 J. A. Bundgård [69]. I cannot follow the author in his attempt to show that the alphabet which the Phoenicians proposed to teach to the Etruscans was their own.
140 G. Glotz, R. Cohen [2], I, 153f.; on colonization in the Black Sea, E. Belin de Ballu [451].
141 We may hope that our knowledge of Chalcidian colonization will be greatly increased by the Swiss excavations at Eretria: K. Schefold [452].
142 Strabo V, 4, 4 (243); J. Bérard [441], 38f.
143 Thuc. VI, 3, 1; J. Bérard [441], 75.
144 Livy VIII, 22, 5; J. Bérard [441], 39; G. Vallet [469], 48.
145 G. Buchner [465, 467], 263f.; J. Bérard [441], 280f.; G. Vallet [469], 30f.
146 G. Buchner, A. Rittmann [464], 43.
147 J. Bérard [441], 42f.
148 J. Bérard [441], 41.
149 J. Bérard [441], 57, n.1.
150 Thuc. VI, 4, 5; G. Vallet [469], 59f.
151 G. Vallet [469], 66f.
152 G. Vallet [469], 56.
153 G. Vallet [469], 164f.
154 G. Vallet [469], 197f.
155 G. Vallet [470], 31f.
156 G. Vallet [469], 81f.
157 G. Vallet [469], 85f.
158 G. Vallet [469], 325f.
159 Thuc. IV, 61, 4; G. Vallet [469], 316, n.5.
160 G. Vallet [469], 234f.
161 G. Vallet [469], 255f.
162 G. Vallet [469], 211f.
163 G. Vallet, F. Villard [518].
164 A. Gitti [502]; K. F. Stroheker [533], 119f.
165 J. Bérard [441], 116f.
166 Thuc. VI, 13, 1; G. Vallet [507], 122f.
167 T. J. Dunbabin [442], 16.

168 Thuc. VI, 3, 1; T. J. Dunbabin
[442], 18f.
169 F. Villard [473b], 50.
170 E. Will [453], 319f.
171 J. Bérard [441], 131f.
172 A. Di Vita [480].
173 P. Griffo, L. von Matt [479].
174 P. Demargne, *La Crète dédalique*,
Paris, 1947, 320f.
175 P. Chamoux, *Cyrène sous la monarchie
des Bacchiades*, Paris, 1952, 124f.
176 T. J. Dunbabin, [478].
177 J. Bérard [441], 287; G. Vallet,
F. Villard [459], 302.
178 Virgil, *Aen*. III, 701.
179 See below, p. 88f.
180 J. Bayet [445], 26f.
181 Plin., *N.H.* III, 95.
182 Pseudo-Scymnus 303; Steph. Byz. *s.v.*
183 Strabo VI, 1, 2.
184 Polyb. II, 39,1.
185 On the origin of the term 'Magna
Graecia' see E. Meyer, *Philologus*, 48,
1889, 274, n.12; E. Pais [449], I, 513f;
E. Ciaceri [446], II, 184f.;
F. W. Walbank [92], I, 222.
186 G. Vallet and F. Villard [471], 301f.
187 T. J. Dunbabin [442], 24.
188 J. Bérard [441], 144.
189 R. van Compernolle [460], 237f.
190 J. Bérard [441], 290;
F. G. lo Porto [494], 8f.
191 F. G. lo Porto [495].
192 Strabo VI, 1, 12.
193 In the anecdote related by Strabo VI
2, 4 Syracuse takes the place of Sybaris;
G. Vallet and F. Villard [471] very
plausibly restore the primitive form of the
tradition.
194 P. Orsi [484], 815f., fig. 77;
J. Bérard [441], 158f. and 290;
G. Vallet [511], 214.
195 J. Bérard [441], 175f.
196 On Siris see J. Bérard [441], 187f.;
T. J. Dunbabin [442], 34f.; for a critique
of the tradition and reconstruction see
J. Perret [491].
197 On Locri see J. Bérard [441], 199f.;
T. J. Dunbabin [442], 35f.; cf. L. Lerat,
Les Locriens de l'Ouest, Paris, 1952, II, 25f.
198 A. Maiuri [498b], 79f., rejecting the
low dates (late sixth century) proposed by
P. Zancani-Montuoro [500] and
P. Sestieri [499].
199 According to J. Defradas, *Les thèmes
de la propagande delphique*, Paris, 1954,
233f., the oracle did not take a hand until

the middle of the sixth century; from then
on it helped to co-ordinate efforts which
had previously been dispersed.
200 J. Bérard [441], 99f., 141f.
201 Thuc. I, 24, 2.
202 Thuc. VI, 4, 2.
203 S. Mazzarino [508], 56f.
204 J. Bérard [441], 140f.
205 J. Bérard [441], 150;
V. Ehrenberg [487].
206 A. Pagliaro [34].
207 Thuc. VI, 5, 1.
208 G. Giannelli [525];
G. Pugliese Carratelli [528].
209 P. Wuilleumier [496], 469f.
210 Plato, *Legg*. VI, 754b;
J. Seibert [510].
211 Diod. XVI, 62, 4; P. Wuilleumier
[496], 77f.
212 F. Sartori [509], 85f.
213 Justin IV, 2, 1.
214 G. Vallet [469], 222f.
215 A. Stazio [514].
216 E.g. at Hyblaean Megara, where the
Sicel king Hyblon led the colonists to the
site (Thuc. VI, 4, 1). Cf. the founding of
Marseilles (below, p. 102).
217 Thuc. VI, 3, 2 (Syracuse);
VI, 3, 3 (Leontini and Catana).
218 J. Bérard [441], 163, n.1;
above, p. 57.
219 N. Degrassi, *Atti del III. Convegno di
Taranto*, 157f.
220 F. G. Lo Porto [495].
221 See above, p. 56.
222 N. Degrassi, *Atti del III. Convegno di
Taranto*, 155f.; cf. P. Wuilleumier
[496], 23f.
223 On the story of Aethra, which turns
up again in the legend of Myscelus the
oecist of Croton, see J. Bérard [441], 167.
224 N. Degrassi, *Atti del I. Convegno di
Taranto*, 228f.
225 D. Adamesteanu [474, 475].
226 G. Vallet [470]; see above, p. 78.
227 Herod. VII, 155.
228 A. Di Vita [480].
229 G. Vallet [470], 31.
230 Diodorus XI, 91, 4; D. Adamesteanu
[474], 178.
231 Diodorus IV, 78–9.
232 G. Glotz, R. Cohen [2], II, 681f.;
D. Adamesteanu [476].
233 See also D. Adamesteanu, in the
archaeological reports on the Basilicate,
Atti dei Convegui di Studi sulla Magna Grecia
(above, p. 32f.), vol. IV onwards.

234 P. Orsi [179]; J. de La Genière [174], 11f.
235 G. Foti, *Atti del III. Convegno di Taranto*, 177f.
236 A. de Franciscis, *Atti del I. Convegno di Taranto*, 215f.
237 J. Bérard [441], 207.
238 J. de La Genière [174], 20f.
239 Strabo VI, 1,14; T. J. Dunbabin [442], 35, n.2.
240 J. Heurgon [741], 76; J. S. Callaway [486], 45; E. Kirsten [504], 141.
241 Strabo VI, 1, 4; Arist., *Pol.* VII, 9, 2.
242 Strabo *ibid.*
243 F. Lenormant [447], I, 262f.; L. Ponnelle [488]; E. Ciaceri [446], II, 226f.; J. Bayet [754], 10f.; J. Heurgon [741], 74f.
244 J. Bayet [754], 48.
245 Timaeus, *F.Gr.Hist.* 566 F. 50.
246 G. Vallet [469], 166f.; cf. J. Heurgon, *JS*, 1958, 161f.
247 The supposed relations between Siris and Pyxous have been disproved by P. Zancani-Montuoro [492]; J. Bérard [441], 196; [443], 185f.
248 A. Maiuri [505], 63f.
249 Diodorus XIV, 101.
250 *IG* XIV, 643; J. S. Callaway [486], 49; A. Maiuri [505], 69; L. H. Jeffery [33], 260, pl. 50.
251 E. Kunze, *VII. Bericht über die Ausgrabungen in Olympia*, 1961, 207f.; P. Zancani-Montuoro [490]; E. Kirsten [504], 139f.
252 G. Vallet [469], 177f.
253 P. Wuilleumier [496], 219f.
254 F. Sartori [489], 152f.; E. Lepore [506], 205, 217.
255 J. G. Milne, *NC*, 1938, 36f.; T. J. Dunbabin [442], 245; G. Vallet [469], 325.
256 L. Breglia [513].
257 L. Breglia [103, 104], 206f.; A. Stazio [514].
258 G. Vallet [469], 167f.
259 A. Stazio [514], 115f.
260 A. Stazio [514], 121f.
261 P. Zancani-Montuoro [492]; L. Breglia [512].
262 A. Schenk von Staffenberg [450], 176f.
263 M. P. Loicq-Berger [526], 189f.
264 F. Altheim [7], II, 292f.; K. F. Stroheker [533].
265 A. Piganiol [5], 156f.
266 M. Sordi [532]. The fourth volume

(1958) of Kokalos is devoted to Timoleon.
267 A. Di Vita [481]; G. Vallet, F. Villard [473].
268 P. Orlandini [531].
269 M. J. Fontana [530].
270 H. Berve [529].
271 S. Gsell [408], III, 18f.
272 G. Glotz, R. Cohen [2], II, 676f.
273 K. F. Stroheker [533], 113f.
274 K. F. Stroheker [533], 117.
275 K. F. Stroheker [533], 132.
276 P. Wuilleumier [496], 51f.
277 P. Wuilleumier [496], 68f.
278 P. Wuilleumier [496], 335f.; [519].
279 Livy I, 18, 3.
280 Diels, *Vorsokratiker* I, 45 A.
281 *ILLRP* 1271a, with the bibliography.
282 F. Altheim [7], I, 114f.
283 G. Giannelli [525].
284 F. Altheim [17], 15f.; H. Le Bonniec [760], 213f.
285 J. Bérard [497], 25f.; J. Heurgon [741], 375f.
286 J. Bayet [754], 10f.; D. Van Berchem [440]; see above, p. 73.
287 D. Comparetti [522], 7, 16f., 25f., 31f.; G. Giannelli [525], 112f., 169.
288 M. Pallottino, *TLE* 2; [64].
289 C. C. Van Essen [332]; J. M. Blazquez [322].
290 F. Altheim [7], I, 129f.; P. Boyance [521].
291 J. Carcopino, *La basilique pythagoricienne de la Porte-Majeure*, Paris, 1926, 161.
292 E. Langlotz, M. Hirmer [515].
293 R. Martin [32].
294 E. D. Van Buren [517]; A. Andrén [336], C-CXV.
295 P. Wuillemier [496], 393f.; S. Mollard-Besques [516], 53f.; 66f, 99f.
296 A. Olivieri [527], 7f.; P. Frassinetti [524].
297 C. Jullian [216], I, 195f.; esp. 197f. Most recently discussed by J.-P. Morel [534, 534b]; G. Vallet, F. Villard [541].
298 See above, p. 65f.
299 H. Rolland [549]; F. Villard [552], 73f.; F. Benoit [542], 29f., 139f. But J.-P. Morel [534] 380f., thinks it better, considering the present state of the documentation, to dispense with the hypothesis of Rhodian trading on the coasts of Spain and Provence in the seventh century.
300 H. Rolland [549], 90f.; F. Villard [552], 74f.; H. Gallet de Santerre [547];

F. Benoit [542], 51f.; J.-P. Morel [534], 383, n. 16.
301 F. Benoit [542], 51; [543], 32f.
302 F. Villard [552], 18; [553].
303 J. Brunel [545]; F. Villard [552], 77f.
304 Justin XLIII, 3, 4f.
305 F. Villard [552], 36f.
306 F. Villard [552], 13f.
307 Herod. I, 162–7.
308 J. Carcopino [535]; J. Jehasse [537], 242f.
309 M. Gigante [536].
310 Thuc. I, 13, 6.
311 Strabo VI, 1, 1 (251), citing (probably inaccurately) Antiochus of Syracuse: Μασσαλίαν seems to be a mistake for 'Αλαλίαν: J. Brunel [545], 10f.
312 Pausan, X, 8, 6.
313 The date conflicts with the archaeological evidence.
314 J.-P. Morel [534], 394f.
315 M. Napoli [539]; G. Vallet, F. Villard [541], 181f.; J.-P. Morel [534], 395.
316 J. Jehasse [537], 276; F. Benoit [542], 44, n. 42.
317 Thuc. I, 13, 6; Justin XLIII, 5, 2.
318 G. Daux [546]; F. Benoit [542], 40.
319 Sosylus, F.Gr.Hist. 176 F.3; S. Mazzarino [538], 8f.; F. Villard [552], 88f.; F. Benoit [542], 46, n.51.; J.-P. Morel [534], 396, n.62.
320 J.-P. Morel [534], 397.
321 Arist., Pol. III, 5, 9; F. Villard [552], 83 and n.5, with the interpretation of J. Brunel.
322 G. Nenci [540], 63f.; S. Mazzarino [87], I, 195.
323 Pseudo-Scymnus, Geogr. Gr. min. I, p. 206; J. Brunel [545], 12.
324 Eustathius in Geogr. Graeci min. II, p. 645; J. Brunel [544], 123f.; F. Benoit [542], 42.
325 R. Dion [380], 32.
326 F. Benoit [542], 98; J.-P. Morel [534], 389f.
327 J.-P. Morel [534], 392.
328 J.-P. Morel [534], 387.
329 F. Benoit [542], 191f.; J.-P. Morel [534], 408f.
330 F. Benoit [542], 91; J.-P. Morel

[534], 410.
331 Aristotle in Athenaeus XIII, 36, 576; Justin XLIII, 3, 8f.; C. Jullian [216], I, 201f.
332 Justin XLIII 3, 4.
333 F. Benoit [542], 92.
334 F. Villard [552], 109f.
335 Strabo IV, 1, 5.
336 F. Benoit [542], 93f.
337 J. Jannoray [234], 296f.; F. Villard [552], 112f.; J.-P. Morel [534], 411.
338 J. Jannoray [234], 302; H. Gallet de Santerre [547], 392.
339 F. Villard [552], 113; H. Gallet de Santerre [547], 393f.
340 See above, p. 96.
341 D. Van Berchem [565].
342 A. Alföldi [554].
343 Ch. Picard [564], after Herod. V, 9–10.
344 P. Jacobsthal [561].
345 H. A. Cahn [556].
346 L. Lerat [563].
347 R. Joffroy [228], 150f.
348 R. Joffroy [226, 229]; see above, p. 96. In his last work, 137f., Joffroy declares that 'everything speaks for the route by Switzerland and the Alps'.
349 J. Carcopino [225], 23f.; F. Villard [552], 141.
350 P. Jacobsthal, J. Neuffer [548].
351 J.-J. Hatt, A. Perraud, Ch. Lagrand [560]; some doubts felt by A. Grenier, CRAI 1959, 91f.
352 F. Benoit [542], 141.
353 F. Villard [552], 141.
354 J.-P. Morel [534], 410.
355 R. Dion [429].
356 J. Carcopino [225], 34f.; R. Joffroy [228], 145; F. Villard [552], 143f., with the texts.
357 J. Carcopino [225], 82.
358 F. Villard [552], 158.
359 F. Benoit [555], 15; cf. P.-M. Duval [206], 289; H. Gallet de Santerre [547], 399.
360 R. Joffroy [226], 32f.; [228], 151.
361 W. Kimmig [562].
362 J.-J. Hatt [559]; F. Villard [552], 128f.
363 J.-P. Morel [534], 411f.
364 Arist., Pol. VI, 7.
365 G. Nenci [540], 87f.

Chapter Four

1 E. Meyer [573], 30f.
2 Dion. Hal. V, 48, 3; Plut., Publ. 23.

3 See below, p. 196.
4 Livy VI, 20, 14; Auct. de praen., 6.

5 Dion. Hal. IX, 15, 2.
6 See below, p. 124.
7 See above, p. 48.
8 See above, p. 38.
9 Festus 300 L.
10 E. Benveniste [592].
11 *XII Tab.* VIII, 21; Virg., *Aen.* VI, 609; Gell., *N.A.* V, 13; XX, 1.
12 For the business of the Marcelli and the patrician Claudii, see Cic., *De Orat.* I, 176; G. Bloch [629], 107f.
13 Livy XLIII, 16, 4.
14 Fest. 288 L.; Fustel de Coulanges [605], 13f.; L. Zancan [729], 13f.
15 J. Heurgon [318], 713f.
16 Livy II, 16, 4; Dion. Hal. V, 40, 3.
17 Livy II, 49, 4; 50, 11; Dion. Hal. IX, 15, 3; Fest. Paul. 451 L.
18 Livy III, 16, 5; Dion. Hal. X, 14, 1.
19 See below, pp. 154, 196f.
20 P. de Francisci [570], 140f.
21 See below, p. 228.
22 P. de Francisci [570], 164f.
23 Livy IX, 29, 10; cf. J. Carcopino [757], 199f.
24 Livy XXIX, 27, 2.
25 Livy X, 8, 9.
26 Livy I, 8, 5; F. Altheim [20], 175f.
27 P. de Francisci [570], 777f.
F. de Martino [571], 49f.; E. Meyer [573], 33f.
28 Th. Mommsen [575], II, 387f.
29 Cicero, *De rep.* II, 16.
30 Fustel de Coulanges [604], 222; E. Meyer [573], 33.
31 Fustel de Coulanges [604], 222.; G. Bloch [594].
32 The different solutions put forward are reviewed by F. de Martino [571], 61; cf. *inter alios* J. Binder [593]; A. Piganiol [576], 251f.; [6], 56.
33 P. de Francisci [570], 777f.
34 Livy I, 8, 7; 17, 7f.
35 H. Last [653].
36 U. Coli [612], 73.
37 Livy IV, 3, 16.
38 P. de Francisci [570], 777f.
39 A. Alföldi [590].
40 A. Momigliano [574], 117f.
41 G. Devoto [117], 214.
42 S. Mazzarino [687], 27f.
43 F. de Martino [571], 33; 67f.
44 U. Coli [612], 77f.; P. de Francisci [570], 511f.
45 P. Catalano [607].
46 A. Ernout [611]; G. Dumézil [610].
47 Livy I, 18, 6f.; on such laying-on of

hands see H. Wagenvoort [24], 35f.
47a P. de Francisci [570], 549f.
48 A. Magdelain [631].
49 S. Mazzarino [687], 218; E. S. Staveley [660], 84f, thinks it does not antedate the beginning of the republic.
50 Festus 198 L.
51 K. Latte [14], 195f.
52 Latest state of the excavation of the Regia: F. E. Brown [615].
53 On the pre-Julian calendar see A. K. Michels [618], 3f.; [617].
54 Varro, *L.L.* VI, 27; Macrob., *Sat. I*, 15, 9–11; on Juno Covella see M. Renard [621].
55 On these letters see A. K. Michels [618], 61f.
56 J. Paoli [619, 620]. In the mutilated text of Festus 346 L. we find: *e nefasto fastus.*
57 Festus 346 L. mentions the *Q.R.C.F.* days in connection with the *regifugium* (*inter tales dies*).
58 Plutarch, *Q.R.*. 63; F. Altheim [7], II, 56f.; K. Latte [14], 128. The year originally began on 1 March.
59 *ILLRP*, I, 3 and II, p. 379; G. Dumézil [670].
59a Mommsen, *CIL* I, p. 361; cf. A. K. Michels [618], 207f.
60 G. Wissowa [13], 31.
61 They can now be best studied in the edition of A. Degrassi, *Inscriptiones Italiae* XIII, 2.
62 K. Latte [14], 36.
63 H. J. Rose [622], 76; F. Altheim [19], 106f.; F. Altheim [7], II, 23f.
64 A. K. Michels [617] and [618], 216f.
65 Livy I, 8, 3; Florus I, 1, 5.
66 A. Alföldi [613], 28, n.1, 29f., 38f.; F. Altheim [7], II, 59f.
67 Livy X, 7, 10.
68 G. Dumézil [608], [609], 151.
69 P. Noailles [627], [628], 16f.
70 J. Carcopino [630]; J. Paoli [632].
71 E. Meyer [573], 22f.; U. Coli [612], 114f.; P. de Francisci [570], 557.
72 Dion. Hal. II, 27, 4; Plut., *Numa* 17, 5.
73 A. Piganio [6], 32.
74 Livy I, 26, 5; P. de Francisci [570], 612f.
75 P. de Francisci [570], 619f.; E. Meyer [573], 39.
76 H. Lévy-Bruhl [625]; see on this topic a suggestion of Carcopino's in *REL* XI, 1933, 284.

77 L. Gernet [623]; but the two *-rr-* seem to be etymological. They are simplified in the text of Festus (Paul. 247 L.) but this is only the archaic spelling which does not double consonants. In any case, on this interpretation, Horatius would have been accused of *parricidium*.
78 Fest. Paul. 247 L.: *si qui hominem liberum dolo sciens morti duit, paricidas esto.*
79 M. Kaser [624], 42f.
80 A. Alföldi [614].
81 Livy I, 13, 6f.; X, 6, 7.
82 G. Devoto [117], 224; cf. the *Sapinia tribus*, Livy XXXI, 2, 6; XXXIII, 37, 1.
83 Varro, *L.L.* V, 35; 55; but see Ernout-Meillet, *Dict. etym.* s.v. *tribus*.
84 Florus II, 6; U. von Lübtow [661], 39f.; G. Devoto [596]; opposed by A. Momigliano [574], 111.
85 E. Taübler [728].
86 G. Dumézil [598], 129f.; [603], 13f.
87 W. Schulze [76], 218, 581.
88 Cic., *De rep.* II, 36; Livy L, 36, 2f.; 43, 9.
89 P. de Francisci [570], 537f.
90 Tacitus, *Ann.* I, 54.
91 P. de Francisci, who thinks that the three genetic tribes were constituted in the late eighth century, will not agree to localize the Tities on the Quirinal, which was not yet part of the community. But the date is very much guesswork.
92 See above, p. 32f.
93 On the curiae see E. Meyer [573], 26f.; P. de Francisci [570], 484f.; most recently A. Momigliano [574], 108f.
94 Ernout-Meillet, *Dict. etym.* s.v. *curia.*
95 E. Vetter [39], no. 222.
96 Festus 182 L.; Fest. Paul. 503; Varro, *L.L.* VI, 23; Livy IX, 38, 15.
97 Cicero, *De rep.* II, 14; Livy I, 13, 6; Fest. Paul. 42 L.
98 Dion. Hal. II, 47, 4; τὰ δ' ἀπὸ πάγων.
99 G. Devoto [43], 352.
100 W. Schulze [76], 543f.
101 F. R. Adrados [589].
102 Dion. Hal. II, 23, 5.
103 Varro, *L.L.* VI, 22; on Angerona see Dumézil [22], 330f.
104 This interpretation is bound up with the meaning of *Quirinus* and *Quirites* held by G. Dumézil [601], 225f.; [22], 154f.
105 K. Latte [14], 143.
106 K. Latte [14], 68.
107 Tacitus, *Ann.* XII, 24;

G. Lugli [25], 400.
108 Livy XXVII 8, 1f.
109 Ovid, *Fasti* II, 512; Varro, *L.L.* VI, 13 ; Festus 304 and 418 L.
110 Ovid, *Fasti* IV, 630.
111 Varro: *qui Furnacalibus suis non fuerunt feriati*; Festus: *qui sollenni die . . . non potuerunt rem divinam facere.*
112 P. de Francisci [570], 575.
113 Varro, *L.L.* V, 13; Macrob., *Sat.* I, 15, 10.
114 W. Schulze [76], 524.
115 Gellius, *N.A.* XV, 27; following Laelius Felix, under Hadrian; he gives a very artificial classification of the different forms of comitia, in which the comitia calata, as being 'called', embrace the comitia curiata and centuriata.
116 Gell. *N.A.* XV, 27; Gaius II, 101; P. de Francisci [570], 585.
117 Gell, *N.A.* V, 19.
118 Gell., *N.A.* XV, 27.
119 P. de Francisci [570], 489.
120 P. de Francisci [570], 580.
121 U. Coli [612], 67; P. de Francisci [570], 586.
122 U. Coli [612], 65f.; P. de Francisci [570], 581f.
123 U. Coli [612], 66.
124 F. de Martino [571], 126.
125 Gell., *N.A.* V, 19.
126 Gell., *N.A.* XV 27.
127 P. de Francisci [570], 484, n.350; F. de Martino [571], 120f.; A. Momigliano [574], 111.
128 Mommsen [575], I, 144f., 182f.
129 H. Last [653].
130 F. de Martino [571], 86f.
131 E. Meyer [573], 27.
132 F. de Martino [571], 130f.; P. de Francisci does not agree.
133 P. de Francisci [570], 430.
134 G. Bloch [629], 105f.; U. Coli [612], 68.
135 On the Ovinian *plebeiscitum* see Festus 290 L.; P. de Francisci [570], 490.
136 Dion. Hal. II, 12, 1.
137 G. Bloch [629], 43f.
138 Livy I, 35, 6; Dion. Hal. III, 67, 1; Cic., *De rep.* II, 20: *duplicavit illum pristinum patrum numerum.*
139 U. Coli [612], 69; P. de Francisci [570], 592; F. de Martino [571], 90, 119.
140 Livy I, 8, 7.
141 A. Momigliano [574], 118, n.93.
142 F. de Martino [571], 117f.
143 U. Coli [612], 67f.

144 Cicero, *De domo* 38; Livy VI, 41, 6f.; A. Momigliano [574], 117, n.92.
145 P. de Francisci [570], 490, 550f.
146 Livy I, 22, 4f.; 24, 3f.; 32, 5f.; 45, 1f.
147 Cic., *De rep.* II, 14; Festus 290 L.; P. de Francisci [570], 548.
148 Livy I, 49, 5 and 7.
149 A. Alföldi [566], 1f.
150 Pliny, *N.H.* III, 69.
151 A. Alföldi [566], 265f.
152 Cato, *Or.* II, 21 J.; *HRR* 68.
153 Livy I, 45; A. Alföldi [662], opposed by A. Momigliano [663].
154 A. Alföldi [566], 34f.
155 E. Gjerstad [572], 37f.
156 J. Perret [636].
157 F. Bömer [634]; A. Alföldi [633].
158 Fest., 326 L.
159 *ILLRP* II, 1271; S. Weinstock [765], 114f.; J. Heurgon [635], 663f.
160 F. Bömer [634], 47f.
161 See above, p. 21f.
162 See above, p. 21.
163 A. Alföldi [633], 23f.
164 A. Momigliano [89], 549f.
165 But Roman reckoning was inclusive; they counted 748 to 504 as being 245 years.
166 O. Leuze [616], 83f.
167 M. Pallottino [196], 9.
168 Dion Cass. XLIII, 45, 3.
169 Divus Claudius ap. *CIL* XIII, 1668 = Dessau 212, col. 1.
170 Dion. Hal. IV, 7, 5.
171 G. Dumézil [599], 34f.
172 G. Dumézil [600], 247f.
173 G. Dumézil [602], 52.
174 G. Dumézil [597].
175 G. Dumézil [598].
176 G. Dumézil [602], 14f.
177 G. Dumézil [598], 182.
178 G. Dumézil [600], 159f.
179 G. Dumézil [600], 199f.
180 G. Dumézil [598], 32.
181 J. Bayet in *REL* 25, 1947, 54.
182 G. Dumézil [598], 85f.
183 G. Dumézil [600], 176, 181f.
184 E. Gjerstad [572], 40.
185 Varro, *L.L.* V, 33.
186 L. Ross Taylor [669], 38; A. Alföldi [668], 206; [566], 310.
187 W. Schulze [76], 579f.; A. Ernout, *Philologica*, Paris, 1946, 22; K. Latte [14], 20.
188 J. Carcopino [756]; below, p. 346f.
189 R. Thomsen [772], III, 153.
190 J. Carcopino [756], 81.
191 *Auct. de praen.* 1; G. Bonfante [595].
192 Livy XXVII, 6, 15; F. Münzer [712], 80f.
193 First attested in 171 (Livy XLIII, 1, 12).
194 The story that Ancus Marcius founded Ostia, which is not older than 335, seems to have been inspired by the victories gained in 356 by C. Marcius Rutilus at the mouth of the Tiber; this was the moment 'when the Marcian family, emerging for the first time into the full light of history, shines with a brilliance which it is never to recapture' (J. Carcopino [744], 34f.).
195 J. Gagé [758], 297f.; J.-P.Morel [637].
196 E. Gabba [84], 154f. has nevertheless found traces of the rise of the legend of Numa in the Pythagorean movement of the fourth century.
197 Dion. Hal. II, 49, 4.
198 Cic., *Brut.* 75; *Tusc. 1*, 3; *Varro, De vita populi Romani*, in Nonius 77 L.; A. Momigliano [88].
199 Livy I, 22, 2.
200 Livy I, 24, 4.
201 See above, p. 119.
202 See above, p. 135.
203 M. Horatius, *praetor maximus* and consul in 509–508; see below, p. 161.
204 Livy I, 25; II, 10.
205 Livy I, 28, 9f.; Enn., *Ann.* 138f.Vahl.
206 M. Pallottino, *TLE* 35.
207 J. Heurgon [647].
208 F. Messerschmidt [648]; M. Pallottino [352], 115f.; A. Alföldi [566], 221f.; on the date see now M. Cristofani [646].
209 A. Alföldi [566], 218f.
210 Plut., *Rom.* 2; J. Heurgon [272], 312f.; S. Mazzarino [87], I, 195f. and 584f.
211 Divus Claudius ap. *CIL* XIII, 1668 (=Dessau 212, col. 1).
212 J. Heurgon [641].
213 Livy V, 33, 7; above, 107f.
214 See above, 72, 108.
215 Vell. Paterc. I, 7; J. Heurgon [741], 62f.
216 A. Alföldi [638], 386; [566], 182f.
217 See above, p. 43.
218 See above, p. 24.
219 E. Gjerstad [192], IV, 494.
220 M. Pallottino [642]; *TLE* 24; *SE* 22, 1952–3, 309.
221 E. Gjerstad [192], I, 21f., 72f.; P. Romanelli, *Gnom.* 31, 1959, 437; H. Müller-Karpe [195], 14.

222 G. Lugli [25], 80.
223 E. Gjerstad [192], III, 321f.;
H. Müller-Karpe [195], 17.
224 E. Gjerstad [192], III, 378f.;
G. Colonna [644].
225 M. Pallottino [353].
226 Dion. Hal. I, 29, 2.
227 Livy I, 38, 6; 56, 1f.; 57, 2.
228 Livy I, 56, 1: fabris undique ex
Etruria accitis.
229 A. Grenier [70]; M. Lejeune [73].
230 ILLRP 3; see above, p. 115f.
231 See above, p. 121.
232 Varro, L.L. V, 46; Livy II, 14, 9.
233 ILLRP 1.
234 J. B. Ward Perkins [266], 22.
235 A. Alföldi [566], 206f.
236 J. Heurgon [272], 305f.
237 A. Alföldi [566], 209f.
238 Cato, Or. I, 12; Festus, 322 L.
239 A. Alföldi [566], 208.
240 See above, p. 131.
241 Livy I, 34, 10.
242 E. Ciaceri [568], 254f.; opposed by
M. Cristofani [640].
243 Ed. Will [453], 362, would lower
this date to c. 620.
244 A. Blakeway [639]; Ed. Will [453],
309 and 325; G. Vallet [469], 185.
245 Livy I, 34, 4f.; 39, 3; 41, 1f.; 48, 5;
J. Heurgon [272], 95f.
246 Livy I, 34, 9.
247 Livy I, 35, 2 and 5; 47, 7; 49, 1.
248 Livy I, 44, 3f.
249 Livy I, 38, 6; 56, 3; Dion. Hal. III,
67, 5; IV, 45, 1.
250 Livy I, 38, 7.
251 Livy I, 55, 2f.; Dion. Hal. III, 69f.
makes Tarquin the Elder responsible
for this.
252 E. Pais, J. Bayet [3], 46, n.58.
253 Livy I, 53, 3; 55, 8.
254 Pliny, NH III, 70.
255 Dion. Hal. III, 51f.
256 A. Alföldi [633], 24f.; [566], 238f.
257 Dion. Hal. I, 29, 2.
258 Divus Claudius, ap. CIL XIII, 1668;
Festus, 486 L.
259 M. Pallottino [352], 115f.
260 A. Alföldi [566], 212f.
261 A. Hus [346], 135.
262 L. Pareti, SE V, 1931, 154f.;
J. Heurgon [741], 70.
263 G. Colonna [664], 139; [645].
264 Dion. Hal. III, 65, 6;
A. Alföldi [566], 215.
265 H. Lévy-Bruhl [606].

266 E. Benveniste [591].
267 F. Münzer, Rh.M. 1898, 607;
G. de Sanctis, Klio, 1902, 96. The word is
attested as designating a magistracy or a
military command in Etruscan inscriptions;
thus TLE 195: macstrev 'he held the post of
magister'. It has been compared with the
old name for the dictator at Rome,
magister populi (S. Mazzarino [687], 188f.):
Servius Tullius could thus have been the
first dictator. We should notice further
that in the war against the Sabines,
according to Dion. Hal. III, 65, 6, Tarquin
put him in command of the Latins and the
other allies.
268 Divus Claudius ap. CIL XIII, 1668.
269 Livy I, 43; Dion. Hal. IV, 16f.
270 Fest. Paul. 100 L.
271 E. Meyer [573], 48f., 482f.
272 G. Piganiol [658]; C. Nicolet [656].
273 G. de Sanctis [10], II, 187.
274 F. Altheim [7], II, 165.
275 Polyb. VI, 23, 15.
276 See above, p. 110f.
277 A. Momigliano [574], 118f.
278 P. Fraccaro [651], 289.
279 It is not easy to accept Mattingly's
theory (see [654]) that these figures
represent the state of affairs after the as
was reduced to ½oz. in 89, and that they
stand for sesterces, not asses. It is hard to
imagine that the census of the first class
was 100,000 sesterces in 70, when that of
the tribuni aerarii was 300,000 and that of
the knights 400,000 sesterces (A. Piganiol
[5], 520; J. Carcopino, César, 956, make
the equestrian and the first-class census the
same—a million asses). Mattingly does not
give any census-figure for the other four
classes; but it is certain that in 169 the
census of the second class was 75,000
asses.
280 Polyb. VI, 23, 15.
281 Livy XLV, 15, 2.
282 Polyb. VI, 19, 2; F. W. Walbank
[92], I, 698.
283 C. Nicolet [656], 358.
284 XII Tab. IX, 2; Cic., De rep. III, 61;
De legg. III, 11; E. Meyer [573], 54f.
285 Fest. Paul. 100 L.; Gell., NA. VI, 13;
A. Momigliano [655], 509f.; [574], 120.
286 XII Tab. I, 4; Cic., De rep. II, 40.
287 H. H. Scullard [12], 425f.
288 G. de Sanctis [10], II, 181f.;
[650], 289f.
289 P. Fraccaro [651], 287f.; cf. 293f.
290 P. Fraccaro [708b], 151, n.9.

291 K. Delbrück, *Geschichte der Kriegskunst,*
I³, 270, quoted by Fraccaro [651], 291.
292 H. Last [653].
293 S. Mazzarino [687], 201f.
294 F. de Martino [571], 149.
295 A. Bernardi [679], 18f.
296 E. Schönbauer [659], 24f.
297 U. von Lübtow [661], 65f.
298 E. S. Staveley [660], 75f.
299 E. Friezer [652].
300 P. de Francisci [649]; [570], 760f.
301 H. H. Scullard [12], 423f.
302 A. Momigliano [574], 120.
303 A. Bernardi [679]; E. Meyer
[573], 56; H. H. Scullard [12], 426.
304 P. Fraccaro [651], 305f.;
E. S. Staveley [705], 30f.
305 A. Bernardi [679], 43f.
306 E. S. Staveley [660], 82.
307 M. P. Nilsson [657], 4f.
308 F. Altheim [7], II, 153f.;
A. Bernardi [679], 21.
309 Accius in *Sc. Rom. Fragm.* I, 367.
310 Livy I, 43, 8.
311 Livy I, 13, 8; 30, 3; 36, 7.
312 Festus 290 L.
313 E. Meyer [573], 491, n.80;
differently interpreted by A. Momigliano
[574], 118, n.93.
314 E. Meyer [573], 48.
315 Livy I, 36, 7f.; 43, 9.

316 P. de Francisci [570], 567f.
317 Cic., *De rep.* II, 39.
318 Livy I, 43, 13; Varro, *L.L.* V, 45.
319 Festus 310 L.
320 F. Castagnoli [664].
321 The conclusions reached by
G. Säflund [667] have been called in
question by G. Lugli [665] and
P. Quoniam [666]. See now E. Gjerstad
[192], III, 27f.
322 Livy I, 44, 4; Tacitus, *Ann.* XII, 24.
323 Dion. Hal. IV, 15, 1; the figure is
defended by F. Cornelius [569], 106f:
the 26 tribes, he thinks, included the
septem pagi taken from Rome by Porsenna.
324 Livy II, 21, 7.
325 H. H. Scullard [12], 46, n.2.
326 J. Beloch [9], 175, 270f.;
E. Meyer [573], 57.
327 A. Bernardi [679], 20, n.2;
L. Ross Taylor [669], 36, n.4.
328 G. de Sanctis [10], II, 18f. thinks
that the territorial tribes were created in
the early fifth century; cf. E. Meyer
[573], 56; L. Ross Taylor [669], 6,
accepts the traditional account.
329 A. Alföldi, [566], 304f; [668].
330 Mommsen, *R.G.* I, 35;
J. Beloch [9], 333f.
331 J. Beloch [9], 334.
332 Fest. Paul. 102 L.

Chapter Five

1 Livy I, 48, 9; II, 1; Dion. Hal. IV,
84, 4; V, 1f.
2 G. de Sanctis [10], I, 390.
3 A. Alföldi [566], 47f.;
J. Heurgon [685], 117f.
4 A. Alföldi [566], 56f.
5 Livy II, 9.
6 J. Bayet, *Tite-Live* II, p. 24, n.3.
7 Livy II, 14, 5f.
8 Livy II, 15, 7.
9 Livy II, 21, 5.
10 Dion. Hal. VII, 3–11; A. Alföldi
[556], 56f; on Aristodemus see
M. Pallottino [692].
11 Cato, *Or.* II, 21 J.; *HRR* 58.
12 Dion. Hal. V, 61, 3; cf. 50, 4.
13 A. Alföldi [566], 47f.; [662]; [753].
14 Livy I, 45; A. Momigliano [663].
15 G. Wissowa [13], 247f.;
R. Schilling [763].
16 E. Gjerstad [572], 44f.; R. Bloch
567], 62f.; [680]; [681];

R. Werner [694], 297f.
17 M. Pallottino [693], 31f.
18 On the conception of a cultural *koin*
see S. Mazzarino [687], 5f., 69.
19 A. Andrén [336].
20 J. Heurgon [685], 101f.
21 R. Werner [694], 474f.
22 M. Pallottino [692], 85.
23 Livy VII, 3, 5f.; Pliny, *N.H.* XXXIII,
19; J. Heurgon [684].
24 K. Hanell [682], 71f.
25 K. Hanell [682], 49f.
26 P. Fraccaro [78b], 5.
27 K. Hanell [682], 121f.; discussed by
E. Meyer [688], 177.
28 A. Alföldi [566], 78f.
29 P. de Francisci[570], 765.
30 J. Heurgon [685], 104f.;
A. Momigliano [691].
31 Livy II, 1,7.
32 Cic., *De rep.*, II, 53; *De legg.* III, 8;
Sallust, *Cat.* VI, 7.

33 Dion. Hal. IV, 73,3.
34 Livy I, 13, 4; A. Piganiol in his *Essai sur les origines de Rome* [576], cf. [5], 86. suggests that the original 'dualism' ought to turn up again in the institutions of the federated communities.
35 J. Beloch [9], 225f.
36 F. Sartori [509], 157.
37 J. Beloch [9], 230f.; S. Mazzarino [687], 86f.; 190f.; F. de Martino [571], 188f.; bibliography in E. Meyer [573], 478.
38 A. Bernardi [679], 5.
39 Livy II, 18, 4.
40 Livy III, 55, 12; Zonaras VII, 19; Fest. Paul. 249 L.
41 G. de Sanctis [10], I, 392f.
42 A. Bernardi [679], 24f.; P. de Francisci [570], 761f.
43 Dion. Hal. IV, 85, 3.
44 Livy VIII, 39, 13; X, 13, 3.
45 Varro, *L.L.* V, 80.
46 A. Walde, J. B. Hofman, *Lat. Etymologisches Wörterbuch*, s.v. *consilium*.
47 Mommsen [96], II, 1⁸, 77, n.3; K. Hanell [682], 204; J. Heurgon [685], 122f.
48 F. Bernardi [678], 3f.
49 P. Fraccaro [78b], 5.
50 Livy VI, 35, 5; Gell. *N.A.* XVII, 21, 27.
51 Diod. XII, 25.
52 P. Fraccaro [78b], 18; A. Bernardi [678], 6f.; M. Pallottino [693], 33f.
53 G. de Sanctis [10], I, 228f.
54 L. Ross Taylor [669], 40f.; but see also A. Alföldi [566], 312; [668], 207f.
55 A. Alföldi [662], 29.
56 G. Niccolini [698].
57 Livy II, 33, 1.
58 F. Altheim [695]; cf. J. Bayet [696].
59 Livy IV, 26, 2; X, 38, 2.
60 J. Bayet [696], 147.
61 Livy II, 33, 3; G. Niccolini [698], 40f.
62 Varro, *L.L.* 81: *tribuni plebei, quod ex tribunis militum primum tribuni plebei facti, qui plebem defenderent*. G. Niccolini [698], 30; F. Altheim [695], 237; E. Meyer [573], 44.
63 Livy II, 58, 1; Cic., *De rep.* II, 59.
64 Livy II, 58, 1; Ascon. *in Cornel.* 76; Diodorus XI, 68, 8; G. de Sanctis [10], II, 24f.; H. H. Scullard [12], 55, opposed by E. Meyer [573], 44f.
65 Cic., *De rep.* II, 58.
66 E. Meyer [573], 46f.
67 In 471: H. H. Scullard [12], 55; in 456: A. Alföldi [662], 28f.

68 G. de Sanctis [10], II, 33.
69 H. Le Bonniec [760], 255f., 266, 277sq., 342f.
70 E. Meyer [573], 43, 481, n.13.
71 H. Le Bonniec [760], 266f.
72 Livy II, 32, 1; III, 54, 9: the assigning of it to the Mons Sacer may have been motivated by the word *sacer*—often given to mountains—and a supposed connection with the *lex sacrata*. But Varro speaks of a 'secessio Crustumerina, which points to the same area: the army, on casting off its allegiance, marched towards the territory of the Aequi.
73 A. Merlin [697], 69f.; A. Alföldi [662], 28.
74 H. H. Scullard [12], 55f.
75 Cicero, *De rep.* II, 61.
76 E. Meyer [573], 60 and 486; F. de Martino [571], 243f.; survey of literature for and against the historicity of the Law of the XII Tables *ibid* 247, n.23; P. Noailles [628], 37f.; J. Bayet [701]; F. Wieacker [703].
77 Livy III, 34, 6.
78 C. G. Bruns [93], 15f.; P. F. Girard [94], 9f; S. Riccobono [95], I, 23f.
79 Livy III, 34, 3.
80 P. Noailles [628], 41f.; J. Bayet [701], 130.
81 Pomponius, *Dig.* I, 2, 2, par. 3.
82 J. Bayet [701], 130.
83 P. Noailles [628], 45f.
84 P. Noailles [627], 187f.; J. Bayet [702], 133f.
85 J. Bayet [701], 145.
86 Livy III, 31, 8.
87 F. Cornelius [569], 29; F. Wieacker [703], 330f.
88 *XII Tab.* VIII, 2.
89 P. Noailles [628], 18f.
90 Polyb. VI, 11; F. W. Walbank [92], I, 674.
91 Livy III, 33, 1.
92 F. de Martino [571], 253f.
93 Livy III, 9, 5; G. Rotondi [97], 198.
94 Livy III, 30, 7; 54, 11.
95 Livy IV, 3, 17.
96 Dion. Hal. X, 58, 4.
97 Appius Claudius Caecus, censor in 312; Ap. Claudius, III vir with the Gracchi; P. Clodius, tribune in 59.
98 Tacitus, *Ann.* I, 4, 3; J. Carcopino [4], 99f., 173.
99 F. de Martino [571], 252f.
100 J. Bayet [701], 133.

101 Livy IV, 3, 6f.; Cic., De rep. II, 63.
102 J. Bayet [700], 129;
F. de Martino [571], 256.
103 H. Last [653], 31.
104 F. de Martino [571], 256.
105 XII Tab. I. 4.
106 Livy III, 55, 3f.; G. Rotondi [97], 203f.
107 See above, p. 171.
108 Livy IV, 7, 3; T. R. S. Broughton [78], 52f.
109 E. Meyer [573], 70f.; J. Bayet [704];
E. S. Staveley [705].
110 Livy IV, 6, 8.
111 J. Bayet [704], 143f.;
F. de Martino [571], 268.
112 Livy IV, 7, 2.
113 Livy IV, 7, 10 (for 444);
23, 2 (for 435).
114 Livy V, 12, 9; VI, 37, 8;
Mommsen [575], I, 95; F. Münzer [712], 10.
115 J. Beloch [8], 247f.
116 A. Bernardi [679], 46.
117 T. R. S. Broughton [78], 82 (for 403).
118 A. Bernardi [679], 41f.
119 G. de Sanctis [10], II, 181f.
120 E. S. Staveley [705].
121 F. de Martino [571], 264f.
122 Livy III, 51, 2.
123 A. Alföldi [566], notably 36f., 101f.
124 Festus 276 L., citing L. Cincius.
125 Festus 276 L.
126 G. de Sanctis [10], II, 232f.;
E. T. Salmon [731], 93f.; [732], 63f.;
A. Alföldi [566], 393.
127 A. Piganiol [730], 298f.
128 Livy III, 4, 10: socialis exercitus.
129 e.g. one Quinctius: A. Piganiol [730], 306.
130 A. Alföldi [566], 121, 372f.;
Tibur and Praeneste, in face of the threat from the Aequi, more often thought of their own danger than of the common interest.
131 E. Kornemann [725], 72f.;
J. Heurgon [741], 116f.
132 A. Alföldi [566], 103f., on the juridical basis of Rome's sovereignty.
133 Livy I, 45, 3; see above, p. 128.
134 Dion. Hal. VI, 13.
135 A. Alföldi [566], 93, 400, pl. 2.
136 ILLRP 1271a; S. Weinstock [765], 112f.; R. Bloch [755].
137 Dion. Hal. VI, 95, 21;
H. Bengtson [721], 22f.
138 Cicero, Pro Balbo 53.
139 Festus 166 L.

140 Livy II, 19, 4.
141 Dion. Hal. V, 61, 3, in describing the coalition of the Latin peoples before the battle of Lake Regillus, only lists 29.
142 J. Heurgon [716].
143 G. Devoto [117], 103; see above, p. 7.
144 Livy II, 16, 4.
145 G. Devoto [117], 112f.
146 The Hernici very soon made their submission to the Latins: Livy II, 41, 1.
147 G. Devoto [117], 113f.
148 See above, p. 143.
149 A. Andrén [336], 407f., 453f.
150 Diod. XII, 31, 1; 76, 5; Livy IV, 37, 1; 44, 12; J. Heurgon [741], 81f.
151 G. Devoto [117], 117f.
152 P. Wuilleumier [496], 54f.
153 See above, p. 179, n.146.
154 Livy III, 15, 4f.; Dion. Hal. X, 14; J. Poucet [585], 106f.
155 Livy II, 33f., III, 26, 7f.; IV, 26f.; Ovid, Fasti, VI, 721f.
156 J. Bayet [734]; J. Hubaux [735].
157 Livy I, 15, 1; 33, 9; Dion. Hal. III, 41, 1f.
158 J. Carcopino [744], 472f.;
A. Alföldi [566], 288f.
159 Hor., Sat. II, 2, 33; Carm. III, 7, 28.
160 Livy II, 15, 6.
161 T. Ashby [714]; L. A. Holland [717], 303f.; [580], 160, 247;
A. Alföldi [566], 232.
162 Livy IV, 21, 2; 31, 4;
A. Alföldi [566], 295.
163 L. A. Holland [580], 247.
164 E. Pais, J. Bayet [3], 84.
165 Livy II, 48, 9.
166 L. Ross Taylor [669], 40f.; opposed by A. Alföldi [566], 312.
167 M. Pallottino [693], 35.
168 J. Hubaux [735], 121f.;
M. Sordi [739], 8f.
169 J. Bayet [737], 141f.
170 M. Sordi [739], 2f.
171 See above, p. 37f.
172 Livy V, 33, 1f.; G. Mansuelli [239], 1085.
173 G. de Sanctis [10], II, 156f.
174 Polyb. II, 18, 2.
175 Diod. XIV, 114; Livy V, 37f.
176 Livy V, 39–48; J. Bayet [736], 167f.
177 Livy V, 40, 9; CIL VI, 1272;
A. Degrassi, Inscriptiones Italiae XIII, 3, no. 11.
178 Pliny, N.H. III, 57.
179 Plutarch, Cam. XXII, 4; M. Sordi [739], 49f. This L. Albinus may be the

same who was military tribune with
consular powers in 379; his daughter or his
wife in 375 vowed a temple to Juno Lucina
(*Fasti Praenestini* in *CIL* I, p. 233;
J. Gage [759], 75). One must admit that
the consular tribune of 379 is called
Lucius in Diod. XV, 71, 1, and Marcus in
Livy VI, 30, 1: possibly there is a confusion
between the two praenomina.
180 M. Sordi [739], 25f.; A. Alföldi
[566], 341f.; 355f.
181 Pliny *N.H*. III, 4, following
Cornelius Nepos.
182 G. Vallet [469], 378f.;
K. F. Stroheker [533], 118f.
183 Justin XX, 5, 4.
184 Diod. XIV, 117, 6; Strabo V,
2, 3 (220).
185 Diod. XV, 14, 3.
186 Livy V, 50, 3; D. Anziani [720], 435f.;
E. Meyer [573], 187; M. Sordi [739], 36f.
187 Livy VI, 2, 3.
188 A. Momigliano [745], 389f.;
M. Sordi [739], 92f.; A. Alföldi [566], 347.
189 Theophrastus, *H.P.* V, 8, 2 =
F.Gr.Hist., 840 F. 24.
190 Diod. XV, 27, 4.
191 Livy XXVII, 38, 3, with the note of
Weissenborn and Müller.
192 Plutarch, *Cam.* II, 3.
193 Justin XLIII, 5, 10.
194 A. Alföldi [566], 348f.;
see below, p. 250f.
195 Livy VI, 42, 11f.
196 Diod. XV, 75.
197 Livy VI, 35, 10.
198 Livy VI, 35, 4f.
199 A. Alföldi [566], 147f.
200 J. Bayet [766], 120f.
201 Livy VI, 38, 5; K. von Fritz [706], 9.
202 Gell., *N.A.* V, 4, 1; *HRR* 10, p. 110;
A. Alföldi [566], 149; the 21 years are
reckoned as starting with 388.
203 A. Bernardi [678], 6f.; eleven if we
omit L. Brutus.
204 K. von Fritz [706], 3f.
205 K. von Fritz [706], 8.
206 Livy VII, 18, 1.
207 K. von Fritz [706], 8, 25, 28.
208 Livy VII, 38, 9; 42, 1f.
209 F. Münzer [712], 8f.
E. Meyer [573], 77f.
210 Livy VI, 34, 5; A. Alföldi [566], 147f.
211 Livy V, 12, 12; VI, 39, 4.
212 Livy VII, 16, 9; Val. Max. VIII, 6, 3;
F. Münzer [712], 22.
213 Livy II, 50, 11; F. Münzer [712], 53f.

214 F. Münzer [712], 34f.;
J. Heurgon [741], 247f.
215 Livy VI, 4, 2.
216 J. Gage [758], 120.
217 In 364: Festus 436 L.; the other may
have been plebeian, C. Poetelius: see
F. Münzer [712], 28.
218 i.e., after M. Marcius, the first plebeian
rex sacrorum (ob. 210), bequeathed
to his descendants the cognomen *Rex*,
which was the pretext for claiming his
descent from the king: Livy XXVII, 6, 16;
F. Münzer [712], 80f. See also above, p. 232.
219 On C. Marcius Rutilus see F. Münzer
[712], 29; J. Suolahti [707], 200f.
220 Livy IV, 8, 5.
221 J. Suolahti [707], 23f.
222 Livy VIII, 12, 13; J. Suolahti
[707], 207.
223 Livy VIII, 12, 16; G. Rotondi
[97], 227f.
224 J. Suolahti [707], 97, table II, 95.
225 Livy VIII, 15, 9.
226 We know only eleven of the praetors
between 326 and 264.
227 F. Münzer [712], 53f.;
A. Piganiol [5], 173, 183, 191, 216;
J. Heurgon [741], 284f.
228 In 310: Livy IX, 38, 15.
229 *XII Tab.* IX, 2; Cic., *De rep.* II, 61;
De legg. III, 11, see above, p. 149.
230 Livy VIII, 12, 15; G. Rotondi [97], 227.
231 For this interpretation of the
assemblies in Rome in the fourth century
see K. von Fritz [699, 706].
232 Pliny, *N.H.* VI, 37; G. Rotondi
[97], 238f.
233 K. von Fritz [699], 903;
[706], 22f., 26f.
234 Cf. the Canuleian plebiscite in
Livy IV, 5, 1: *oportet licere populo Romano,
si velit, iubere legem*.
235 Cf. the *leges Liciniae-Sextiae* in Livy VI,
42, 9: *per ingentia certamina dictator
senatusque victus, ut rogationes tribuniciae
acciperentur*.
236 E. Meyer [573], 65f.; H. H. Scullard
[12], 433.
237 Cic., *Tusc.* IV, 2, 4.
238 Ap. Claudius was subsequently to be
consul twice (307, 296), dictator once
(between 292 and 285), and to command
against the Etruscans and the Samnites.
But, contrary to normal practice, he spent
the year of his first consulate at Rome,
'to strengthen his power by civilian
activities' (Livy IX, 42, 4), and it was his

censorship in 312 which made his name
famous: J. Suolahti [707], 220f.
239 R. E. A. Palmer [710], 294f.
240 G. Rotondi [97], 233.
241 Diod. XX, 36; Livy IX, 46, 10f.
242 C. Nicolet [709], 691.
243 Mommsen [96], II, 400f.;
G. de Sanctis [10], 213f.; J. Carcopino
[4], 20.
244 P. Fraccaro [708b], 157f.
245 Livy IX, 46, 14.
246 L. Ross Taylor [669], 11 and 135f.
247 Livy XLV 15, 1; L. Ross Taylor
[669], 11, n.24.
248 J. Heurgon [272], 79f., [319], 70, n.5.
249 Livy IX, 46, 5; Livy, *N.H.* XXXIII, 17.
250 B. V. Head [99], 64;
S. P. Noe [771], 32.
251 A. Delatte [523], 259.
252 A. Momigliano [738], 111.
253 A. Alföldi [566], 159f.;
see above, p. 171.
254 Cic., *Brut.* 55; [Aur. Vict.]
De viris illust. 34, 3.
255 Livy X, 7, 1f.
256 Livy IX, 33, 4.
257 Suet., *Tib.* 2, 5, with Mommsen's
correction [575], I, 308f.; L. Ross Taylor
]669], 147.
258 A. Garzetti [708].
259 J. Carcopino [4], 21, 99f., 173.
260 C. Nicolet [709], 717.
261 E. S. Staveley [711], 410.
262 Mommsen [575], I, 306.
263 The importance of this date was
remarked by L. Cincius: Festus 276 L.
264 P. Boyancé [722].
265 J. Heurgon [741], 85f.;
see above, p. 180.
266 Livy VII, 19, 4; E. T. Salmon
[122], 187f.
267 Livy VII, 30–31; J. Heurgon
[741], 168f.; W. Dahlheim [723], 30f.
268 J. Heurgon [741], 165f.
269 A. Alföldi [566], 411f.
270 See above, p. 176.
271 Livy VIII, 14, 2: *relatum igitur de
singulis decretumque.*
272 A. Alföldi [566], 40f., 416f.
273 Livy VIII, 11, 13
274 J. Heurgon [741], 255f.
275 J. Heurgon [741], 260f.
276 Livy XXXI, 31, 11; J. Heurgon
[741], 182f.
277 A. N. Sherwin-White [727], 40.
278 A. Piganiol [5], 186.
279 Lycophron, *Alex.* 1271–1280;

J. Heurgon [741], 279f.; on Lycophron
see K. Hanell [85], 151.
280 J. Heurgon [741], 187f.
281 J. Heurgon [741], 201f.
282 J. Heurgon [741], 209f.;
R. Thomsen [772], II, 108f.;
J.-B. Giard [768].
283 Livy IX, 20, 5; J. Heurgon [741], 231f.
284 Mommsen [96], III, 1, 570f.
285 M. Napoli [742], 11f.
286 Strabo V, 4, 7.
287 F. Sartori [509], 45;
M. Napoli [742], 20f.
288 H. Le Bonniec [760], 381f.
289 Livy X, 31, 10; E. T. Salmon,
[122], 214f., 255f.
289a Livy VIII, 39, 13; X, 13, 3;
E. T. Salmon [122], 95f.
290 See above, p. 179.
291 Livy X, 38, 2f.; F. Altheim [695], 221f.
292 Livy IX, 40, 1f.; disputed by
P. Couissin [718], 181f.; J. Harmand
[719], 61f., 67.
293 G. de Sanctis [10], II, 299.
294 Livy XXXI, 31, 10.
295 G. de Sanctis [10], II, 281.
296 Cic., *Cat. mai.* 41; P. Wuilleumier
[496], 69, 89.
297 P. Wuilleumier [496], 77f.
298 Livy VIII, 37, 4: *socios eius gentis
populos ab Samnitium vi iniuriis defensos*
(following Fabius Pictor).
299 A. Grenier [715].
300 G. de Sanctis [10], II, 290;
A. Piganiol [5], 190.
301 Livy IX, 2, 6.
302 Livy IX, 4, 4; 12, 5.
303 Livy IX, 5, 2.
304 G. de Sanctis [10], II, 297.
305 A. Magdelain [726];
F. de Visscher [724].
306 Livy IX, 29, 1.
307 Livy IX, 32, 1f.; 37, 1; 39, 4.
308 Livy IX, 20, 2; 35, 2f.
309 Livy X, 10, 7; 16, 6.
310 G. de Sanctis [10], II, 315, n.103;
A. Piganiol [5], 189.
311 Livy X, 16, 7.
312 Livy X, 37, 4.
313 Livy X, 46, 10.
314 See above, p. 197.
315 A. J. Pfiffig [746].
316 J. Poucet [585], 415f.
317 See above, p. 33.
318 Livy X, 38, 4.
319 Clitarchus in Pliny, *N.H.* III, 57;
Aristobulus in Arrian, *Anab.* VII, 15, 6;

G. de Sanctis [10], II, 405, n.109.
320 Strabo V, 3, 5 [232].
321 J. Carcopino [744], 32f.
322 Polyb. XXX, 5, 6; G. de Sanctis
[10], II, 406, n.114; disputed by
M. Holleaux [752], 30f.; J. Carcopino
[751], 71.
323 Polyb. III, 26, 3f., denying the
existence of Philinus' treaty; P. Pédech
[91], 188f.; the identification is rejected by
F. W. Walbank [92], I, 354; but see
A. Piganiol [6], 64; P. Wuilleumier
[496], 95.
324 M. Cary, JRS, 9, 1919, 75, quoted by
P. Pédech [91], 189.
325 Claudius Quadrigarius, HRR, 31.
326 P. Wuilleumier [496], 95.
327 Diodorus XIII, 44, 1; XIV, 9, 2;
XVI, 82, 4.
328 J. Heurgon [741], 24f.
329 On the date see J. Beloch
[8], IV, 2, 479f.; P. Wuilleumier
[496], 101, n.7; J. Heurgon [741], 203f.;
P. Lévêque [750], 246, n.4
330 P. Wuilleumier [496], 183f.;
F. Sartori [509], 87; P. Lévêque
[750], 247, 308.
331 F. Cassola [713], 159f.
332 P. Lévêque [750]; J. Carcopino [747].
333 P. Lévêque [750], 538.
334 P. Lévêque [750], 347f.
335 A. de Franciscis [748, 749].
336 Livy, Per. XV; Polyb. I, 20, 14;
P. Wuilleumier [496], 139f.; F. Sartori
[509], 89; F. W. Walbank [92], I, 75.
337 Dion. Cass. I, 139; M. Holleaux
[752], 81; J. Carcopino [751], 73;
P. Lévêque [750], 582.

338 Livy, Per. XIV.
339 Lyc., Alex. 1229; cf. 1446–50; on the
interpretation of the passage see
P. Lévêque [86], 40f.
340 A. Momigliano [89].
341 Dion. Hal. I, 74, 1.
342 Polyb. I, 5, 1.
343 Livy VII, 29, 1; J. Heurgon [741], 283.
344 A. Piganiol [5], 216; J. Heurgon
[741], 285f.
345 See above, p. 194.
346 Livy IX, 46, 14; see above, p. 196f.
347 Pliny, N.H. VII, 133; F. Münzer
[712], 53f.
348 F. Cassola [713], 5f.
349 A. Piganiol [5], 173, 196.
350 S. Weinstock [764].
351 W. Schulze [76], 150f.
352 Livy X, 6, 6f.
353 A. Grenier [15], 140, 154;
K. Latte [14], 225f.
354 Livy X, 23, 12.
355 J. Carcopino [756].
356 P. J. Riis [358], 90f.
357 Pliny, N.H. XXXIII, 42–6.
358 R. Thomsen [772], I, 216f.
359 H. Mattingly [769, 770]; results of his
articles analysed in R. Thomsen [772], I, 231f.
360 T. V. Buttrey [767], 261f.
361 R. Thomsen [772].
362 Pomponius, Dig. I, 2, 2, 30f.;
R. Thomsen [772], III, 172f.
363 R. Thomsen [772], III, 85f.
364 R. Thomsen [772], III, 92f., 153f.
365 R. Thomsen [772], III, 119f.
366 R. Thomsen [772], III, 124f.
367 R. Thomsen [772], III, 170f., 179f.
368 R. Thomsen [772], III, 170.

Part Two   Research: Its Problems and Directions

1 G. Kossinna [108], 4.
2 V. Gordon Childe [106], 1.
3 L. Halphen, Les Barbares, 1926, 4: The
Germanic invasions of the fourth and fifth
centuries set in motion 'groups which were
very strong numerically and were squeezed
up against the frontier.' C. Courtois, Les
Vandales et l'Afrique, 1955, 51, estimates
the number of Vandal effectives who
crossed Gaul between 406 and 409 as
from two to three hundred thousand.

4 C. Coutois, ibid., 49.
5 U. Rellini [148], 76.
6 U. Rellini [148], 63.
7 G. Patroni [112], 215. The idea which
he slips in parenthetically here, viz. that in
primitive society pottery was left to the
women, and that consequently the
appearance of new pottery-types show the
presence of foreign women and hence
foreign families, has enjoyed a certain
vogue: H. Hencken [107] 3; some doubts

felt by E. Pulgram [113], 81, n.32.
8 G. Patroni [112], 221.
9 G. Patroni [112], 225.
10 E. Pulgram [113], 126f.
11 M. Pallottino [278], 32.
12 M. Pallottino [110], 20.
13 M. Pallottino [110], 24.
14 Livy II, 16, 3f.; Dion. Hal. V 40;
Plut., *Popl.* 21; Sueton., *Tib.* 1. See also
above, p. 179.
15 Diod. XII 31, 1; Liv. 37, 1, and
see above, p. 199.
16 For Cumae, Diod. XII, 76, 5; for
Naples, Strabo V 4, 7; for Messina,
Polyb. I 7; Dion. Hal. XV 3; Festus 150L.;
for Rhegium, Diod. XXIII 3.
17 J. Heurgon [716].
18 M. Pallottino [110], 15, is sorry to
find Mme Laviosa-Zambotti 'in some recent
studies adopting palpably invasionist
positions'. Yet J. Loicq, *RBPh* XLI, 1963,
126, n.1, observes that Pallottino himself,
having long championed the theory that
the Etruscans were indigenous, 'seems to
be turning towards a solution which
would not exclude an eastern contribution,
coming from the Aegean area originally'.
19 See above, p. 179. Dionysius says that
Atta Clausus had 'not less than 5,000 men
capable of bearing arms'; Plutarch speaks
of 5,000 families, including women and
children.
20 On this figure see J. Heurgon
[741], 204f.
21 P. de Francisci [570], 129.
22 P. de Francisci [570], 149f.
23 P. de Francisci [570], 161.
24 P. de Francisci [570], 162f.
25 P. de Francisci [570], 168f.
26 Paul. ex Fest. 22 L.
27 Pliny, *N.H.* XXXIII 21.
28 P. de Francisci [570], 163, n.303;
F. de Martino [571], 27, n.27.
29 P. de Francisci [570], 166f.
30 P. de Francisci *ibid.*
31 F. de Martino [571], 10.
32 F. de Martino [571], 9.
33 B. Paradisi, *Atti del Congr. intern. di
diritto romano,* Verona 1948, 4, 3f.; *Ann. di
Storia del Diritto,* I, 1957, 183f.
34 U. Coli, *Stati-citta e unita etniche nella
preistoria greca e italica.* Studi de Francisci,
4, 507f.
35 P. de Francisci [570], 131.
36 Pliny, *N.H.* III, 69; see above, p. 127.
37 Herod. I 94.
38 Dion. Hal. I 30, 2.

39 P. Ducati [254].
40 A. Piganiol [262].
41 See above, p. 51.
42 See above, p. 49.
43 G. M. A. Hanfmann [344]; cf.
G. Q. Giglioli [342], pl. 87, 88, 90.
44 See above, p. 42.
45 G. Buonamici [57], 88f.;
M. Pallottino [278], 99f., pl. 6;
M. Lejeune [72], 168f.
46 A. Piganiol [262], 336.
47 P. Bosch-Gimpera [252], 646.
48 M. Pallottino [258].
49 F. Altheim [251], 34.
50 M. Pallottino [110], 20;
see above, p. 228.
51 See above, p. 76.
52 See above, p. 19.
53 H. Hencken [256]; [257], 601f.
54 H. Hencken [256], 205;
cf. J. Bérard [441], 500.
55 H. Hencken [256], 208.
56 See above, p. 18f.
57 A. Piganiol [5], 32.
58 M. Pallottino [110], 31f.
59 H. Hencken [256], 209f.; [257], 631f.
60 Herod. I 94.
61 Herod. I 57; M. Pallottino [259], 16.
62 Dion. Hal. I 28, 2;
H. H. Scullard [265], 227f.
63 Dion. Hal. I 28, 3.
64 Dion. Hal. I 17, 2.
65 L. Pareti [261], 28f.;
M. Pallottino [259], 13f.; J. Bérard
[441], 503f.
66 J. Bérard [441], 470f.
67 Dion. Hal. I 18f.; cf. Herod I 57.
68 Thuc. VI 3–5.
69 G. Vallet, F. Villard [471], 312f.
70 J. Bérard [441], 91.
71 F. Villard [461].
72 G. Vallet [469], 30f.; G. Buchner
[467], 263f.; see above, p. 76.
73 T. J. Dunbabin [442], 457; the date
is corrected by G. Vallet and F. Villard
[471], 318f.
74 T. J. Dunbabin [442], 458; F. Villard
[461], 33; G. Vallet and F. Villard
[471], 344.
75 G. Vallet [469], 56.
76 G. Vallet, F. Villard [471], 312f., 343f.
77 B. Schweizer [458].
78 K. Johansen [455].
79 H. Payne [456, 457].
80 F. Villard [461], 23.
81 J. Bérard [441], 279.
82 J. Bérard [441], 91f.; T. J. Dunbabin

[442], 447f.
83 J. Bérard [441], 94; G. Vallet
[469], 61.
84 R. van Compernolle [460].
85 R. van Compernolle [460], 257.
86 Ed. Will, *RPh* XXXVI, 1962, 305f.
87 J. Ducat [454], 169f.
88 Ed. Will, *loc. cit.*, J. Ducat [454], 170.
89 Strabo V 4, 4 (243); J. Bérard [441], 38.
90 G. Vallet, F. Villard [471], 322.
91 J. Ducat [454], 166.
92 F. Villard [461], 28f.;
T. J. Dunbabin [442], 460f.
93 F. Villard [461], 32.
94 T. J. Dunbabin, 'The chronology of
Corinthian Vases', *Mel. Oikonomos*, quoted
by R. van Compernolle [460], 509.
95 J. Ducat [454]. But, as the author
reminds us in his table of chronologies
following Payne's principles, Matz said
590, Buscher 'about 590', and Kübler 580.
96 Livy VI 1, 2.
97 Cic., *Brut.* 62; Livy VIII 40, 4;
XXII 31, 8.
98 E. Pais and J. Bayet [3], 3.
99 A. Piganiol [5], 623; [6], XVII.
100 A. Piganiol [5], ed. 4, 463, n.1.
101 E. S. Staveley [660], 95.
102 See above, p. 54f.
103 See above, p. 27.
104 See above, p. 19.
105 See above, p. 138.
106 See above, p. 97.
107 See above, p. 129.
108 F. Altheim [7], I, 27f.
109 P. Fraccaro [78b], 15f.
110 A. Alföldi [566], 101f.
111 Prop. IV 1, 1f.
112 Livy *Praef.* 9; II 1, 6 (*res nondum
adultae*).
113 A. Piganiol [5], 109.
114 Dion. Hal. IV 26, 5.
115 See above, p. 173.
116 See above, p. 110.
117 See above, p. 268.
118 See above, p. 279.
119 P. Fraccaro [78b], 5.
120 See above, p. 273f.
121 Livy VI 1, 2, 10.
122 M. Pallottino [196], 8f.

123 E. Colozier [672], 90; H. Bengtson
[721], 1962, 16f. (21 for, 13 against);
A. Alföldi [566], 350, n.2 (30 for,
19 against; this in 1964).
124 Polyb. III, 22, 1f.
125 Diod. XVI, 19, 1.
126 Livy VII 27, 2.
127 Livy IX 43, 26.
128 Livy, *Per.* XIII.
129 Livy VII 38, 2.
130 Livy XXIX 27, 8.
131 O. Meltzer [674] I, 181, 488;
G. de Sanctis [10], III 2, 580f.; S. Gsell
[408], I 457; F. W. Walbank [92], I 342.
Polybius' interpretation is defended by
J. Désanges. *Cah. de Tunisie*, 1963, 9f.
132 See above, p. 337.
133 A. Alföldi [566], 295, 352f.
134 A. Aymard [671].
135 One year after Aymard's study,
F. Hampl [673], equally struck by the close
resemblances between the two treaties,
reached the opposite conclusion that the
second must have been shortly after 509,
the date admitted for the first.
136 A. Alföldi [566], 346f., 354.
137 The clauses relating to the protection
of the Carthaginian coasts are in accordance
with ancient maritime law: Herod. II 179
(Naucratis), and particularly with
Phoenician maritime law (R. Rebuffat
[675], 259f.).
138 S. Gsell [408], I 459, n.1;
F. W. Walbank [92], 347.
139 G. C. Picard [412], 31.
140 Diodorus XX 14; R. Rebuffat [438],
31, n.3.
141 G. C. Picard [412], 45.
142 S. Gsell [408], II 93f., 144;
G. C. Picard [412], 44.
143 Polyb. III 24, 7; P. de Noailles
[628], 143f.
144 See above, p. 237.
145 A. Alföldi [566], 372f.
146 H. Bengtson [721], 8, 10, 15.
147 R. Rebuffat [438], 35.
148 A. Alföldi [566], 191
149 Livy XXVIII 37, 10; Cicero,
pro Balbo, 14.
150 Tac., *Ann.* IV, 55, 8.

Index

DUE DATE